THE ARCHETYPAL ACTIONS OF RITUAL

OXFORD STUDIES IN SOCIAL AND CULTURAL ANTHROPOLOGY

Oxford Studies in Social and Cultural Anthropology represents the work of authors, new and established, which will set the criteria of excellence in ethnographic description and innovation in analysis. The series serves as an essential source of information about the world and the discipline.

OTHER TITLES IN THIS SERIES

Organizing Jainism in India and England
Marcus Banks

Society and Exchange in Nias
Andrew Beatty

The Culture of Coincidence:
Accident and Absolute Liability in Huli
Laurence Goldman

The Female Bridegroom: A Comparative Study of Life-Crisis Rituals in South India and Sri Lanka
Anthony Good

Of Mixed Blood: Kinship and History in Peruvian Amazonia
Peter Gow

Exchange in Oceania: A Graph Theoretic Analysis
Per Hage and Frank Harary

The Interpretation of Caste
Declan Quigley

The Arabesk Debate: Music and Musicians in Modern Turkey
Martin Stokes

THE ARCHETYPAL
ACTIONS OF
RITUAL

A THEORY OF RITUAL ILLUSTRATED BY
THE JAIN RITE OF WORSHIP

CAROLINE HUMPHREY

and

JAMES LAIDLAW

CLARENDON PRESS · OXFORD
1994

Oxford University Press, Walton Street, Oxford OX2 6DP

Oxford New York Toronto
Delhi Bombay Calcutta Madras Karachi
Kuala Lumpur Singapore Hong Kong Tokyo
Nairobi Dar es Salaam Cape Town
Melbourne Auckland Madrid
and associated companies in
Berlin Ibadan

Oxford is a trade mark of Oxford University Press

Published in the United States
by Oxford University Press Inc., New York

British Library Cataloguing in Publication Data
Data available

Library of Congress Cataloging in Publication Data
Humphrey, Caroline.
The archetypal actions of ritual: an essay on ritual as action
illustrated by the Jain rite of worship / Caroline Humphrey and
James Alexander Laidlaw.
— (Oxford studies in social and cultural anthropology)
Includes bibliographical references.
1. Jainism—Rituals. 2. Worship (Jainism) 3. Ritual.
I. Laidlaw, James Alexander. II. Title. III. Series.
BL1376.H86 1994 294.4'38—dc20 94–1005
ISBN 0–19–827788–1
ISBN 0–19–827947–7 (Pbk.)

1 3 5 7 9 10 8 6 4 2

Typeset by Best-set Typesetter Ltd., Hong Kong
Printed in Great Britain
on acid-free paper by
Biddles Ltd., Guildford and King's Lynn

PREFACE

ONE day we went to see our Jain friend Ravindra Golecha in his villa in the suburbs of Jaipur. We had both worked before, at different times, among Jains in Jaipur. This visit was to start a new project together, one which we confidently expected to be manageable in a short time, on the symbolism of the *puja*, the ritual of morning worship performed in Jain temples. Golecha had offered to tell us all about it. When we arrived, a man dozing in the shadow of the verandah rose to show us through to a ground-floor room, which was tightly shuttered against the sun. Here we found Golecha, and some other dignified old men, comfortably reclined on a huge mattress, playing cards. Several younger men lounged at the sides watching and a little girl lay sprawled asleep in the centre of the group. Slightly taken aback at our arrival, Golecha nevertheless jumped to his feet, and brushing aside our apologies for disturbing him, took us inside the house to a more suitable place for our conversation. This was his bedroom, which was on an upper floor, reached by passing through the dining room and skirting round the kitchen where some of the women of the house were preparing food. Here in the bedroom we found Golecha's wife fast asleep on a capacious bed. To our embarrassment she was unceremoniously dismissed and sent to bring tea and biscuits. We were all seated on the bed: Ravindra himself, James, Caroline, and Anju Dhaddha, our assistant, who comes from another of Jaipur's prominent Jain families. 'Now', said Golecha, with a beaming smile, 'ask me your questions. It is my duty to tell you about Jainism, it is a religious duty.' He proceeded to tell us about some of the minutely detailed 'rules which must be followed' to be a good Jain.

This encounter was not exceptional, just one of many conversations we had with Jain people in their homes. But it hints at some of the things we came to find so difficult to understand and which transformed our limited project into something unmanageable (and to which this book is only a partial and imperfect answer). What was this combination of languid informality with the exacting and multifarious 'rules which must be followed'? What was this 'religious duty' which so firmly and generously displaced everything else going on in the household? Though we knew Golecha quite well, it was apparent that it was because of our religious purpose that we were invited into the sanctum of his bedroom. It was because he thought of us as seekers after the truth about Jainism that he said, 'You are my family.' There was nothing set apart about his religion, no hint that it only really applied to particular places (the temple) or with particular people (other Jains). In fact, the rules and precepts of Jainism are fastidiously, even relentlessly applied to every aspect of life. The very biscuits which were brought to us had to conform, and were used as an occasion to explain how the central Jain doctrine of non-harming (*ahimsa*) is applied. Each of their ingredients is classified and rigorously inspected for the presence of tiny life-forms, and they must be produced by non-violent means; the heat of the stove, for example, should not harm insects. Could we possibly describe how 'Jain sentiments' arise from an infinite number of such occasions?

Most of our work was conducted in the Dadabari temple, where we knew many of the congregation from our previous visits. Just after dawn, in the comparative cool of the early morning, the bicycle repair shops and dried-dung makers were already busy in the streets outside, and a steady stream of immaculately clad Jains was arriving at the temple: making their way on foot, or alighting from cars and rickshaws, bearing their offerings to the Jinas, the founding teachers of the Jain religion. The temple is a clean-swept, quiet enclave, with its own garden and dwelling-hall for the occasional passing ascetics, Jain monks or nuns, who spend their time wandering from town to town, preaching Jain doctrines to their followers. We used to station ourselves in a shaded alcove in the garden, between the entrance and the temple itself. Here, we would talk with lay Jain worshippers as they came by. We spent many hours watching people perform the *puja*, and then discussing with them what they had just done. In time, we too learnt to perform the *puja*. After morning worship people used to drift home for a meal before the day's work, but no one was in a rush, and as with Golecha, we felt that people were genuinely happy to talk about their religion. Little groups would form in the shade of our alcove. A temple servant brought tea and listened genially to our conversations. Occasionally he would rouse himself to chase away a monkey or a peacock. A single bell would clang as a worshipper entered the temple; every so often the birds in the garden would screech or chatter.

The *puja*, we discovered, is a 'forest of symbols'; but these symbolic meanings were different from the religious meaning of objects in everyday life. In *puja*, each item brought as an offering is likely to be given one or more propositional meanings. For example, sweets might be given the meaning, 'these are for the attainment of spiritual contentment'. In the everyday world things such as biscuits must be made and used in accordance with Jain principles, and they can become the subject of a lengthy religious discourse, but the biscuits remain just biscuits, items of food. They have 'significance' in the widest sense, but they do not refer to or express propositions. With *puja* offerings, on the other hand, people were happy to declare multifarious, but in each case specific 'meanings'. Sometimes these seemed to have been plucked from the air in response to our questioning, and no one was perturbed that different individuals proffered quite different such definite 'meanings' for the same object or act. As the days passed we grew increasingly puzzled: what were these 'meanings' which seemed so weighty in import, and yet so lightly and variously applied? Why did they not, as we had expected, add up to a system?

Our Jain respondents were invariably and unfailingly polite, but it was not long before we were being given the idea—particularly by some of the older men—that we had chosen the wrong subject. Why were we so interested in this mere 'empty ritual'? Some tried to guide us away from our topic, the kind of secondary and 'external' thing that foreigners would latch on to. We knew, of course, that other Jain orders had renounced temples and worship of statues of the Jinas. It was disconcerting to find nevertheless that some adherents of these orders came regularly to the Dadabari to perform *puja*. And it was not only these people who expressed restrained disapproval of our research. The basic idea was universal: anything of any religious value that can by done through *puja* can be done better in other ways.

Part of the reason we had chosen this subject was that even casual observation reveals that this form of worship is performed with sincerity and piety, and is a central part of people's religious lives. But our Jain friends' opinion was to change the direction of our own ideas completely. It became clear to us that to develop an adequate account of Jain religious practice we had to raise some difficult questions about the problematic status of ritual in general. We had to make sense of the variety of meanings that we were told the *puja* has, and yet to take seriously the fact, inseparable ethnographically from this feast of 'meanings', that the ritual is declared by those who practise it to be meaningless. To do this, we had to raise fundamental questions about the understanding of ritual in general, and abandon many of the assumptions behind current anthropological thinking about ritual. In the end we had to develop a new theory of ritual action.

ACKNOWLEDGEMENTS

WE are very grateful to all the people in Jaipur, Ahmedabad, and other parts of western India, who helped us with our enquiries about Jainism and the *puja*. The following people were especially kind and generous with their time and knowledge: the late Pravartini Sajjan Shri ji Maharaj Saheb, Gani Shri Mani Prabh Sagar ji Maharaj Saheb, Sadhvi Priyadarshana Shri ji Maharaj Saheb, Dr N. K. Baz, Dr Narendra Bhanavat, Dr Hukamchand Bharilla, Mr and Mrs P. L. Dagga, Mr Kamal Kant Dagga, Mr and Mrs H. Dhaddha, Mr S. L. Gandhi, Mr Prem Chand Jain, Mr and Mrs S. C. Jain, Shri Jyoti Kumar Kothari, Mrs Sunita Meharchandani, Mrs Anju Dhaddha Mishra, Shri Dhanroopmal Nagori, the late Mrs Phophalia, Mr Rajendra Kumar Shrimal, the late Shri Rajroop-ji Tank, Mrs Saceti, Dr K. C. Sogani, Kavita Srivastava, Meenu Srivastava, and Dr (Mrs) Pawan Surana.

All through our research, but especially in 1985, we were given encouragement, academic advice, and most generous practical help by the then Vice-Chancellor of the University of Rajasthan, Professor T. K. N. Unnithan, and by Mrs Unnithan. We are grateful also to Professor N. K. Singhi, of the Department of Sociology in the University of Rajasthan, for his valuable insights into Jain society. The original intention of our 1985 fieldwork was to make a video film together with a paper about the Jain *puja*, so we were accompanied by our colleague Marcus Banks, who shot the film. We joined Marcus in editing the film, 'The Jains: a religious community of India', which was produced in the Department of Social Anthropology, Cambridge University, in 1985. We benefited much from Marcus's knowledge of Jainism.

This work started life as a longish paper which we read to an informal seminar in King's College, Cambridge. It was the interest of Pascal Boyer, Keith Hart, Tanya Luhrmann, and Nicholas Thomas that encouraged us to turn the paper into a book. All along, Pascal's friendly typed missives from across the court have pointed us in the direction of new ideas, and he has commented in detail on successive versions of the work. The following people have read all or parts of earlier drafts of the book, and we are extremely grateful for their comments: Peter Allen, Alan Babb, Stephen Cherry, John Cort, Paul Dundas, Alan Fiske, Chris Fuller, Alfred Gell, Tanya Luhrmann, Gananath Obeyesekere, David Owens, Fitz Poole, Quentin Skinner, Tony Tanner, Giles Tillotson, and Harvey

Whitehouse. An anonymous reviewer for Oxford University Press made particularly detailed and helpful comments and for this too we are grateful. Other people with whom we have discussed our ideas or who have suggested examples or arguments to us include Bill Brewer, John Drury, Naomi Eilan, Ernest Gellner, Stephen Hugh-Jones, Nick Humphrey, and Julian Pears. In April 1991 we read a paper, based on this work, at the Collège de France and we profited much from long discussions of the material with Michael Houseman and Carlo Severi.

We should like to acknowledge the generous financial support given by the Nuffield Foundation and King's College, Cambridge, which enabled us to undertake fieldwork together. More generally, James Laidlaw is grateful for research funding to the Economic and Social Research Council and for a research fellowship to King's College, Cambridge. During the final period of writing the book, 1990–2, Caroline Humphrey was supported by a British Academy Research Readership.

CONTENTS

List of Figures and Plates   xii
Notes on the Text   xiii

1. Introduction   1
2. Jainism and the *Puja* Ritual   16
3. What Kind of Theory Do We Need?   64
4. The Ritual Commitment   88
5. Getting It Right   111
6. Apprehension and Cognition   133
7. The Disconnection of Purpose and Form   167
8. Looking for Meanings   191
9. Meaning to Mean It   211
10. The Evocation of Mood   227
11. Stances of the Self   247
12. Conclusion   260

Glossary   269
References   275
Index   289

FIGURES

1. Plan of Dadabari temple compound 22
2. Interior of Dadabari temple 23
3. Standard pattern formed from rice grains during *puja* 27
4. 'Nesting' model of *puja* 33

PLATES

    I The Dada Guru Dev shrine at the Dadabari temple in Jaipur 30
   II The same idol, at the climax of an elaborate *puja* 30
  III The offering-table in the Dadabari temple 31
  IV Three Shvetambar nuns 148
   V A layman and his wife as Mahavir's parents 148
  VI A standing Jina idol 173
 VII Idol of Manibhadra Vir 173
VIII A collective *snatra puja* in the Dadabari temple 184
  IX and X Pages from a *puja* manual 195
  XI A *samavasarana-patta* 251

**PLEASE RETAIN THIS
COPY FOR YOUR RECORDS**

**PLEASE RETAIN THIS
COPY FOR YOUR RECORDS**

NOTES ON THE TEXT

A NOTE, first, about the 'we' which, perhaps all too frequently, peppers this text. All parts of this book have been written by both Caroline Humphrey and James Laidlaw. The chapters grew from sketchy passages in the original paper, drafted by one or other of us. These were then revised by the other and then handed back, often several times. Crucial passages were put together over the telephone, with each of us noting down what the other was saying. The final text was produced by both of us, sitting before the word-processor screen together. There were surprisingly few disagreements. Sometimes we found a good deal of surprise and amusement in what the other had written, often we have even forgotten who first came up with a given passage.

We have used the standard system for transliterating words from Sanskrit and Hindi into English, with the following exceptions. We have substituted *sh* for *ś* and *ṣ*, *ri* for *ṛ*, and *w* for *v* where this seems appropriate. Except for terms, such as *karma*, which are very well known in their Sanskrit forms, we have preferred modern vernacular Hindi and have generally omitted the final *a*. In the main body of the text we have omitted diacritical marks. In passages quoted from other published works we have adapted transliterated words to conform to the conventions used in this book. A glossary at the end of the book provides full transliterations, with diacritical marks, for the most important terms used, and brief glosses on the meaning of these terms, to facilitate recognition.

1

Introduction

RELIGIOUS rituals can provoke a deeply ambiguous reaction in those who practise them. This book attempts to see what this kind of reaction can tell us about ritual. What happens in religious traditions when the nature of ritual is questioned, but the practice of performing rituals is not itself abandoned? Much anthropological analysis simply equates religion and ritual, or regards them as forming some kind of indissoluble whole, yet in many cases a religious attitude, a searching for spiritual perfection perhaps, can turn upon its own vehicle, ritual, to regard it with distrust, deprecation, or even fear. Ritual is still assumed to be efficacious, in the sense that nothing more than performing it brings about a desired transformation. Yet this very effectiveness now becomes suspect, and ritual comes to seem dangerous, almost impious, unless accompanied by a further religious act—the giving of 'meaning' to the ritual. We think that these reactions to ritual tell us about more than just particular religious ideologies, for there is a sense in which, when different religious traditions act in this way, they are reacting to a common phenomenon. Such reactions therefore reveal the essential features of ritual action. The example we shall use to lay bare these features is the *puja* ritual of the Shvetambar Jains of western India. But we should stress that our book is not meant to be primarily a study of Jainism. We are proposing a theory of ritual action.

Forms of the word *puja* are used throughout the Indian subcontinent to denote a rite in which a deity, usually present in the form of an idol, is worshipped. *Puja* is found in all the indigenous Indian religions. The daily Jain *puja* consists of bathing, anointing, and decorating a consecrated idol, a *murti*, and then making a short series of 'offerings' to the idol.[1] Notionally there are eight of these operations, so the rite is often referred to as the 'eightfold' (or *ashta prakari*) *puja*.[2]

We went to Jaipur in 1985 with the idea of exploring the range of symbolic meanings which the restricted series of acts of the Jain daily *puja* might have. As we had hoped, the Jains we spoke to had a lot to say about the symbolism of the *puja*, and we collected many elaborate commentaries and explanations. We talked with ordinary lay householders, lay experts, and religious teachers, and their responses were often highly sophisticated and complex.³ Our most puzzling problem arose from the fact that our respondents, eloquent though they were about the ritual they had just performed, had the disquieting habit of insisting, complaining, warning us, that the *puja* is meaningless.⁴ They said this not only about the *puja*, for their complaint was about ritual in general. This was despite the fact, which points to the ambiguity referred to above, that these Jains are happy to be known as the Murti Pujaks—those who conduct the ritual to the idol.

Now we too shall claim that the ritual actions of *puja* do not convey 'a meaning', and that anthropologists have been mistaken in thinking that the communication of meanings is distinctive or definitional of ritual; but it must be emphasized that while our Jain friends' comments helped us to reach our views, we are not involved in the same kind of argument as they are and we are not saying the same thing. We argue below that ritualization severs the link, present in everyday activity, between the 'intentional meaning' of the agent and the identity of the act which he or she performs. The Jains, on the other hand, were using the word 'meaning' in a religious sense. All rites and rituals (*vidhi-vidhan*), we were told, are mere 'empty ritual'. They are 'external' actions and therefore irrelevant to an understanding of the transformation of the soul which, our respondents insisted, is the heart of Jainism. It was to this end that they claimed that meanings must be put into ritual, to infuse its emptiness with spiritual significance. This, it was agreed, is no easy or straightforward matter: the meanings should come from inside the self and some people are more spiritually gifted and so better at this than others. Thus the chapters which follow will explore two distinct, but in this case ethnographically related problems about meaning in ritual. Our own discussion of the senses in which ritualized actions can be said to have (or not to have) meaning, will be interleaved with, and we hope will illuminate, an ethnographic account of the Jain *puja*, and of the distinct Jain sense of what meaning is in ritual, as an input which is spiritually significant.

Ritual as Action

The book offers an analysis of ritual as action. Although ritual in world religions prominently includes language, these uses of language are always also forms of action. In other words, even the language materials (prayers, hymns, and so forth) must be seen first as linguistic acts. Our task then is to contrast ritualized action, including linguistic acts, with action which is not ritualized. We do not claim that our analysis explains everything about every event and practice which might reasonably be called 'a ritual'. We shall argue below (in Chapter 3) that no useful theory of the whole range of such phenomena is possible, and that the term 'ritual' does not pick out a class of events or institutions in an analytically useful way (although it remains useful as an informal descriptive term). We suggest instead that ritual is a distinctive way in which an action, probably any action, may be performed. Thus a 'theory of ritual' is an account of the transformation of action by ritualization. There is no point in trying to frame generalizations about the social function, or whatever, of all rituals, because ritualization can happen to anything. The proper focus of theoretical attention is therefore the distinctive quality which action, performed in this way, comes to have. We shall address this question in the abstract, although we shall be concerned primarily with ritualization in the context of religion. The view that ritual is a quality of action, and not a class of events or institutions, draws our attention to new aspects of ritual action and allows us to ask new questions about it.

In Chapter 4 we begin the task of describing the phenomenon of ritualization. The chapter is very abstract and unethnographic, but it launches us on our theory by raising the philosophical questions involved in distinguishing between ritualized and unritualized action. Because we set out in this way, a host of new questions and possible objections immediately come into view, but it takes us to the end of the book to visit them all. So it must be emphasized that despite appearances, this chapter does not contain a 'summary' of the theory. We think that ritualization works by means of a single crucial transformation, but it is a unique concatenation which nevertheless has numerous components. They are discussed in turn as the book proceeds. It is important to realize that some of these components are not unique to ritual, and can also be seen, though not all together, in other kinds of action (theatrical performance, acting under orders, habit, conventional behaviour, games, etc.).

In a recent survey of anthropological and other theories of ritual, Catherine Bell (1992) has drawn attention to a pervasive tendency to employ a distorting separation between thought and action, and to fit ritual into the latter, devalued category. We are much in sympathy with the point Bell makes here. But we prefer not to adopt her solution, which is to refer to ritual as practice rather than action. Bell has concluded, as we have ourselves, that it is best to abandon the focus on rituals as a set of independently existing objects in favour of a focus on the common strategies of ritualization (1992: 219). However, her use of the word 'practice' draws with it a cloud of associations which we feel are unproven for ritual action in general, namely, the idea that ritualization produces 'practical knowledge' and 'the ability to deploy, play, and manipulate basic schemes in ways that appropriate and condition experience effectively' (1992: 221). Bell's choice of the word 'practice' also stems from her perception that ultimately the notion of ritual is constructed in the practice of anthropological theorizing about it within the concerns of a particular academic era. This must be true, but it is confusing to conflate this sense of 'practice' with the 'practice' of people from other cultures engaging in ritual. All in all, it seems a pity to relinquish an indispensable word (action) in this way, especially since, as Bell also says, to regard 'action' as divorced from and devoid of 'thought' is an impoverished understanding of human activity.[5]

Perhaps we should say a few words about the view we take of action in general. Charles Taylor's paper 'Hegel's Philosophy of Mind' (1985: 77–96) is helpful here. Taylor's view, drawn from Hegel, is that actions are qualitatively different from other kinds of event. They cannot be reduced to a combination of separate and allegedly more basic entities, such as a physical movement and a peculiar kind of cause, for they are, as Taylor says, 'intrinsically directed'. 'Actions are in a sense inhabited by the purposes which direct them, so that action and purposes are ontologically inseparable.' In this 'qualitative' view, action is directed, aimed to encompass ends or purposes, and this notion of directedness is part of the concept of agency. The agent is the being 'for whom and through whom action is directed as it is', and so must necessarily have a direct, unmediated awareness of the action itself. This is the basis, in so far as we bring this inarticulate sense to conscious formulation, of a kind of knowledge, and this agent's knowledge, although it may remain dim or partly subliminal, and is always certainly partial, is qualitatively different from the kind of knowledge that is possible of things encountered and perceived only from outside. The 'subjective' awareness and attitude of the agent is part of the 'objective' reality which he or she knows, so that the character of an action is in part constituted by the attitude which the agent takes to what he or she does.[6]

This 'qualitative' view of action, which does not see action as opposed to thought, will guide us throughout this book, and it is the reason why we explore the character of ritual action by looking through the lenses provided by people's attitudes and reactions to their ritualized action. The view of action as intrinsically directed enables us, we hope, to pinpoint the difference between ritualized and unritualized action; although neither Taylor, nor, to our knowledge, any other philosopher of action, has given serious consideration to ritual. Ritualization implies an agent's adopting a particular attitude to his or her action, and enacting what he or she does, therefore, in a particular, qualitatively transformed way. We shall argue below that ritual action is still 'directed', but the relation between intention and action is subtly transformed, so that it is different from action in general. In ritual, the celebrant has agent's awareness of his or her action, and indeed an aspect of this awareness is distinctive of ritual action, but this is also preceded and accompanied by a conception of the action as a thing, encountered and perceived from outside. This distinctive quality of agents' awareness of their action, which can only be grasped from the perspective of the 'qualitative' view of action in general, we shall call the ritual commitment or stance.

The argument set out in the chapters which follow is that ritual is different from other forms of action. But it remains, none the less, a mode of human action, so its study does lay bare more general truths. It simply is not possible, even if one thought this were the way to go about explaining human action in general, to explain the ritual acts which people perform only by their individual motives, intentions, or purposes. On the other hand, it is just as implausible to tidy away such intentions by subsuming them in historical and sociological 'causes'. Ritualized acts in liturgical traditions are socially prescribed and present themselves to individual actors as 'given' and external to themselves. Because ritualized acts are stipulated in this way, a new situation arises: instead of, as is normally the case in everyday life, a person's act being given meaning by his or her intentions, with ritual action the act itself appears as already formed, almost like an object, something from which the actor might 'receive'. In this transformed situation the intentions and thoughts of the actor make no difference to the *identity* of the act performed. You have still done it, whatever you were dreaming of. Furthermore, a wide variety of actions may 'count as' the ritual act. This situation is neither an accident nor is it a matter of absentminded habit. It results from a positive act of acquiescence in a socially stipulated order (the ritual commitment). In effect, these features of ritualization remove the possibility of there being intrinsic meaning in ritual acts, as we argue in detail in Chapter 4.

Nevertheless, actors in ritual are of course conscious and normally voluntary agents, and it is in this situation that ritualized acts may be apprehended and meanings may be attributed to them. The peculiar fascination of ritual lies in the fact that here, as in few other human activities, the actors both are, and are not, the authors of their acts. It is the implications of this situation that our book explores.

What Kind of Ritual is the Puja?

There are two ways in which 'ritual' is various: a variety of different kinds of actions are ritualized in different social, institutional, and ideological contexts, and in these different contexts agents can adopt a range of attitudes in reaction to ritual. We take it as essential that our explanation should account for ritualized action not only as a social phenomenon, as anthropology normally does, but also as it is cognized by individual persons. This book develops the idea that reactions to ritual occur at both the social and individual levels, that the two cannot be understood separately, and that what is interesting about ritual in general is their relation to one another.

The daily form of the Jain rite of worship has been described in some detail by Humphrey (1985), Babb (1988), and Cort (1989). As in all liturgical traditions, the acts of which the *puja* can consist are stipulated. However, all these accounts give the impression, which we now think is mistaken, that there is some set of ideas held in common, from which individuals may perhaps deviate, but which constitutes the 'meaning' of the *puja*. We shall argue that no such underlying meaning exists, but that people do attempt to counteract the meaninglessness of ritual by imposing religious meanings which they have been told about, have read about, or have thought up for themselves. We shall argue too that this tells us something important about ritual action in general.

Each specific local ethnography is of course a special case, and as we hope our discussion will show, Jain religious ritual is of the greatest intrinsic interest. But we think too that the Jain *puja* provides an important and revealing case for the understanding of ritual in general, for it enables us to separate a consideration of the intrinsic character of ritual action from observations on the coercive ideological power of religious institutions. Jain rituals are in fact rather free and non-coercive. This enables us to see that the question, which has often fascinated anthropologists, of how and why ritual can be used in the service of power is logically separable from an understanding of ritual as such. The question of ritual's relation to power cannot possibly be answered satisfactorily without understanding ritualization *per se*. Whether because Jainism has so rarely enjoyed direct political patronage, or because its religious adepts are so rigorously separated from wealth and worldly power, or because its lay practitioners are generally so affluent and independent, or because its philosophical orientation is so rigorously individualist, or because it is so deeply equivocal about the religious validity of ritual, the revealing fact from the point of view of a general understanding of ritual, the fact that makes this special case an especially instructive one is that Jain religious tradition is remarkably free of coercive or inquisitorial institutions and Jain religious practice, even weighty collective rituals, are organized in a remarkably un-authoritarian way. In Christianity, for example, religious authorities have often been able to give fairly stable, agreed meanings to a ritual, and to enforce allegiance to those meanings, so that it might seem that the meaning belongs to the rituals themselves, but we argue instead that this is something which social power can achieve *against* the effects of ritualization. Why religious authorities should want to do this—why, so to speak, power is drawn to ritual—is another question to which we shall also suggest some answers. The Jains, who do not have an authoritative priestly office, provide a clear illustration of how meanings are not found in rituals, but must be given to them.

Although at several points in this book we shall make comparison with Christian attitudes to ritual, readers should bear in mind that the Jain religious culture is quite foreign to the Judaeo-Christian tradition. Its characteristic style is not the use of humanistic symbolic ideas, but meta-physical analysis and exhaustive arithmetical inquiry. Jainism specializes in the production of elaborate classificatory charts and geographic-cosmic diagrams. These simply depict the facts of the nature of the universe. One could say, indeed, that Jainism in a sense rejects mystery.

Nevertheless, there is a mystery at the heart of Jainism, which is the destiny of the human soul. No one has put this better than Caillat and Kumar in their study of Jain cosmology.

The fact that the continents, zones, and kingdoms which [humankind] is capable of inhabiting are thus apportioned into clearly defined territories comes partly from the need to define the countries where Release is possible. . . . A gigantic theatre where transmigrations and reincarnations take place, in one or other of the four modes of life—infernal, animal, divine and human—the cosmos is capable, at the cost of strenuous efforts and long struggles, of being understood and overcome by man's purely spiritual cognition. (1981: 34–5)

One of the ways, and in fact for our lay Jain friends the daily cosmic theatre for the engagement in this 'spiritual cognition', is the performance of ritual.

Jains are nevertheless aware that ritual is only one path in the religious life and they generally insist that it must be made meaningful. It is through the lens of such reactions that we hope to see what ritual is (an approach which is required if one takes the qualitative view of action). We recognize that people in different societies look through different lenses. The Jain case is clearly different, for example, from the performance-centred rituals which predominate in the inspirational cults and life-cycle ceremonial of non-literate societies. There, where religion is not constituted as a separate domain from ritual, the response we are concerned with is bound to have a different nature. Another, more pertinent case is the highly ritualized practices of hieratic religions, where correct performance alone is held to be automatically effective. In India, the paradigm of such ritual has been the Vedic sacrifice. As we shall describe below, the Jains have always been hostile to this ancient tradition and are deeply equivocal about the aspects of their own ritual which resemble it. Different again in their attitudes to ritual are post-Reformation Protestant contexts where faith in the efficacy of ritual has been terminally undermined. In this case, churches conduct their own services with the degree of ritualization they wish. Thus the service may be changed from time to time, with a view to engaging the religious participation of different congregations. With this has come the triumph of the idea that this changeable ritual is, or should be, only a way of communicating or expressing the religious beliefs and moral ideas of the participants. So pervasive is this idea that ritual on its own, without subjective convictions, comes, for many, to seem mere mumbo-jumbo.

The *puja* is an example of liturgy-centred, as opposed to performance-centred, ritual (a distinction we owe to Atkinson 1989). It is worth explaining this distinction at some length, since in anthropology such a great emphasis has been placed on the latter that it has come to seem paradigmatic of ritual in general. We, on the contrary, think that performance-centred 'rituals' are commonly very weakly ritualized. If we are thinking about what ritualization 'does' to action, such performances provide only confusing clues, because their central concern, with the genuineness or truth of the supernatural quality of the event, is one that need not be demonstrated *ritually* at all—it may be revealed in quite other ways.

As examples of performance-centred 'rituals' let us take inspirational shamanism and initiation ceremonies. Such events are never regarded as unproblematic, but neither the reasons for this, nor the responses to it, are those which we shall find in the scriptural religions. Claude Lévi-Strauss, Pierre Smith, and Pascal Boyer, amongst others, have shown how such 'rituals' rest on a simulation, a half-believed fiction that some unseen supernatural event really happens as they are performed. Smith, analysing initiation, writes as follows.

Throughout the world, in black Africa, Amazonia, Australia, Melanesia, and elsewhere, men on one side, women and children on the other, clearly divide ritual roles between them: the former convince the latter that the gods, spirits, or ancestors are among them in a perceptible way. To do this they put on masks or costumes, or change their voices and their bearing, or play instruments which the others do not see, such as bullroarers, flutes, hand drums, and so on, and the women and children believe, or are supposed to believe, or at least are supposed to act as if they believed, often under pain of death, that these really are supernatural manifestations. The central theme in the collective initiation of young men is their passage from the second group into the first, and it involves the exposure of the simulation. But what is even more striking is that this passage takes nothing away from their beliefs; on the contrary, when they are given the mission of simulating the manifestations, they only become closer to the gods and come to consider this the most excellent way of worshipping them. . . .

I have been able to observe these ritual performances, well-known to ethnologists, among the Bedik of eastern Senegal . . . and I took down these significant words from an initiator: 'When we announce to the future initiates that the masks are going to cut off their heads, they should act as though they believe it. If one of them acts sceptical or put out, it is very serious and he must be severely punished. But if one of them believes too strongly and gets upset, tries to run away or loses control, it is even more serious. This is the sign that he will never live among us as a man, and in the old days they preferred to kill him and be done with it'. This statement bears out the paradoxical viewpoint suggested above. (Smith 1982: 105–6)

Smith sees this 'snare for thought' (*piège à pensée*) as the kernel of 'ritual' (not that we would agree with him). Lévi-Strauss, and later Pascal Boyer, suggest that something similar also occurs in exorcist and 'inspirational' rituals. Lévi-Strauss's example (1968) concerns a shaman who is considered by some, including himself, to be a trickster, yet is also believed to have effected successful cures. Boyer, using observations drawn from Kapferer's analysis of exorcism in Sri Lanka (1983), makes the point that performance rituals of this kind always involve a fundamental uncertainty.

This episode of the trance is of course the crucial part of the seance, in that the result of the rite as a whole depends on its successful performance. As Kapferer points out, the relationship between possession and the exorcist's trance is both 'iconic' and direct. The exorcist is miming a process of possession; at the same time, however, he is supposed to be literally possessed, so that his dance is directly caused by the demon. This latter aspect is a condition *sine qua non* for the seance to be held valid. Kapferer observes that 'the audience . . . is generally concerned with the authenticity of the exorcist trance, and much discussion usually follows concerning whether or not the demon actually entered the exorcist's body' (1983: 196). . . . The problem here concerns the 'reality' of the enacted performance. (Boyer, forthcoming).

Boyer concludes that in these performances every step of the ritual may be enacted as it should be, and yet the audience may doubt that the possession was 'authentic'. In fact, in this kind of ritual it matters far more that the audience is convinced, or consents to appear convinced, than that a stipulated sequence of ritual acts be enacted. As will become clear as this book proceeds, we think that the proper way to describe this is to say that their being ritualized is not the most pronounced and important aspect of these events. They are ritualized religious 'performances' of a quasi-theatrical kind, where success and failure is of the essence.

Not uncommonly, in many parts of the world, such performances include relatively spontaneous miraculous tests: the shaman cuts his own stomach which immediately heals, or he eats fire, and so on. These seem to have no purpose except to convince the audience (and perhaps oneself) that something supernatural is taking place. In shamanic performances it is common to find improvization, and the selection of what is enacted from a wide range of possible scenarios. Atkinson, in her book *The Art and Politics of Wana Shamanship*, writes, 'As a performance-centered ritual, a *mabolong* [shamanic seance] cannot be described or analyzed as a preordained progression of delineated steps to which ritual practitioners and congregants collectively conform. It is rather a repertoire of ritual actions available to performers acting independently in the ritual arena' (1989: 15). Wana shamanic song, like that of many other inspirational traditions, is formulaic, but not at all fixed. Atkinson observes, 'A mixture of stock formulae and improvisation, the songs reveal the challenge their performers face: to create distinctive reputations for themselves, but to do so in ways that conform with audience expectations of what powerful shamans are' (1989: 16).

The point here is that shamanic success is not really defined by control over disease or other afflictions. An excuse or an alternative diagnosis can always be found if a patient dies. It is a matter, rather, of creating and confirming personal shamanic power, and this is achieved through discourse in which the audience is an essential partner. Atkinson rightly insists that such ritual cannot be seen as a reflection or representation of existing social relations. Rather, in a real sense, the seance constitutes these social relations and hence becomes a political arena. It is through successful performance that shamans achieve status and power. The 'audience' in rituals of this kind is never passive, and indeed Atkinson later argues, 'Instead of ascribing political initiative solely to political leaders, I would argue that Wana communities seek—and thus create—their shamans every bit as much as individuals strive to become shamans on their own' (1989: 292).

Just as the *mabolong* shamanic rituals are part of the same process as non-ritual political contest, the authenticity of shamanic possession is not separate from non-ritual experiences of magical power. Such experiences can be sought or encountered by any Wana person. They occur during lone foraging in the forest, in spells and chants, or in strange events in a host of everyday situations. Thus shamanic ritual performances do not assume and then overturn the contours of everyday existence, but pose an order that exceeds the order achievable in non-ritual reality, and then—Atkinson argues—threaten their audiences with disruption of that ideal order (1989: 18–19). This posing of a supernormal reality as a potentially shared experience could not perhaps be achieved without ritual (see Chapter 5). But nevertheless ritualization is not the most important thing going on here—it is submerged in the intense experience of enchantment and the fluid, ever-changing, interpersonal recognitions of hidden powers (all of which also occur in non-ritual contexts). Above all, inspirational ritual tends not to be self-conscious. There may be discussion about whether the supernatural event really happened, about whether the best ritual method was chosen, and about whether it was performed well or not. But people in general do not agonize over initiation ceremonies, offerings to mountain-spirits, or shamanic trances *as rituals*, if only because these activities are not assessed in relation to religious values and set apart from them, but are primarily conceived as ways to get results.

We should emphasize that we are not saying that performance-centred rituals are not rituals. When we say that they are less ritualized, we have in mind that the question most insistently asked of them, 'Has it worked?' is different from, and in these contexts eclipses, the question asked of liturgical ritual, 'Have we got it right?' This latter concern, construed in the particular way we describe in Chapter 5, is, we think, one of the elements intrinsic to ritualization.

That there is a distinction to be made between types of ritual has of course been remarked before, and characterized in a number of different ways. Marcel Mauss (1972) compared 'religious rites' with 'magical rites', Max Weber (1978 i. 422–39) distinguished routinized from charismatic religious practice, and John Skorupski (1976) contrasts interactive with operative ceremonies. Let us emphasize, however, that our distinction between liturgical and performance-centred ritual is not intended to characterize whole societies. So-called 'shamanic societies' invariably seem also to have liturgical ritual,[7] and societies dominated by the most hieratically liturgical religious traditions invariably have niches occupied by more ecstatic, performance-centred practices. The same Jains who practise the liturgical *puja* we are concerned with here also visit another Jain temple, only twenty miles or so from Jaipur, where those possessed by malevolent spirits are induced into states of trance and 'cured' through performance-centred exorcism (see Chapter 10).

Ritualized Action and Religious Reaction

We shall argue in this book that the degree of ritualization of action corresponds to the degree to which actions are felt to be stipulated in advance and thereby separated from people's intentions in acting. This stipulation determines what acts are to be 'counted as', and thereby names and objectifies such acts as social phenomena. The form taken by ritualized actions is not only divorced from individuals' intentions and purposes but is also separate from everyday functional action in time; the more ritualized a sequence of action, the greater the possibilities of changes in order, abbreviation, lengthening, and reversals. Such manipulations are justified not by practical necessity but by reference to previous ritual enactments, hallowed precedents which establish the 'archetypal' nature of the present act. (This does not mean that ritual need be any less practically effective than everyday action. In some cases it might be, but it is not possible to define ritual by a lack of instrumental effectiveness). All of this establishes the ritual act as object, as something separated, constituted, and awaiting, as it were, apprehension by the actors. It is for this reason that ritual can posit a transcendence of ordinary functional action. This is also why strongly ritualized acts evoke responses— and these responses may be as various as the interpretative vantage points in the everyday world from which people approach ritual. We argue indeed, in Chapter 7, that a custom does not become 'a ritual' until people can disagree about its meaning.

The scriptural religions have all experienced reforms of ritual conceived as returns to the original meaning of a text or the original form of a rite. These are thought of as standing above and beyond contemporary ritual practice. In such searching for the 'true' prototypical form we can see a characteristic of liturgical ritual which is much weaker, or altogether absent, in performance-centred ritual. Often, however, such reforms have

left in place liturgical rituals which are believed to be automatically efficacious—the 'material' version of the sacraments in Catholicism, the
Vedic sacrifice in Brahmanism, Confucian state rituals in T'ang China,
lamas' blessings in Tibetan Buddhism. But for the Jains, for Protestants at
the time of the Reformation, and for today's Buddhist reformers in the
Theravadin world, such ritual has also come to be questioned *as ritual* (i.e.
as a mode of action). The issues of which rituals to perform and how to
perform them correctly remain, as they appear always to have been, at the
centre of religious concern and debate. However, in the latter 'protestant'
cases, as we shall show later for contemporary Jains, there is a double
questioning: no longer simply a matter of what the correct act should be,
the terms of debate here call into question the very premises of liturgical
ritual activity. Our book focuses on cases of this kind. Liturgical
correctness, the necessity of conforming to some unquestioned idea of
rightness, remains important, as it no longer does in some 'post-Reformation' religions, because the efficacy of ritual is still assumed. But just
performing the right act is not enough: the archetypal action should be
apprehended by its conscious agents and given meaning. Some meanings
are shared, others are not.

Although we focus on a particular example, we think that the
ritualization of action is a universal phenomenon, and that while rituals
and their place in society vary across different social contexts, there is
something invariant in the difference between ritualized and everyday
action. In other words, as we said above, when religions react in their
different ways to ritual they are reacting to a common phenomenon.
Tambiah (1985: 125) similarly comments that notwithstanding the differences between ritual traditions, the differences in the use societies make of
ritual, and the extent to which both can change over time, 'I am persuaded
that human beings everywhere commonly structure certain events which
they consider important in a similar way, events which we can recognize
as *ritual*, and that there are good reasons why they should do so.' If we
substitute 'enact' for 'structure' in this passage (the reasons for which
should become clear as we proceed), we can agree.

We are well aware how contentious these issues are. This is why, in
order to substantiate our case, we must now, at some length, describe the
practice, theory, and history of our chosen example. We shall then take
some time to argue against certain approaches to ritual prevalent in anthropology, and, in the second half of the book, we begin to use our theory
to make some points about ritual in general. We feel this gives us a
distinctive and fruitful way of developing an ethnography of Jain religious

life through its rituals. Although most of our book proceeds through discussion of Jain ethnography, what we have to say applies, we hope, to all ritual.

Notes

1. We have placed 'offerings' in inverted commas because, as will become clear through this book, there are so many purposes and motives for performing *puja* and so many meanings given to these items, that the term 'offering' cannot be more than shorthand for 'things brought to the temple and laid before the god and which sometimes are thought of as offerings'.
2. The Jain rite has much in common with *puja* in other traditions. However, although many scholars have thought that the kernel of the *puja* is *prasad*, in which worshippers give offerings to a deity and receive them back as a blessing, the Jain ritual does not normally include this.
3. Sometimes, in this urban community of well-travelled business people, our conversations were in English or in a mixture of Hindi and English. Of course, the central religious concepts are most naturally expressed in Hindi or Sanskrit and some people preferred to speak in Hindi even if they did know English. Rather than interrupt the flow of conversation with questions arising from our patchy knowledge of Hindi or with questions about the particular meaning of Sanskrit terms, we recorded many of these interviews and spent a great deal of our research time translating and transcribing them with the help of our assistant, Anju Dhaddha. As Anju was not only a gifted linguist but also a practising Jain, she was able to provide us, as this work proceeded, with a valuable commentary of her own.
4. This idea was commonly expressed to us in English. In Hindi, people said that there is no meaning (*arth*) in the *puja*.
5. Bell's book appeared after this book had been virtually completed. We are greatly in sympathy with much of what she says and have profited from reading her critique, which in its broad sweep deconstructs and undermines much of the anthropological literature. We are not dissuaded, however, from adding our own theory to the fray.
6. In a similar vein, Moya (1990) argues that what distinguishes action from happenings (what we do from things which may merely happen to us) is most clear in the case of expressive, or what he calls 'meaningful' actions, and therefore it is these, and not the decontextualized 'raising the arm' and so on, beloved of the 'causal' theory, which should properly be called 'basic actions'. Moya argues that the nature of human action can only be understood against the background of the intentional character of mind: action is intrinsically intentional. The precise relations between intention and action are of course various: there are some actions which cannot be performed unintentionally (conspiring, murdering, marrying) and others which can (offending someone,

pulling a trigger, raising one's arm). But even in the latter case it is only because they *can* be performed intentionally that they are *actions* at all.

7. These are often focused on chiefly or priestly calendrical and fertility rites. The relative importance of these kinds of ritual varies over time in a given social entity (Atkinson 1989: 15) and it seems in many cases that there may be an inverse relation between the two (Thomas 1988).

2

Jainism and the *Puja* Ritual

THE central objects of veneration in a Jain temple are statues of human figures in marble, stone, or metal. These austere and rigid figures, always sharply sculpted and finely polished, sit with their hands folded on their lap or stand bolt upright in meditation. They are the Jinas or Tirthankars, the twenty-four divine ascetic renouncers who have founded and re-founded the Jain religion. Although there are many other idols[1] and sacred representations in Jain temples, it is essentially to the Tirthankars that the *puja* is addressed. Each temple is named after its one main Tirthankar, but statues of others gleam from every wall and dark corner, and it is as though, going into the temple, one enters a space which is already peopled by a crowd of silent identical predecessors.

In this chapter we shall introduce the Jinas and explain the general outlines of the Jain religion. Our exposition is brief because excellent studies of Jainism by Jaini (1979), Dundas (1992), and others, are available to interested readers.[2] However, we do make a detailed description of the daily morning *puja* as it is actually practised (this not being provided elsewhere), and we indicate its place among other Jain religious rituals. Throughout the book we shall make most of our points about ritual in general through the example of the Jain *puja* and this is why a certain minimum of information about the religion is provided here, but readers interested mainly in the theory of ritual as a mode of action could proceed directly to Chapter 3. The latter part of this chapter will show that even one religion (Jainism) may react to ritual through various understandings. In the case of the *puja* these responses range from devoted participation to outright rejection. Since such reactions emerge in specific historical and social contexts, we describe the present socio–economic position of the Jains, and we also provide a short history of the reforms and debates about ritual in the Khartar Gacch, the Jain tradition to which most of our friends in Jaipur belong.

The Jain Religion

Jainism, like other indigenous Indian religions, conceives of time in im-mense cosmic cycles, in which, by turns, the moral and physical condition of the universe improves and declines. It is part of the established order of the cosmos that twenty-four Jinas appear in India during each of these world-eras. By severe asceticism and meditation, they each discover the truth about the nature of the universe and the causes of suffering. Realizing that all living things are trapped in the cycle of death and rebirth, they achieve gradual awareness of the way to escape rebirth and achieve permanent release (*moksh*).

The early Jinas in our era are mythological figures, living for thousands of years in a distant Golden Age and establishing the institutions of human society. The last, Mahavir, is a securely historical figure, an elder contemporary of the Buddha, living some time during the 5th and 6th centuries BC. Both Mahavir and the Buddha were prominent in the schools of religious thinkers of the time known as *shramana*s. These teachers emphasized universal ethical precepts and individual salvation. Groups of mendicant renouncers experimented with a range of meditational, ascetic, and magical practices, and they repudiated the Vedic sacrifice and the intrinsic authority of the Brahman priestly caste. However, although the metaphysical and ethical doctrines they espoused were heretical at the time, they have in turn had considerable influence on Brahmanical tradition and so on modern Hinduism.

The Jains regard Mahavir as more than just a great religious innovator, for as a Jina he has a literally cosmic significance. Because of his actions during his previous births, he was born *destined* to (re)found the Jain religion, to be worshipped by gods, men, and animals alike, to achieve omniscience and eternal release, and to give the chance of salvation to countless souls. In this sense, despite the various popular stories attaching to the Jinas, including their individual adventures in previous births, the final life of each of them is summed up in five essentially identical supreme events. These are the five auspicious moments (*panc-kalyanak*): miraculous conception, auspicious birth, renunciation, omniscience, and release. These five moments are re-enacted in a long *puja* when a Tirthankar idol is consecrated and on a smaller scale in many other *puja*s. The truths of Jainism are eternal, and it is the unique contribution of the Tirthankars to rediscover these truths and to present and interpret them for the age in which they live. They preach from a great assembly hall, constructed for them by the gods. Thus they establish an order of Jain renouncers: men and women who will follow the path of wandering asceticism.

Jain renouncers are ordained at great public rituals, called *diksha*s, which along with the consecration of Jina idols constitute the major

religious events of Jain communities. Thereafter, they live with virtually
no possessions, according to strict codes of discipline, under the direct
authority of a guru. They are homeless, and except during the four
months of the rainy season when they should stay in one locality, they
journey on foot between villages, towns, and important Jain temples.
They practise regular self-mortifications, such as fasting and pulling out
their hair by hand; they give sermons to the laity, exhorting them to
practise austerities and make donations to religious and charitable causes;
and they lead them in ritualized meditation and confession. The Jain
religious community, or *sangh* (unlike the Buddhist use of this same
term), includes the laity as well as the renouncers.[3] Everyone should try to
follow, according to their circumstances, the precepts which form the
central monastic vows of the renouncers: non-violence, truth, not taking
anything which is not given, sexual restraint, and non-possession or non-
attachment. These precepts, as we shall see, are taken very seriously by
Jains. The great renouncers are a religious and ethical model for all and lay
piety includes ascetic and penitential practices modelled on those of the
renouncers.

Ascetic practices are thought to be directly effective in altering the
condition of the individual's soul, and it is the individual soul, the *jiv* or
atma, which is the focus of Jain religious and philosophical interest.
Unlike much Brahmanical thought, as expressed for example in the
*Upanishad*s, Jainism does not posit the equation of the individual soul
with a universal or cosmic soul. Nor have Jain thinkers, as have the
Buddhists, denied the existence of a permanent individual soul, and regarded existence as a momentary assemblage of conditions. And unlike
Christianity, Jainism has little place for a doctrine of the salvation of
society as a whole, alongside that of the individual. The closest that
Jainism gets to this idea is the miraculous preaching of the Tirthankar to
the 'assembly of listeners', which converts all those present to Jainism and
showers blessing upon them. But the people converted in this way must
still work towards their own personal salvation by asceticism and meditation. Thus for Jains the goal of religion is the transformation of the
individual soul throughout many lifetimes, and this occurs by ridding the
soul of *karma*.

What is the Jain theory of *karma*? The Jains believe the universe to be
governed by natural laws. These laws comprehend the moral as well as the
physical aspects of the universe, for the moral quality of an individual's
actions affects his or her future for good and ill in a directly mechanical
way. All indigenous Indian traditions maintain that the moral quality of

your previous acts, your *karma*, will affect your fate in this and in future lives, but the Jains are alone in seeing *karma* unequivocally as matter.[4] The individual embodied soul is encumbered and obscured by the tiny particles of matter which are attracted to it because of its mental and physical acts. The inevitable fruit of the *karma* from each sinful act is a later misfortune, including the desire and attachments which give rise to further sinful acts. Only by removing all this *karma* can the soul realize its true nature, which is to achieve omniscience (*keval gyan*) and then to become perfected (*siddha*). The soul which achieves this latter state leaves its earthly body and rises to the summit of the universe, there to experience eternal omniscience and bliss. But the universe itself is teeming with embodied souls, souls which, because of the *karma* they have acquired, have been reborn as gods in heaven or demons in hell, as plants, animals, or humans, or as tiny single-sensed beings which flourish briefly in the air, the earth, in water, or in fire. When their *karma* dictates, all these beings, including the gods, will die and be born again in some other form.

The existence of these innumerable living beings, each possessing a soul which in essence is the same as a human soul and thus ultimately capable of perfection and release, means that the ethical principle of not causing harm to others (*ahimsa*) acquires a peculiar importance and an all-embracing range. Taken to its limits this doctrine has shocking implications: any action might hurt these infinitesimal beings and cause one's own soul to accumulate harmful *karma*. This includes ritual. Thus, all worldly activity is strictly incompatible with the full realization of 'non-violence'. Unable to realize this ideal, all Jains nevertheless pursue it as best they may: they are strict vegetarians and they also avoid many vegetables and fruits which are believed to contain many souls. The daily routine of renouncers is dominated by the closely specified procedures by which they must obtain their food as alms from lay householders, and by ritualized forms of meditation, confession, and penance. Jainism permits and even recommends a controlled, ritualized fast to death for the spiritually advanced.[5] However, although both physical and mental discipline are the most highly valued and central goals in Jain tradition, inspirational and ecstatic practices, as we shall see later, also find their place within it.

The Jains

The tradition established by Mahavir split early on into two separate and frequently mutually hostile branches, Shvetambar and Digambar.[6] Spiritually advanced renouncers among the Digambars go naked and stand to take the food offered to them in the palms of their hands. They deny that women can attain enlightenment and allow female renouncers only a very subordinate status. The clothes worn by the Shvetambars are simple white robes. The majority of Shvetambar renouncers are women, although the highest-ranking are men, and this tradition believes that many women have attained enlightenment and release. They maintain that the nineteenth Tirthankar of our age, Mallinath, was a woman. The doctrinal differences between the Digambars and Shvetambars imply a different view of the body, a subject which we shall return to in Chapter 11.[7] Both the Digambar and the Shvetambar traditions have subsequently subdivided. The community of Jain renouncers has always been prone to segmentary division, and texts record heterodox and dissident groups from the very earliest times. Now in both traditions some groups sanction the worship of Jina idols and some do not. Indeed, debate over the validity or the importance of *puja* has frequently been a central issue in sectarian schism.

The general picture today among the Shvetambars, who are found mostly in western India, is as follows. There are two broad and loosely organized groupings, the Murti Pujaks ('idol-worshippers'), and the Sthanakvasis ('those who dwell in halls'). The latter do not maintain temples, worship idols, or celebrate the *puja*. There is another more recent group, the Terapanth, which, like the Sthanakvasi order, is against the *puja*, but which, unlike either of the other two groupings, is a tight sectarian organization under the authority of a single leader, called an *acarya*. The major divisions within the Murti-Pujaks are called *gacch*s. Although some of these are more cohesive than others, they tend to have more than one *acarya*, and all are further subdivided into smaller informal groupings around particular senior or charismatic renouncers. The lay followers of each *gacch* maintain temples, renouncers' dwelling-halls, and other religious buildings. Jaipur has substantial lay followings of both Digambars and Shvetambars. All the main Shvetambar groups are represented, including the Terapanthis, the Sthanakvasis, and the two most important Murti-Pujak *gacch*s: the Tapa Gacch and the Khartar Gacch. This book is about followers of the Khartar Gacch in Jaipur city.

The stereotype of a lay Jain is that he or she is an affluent *baniya*, that is, from a grouping of high castes traditionally associated with trade, retailing, and money-lending. Indeed a large number of Jains are wealthy, and their pursuit of profit is notoriously unstinting. Nevertheless, as we have said, the principles and practices of the possessionless renouncers are highly influential among them. Lay Jains can rival the monastics of most other religious traditions in the prohibitions they apply to their daily routine, in sexual abstinence, in penitential fasting, and in their avoidance of personal adornment and self-indulgence. The Khartar Gacch Jains of Jaipur certainly conform to the stereotype. Concentrated in the most expensive trading quarter of the old walled city, many of them are emerald and diamond traders in the large and lucrative gem market there. They own rambling *havelis*, mansions which serve both as homes for joint families and as business premises. The major families can afford to build themselves modern villas in a smart residential suburb about a mile from the city gate. Still, the older men in particular maintain a frugal demeanour. As the end of life approaches both men and women spend more and more time at worship.

The Jain suburban villas in Jaipur cluster round the Khartar Gacch temple in which we did most of our work.

Puja *in the Dadabari Temple*

The descriptions of the Jain ritual of worship used as our main example in this book derive from what we saw in the Dadabari temple in Jaipur. Here, the central idol is of the twenty-third Tirthankar, Parshvanath, and there is a separate shrine to the *Dada-guru-dev*s (see Plates I and II).[8] The *guru-dev*s are the four patron saints of the Khartar Gacch, leading renouncers who lived between the eleventh and seventeenth centuries and performed miracles to protect their followers and attract new converts to the religion. The worship of renouncer-saints, both living and dead, is a prominent part of devotional practice in Jainism, as it is in many Hindu traditions. The Khartar Gacch *guru-dev*s are highly popular in the Jaipur area. They are believed still to perform miracles, and this shrine even attracts worshippers from the nominally non-idolatrous Jain traditions.

Let us first take a look around the Dadabari. Apart from its central statue, the temple in the Dadabari, like other Jain temples, contains many other Jina (Tirthankar) idols (see Figs. 1 and 2). In most temples there are idols of all twenty-four Jinas as well as several examples of the four or five who are most popular. In front of the central shrine in each temple stands a metal structure about a metre high, colloquially called a *samosaran*. This is a three-tiered podium which is said to represent both Mount Meru, the mythical mountain at the centre of the world, and the sacred assembly hall from which the Jina delivers his sermons. At certain times a tiny metal idol of the Jina to whom the temple is dedicated is placed here and *puja* is performed to it. The reason for this duplication is that this small idol can

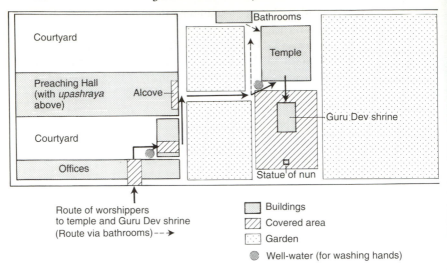

F IG. 1. Plan of Dadabari temple compound.

be moved during *puja*s, unlike the ritually 'placed' (*pratishthit*) stone and marble idols. It is also used on festive occasions in noisy processions through the streets around the temple.

Jain temples contain a profusion of other sacred representations, all of which are the object of prayers and offerings in *puja*. By the doors to the central sanctuary one often finds statues of some of the other great Jain saints. The most common of these is Gautam Swami, Mahavir's own most devoted disciple. Still other more recent saints are represented either in statues or in more simple footprint shrines (*caran*s). Then each of the Jinas is associated with a pair of powerful, miracle-working protector deities, a god (*shasan-devta*) and a goddess (*shasan-devi*), also known as *yaksha*s and *yakshi*s.[9] One or two of these protector deities, especially the goddesses, have been picked out for veneration in their own right, and are rather like the powerful goddesses of Hinduism.[10] They are often found in shrines around the walls of the main temple. Unlike the austere Jina statues they are often adorned with brightly coloured, embroidered clothes, and carry weapons, conch shells, wheels, thunderbolts, and other emblems and attributes.

Other representations include *papier-mâché* panels showing events from the lives of the Jinas and gaudy schematic pictures of important pilgrimage sites. There are stone bas-reliefs depicting all twenty-four

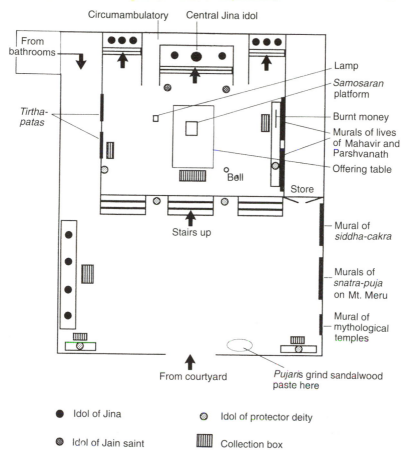

FIG. 2. Interior of Dadabari temple.

Jinas sitting together in serried ranks, and various geometrical diagrams such as *yantras* and *mandalas*, which are endowed with magical power. The Dadabari temple has one popular object of worship, which is a picture frame containing the remains of several burnt rupee notes. This commemorates a famous act of renunciation by a local Jain merchant.

Nearer the outer door one finds idols of a range of powerful gods and goddesses who are rooted in local Rajasthani and Gujarati 'Hindu' tradition but also incorporated into Jain religious practice. These include the *bhumiyas* ('lords of the soil') and the *kshetrapals* ('guardians of the place'), both of whom are often represented as almost featureless silver-covered blobs, and the *bhairus*, depicted as armed, mustachioed warriors. Unlike the Jinas and renouncer-saints, these deities are not Jain and consequently are not bound by vows of non-violence. Their supernatural power is potentially harmful. They inflict illness on those who violate the places they guard or who show disrespect to the Jain religion. Lay Jains pray and make vows to them to obtain their power in granting worldly success and destroying enemies. Ideally, although this is not always adhered to, *puja* should be performed to these various idols in order: first to the central idol of the temple, then to the other Jinas, to the Jain protector deities and renouncer-saints, and finally to the powerful gods.

So how is the daily *puja* performed? Each morning from just after dawn, people who wish to perform *puja* first bathe to purify themselves, dress in clean clothes, and make their way to the temple. Each worshipper arrives bearing a small tray, bag, or box full of offerings. These may include rice grains, fresh flower heads, sticks of incense, nuts, fruits, sweets, and money. Just outside the temple, worshippers remove their shoes and rinse their hands at a tank of well-water near the door. As they enter, they bow, and many touch the threshold with their right hand, uttering a short salutation, *nissahi*, and so declaring that they are leaving worldly cares and concerns behind. Inside, a servant grinds sandalwood with saffron and water into a smooth yellow paste and each worshipper takes a little of this in a small metal pot, adding it to his or her tray of offerings. By a small mirror nearby, more sandalwood paste is provided so that worshippers can put a small dot, a *tilak*, on their forehead. The final preparation which worshippers make, before approaching the central shrine, is to cover their mouths with a piece of cloth.[11]

The *puja* is not performed in unison. Each celebrant acts alone and chooses his or her own way. There is no set time for performing the daily *puja* and no congregation which holds a common service. Worshippers are free to come to the temple and worship at any time during daylight hours, and they have direct access to the idols. They spend as long as they like at their devotions and put together their own separate performances. As mentioned above, Jain teaching stresses the need for each individual to work towards his or her own salvation. Fittingly, then, there is no need for officiating priests in Jain temples. In theory all consecrated idols should be worshipped at least once every day, but it is lay people themselves, rather than priests, who perform these regular repeated rituals, unlike in many Hindu temples. Servants employed in the temple are called *pujaris*, which is the term Hindus use for priests, but rather than actually performing the *puja*, they merely assist lay worshippers to do so. Their tasks include cleaning the temple, and removing the previous day's offerings. They lay out utensils, collect flowers, prepare sandalwood paste, light lamps, fill water vessels, make sure that incense burners are kept filled, and blow conch shells and ring the temple bell to accompany particular kinds of offering.[12]

The individuality of the daily *puja* is emphasized by the fact that Jains are not supposed to greet, or even recognize each other while at worship, and as they make their way about the temple, it seems almost that they cannot see the kinsmen, neighbours, and colleagues around them. One is alone in one's religious practice. In this respect the Jain morning *puja* seems unlike most rituals studied by anthropologists. But *puja*s can on occasion be communal affairs, as we describe below. So the point to note here is that *communitas* is not intrinsic to ritualization. The Jain daily *puja* is perhaps something of a limiting case as rituals go, and our discussion of the mental representations and actions that are shared even here allows us to think further about what it is in ritualization in general that is held in common. But before we can reach that point, and in order for readers to be able to follow what we have to say about the ritual later in this book, we should now describe the 'complete' morning *puja* itself. What follows is based on what we observed in the Dadabari and other temples in Jaipur. We must stress that it would only rarely be possible to see a particular person doing exactly what we describe, and we have indicated here only the main points of divergence between individual worshippers. Some devout Jains would certainly want to quarrel with some detail or other, and to suggest an improvement of their own.

A performance of *puja* consists of a number of specific, named acts, also called *puja*s.[13] The ritual usually begins with a sequence of acts in which the idol is bathed: in water, in milk, and sometimes in more lavish mixtures of curd, ghee, milk, and sugar, mixed with sandalwood, camphor, and other perfumes. Often, in preparation for this, it is first dusted with a peacock feather. Then, after being scrubbed vigorously with little brushes of dried grass and rinsed in fresh water, it is dried with three soft woollen cloths. The central idol is bathed shortly after the temple opens in the morning, so only those who arrive early can take part in this.

As part of the bathing stage of the *puja*, the tiny movable Jina idol is bathed each morning in a ceremony called *snatra puja*, which a small group of early worshippers performs together (Plate VIII). The idol is placed on the *samosaran* and those who take part join in singing songs from booklets provided in the temple. This ritual is a re-enactment of a famous story in the life of all the Jinas: just after his birth, the gods and

goddesses (*devtas/devis*), led by Indra, king of the gods, take him to
Mount Meru to worship him and to give him his first bath in water
brought from the heavenly milky oceans. In the *snatra puja*, worshippers
take on the role of the gods, as the Jina's first and paradigmatic worshippers. Various details from the mythic story are enacted: fly-whisks
(*camars*), traditional symbols of royalty in India, are waved as the gods pay
homage to the infant prince; a jug in the form of a bull is used, because one
of the gods in the myth took the form of a bull and produced milk from his
horns; and so forth. In *snatra puja* people mimic actions in a story, but
they also do things which are not in the story.[14] On an average day in the
Dadabari, only two or three people perform the *snatra puja*.

    Throughout the morning people continue to arrive and perform their
own bathing rite, by washing one or more of the other Tirthankar idols.
Worshippers arrive in ones and twos, and on entering the temple they may
circumambulate the central idol in its sanctum and then ring the bell
which hangs from the ceiling in the centre of the main hall. As the
morning progresses, other lay Jains come dressed in ordinary clothes,
perhaps on their way to work, content only to bow before the idols and
take a *darshan*, or 'vision' of them.

    The next stage of the *puja* is often to dab a little sandalwood paste on
nine parts of the idol and to place fresh flowers on its lap, its knees, its
shoulders, or the top of its head. This is known as *anga* ('limb') *puja*. The
process of anointing and decorating may be completed by applying perfumed oil or sheets of silver foil and by dressing the idol with jewelled
ornaments and a silver crown. Worshippers may recite prayers internally
in silence, or in a distinctive, low but relentless, mutter. As they wander
from statue to statue, adding a rose here, a jasmine flower there, or a dab
of sandalwood paste on a favourite idol, they might recite as they choose
various chants, magical formulas, prayers, and songs. Some people read
prayers from printed manuals which are provided in the temple, and there
is a large stock of hymns and devotional praise-songs, some of which are
quite widely known and are set to popular Hindi film music. Others have
Jain lyrics, often penned by leading Jain renouncers, fitted to tunes which
are also sung in Hindu temples. But what most people do is to repeat
under their breath time and again one well-known sacred formula—the
namaskar-mantra—either in full or in a shortened form.[15] Occasionally
someone will sing out loud or a bell will be rung, but usually there is
virtual silence in the temple, broken only by the gentle padding of bare
feet as people criss-cross the floor, intent on their own devotions. A lamp
is lit at the beginning of the morning and placed in the central hall before

the main idol, but many worshippers also take small oil lamps, and then a large incense burner, on further perambulations around the various idols in the temple.

After anointing the idol and burning incense and lamps before it, the worshipper makes a number of offerings, of rice, fruits, sweets, and money, which are placed on benches or tables in front of the idols. This is *agra* ('in front') *puja*. Most offerings are placed on the table which stands in the middle of the central hall in front of the main statue, but there is space for offerings in front of the other Jinas, and smaller tables and collection boxes stand before many of the other idols. So there are always little arrangements of rice, sweets, fruits, and coins lying here and there around the temple. Sometimes the rice is simply scattered or placed in a little pile, but many people conjure a more elaborate arrangement. In this, the rice is laid out to form a swastika, with three dots above it, and above this there is a further single dot, sitting in a crescent shape (see Fig. 3 and Plates III and VIII). Fruits, sweets, and money are placed on or around this rice pattern. Everyone lays out their offerings themselves, and when the offering tables become crowded they push aside those left by earlier worshippers to make room for their own. Every so often a *pujari* comes and sweeps up everything from the tables, leaving them clear for later worshippers. People can choose to perform a range of other actions, using coconuts, mirrors, flags, and fly-whisks, and they can also decide whether or not to employ a range of ritual postures and gestures.

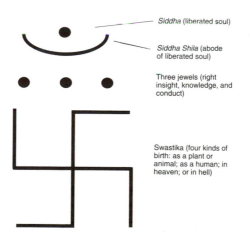

Siddha (liberated soul)

Siddha Shila (abode of liberated soul)

Three jewels (right insight, knowledge, and conduct)

Swastika (four kinds of birth: as a plant or animal; as a human; in heaven; or in hell)

FIG. 3. Standard pattern formed from rice grains during *puja*.

The last stage of the ritual, *bhav puja*, is a period of meditation and prayer, performed without the use of objects or substances.[16] Some people do this by sitting before the pattern of offerings they have laid out, often in silence, but sometimes singing quietly or using their fingers as a rosary to count their recitation of prayers. Others go through an elaborate series of prostrations before kneeling, with the left knee raised in front of them, and reciting ancient verses in Prakrit, the language of the Jain scriptures. In this they are drawing on rituals which are prescribed for the veneration of renouncers. These are called *vandan* and are performed in slightly different forms to the Jinas (*caitya vandan*) and to a living renouncer (*guru vandan*).[17] Jain renouncers are eager to instruct the laity on how to perform these salutations, perhaps because they are the most respectful forms for householders to use when approaching the ascetics themselves. But only a few lay Jains know a full text of this ritual (which varies slightly between different sects and the followers of different leading renouncers), and of those who have learned it by heart fewer still can understand the Prakrit. So what generally happens is that people adopt the well-known crouching posture for the rite, or just sit cross-legged on the ground, and either read from a manual or sing their own favourite hymns and prayers.

During the course of the morning this flow of individual and independent performances of *puja* is interrupted by the performance of *arti*. *Arti* is a ritual act in which an oil lamp is waved in front of an idol. The celebrant holds up the *arti* lamp with both hands in front of his or her face, and with eyes fixed on the idol beyond, uses the lamp to describe a circle in the air, framing the idol in rhythmic clockwise motions. Some people come to the temple in the evening, around sunset, just to perform *arti*. But while it can thus be a separate ritual, *arti* is also an element in many elaborate sponsored *puja*s, and it is part of the routine of the daily morning *puja* too. Suddenly a *pujari* stands beneath the temple bell and starts to ring it, continuously and insistently. All those in the temple break off what they are doing and come up in turn, usually all the men followed by all the women, and for a few seconds each waves the lamp before the central Jina idol, while everyone else claps and sings a song of praise to the Jina, this song in most temples being printed on a board near the entrance to the sanctum. In large city-centre temples and at famous pilgrimage places auctions (*boli*) are held each day for the privilege of performing *arti* first, and this practice is also used in other temples on certain special occasions and auspicious days. Thus it is a curious feature of Jain ritual that, despite the emphasis in the religion on detachment and equanimity, certain key acts become the focus of passionate intention. *Arti* is abrupt and noisy, and rather a sharp change in tempo and tone from the leisure and quiet of the rest of the morning *puja*. As they finish their turn, each celebrant puts a small coin in the tray on which the *arti* lamp stands. In some temples another *pujari* bangs on a kettle-drum behind the scenes. Some Jains travel to other temples outside the city to take part in wild, ecstatic *arti* performances which can culminate in spirit exorcism (see Chapter 10).

The links between the Jain *puja* and popular Hindu forms of worship, which are suggested by the pantheon of powerful gods in the temple, is clear also in the simple *puja*s performed by Jains at home. Many Jain families have a small shrine in the house, a separate room, a cupboard, or just a small shelf in the corner of a room. Exactly what these shrines contain varies from family to family, but typically they include a few small Jina idols, statues of some Hindu deities such as Ganesh and Lakshmi, pictures of Jain saints, and oleographs or amulets from important pilgrimage sites that members of the family have visited. Just as Jain shopkeepers and businessmen, in a practice which parallels exactly that of their Hindu counterparts, take a small incense stick around their shops and offices every morning, waving it before pictures of Jinas and protector deities, which they also garland, so in many Jain homes this small shrine is attended by one or two members of the family, usually women, with a few simple *puja* acts and a short prayer each morning.[18]

At the other extreme, the major events of the Jain religious year are marked by lavish public *puja*s, sponsored by local caste or sect organizations or by wealthy private patrons. Murti Pujak Jains hold a bewildering variety of ceremonial *puja*s on a wide range of occasions, at most religious gatherings and to mark many of the important events in the life of a community or its prominent individuals. The form of these *puja*s depends on the particular occasion which is being celebrated, and more especially on the patron's preference. The *siddha cakra puja*, for instance, focuses on the worship of a sacred diagram (*yantra*) which represents the Jinas, the liberated souls (*siddha*), and renouncers of various levels of seniority, together with the qualities of spiritual insight, knowledge, good conduct, and asceticism; and 'offerings' are made in turn in worship of each of these categories. Other public *puja*s take as their theme different magical diagrams, certain kinds of *karma*, a specific Jina, or a renouncer-saint such as a *guru-dev*. These *puja*s usually involve bounteous heaps of offerings—of fruits, grains, perfumes, and sweets—but they are basically amplifications of the everyday morning rites. Members of the sponsoring family, or those who have won auctions for the honour, go through very lengthy series of the same *puja* acts which are performed by individuals each

PL. I. *The Dada Guru Dev shri at the Dadabari temple in Jaipur*. On the left a *pujari* is cleaning off sandalwood paste left by previous worshippers. The hand appearing from the right is pouring water on a representation of the Guru Dev's footprints.

PL. II. *The same idol, at the climax of an elaborate* puja. The whole shrine has been hung with garlands of flowers, and the idol has been covered with silver foil and decorated with coloured paste and beads.

Pʟ. III. *The offering-table in the Dadabari temple.* Individual worshippers leave their own arrangements of offerings, and when the table is full they clear away those left by others to make room. They make patterns which elaborate and alter, in various ways, the basic design shown in Fig. 3.

morning, under the guidance of temple servants, while a large gathering of relatives, friends, neighbours, and indeed anyone who happens to come to the temple, sings songs and chants prayers from books and pamphlets provided in the temple (see Chapters 5, 6, and 8 for descriptions of such public *puja*s).

Models and Meanings

All these acts of washing, anointing, decorating, offering, manipulating, singing, chanting, and gesturing are well-known in Jain communities. From our conversations and interviews, it is clear that the *puja* is described in language by those who perform it as a prescribed and structured series of specific acts, and it is an anthropological task of no great difficulty to abstract from people's accounts one or more authoritative 'models' for the ritual. We call these 'discursive models', to make clear that they refer to what people said, to one another or to us, as opposed to what they did, or what they thought to themselves (in so far as it is possible for us to talk about this). Two fairly simple discursive models of the *puja* emerged as dominant in the Dadabari community in Jaipur: a linear, sequential model, and an analytical, 'nesting' model as follows.

1. *'Sequential' model of the* puja. The sequential model is abstracted from accounts people gave us of what one does in *puja*—'First I do this, then I do that . . .'. The lists of stages people gave us were various, and sometimes included repetitions of stages, but most resembled more or less closely the standard list of eight things, the 'eightfold' or *ashta prakari puja*. This model lists eight substances in sequence, but does not distinguish between different kinds of operations performed with these substances, such as the pouring of water, the dabbing of paste, the waving of lamps, and so on. This model also leaves out all other bodily movements—bowing, circumambulating the statue—as well as prayers, and the use of milk and silver foil, and it disguises the use of the same substance, such as sandalwood paste or rice, in different operations which are clearly distinguished in the second model.

→ 1. *jal* (water) → 2. *candan* (sandalwood) → 3. *pushpa* (flowers) → → 4. *dhup* (incense) → 5. *dip* (lamp) → 6. *akshat* (rice) → → 7. *naivedya* (sweets) → 8. *phal* (fruit)

2. *'Nesting' model of the* puja. The nesting model (see Fig. 4) is abstracted from more analytic statements about what the *puja* is, for instance, where people said, 'There are two kinds of *puja*—*puja* with things and *puja* with thoughts', or, 'Rice *puja* is part of "in front" *puja*, and so is fruit *puja*.' Although this model is more comprehensive than the sequential model, it leaves the position of the incense and lamp *puja*s ambiguous. Informants were divided on whether they counted as *anga* or *agra puja*, and some refused to assign them to either category which leaves them anomalous from the point of view of this model. This model is also open-ended in a way that the sequential model is not. Different informants provided versions of widely differing detail and complexity and there seemed to be no 'complete' version.

A few points by way of explanation. *Prakshal puja* is bathing the idol. This is grouped with acts of anointing and decorating into *anga puja* ('*puja* of the limbs [of the idol]'). *Anga puja* involves doing things to the idol itself, and it is opposed to another group of acts called *agra puja* ('*puja* in front') in which worshippers place offerings on small tables before the idol. At the most inclusive level, we have a further distinction for *anga puja* and *agra puja*, taken together, are called *dravya puja*, or 'material'

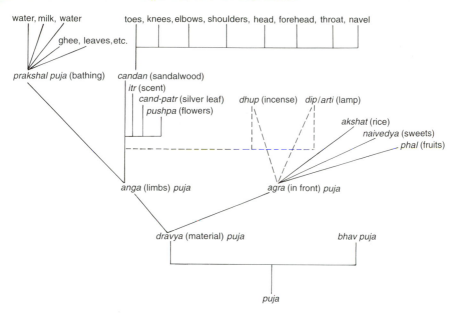

water, milk, water

ghee, leaves, etc.

toes, knees, elbows, shoulders, head, forehead, throat, navel

prakshal puja (bathing)   *candan* (sandalwood)

itr (scent)

cand-patr (silver leaf)   *dhup* (incense)   *dip/arti* (lamp)

pushpa (flowers)

akshat (rice)

naivedya (sweets)

phal (fruits)

anga (limbs) *puja*   *agra* (in front) *puja*

dravya (material) *puja*   *bhav puja*

puja

FIG. 4. 'Nesting' model of *puja*.

puja, as they are acts done with material objects and substances. This is distinguished from *bhav puja*, which may be translated as 'devotion *puja*' (but see further discussion in Chapter 9). In *bhav puja* the only visible action is the adoption of specified bodily postures, and the worshipper either meditates, or, often silently, rehearses prayers or songs. We have arranged this diagram to reflect a general temporal ordering of these segments of the *puja*. Most people's performances progress roughly from left to right.

Even though the grouping of *puja* acts into the categories provided by these models is, we found, fairly generally agreed, we can see no serious sense in which these discursive models can be thought of as 'underlying' the *puja* as action. Agreement among celebrants about the constituents of the *puja* does not lead everyone to identical performances. Far from it. People choose when and for how long to come to the temple, and which particular *puja*s, under each more general heading, to perform. They select the things of each general type to offer, and how much to leave before each of the many idols. Of each act they perform, they choose likewise how much time and care to take, whether or not to repeat it before any particular idol and whether to perform it before every idol in the temple or only before a few. From a bewildering range of available songs and prayers in Sanskrit, Prakrit, and Hindi, they choose which, if any, to recite. As in so many cases described in the anthropological literature, the 'repetitions' of the ritual are observably various. It becomes difficult to describe how models such as these might in any way actually inform ritual performance, although it is usually blithely assumed in anthropological monographs that somehow or other they do. We shall return to these difficulties, and consider their implications for the understanding of ritual in general, in Chapters 5 and 6.

As with any ritual, the celebrants of the *puja* may content themselves with simply performing what they see as the correct acts, without attributing any particular meaning to them. But if they do lend meaning to their actions, the sources they can apply to are many and various. Learned or influential renouncers, lay religious specialists, and amateur historians produce a stream of books and pamphlets on a wide range of religious topics and these are widely circulated in Jain communities. Sponsorship for religious publications is easy to find, and religious books are the only kind allowed in many devout households. Booklets in Hindi and Sanskrit also provide a substantial number of songs and prayers for use in *puja* although few of these are much used by ordinary worshippers. The meanings offered in these various media draw on episodes in mythology, most especially the lives of the Jinas, and from Jain doctrines about asceticism, non-violence, psychology, cosmography, and the karmic causality of human affairs. Such is the wealth of this material that there is no one authoritative source which links a given ritualized act with a specific meaning. This crucial link is left for the individual worshipper to make.

Thus, when we asked about the *puja* they had just performed, the meanings which different people assigned to the same offerings and acts varied considerably. Let us look, for example, at the range of meanings we were given for *pushpa puja*, the placing of flowers on the statue.

1. *An elderly female renouncer.* 'When flowers are offered people should think, "As this flower has blossomed and attained completion, so should my soul, so should my knowledge (*gyan*), blossom".'

2. *A middle-aged man.* 'The flower is soft. Like this our heart must be soft. By putting flowers we remove anger and put good morals in our heart.'

3. *An elderly woman.* 'We put flowers because of the smell. Flowers must smell or they are not allowed.[19] If you have no flowers, then you can use cloves, as they

have a flower shape and a good smell. The smell helps to concentrate the mind, it fascinates and attracts people, so they will take pleasure in worshipping.'

4. *A young girl.* 'We put things like flowers to God so that in real life we don't get distracted and lose our way. This is not my idea, but said by the *muni*s (male ascetics).'

5. *A young businessman.* 'It is said that flowers have scent. We know many smells in this life. We put flowers so that we don't get distracted by beauty and pleasant scents. We give them to God instead.'

6. *A middle-aged woman.* 'We do the offering of flowers (*kusum-anjali*[20]). This is like when our grandfather is dead and we do homage (*shraddh-anjali*), or like giving flowers after Gandhi-ji's death. If it is God's birthday we offer flowers.'

7. *Another young girl.* 'I do not know the reason why I put flowers, I just do it. But they should not be picked. Take only those which have fallen, and then wash them and clean them. See that there are no insects in them. The flowers must first be purified with incense. This is why I burn incense first when I come to the temple.'[21]

8. *A young female renouncer.* 'You consider your Being as having many circles (*cakra*s). With every stage of knowledge one new circle opens out. Each *cakra* gives us a new strength. The entire blossoming of the flower is *keval gyan* (omniscience). As you, the Tirthankar, have this, this is what we want.'

9. *A middle-aged businessman.* 'It is just emotion (*bhav*) from the heart.'

10. *An old woman.* 'Flowers are pure and good, so we offer them to God for his decoration.'

11. *A young jeweller.* 'Flowers? I do not offer any flowers; I do not believe in these things. Only devotion (*bhakti*) is important.'

People thus gave not entirely random, but certainly very different meanings to the flower offering, and in some cases the meanings were diametrically opposed (compare 3 and 5). So we are not just dealing with a limited *range* of meanings, of which one might, for instance, chart the limits. In attributing meaning to an act, worshippers take their cues from the characteristics of the act itself, from their experiences of it, from official teaching, and so on. It is worth noting that there is nothing one might call a single core meaning, such that the variations could be explained away as more or less close approximations to a norm or ideal.

Worshippers drew freely on the various competing sources of authoritative interpretation, but they also provided idiosyncratic interpretations of their own, and cited as support for these both their own feelings and thoughts as they performed the ritual, and their particular understanding of the 'fundamentals' of Jain philosophy. Our informants were certainly deferential to the religious authority of renouncers and religious specialists, but they also referred confidently to their own understandings and opinions. Equally readily, they might admit that they knew no rationale behind the meaning they assigned to an act, or indeed that they knew no meaning for it at all. In this latter case they might venture a speculation, plucked almost at random, about what the 'correct' meaning might be. To the observer, the problem appears to be a superabundance of meanings—meaning untamed. In what sense can these very same Jains be saying that the *puja* has no meaning?

The Religious Reaction to Ritual

As one of the themes of this book is to question the anthropological orthodoxy that rituals are essentially systems of meaning, it is crucial to make clear that when our Jain friends warned us that the *puja* is meaningless they were not advancing a version of our anthropological argument. Nor do we take the essentially religious point they were making to be in any direct sense evidence in support of our own position. Nevertheless, such statements did force us to think about the religious contentiousness of ritual, and this in turn led us to see that ritualized action has its own characteristics which can disturb or entrance the religious imagination.

Religious traditions objectify and appraise ritual in their own quite different ways. Clearly, then, a study of these religious reactions cannot be identical to the anthropological analysis of the distinctiveness of ritual action. Yet, because ritual is human action, and not an object in the world like a tree or the sun, any theory about it must involve the fact that the subjective attitudes which are taken towards it in any particular context will shape the specific manifestations of the general phenomenon which are there for the observer to see. In order to set the *puja* properly in context, we need to describe the ways in which ritual in general, and the *puja* in particular, have perennially evoked religious doubts, claims, and counter-claims among the Jains. Ritual has frequently been the target of religious 'reform', although the direction and results of such reform are by no means always the same.

Early Jainism, in common with other *shramana* movements, rejected the validity of the dominant religious tradition of its time, that of the priestly Brahmin caste, which was focused on ritual (the Vedic sacrifice). Now, there is very little evidence, and certainly no direct ethnographic observation, to tell us exactly how these rites were performed and what participants thought about them at the time. However, textual scholars are able to tell us a certain amount on the basis of Vedic ritual texts, which contain specific instructions on how to perform sacrifices and lengthy hymns to accompany them; and, more importantly, we know from the writings of opponents of the sacrifice, such as the Buddhists and the Jains, what they found objectionable in these rites.

There is virtual unanimity among scholars that the Vedic sacrifice was rule-bound, that the actions and songs are minutely specified in the Vedic texts, and crucially that the sacrifice was understood to have a necessary effect on the reproduction of the cosmos. This was a classic example of an automatically efficacious ritual. Brian Smith writes, 'The ritual order lends its form to a cosmic order, a universal structure emanating from the structured sequence of rites. Such grand results, however, depend on the perfect performance of the ceremonial. In the construction of a ritual production, each detail must be attended to and properly executed' (B. K. Smith 1989: 53–4).[22] Sacrifice is the womb of order (*ritasya yoni*) and the rite is efficacious because it is considered to act directly on the world according to the same ordered conditions of existence (Herrenschmidt 1982: 27). There are no means whereby the desired outcome can be achieved other than by sacrifice. The same may be true of ritual in other traditions, such as Taoism, in which the universe is thought to function according to a natural order (Schipper and Staal 1986). Now the Jains also believe the universe to be subject to fundamental laws within which a ritual such as the *puja* and other rites for the removal of *karma* are seen as effective acts. But on the other hand the earliest and most authoritative Jain scriptures, those of the Shvetambar canon, are unlike the Vedas in that they are not liturgical. They contain neither prescriptions for ritual acts nor hymns to be sung. The canon includes Jain cosmology and philosophy, the refutation of false views, the delimitation of pious and impious acts, the rules to be followed by Jain ascetics, stories of the lives of the Jinas, and edifying narratives for the laity and potential converts. With these texts we are immediately faced with the demand for a moral life, and within this explicit anti-ritualistic criticism of Vedic sacrifice is one of the founding protestant gestures of the Jain religion.[23]

The twenty-fifth lecture in the canonical *Uttaradhyayana Sutra* tells of a Jain ascetic who approaches a Brahmin priest to beg for alms while the latter is sacrificing. He is refused, and so discourses to the priest as follows on the nature of the 'true' Brahmin and the 'true' sacrifice.

He who is called by people a Brahmin and is worshipped like fire (is not a true Brahmin) . . .

He who is not greedy, who lives unknown, who has no house and no property, and who has no friendship with householders, him we call a Brahmin . . .

The binding of animals (to the sacrificial pole), all the Vedas, and sacrifices, being causes of sin, cannot save the sinner; for his works (*karma*) are very powerful.

One does not become a *shramana* by the tonsure, nor a Brahmin by the sacred syllable *om*, nor a *muni* by living in the woods, nor a *tapasa* (ascetic) by wearing (clothes of) *kusha*-grass and bark.

One becomes a *shramana* by equanimity, a Brahmin by chastity, a *muni* by knowledge, and a *tapasa* by penance.

Thus sacrifice, as a ritual act separated from life in general, is contrasted with 'sacrifice', as renunciation governing a whole way of life. The priest is convinced and enters the Jain order with the declaration, 'You have well declared to me what true Brahminhood consists in. You are a sacrificer of sacrifices' (Jacobi 1895: 138–41). It is not only that the Brahmanical Vedic sacrifice involves killing living beings, and is therefore a sin, but any ritualized act, any simple 'mark' which stands for a way of life without actually being it, is insufficient. This does not affect the question of the efficacy of ritual—rituals are still regarded by Jains as effective ways to change one's state—but it gives rise to the double question: is it ideally by ritual that such results should be obtained? and are the results of ritual the best ones from the religious point of view? Thus the same text describes the benefits of yet another kind of 'sacrifice', the kind of magical powers one can acquire by practising Jain ascetic rituals, and the help and protection which gods, pleased by the ritual penances performed by Jain adepts, render to the Jain religion. That such Jain 'sacrifice' has its benefits is not doubted, but the superior form of religion is to sacrifice sacrifice.

To repeat, such Jain polemical texts are probably of rather limited value if one wanted to reconstruct the practice of ancient Vedic sacrifice, but there can be no doubt that the Vedic rituals have come to be generally *represented*, within both Jain and much Hindu tradition, as necessary and automatically effective rites. This can serve either as a spectre of superstition and false religion, or as a paragon of an age in which the prescribed conduct (*dharma*) of men, governed by the Brahmins and the Word in the Vedas, was in complete conformity with the order (*dharma*) of the cosmos. The point, for our purposes, is that the idea of automatically efficacious ritual, while it has never been uncontroversial, has never left the Jain tradition. As the passage above from the *Uttaradhyayana Sutra* intimates, Jains have often described physical austerity as a fire sacrifice, conducted inside one's own body (see further discussion in Chapter 11). And to this day the central practices of monastic asceticism are widely regarded as rites in which accurate physical movements and correct recitation of texts produce unseen changes in the condition of the soul. These rituals, in various forms, are common to all Jain traditions, both Digambar and Shvetambar. They include: *samayik* (a ritualized form of prayer and meditation), *pratikraman* (a rite for 'casting off' past sin), *vandan* (a rite of obeisance performed to renouncers), *kaussagg* (a combination of penance and meditation in prescribed bodily postures), *paccakkhan* (a ritual formula for taking a vow, typically a vow to fast), *diksha* (initiation of renouncers), *baharana* (the presentation of alms to renouncers) and *updhan* (the adoption, by householders, for a fixed period of time, of all the vows and restrictions of renouncers).

The mechanical causality of *karma* provides a partial basis for the explanation of ritual efficacy in that *all* action must eventuate in an appropriate reward or retribution. The type of action, moreover, determines the specific nature that karmic matter now assumes. One's attempt to withhold knowledge from another out of jealousy, for example, develops *karma*s which will at a later time function to obscure one's own knowledge (Jaini 1979: 113). The precise amount of *karma* that engulfs the soul after a given action is said to depend on the degree of volition with which that activity was carried out. Yet it is also by intentional ritualized acts, such as ritual fasts, *pratikraman*, meditational exercises, and indeed *puja*, that the effects of *karma* may be undone. And furthermore, these acts, as acts, might themselves be the cause of further *karma*. Behind this dizzying paradox lies the fact that *karma* is the source of all suffering, and is therefore that which the Jain religion avowedly aims to overcome. The karmic trap, which Jaini calls the 'mechanism of bondage', is unlocked by an extraordinary and mysterious quality of the soul called *bhavyatva*, its capacity to become free. There is a moment of essentially non-volitional spiritual awakening (*samyak darshan*) when the *bhavyatva* is moved to exert its catalytic influence on the energies of the soul, directing it away from actions which cause karmic influx, towards insight and freedom (Jaini 1979: 138–41). So while all action is defined as the cause of *karma*, some forms of action, particularly ritual, might be having the opposite effect, though one can never know. These matters are discussed further in Chapter 9, and we observe here only that this insistence on both the 'mechanical' effect of action and the transcendent effect of spiritual awakening must surely give a particular form, and a particular urgency, to the perennial contentiousness of ritual in Jainism.

Nevertheless, whatever the logical paradoxes, religious practice turns on the hoped-for effects of ritual. One of the effects of ritual fasting, for instance, is an arithmetical reduction of the time the soul will spend in hell. One day of fasting brings a reduction of one hundred years, two days brings two hundred years, and so on. Popular stories give much more baroque illustration of the instantaneous, flick-a-switch-like effect on someone's destiny of performing rites such as fasting and *puja*. A woman told Caroline:

Ambika was an ordinary laywoman. She was a Jain, but she married into a Hindu family. Her mother-in-law was very wicked and used to harass Ambika and tell lies about her to Ambika's husband. She forbade Ambika to perform *puja*. But Ambika went against her wishes, made a *puja* to the Jina and also gave alms to a Jain renouncer. For this, the mother-in-law got the husband to throw her out. Ambika took her two children and went to take shelter under a big mango tree. Now, normally this tree bore no fruit, but because Ambika had performed meritorious deeds, it began to bear fruit and the lady and her children did not starve. Ambika then decided to fast for three days. Her children however needed water. Because Ambika fasted, she achieved omniscience and she therefore knew that there was water. She just scratched the surface of the ground and water appeared. But she was sad, and threw herself in a well with her two children. She died and went to heaven, where she became a *shasan-devi* (protector goddess) of Jainism.[24]

The fact that ritual is both effective and unequivocally directed towards the self rouses in many Jains a moral ambivalence; one which non-Jains can feel even more acutely. We met one Brahmin *pujari*, the lackadaisical custodian of a dusty, seemingly permanently closed Jain temple in Sanganer, who said simply, 'The Jain *puja* is just selfish.' This man felt that *puja* should be 'for God', or 'demanded by *dharma* (religious law)', and the Jain insistence that the proper religious end of *puja* is the transformation of the self seemed to him almost irreligious.

The religious validity of ritual has of course been equally contentious in other religious traditions. In Judaism, Herrenschmidt notes a tension which is comparable to the Jain case, for there, effective sacrifice came to exist alongside a theology of divine creation of the cosmos, a theology which renders sacrifice inexplicable. After the Exile new ideas, which penetrated the Judaic from the Hellenistic world, represented the universe as a systematically organized whole, with its own 'natural law'. Together with this was found the affirmation of ritualism and the monopoly of a priestly class over the performance of effective sacrifice. But this, contradicted too profoundly the idea of *creation*—and, therefore, the idea of transcendence. In so far as a 'natural law' appears, it certainly does not rule God in the way it may rule nature or mankind—and we have seen that the law of nature is totally distinct, even as to its time of formulation, from the law of mankind. Yahweh remains the origin and the guarantor of this law, which is to say that he cannot be subject to it, any more than he can be within the cosmos. Sacrifice acts upon the ultimate reality, which is not the universe but the divinity. But because divinity is transcendent, there can be no valid explanation of the action of sacrifice upon him. And so this system cannot go beyond the simple affirmation of the effectiveness of sacrifice itself: it cannot be rationalized, it cannot be made into a 'theory'. (1982: 33)

In Jainism too there is no authoritative theory of the *puja*. Even its central purpose is unclear and on the most central question of the nature and effectiveness of the act, there are competing views.

So why have we chosen to write about *puja*? In some ways ascetic rites, such as *pratikraman* (ritualized confession), could be said to be more central to the Jain religion, because they are accepted by all sects and schools. But on the other hand, the majority of Jains belong to one or other of the idol-worshipping groups and the *puja* is absolutely central to their religious lives. For most lay Jains a rite such as *pratikraman*, which they are enjoined in theory to practise every day, is a rare and special event which they never learn to perform unaided and which they attempt no more than once or twice a year. The *puja* is more interesting for our purposes for two reasons. First, unlike the ascetic rites, we found that many of those who perform the *puja* regularly attribute symbolic meanings to it, whereas *pratikraman* for instance is described almost exclusively in terms of the effects it has, and while the texts which are recited during it certainly have meanings, almost no one understands them and this does not invalidate their performance of it. So from the point of view of our attempt to understand just how and to what degree there is meaning in ritual, the *puja* is a much more interesting case. The less symbolic and much more unambiguously effective ascetic rites would appear too easy a base for our argument that meaning is not essential to ritual, and too much a special case to anthropologists who have not worked in ancient, hieratic, and liturgical traditions. Forms of *puja* are practised in all indigenous Indian religious traditions, and we hope that our discussion of Jain practice might encourage others to look again at other cases.

The second reason for choosing to concentrate on the *puja* is, precisely, the fact that it has been so controversial in Jainism. If ritual in general is a paradox for Jain religion, the *puja* has often been regarded as particularly suspect, because it is practised outside Jainism in all kinds of 'Hindu' and Buddhist contexts. That is to say, it differs from ascetic rites such as *pratikraman* not in being an effective rite, for both are that, but in being effective for dubious purposes which may not be limited by Jain ethical teaching. So Jain teachers have been much more equivocal about *puja* than they have about other rites. What is so interesting is that the most insistent form this reaction to ritual now takes in Jainism, a reaction which power-fully shaped the way our friends in Jaipur talked about the *puja*, is the idea that to make it more than an empty ritual the celebrant should endow it with symbolic meaning. People did also claim that one should 'give mean-ing' to other rituals, such as *samayik* and *pratikraman*; but on closer investigation it turned out that very little imaginative work was being done on this. We did not find pamphlets by leading renouncers giving symbolic and spiritual meanings to parts of these rites, and no such meanings seemed to have been disseminated among the laity. In striking contrast to the case of the *puja*, the people we spoke to had very little exegesis to offer of these rites. So despite the impression given by some published accounts that the *puja* is in some sense peripheral to Jainism, it turns out that at a popular level it is pivotal, for it provides a rather intense focus for popular discourse about what the central beliefs of Jainism are.

We should note too that although Jains tend to talk about the Hindu *puja* as if it were always a cynical bargain with a deity for purely material ends—always, like the Vedic sacrifice, a paradigm of efficacious but irre-ligious ritual—much Jain questioning, rethinking, and 'reform' of ritual in fact has very close parallels in Hindu tradition. The idea of the subject-ive experience of devotion (*bhakti*) as the animating force of ritual efficacy, which has been highly developed in certain Hindu traditions, is one to which, indeed, the Jains are indebted for much of their language and thinking on the matter.

Jain Interpretations of the Puja

There is no single or authoritative theory which gives an indigenous explanation of the Jain *puja*.

The first liturgical texts to describe the *puja* are later than the Shvetambar canon. They are part of a large body of treatises prescribing a proper life for lay Jains (*shravakacar*—the householder's conduct) which begin to appear in the eighth century.[25] The difference between these and the canonical texts is broadly equivalent to that between publications such as the Rites and Ordinances of the Church and the Bible, but even here, in the Jain case, the texts related to the *puja* and other comparable ritualized activities such as confession, pilgrimage, and the setting-up of temples and images, are only a small part of a corpus which is dominated by ethics in general: the delineation of right and wrong thoughts and actions, non-violence, chastity, dietary rules and fasting, study, giving of alms, the correct ways of gaining a living, and so forth.

Noting that *puja* is not discussed at all in the earlier canonical texts, Williams states that, 'The custom of *puja* is manifestly one of Jainism's earliest conscious imitations of the Hindu world around' (1963: 216). Many of our Jain respondents were of the same opinion. But though many of the particular ritual acts in the *puja* are paralleled in Hindu ceremonies and although it might even be possible to trace historically the points at which Jains took them up, it is clear that from its earliest adoption the *puja* has been part of specifically Jain polemic, and interpreted in Jain ways.[26] Justifications of the rite within Jain tradition, aimed at deflecting specifically Jain criticism, appear early. One, attributed to the great sixth-century saint Haribhadra, uses an analogy between building a temple for worship and digging a well. Although both are violent actions, causing the deaths of untold numbers of life-forms and as such sinful, this sin is outweighed by the benefits, both spiritual and material, which ensue (see Dundas 1992: 213–14).

Jaini puts well what is certainly the dominant, and perhaps also the most generally held view of *puja* today.

Building, consecrating, and regularly venerating images of the Tirthankars today constitute the primary religious activities of lay Jains. The popularity of these practices should not, however, be construed to mean that Jains expect worldly help of any sort from the Jinas thus worshiped; they know full well that these perfected beings are forever beyond the pale of human affairs. In other words, there is basically no 'deity' present in a Jaina temple; a one-way relation obtains between the devotee and the object of his devotion. Hence we must understand Jaina image-worship as being of a meditational nature; the Jina is seen merely as an ideal, a certain mode of the soul, a state attainable by all embodied beings. Through personification of that ideal state in stone, the Jaina creates a meditative support, as it were, a reminder of his lofty goal and the possibility of attainment. (1979: 193–4)

But Williams detects in the medieval liturgical texts a different view of *puja* which draws again on the (bewilderingly variable) term 'sacrifice'. This was a view some of our respondents also held: '*Puja*, often called *ijya* or *yajna*, [is] the one form of "sacrifice" possible to a Jain' (1963: 216).

Without developing this idea, Williams then also notes a possible evolution in the aims of ritualized worship. The *puja* is understood variously in the medieval literature, as either a constituent part of, or equivalent to, or indeed encompassing the veneration of the Jina image, the *caitya-vandan* (1963: 187, 216). Williams comments that the *samayik*, which is part of the *caitya-vandan* and was originally conceived as a period of contemplation, 'gradually took on the character of a formal act of worship, in which praise was offered to the Jina. It was then but a short step to the offering of material objects—the *puja*' (1963: 216). This suggests that the idea of the *puja* as a contemplative or meditational act was superseded by the idea that it is an act of worship of the Jina. But there is absolutely no reason to think this was the case. Not only is there evidence that image-worship was present at the earliest times, but it is almost impossible to conceive of the *puja* other than as containing both components. Certainly, such meditation remains a strong preoccupation of the Jains. The Jains we know maintain that meditational states can be achieved through worship, and indeed in a ritualized form.[27] To 'offer' material objects can thus be understood according to the rationale of meditation, and the offerings thereby become material adjuncts of the meditation process. Since this process consists of a transformation of the self, ideally a shedding of *karma*s, the *puja* seen in this way is consonant with the ethical and soteriological concerns of the earliest scriptures.

There are further variants to add. The *puja* can be seen as something like a Jain version of the Judaic covenant, man's acknowledgment of obedience to God's law.[28] Many of our respondents saw the reciting of the *namaskar-mantra* as an essential part of the *puja*, and it is certainly the prayer which is most often recited. The *namaskar-mantra* is, as Williams says, 'the basic ritual formula of Jainism', one which 'comes to be synonymous with the acceptance of the Jain creed' (1963: 185–6).[29] The use of a magical formula in this way, as a badge of religious affiliation, is exactly paralleled in some Hindu 'sects'. Correct recitation is believed to be automatically effective, but this is interpreted in various ways. As it claims for itself, the *mantra* 'destroys all sin'. But while some Jain teachers stress that 'correct recitation' requires strict adherence to Jain doctrine, this does not preclude claims for more immediate efficacy and stories abound among Jains today of merchants who escaped from disaster on the road, and maidens who saved their virtue, by remembering and reciting it in moments of danger. One woman told James that if he were to kill a fly accidentally he could reduce the sin which would attend on this by saying the *namaskar-mantra* and praying that the fly would go to a better rebirth.

In religious practice the *mantra* is a fundamental declaration of faith, a collective recitation of which begins virtually all Jain meetings and ceremonies. Use of the *mantra* is highly ritualized, and although the meaning of the Prakrit verse is very well known, it is typically recited extremely quickly, and is often reduced in a formulaic way to sixteen letters, three sets of six letters, the five initial letters of each line, three sets of two letters, and even to one syllable, *om*.[30]

Finally, many of our respondents, without denying these understandings of the *puja*, see it primarily in terms of gaining religious merit (*punya*), the fruits of which are success and good fortune in this life and desirable future births. Performing a good action, directly and of itself, it is said, causes the acquisition for the soul of 'good *karma*', or religious merit. Whatever the occluding effects of *karma* in general, for most people the 'merely worldly benefits' of good *karma* are definitely desirable. Now the paradigmatic way to earn merit is by making gifts, and performing *puja* can be seen as an act of 'giving away', even though most Jains are clear that the Jinas, being liberated from worldly existence, do not 'receive' *puja* offerings. Renouncers, it is true, do not use this interpretation (you cannot give away what you do not own and renouncers, because they are supposed to have no material possessions, are forbidden from making *puja* offerings). For lay Jains, however, the smallest act of *puja* offering can be seen in the light of 'giving away' (Babb 1988), and as one might expect, performances of *puja* are often the occasion for making large gifts to religious and charitable causes. The sponsorship of an elaborate and expensive public *puja* is itself seen both as 'renunciation' and as an act of public service and generosity. The *puja* has been listed by Jain teachers among the seven 'fields of merit' (*punya-kshetra*), where the harvest from good conduct is especially plentiful. These include the setting up of Jina images, the building of temples, causing Jain scriptures to be copied and circulated, giving alms to renouncers, and charity.

We should note, however, that subjectively it is impossible to know what one has 'got' from performing ritual. While there is a clear conceptual distinction between gaining merit (good *karma*) and removing or 'burning off' *karma* (whether good or bad), there is no correspondingly clear distinction between the actual practices which cause these different sorts of internal process. The workings of karmic cause and effect are subtle, and except to those with supernatural insight, unknowable. Thus what appears from the outside to be two instances of the same act will have different effects, depending on the *karma*s already present in those who perform them. That the *puja* so often brings *punya* (merit), and so luck, good fortune, and good rebirth, does not mean that it might not also effect the purification of the soul. This applies to other ritual actions too, such as fasting and confession. Shvetambar Jains do not believe, as appears to be widely held by Sri Lankan Buddhists (Southwold 1983), that only ordained renouncers are entitled to aspire to enlightenment and release from the bondage of *karma*. Therefore lay people do not resign themselves only to merit-making. The actions of a renouncer or a pious lay person alike might cause either the accumulation of good *karma* or the destruction of all *karma*. Thus not only can the *puja* be seen in a number of different ways, and described as fitting into different conceptual frameworks, but there is no logical requirement even for any particular worshipper to choose one from among these different interpretations and to reject the others. They have it every which way, one might be tempted to think.

Nonetheless, some Jain religious teachers have felt moved to reject this indeterminacy and to call for just that kind of choice. The fact that this ritual can be understood in ways which include a whole range of religious and philosophical positions has meant that it has been possible to conduct debates about these philosophical issues by disputing the legitimacy of particular ritual rules and practices. If ritual achieves its effects automatically, through the deterministic workings of a mechanically causal universe, can these effects include spiritual transformation, enlightenment, and eternal liberation? And if rituals can achieve spiritual and also practical and material effects, what then becomes of the cardinal religious distinction between enlightenment and good fortune, between release from the world of death and rebirth and mere success within it?

It is not hard to see why Jain religious teachers should find in ritual a cause for concern, and why true religiosity should seem to some of them to require that one does without ritual. For what they are struggling against is the fact that ritual, being at the same time religiously effective yet ultimately unknowable in its effects, can come to stand for the religious life as a whole. Abandoning ritual, which might be cleansing your soul, in the hope that a purifying spiritual insight might arise from within the soul, is in effect a religious gamble.

Equivocation and Reform in Jain Religious History

The renouncers of the idol-worshipping traditions exhort their followers to perform *puja*, but they themselves are forbidden to do so. There are many reasons for this. Renouncers are, by the vows of their initiation, possessionless, so they can hardly make offerings. The acts of washing and scrubbing are, though not gross, none the less forms of violence (*himsa*) which renouncers should always avoid. Furthermore, renouncers are forbidden to make use of fresh, unboiled water, which is held to harbour countless souls, and it is fresh well-water which is prescribed for the *puja*.[31] This avoidance of fresh water means that Jain renouncers hardly ever bathe, and a bath immediately before *puja* is prescribed. Anyone who touches a statue without having bathed is considered to have polluted it, so although it is a senior *acarya* who performs the rites of consecration for a Jina idol, renouncers are not allowed to touch the idol once consecrated. All of this shows how the materiality of the *puja* is transcended by the higher religious point of view of the renouncer.

Though renouncers are not allowed to perform physical *dravya puja*, they do sometimes go to the temple to perform meditational *bhav puja*, and the usual way for them to do this is to adopt the posture and recite the verses of the *caitya-vandan*. In addition, they are permitted, and virtually required by popular sentiment, to be present at the great public *puja*s. Shvetambar renouncers sometimes chant some of the Sanskrit prayers and join in with the singing. But often they contribute only a silent presence. A naked Digambar *muni*, sitting still and alone like a sentinel for religion, can seem utterly removed from the busy, festively costumed, and purposefully active celebrants all around. At one mass *puja* which Caroline attended, as the loudspeakers blared the bids for the right to perform bits of ritual and people pressed forward eagle-eyed to see some crucial action, the renouncer slipped away unobserved, and it later became clear that no one knew where he had gone.

The validity of religious ritual has never been decisively rejected in Jainism, any more than it has in any other religious tradition. The reform of ritual 'misuse' has remained central to all varieties of Jain religious identity, and no present group of Jains sees itself as the bearer of an unreformed tradition, from which all the others have foolishly departed. The contemporary Jain orders each claim to have returned to the true practices of early Jainism by schism and reform. Thus even the idol-worshipping orders, such as the Khartar Gacch, are reformers, in the sense that their ritual has been adapted to their identity *vis-à-vis* other groups. These differences in ritual can seem quite minimal when seen from outside. The token nature of such distinctions is something which we think is intrinsic to ritualization and we suggest an explanation for it below. However, the emergence of varying religious identities is a separate matter which must be accounted for outside a discussion of what is properly ritual about these events (by explanations, for example, in terms of new schools of thought, charismatic personalities, or political confrontations). We cannot possibly present here a comprehensive account in this respect of Jain sectarian history. We want only to illustrate how questions of the validity of ritual, and particularly the *puja*, have remained at the centre of religious controversy. To do this, we shall look briefly not at the Jain sects which now more or less completely reject *puja* (see Dundas 1992), but at two more equivocal reactions to the rite: the 'reforms' which led to the founding of the Shvetambar Khartar order, to which the Dadabari temple belongs, and the experience of the seventeenth-century Jain merchant Banarsidas, who was born into a family which followed the Khartar Gacch, but who developed such deep doubts about ritual that he joined a Digambar reform movement, and became one of the most influential religious figures of his day.

The Khartar Gacch emerged in the eleventh century, from attempts to reform what some leading renouncers regarded as corrupt practices, and to revive the ancient way of life prescribed in the Jain scriptures. Under the patronage of kings ruling in what is now Gujarat and southern Rajasthan, Jainism in this period achieved a cultural dominance which was matched nowhere else. But Jain identity was threatened by the potent attraction of popular revivalist Hindu devotionalism (*bhakti*). Religious dispute in Jainism focused on the way of life of so-called renouncers, the *caitya-vasi* monks who had come to live permanently in temples (*caitya*s) or monasteries (*math*s). Large temple complexes had been specially built for these monks, ignoring the scriptural injunction to the wandering life. The *caitya-vasi*s, the reformers alleged, were disregarding the rules on alms-begging and on avoiding injury to all life-forms. They took baths, adorned their bodies with all sorts of powders and oils, wasted their time in sleep, in buying and selling, and in gossip. They bought young children to become their disciples and also made money by selling Jina images. They were appropriating temple funds for their own uses, which included the staging of elaborate ritual in a conspicuously Hindu idiom (Dundas 1987: 182–3).

That these rituals included versions of image-worship can be seen from Paul Dundas's discussion of an eleventh-century diatribe written by Jineshvara Suri, who together with his guru Vardhamana is credited with founding the Khartar order. Jineshvara Suri caricatured the temple-dwelling monks, and presented them as teaching their followers thus.

If someone makes an image [of a Jina] no more than the size of a thumb, then he will attain deliverance through the gradual achieving of enlightenment after a series of happy rebirths. But whoever constructs a temple will have still greater awards. Therefore, sirs, build temples, and we shall strive in those areas in which you are not competent. (1987: 183)

Although noting that a preoccupation with temple ritual could lead to false doctrines of this kind, the Khartar Gacch did not actually reject either temples or image-worship, as some later groups were to do. But they opposed the teachings of conservative ritualists, such as Sura, who argued that austerities and meditation were too difficult for the laity in the Kali Yuga (our present degenerate World Age), and who attempted to establish *dan*, religious giving, as the main religious duty of lay Jains. Sura taught that *dan* supported the monks and hence the entire Jain religion, and he argued that although monks might be degenerate, they should nevertheless be respected, in the same way as a king's messenger is honoured, although he in no way resembles the king. This then was a defence of the 'domestication of the *sangha*', a process which occurred also in Buddhist societies (Dundas 1987: 188, citing Carrithers). But despite their opposition to Sura, the followers of the Khartar Gacch continued to respect teachers who saw the building of temples as a form of spiritual sacrifice (*bhav-yagya*), and they never actually rejected the giving of *dan*. The Khartar Gacch thus retained ritual while maintaining that there are other forms of spirituality, accessible to lay people, which are superior to it.

The Khartar reformers linked temple-dwelling with ignorance or mis-use of the sacred canon. Jineshvara states that his authority to speak rests on the authority of ancient scriptures rather than upon the results of contemporary disputes, and Dundas recounts an episode from the early life of the reformer Jinavallabha in which his temple-dwelling master hid the scriptures from him. Only after secretly inspecting these texts did he realize that his teacher had been deceiving him and was on the wrong path (1987: 192). But the Khartars' opponents, such as Sura, also referred to the importance of scriptures, though in a different way. Dundas notes,

a vagueness or uncertainty as to what constituted scriptural injunctions . . . terms like *agama* [scripture] and *vidhi* [injunctions] may have come to signify for many monks not so much a body of texts and specific ordinances based on them as, more nebulously, the totality of current and traditional religious behaviour which was perceived as deriving from an amorphous source loosely defined as scripture. It was this vague view of scripture and its contents which has been repeatedly challenged throughout mediaeval and more recent Jain history by recourse to actual texts . . . thus providing one of the most important dynamic elements in the history of the religion. (1987: 193)

However, Dundas also makes the interesting observation that the Khartar reformers seem to have won, 'by imposition of their own charismatic authority established in debate, and by what the hagiographers describe as the performance of miracles and feats of prescience, rather than through any marked adherence to the "great truths" of Jainism' (Dundas 1987: 191). Some of these reformer-saints have become the miracle-working *guru-dev*s, whose bright images were so prominent in our Jaipur temple. If they are remembered today for their knowledge of scripture, it is for having memorized, as children, countless volumes of text, and this as a demonstration of supernatural spiritual power. Similarly, their renunciation of the ritualism and luxury of the *caitya-vasi*s, and their conquest of the hardships of itinerant mendicancy, endowed them with forms of magical power from which their followers today, by means of the *puja* ritual, still hope to benefit.

The reformers of the Khartar Gacch seem to have triumphed, but they brought about neither a unidirectional nor an irreversible change in Jainism. The 'misuses' they had identified did not die out, indeed versions of them continued within these same orders. The descendants of the *caitya-vasi*s remained powerful religious leaders, with close links with the ruling Rajput and Muslim courts, control of considerable property, and with large lay followings which included followers of the reformist *gacch*s. Only in this century have these figures, who came to be known as *yati*s, been decisively displaced in most of India by itinerant renouncers. At the same time the impulse to reform has persisted, further schisms have followed, and new orders arisen, each tracing their origin to some kind of reform: reforms of the codes of conduct and organization of renouncers, and reform of rituals of worship, meditation, and confession.[32]

In the fifteenth century a Gujarati layman named Lonka Shah laid the foundations for a new sect, the Lonka Gacch, when he opposed idol-worship completely, claiming that there was no sanction for such practices in the ancient texts. The Lonka Gacch is now almost extinct (Dundas 1992: 215), but the major anti-idolatrous Shvetambar groups, the Sthanakvasis and the Terapanth, both ultimately derive their inspiration from this shadowy figure. The Sthanakvasis, whose forebears split from the Lonka Gacch in the seventeenth century under the leadership of another lay reformer Lavaji, have no temples, no *yati*s, and exercise their religion in the bare and spartan halls (*sthanak*s) also used as rest-houses by the renouncers. They reject not only image-worship in temples, but also the use of idols in meditation and confession.

But reforms of this kind do not mean that ritual itself disappears. Other rites, including elaborate ritualized reverence for living renouncers, play a more prominent part. Sthanakvasi teachers, for example, emphasize the efficacy of *jap* (ritual recitation of prayers or formulas such as the *namaskar-mantra*). If you do this nine hundred thousand times during your life, you can avoid rebirth in hell. Similarly the Shvetambar Terapanth,[33] although it rejects worship of Jina idols, has developed new forms of congregational ritual worship and meditation focusing on the person of the living *acarya* (not so very different from the focus on a Jina idol in the Murti Pujak traditions). The reader should thus beware of thinking that reform in Jainism invariably implies a one-way movement away from ritual. In the latter half of the nineteenth century, large numbers of Sthanakvasi renouncers were converted to the idol-worshipping Tapa Gacch. They contributed to a striking rise of the numbers and influence of the renouncers of this order (this movement also contributed to the demise of the *yati*s) (Cort 1989: 99–100, 344).

Among the Digambars too there were similar controversies and schisms, such as that which led to the formation of a new sect, in the fifteenth century, around the monk Tarana Swami. The Taranapanth rejected the worship of Jina images, substituting marble models of sacred books for the customary image of the human body as the central objects of temple rituals (S. Jain 1971).

A Digambar reformer of unique interest, who was actually born a Shvetambar, is the layman Banarsidas who left a remarkable autobiography, *Ardhakathanaka* (Half a Tale), written in 1641.[34] In this he describes his motivations for dissent from the tradition in which he grew up and his many attempts to become a good Jain. Banarsi grew up in a Khartar family in an atmosphere of popular religiosity. Soon after his birth the baby Banarsi was taken by his father on a pilgrimage to the Parshva shrine on Mount Samet to make a *puja* to the Jina for his personal protection, an appeal which, as he notes, was both heretical and absurd, since the Jina is a liberated soul and beyond all worldly affairs. Banarsi, following the tradition of his family and caste, became a merchant, but was frequently in deep trouble, attributable variously to robbery, arbitrary persecution, and his own mercurial temperament. On one occasion in his youth, as he ironically notes, he tried to use a *puja* to bargain with the Jina: 'O Lord, grant us wealth, for then we shall have occasion to come and offer worship at your shrine again' (Lath 1981: 56).

An inveterate backslider from his own higher ideals and basically apolitical, Banarsi's doubts about ritual were certainly not the result of his bowing to the ideas of the powerful Muslim rulers of his time. According to Meghavijaya, a contemporary Shvetambar opponent, Banarsi was led by the 'false vision induced by the current phase of cosmic moral degradation' to accept that ritual could lead to enlightenment only if practised with full awareness of its true import.[35]

Once when he was in the midst of a rigorous fast (*vrat*) he developed an inordinate craving for food and drink. This led him to question his earlier resolution.

He asked the monks whether a man who observes a practice in its external form while his mind remains full of impure thoughts can ever achieve the desired goal.

He was told that a man who errs in his intentions and thoughts but mechanically observes rituals can never attain anything. This convinced Banarsi of the meaninglessness of observing rituals and decreed practices. (Lath 1981: 216)

It is significant (and characteristic of a certain kind of pro–ritualist Jain thinking) that Meghavijaya saw this as 'deluded' and 'skeptical towards sacred precepts'. When asked, 'What has made you give up religious practices?', Banarsi apparently replied, his mind 'full of doubt',

I have no use for formal practices.[36] The soul becomes bound to the world through *karma*, a bond which arises out of falsehood. . . . Therefore a man desiring liberation should give up falsehood. And this can be done only through acquisition of Truth (*samyaktva*), and consists in the attainment of a spiritual state of being. No amount of effort can help one reach this state, which emerges on its own when the time is ripe. It is profitless, therefore, to perform rituals or ascetic exercises for this purpose, for these can never lead to salvation (*moksh*). The right path for a man striving after enlightenment is to examine and meditate over the nature of truth, because practices enjoined in the *Avashyaka* and other scriptures can get him nowhere. (Lath 1981: 217)

Although many differences, of course, separate them, Banarsi's line of thought is reminiscent of the transcendentalist stream of the Christian Reformation, and its preoccupation with the theology of the sacraments and the inscrutability of the divine Spirit. Zwingli, for example, presented a fundamental objection to the view that, at the same time as the sacraments are administered outwardly, what they signify happens inwardly. With such a view, 'the freedom of the divine Spirit would be bound, who distributes to each, as he wills, that is: to whom, when, and where he wills' (quoted in Stephens 1986: 184).

One of the reasons why Banarsi's text is so interesting is that he reveals how, even in the context of a religion such as Jainism with its perennially protestant reformism, abandoning ritual can lead to a form of despair virtually equal to the loss of religion itself. In 1623 Banarsi was introduced the Adhyatma Movement, a group of Digambars based in Agra, interested in the mystical doctrines of the second-century Digambar saint, Kunda-Kunda. Once again we see the ongoing dialogue between Jains and their various 'Hindu' neighbours, for this Digambar movement, which sought a spiritual revival of religion through the reform of 'dead, meaningless forms' was clearly influenced by Nirguna saints, and writers of *bhakti* poetry such as Kabir, Dadu, and the Sikh saint Guru Nanak. But the Adhyatma movement was distinctive, and distinctively Jain, and as Lath writes, 'Its moving force was apparently not a deep mystic impulse but a sense of discursive inquiry, a questioning rooted in excogitation' (Lath 1981: xliv). But for Banarsi, the initial result of his inquiry was disillusionment and spiritual crisis. He began to study the *Samayasaranataka*, attributed to Kunda-Kunda.

I began earnestly to study it, pondering over each word and its meaning with great earnestness, but I found that I was incapable of unravelling the mysteries of the true mystic doctrine. But my studies had the effect of completely shaking my faith in rituals and in everything else in religion which was just a conventional, outward form. I had wandered into a spiritual void, for although I had lost faith in Form, I was unable to savour Spirit. I hovered between earth and heaven, befouling the air like a camel's fart.

At this point, Banarsi seems to have broken finally with his own Khartar Shvetambar community.

I renounced all rituals, giving up every form of ordained, conventional precept I had so long been religiously observing, namely, the uttering of *mantra*s, the keeping of *vrat*s, the *samayik*, the *pratikraman* and the like. I even broke my vow of never eating green vegetables. In fact, there was no end to my disillusionment with outward forms. I felt strangely isolated and everything began to seem alien to me.

As Banarsi writes, he found that as he abandoned 'outer forms' he found his 'inner' dispositions changed too. He found, at a *puja*, that all he could think of was gobbling up the sweets being offered at the shrine.

During these days I had three ungodly, blasphemous friends, who were much given to jests and droll humour. . . . Often we had great fun devising impious games . . . we would shut ourselves in a small room, shed our clothes and dance in the nude explaining that we had shed the world and had become *muni*s.[37] . . . We composed verses which were parodies of well-known songs or sayings, and then amused ourselves by reading into them a bawdy, spiritual meaning. (Lath 1981: 86–8)

This 'hovering between earth and heaven' lasted for many years until study of another famous Digambar text, the tenth-century *Gommatasara* of Nemichand, allowed him to achieve his own vision: 'For me its study was a revelation. All my doubts and questionings were put to rest and I became a new man. I had, at last, gained true and profound insight into the Jain doctrine of relativism (*syadvada*)' (Lath 1981: 91). Briefly, what gripped Banarsi's interest was the doctrine according to which the soul passes through many states or stages (*gunasthana*s) on its journey from the bondage of *karma* to freedom. There are fourteen of these stages, beginning with false vision, passing through those in which the soul becomes aware of a partial truth (thinking it is the whole truth), to a fleeting awareness of the true goal, and finally to the removal of the veils of *karma*, and the attainment of omniscience (*keval-gyan*). To quote Mukund Lath,

Banarsi found the *gunasthana* doctrine profoundly satisfying for it gave meaning to much that he had found pointless and revolting: ritualistic practices and ordained formal behaviour which he had so long rejected as dead and empty. These now fell into place as significant and purposeful within the total spiritual journey. Rituals were necessary in the early stages of a man's spiritual progress because they helped formulate his quest and give it the right direction. Later, when the spiritually advanced seeker had transcended them, he could in the light of his perfected knowledge, realise their relative importance with fuller understanding, recognising and synthesizing them as an essential part of an indispensable scheme. Banarsi speaks of this total scheme as *syadvada*, the Jain doctrine of relativism. (1981: 206–7)

Here again we can see a parallel with the Christian Reformation.[38] But whereas the issue of the presence of the Spirit in the material became the great watershed of the Reformation, dividing Luther, for whom the spiritual life could never be entirely disembodied, from Zwingli, who affirmed the incompatibility of spirit and matter, the Jain reformers were able to employ the doctrine of relative truth to 'reconcile' these positions. However, as we shall see, this philosophical reconciliation was not widely accepted in Jainism and did not prevent further schisms over matters of practice.

The ritualization of so much of 'good action' in Jainism means that ritual has a rather different place in this religion from Christianity. Banarsi had been in despair because he had found from his own experience that rejecting ritual was also the rejection of ethical behaviour as a whole. Let us remember that during his many years of 'hovering between earth and heaven' he had rejected not just the *puja* but also vows and rituals of meditation and confession. Such a view, opponents said, attracted followers who were lazy and without self-discipline. Banarsi himself acknowledged that although he had attained a 'knowledge akin to supreme realization' (Lath 1981: 92), he still had 'bad points':

I do not perform sacred rituals; I never utter the holy *mantra*s, never sit for meditations and never exercise self-restraint. Neither do I perform *puja* nor practise charity. I am over fond of laughter and love to poke fun at everything. . . . When I am in the mood for fun, nothing can restrain me from telling fanciful lies or untruths. I sometimes break into a dance when I am on my own. Yet I am also prone to sudden, irrational feelings of dread. (Lath 1981: 94–5)

In contrast to his own personal licence Banarsi advocated for Jains at large exceedingly austere versions of the *puja*, with no decorations of the idol, and so on, the opposite of what they were accustomed to. Perhaps the ardent Banarsi and his light-hearted merchant friends were in the end too alien to the *culture* of Jainism, with its mixture of personal self-restraint and public lavishness, to have a lasting institutional effect.

After Banarsi died, the Adhyatma movement soon withered away, though Banarsi himself had influenced the group of dissenting merchants who founded the Digambar Terapanth. This group, unlike the Shvetambar sect of the same name, sanctions the *puja*, but opposes the use of flowers, fresh fruits, green vegetables, milk, and ghee, as these are said to involve harm to tiny creatures. Instead, water, nuts, and dried fruits are used. Like the much earlier Shvetambar Agamikas, the Digambar Terapanthis protested at the presence of 'Hindu' protector deities in Jain temples and abandoned the *arti* rite because it was thought to be too 'Hindu'. Yet a century after Banarsi, in 1764, a contemporary observer, Raimalla, describes a vast *puja* held by Terapanthi Digambars in Jaipur to consecrate a flagstaff of the great Vedic god Indra, who is often worshipped by Jains as a generic 'king of the gods'.

The *puja* was celebrated with all the pomp and ostentation that the affluent Terapanth could afford. Over 150 skilled craftsmen were employed at great expense to erect a huge platform, 64 yards square, in order to house a miniature model of the cosmos as conceived in Jain mythology. The result as the charmed Raimalla describes it, must have been spectacular: on display was a gilded, glittering, toy-world of houses, temples, palaces, rivers, trees, oceans, mountains, woods and myriad other terrestrial and heavenly things which make up the visible and supramundane world as conceived by the Jains. . . . Tents were erected all around the platform on which the toy-cosmos had been assembled, and hundreds of devotees, from as far as Agra, Delhi, Udaipur, Bikaner, and even Aurangabad and Multan, came to attend the festivities, which lasted for many days. (Lath 1981: lxiii. See also Roy 1978: 56–7)

How can we characterize the dynamics of the historical process of Jainism's relation to ritual? If we look very generally at the process it has a notably different 'feel' to that of the Christian churches in the West, because religious institutionalization in Jainism has never been able to impose universally acknowledged meanings for ritual acts. There is no equivalent in Jainism to the Western Churches, the Pope, encyclicals, or the Inquisition. But the Reformation is evidence that, in the West too, generally acknowledged meanings can be so only for a time. In the history of Jainism we can also identify radical turning-points, the invention of totally new meanings for ritual, such as happened with successive Christian reinterpretation of the Passover. However, in Jainism the more usual process of religious change has involved the adoption of already-formed cults and ritual acts from surrounding popular practice and their absorption into rituals of worship. Subsequent reaction against burgeoning ritualism took the form of the elimination of these acts, or the substitution of others on the basis of new religious ideas. The watersheds in Jainism, on the other hand, occurred with the rejection of the idol of the Jina as the object for worship, with the emergence of the Taranapanth among the Digambars and the Sthanakvasi order among the Shvetambars. The rejection of worship of the statue in human form implies a radical rethinking, since generally in Jainism (and not just in temple ritual) religious action is performed by means of the body, and spiritual qualities are identified with or 'written on to' the body (hence the idea that the statue of the Jina must be perfect, that physically deformed people cannot become renouncers). Thus to eliminate the statue, as the Sthanakvasis have, or replace it, as the Taranapanth has, with idols of books, is evidence of genuinely new thinking.

But most Jain reform of ritual was much less radical than this. Much of Jain reformism has a slippery quality, perhaps because everyone is aware that, on a really strict interpretation of Jain ethics, nothing would be allowable, one should not actually 'do' anything. The Jain rejection of the Hindu custom of *prasad* (the giving back to worshippers of sanctified offerings they have made to the deity) may serve as an example. Jains reject this because the Jina, being outside this world, cannot accept offerings or give them back. But sometimes sponsors of *puja*s arrange to have sweets given out at the door of the temple as people leave. Correctly these are not called *prasad*, but *prabhavana*.[39] However, we found that most people do casually refer to them as *prasad*. Ritual is peculiarly apt to be carelessly given meanings which no one really holds to. Banarsi and others rejected ritual precisely because the disjunction between the act and the mental state of the actor allows the meaning of ritual acts to slip so easily between themes which people could defend religiously and others which they could not.

The various but specific meanings for the component acts of the *puja* which our Jaipur respondents gave us seem almost certainly to post-date the development of a complex textual liturgy for the ritual. Historically we have seen new movements emerge on the basis either of individual study of canonical texts or of personal ritual practice, and in all of this the liturgical texts are largely ignored. Yet the correct performance of the *puja* matters to people intensely. While their concern does not usually take a confrontational form, it matters to people that they themselves should get it right. All Jains are aware that religion can be conducted in non-ritual ways. Indeed, as we have seen, the most admired people, the renouncers, are forbidden from taking part in the material form of the *puja*. So why choose a ritualized way? We shall begin to answer this question by stepping back from the Jain experience to consider the problem of ritual in general.

Notes

1. Many of those who write about Indian religions prefer to avoid the term 'idol', even when, as is the case with the Jains, English-speaking adherents of the religion happily use this word, and even though no one disputes that 'idol' is a valid translation of *murti*. The thought appears to be that the word is likely to rouse disapproval in Western readers for whom idolatry may be associated with superstition. This is, on one level, a nice indication of how avowedly atheist academics routinely display deep Protestant prejudices. On another level, while of course the intention is benign, it seems to us in danger of being patronizing. Idol-worshipping Jains are frequently perfectly aware of the kinds of associations idolatry has in certain Judaeo-Christian circles. Through missionary activity, and, more effectively, through the activities of 'reformed' Hindu organizations, these attitudes have been widely disseminated. Moreover, as we describe below, the worship of temple idols has always been surrounded by similar controversy in Jain tradition too. Their use of the word, like their retention of the practice, shows that they think the associations and

prejudices in question are mistaken, so to use a euphemism in order not to offend these prejudices would be, among other things, to misrepresent our Jain respondents. Fuller (1992: 62) notes that the vast majority of Hindus have similarly been unmoved by criticism of idolatry and although he writes 'images' rather than 'idols', he makes the relevant point very well, 'They know, as any sympathetic observer must also recognize, that in popular Hinduism devotion and respect for deities are not diminished, but most completely expressed, though the use of [idols] in worship.'

2. There are now several excellent published works on various aspects of Jain religion and society available. Padmanabh S. Jaini's *The Jaina Path of Purification* has been the standard source on the textual religion since 1979 and remains indispensable. Its rather cursory historical treatment, and its slightly Digambar perspective, have now been compensated for by Paul Dundas's excellent book, *The Jains* (1992), which includes the first accessible and authoritative treatment of the crucial medieval period in Jain history. The ethnographic record of Jain religion and society has been much enriched by the publication of Marcus Banks's *Organizing Jainism in India and England* (1992), based on fieldwork in Jamnagar in Gujarat, and in Leicester, England. A conference collection, *The Assembly of Listeners* (1991), edited by Michael Carrithers and Caroline Humphrey, provides the most general overview currently available of Jain society in different parts of India.

3. The life of a Jain renouncer is very austere, and they are few in number. There are probably only about 7,000 renouncers, out of a total of over 3 million Jains in India. We should add that while most do, not all Jain renouncers come from Jain families.

4. As both Jaini (1980) and O'Flaherty (1980) remark, judged by sheer volume of literature, Jainism has shown more interest than any other Indian religious or philosophical school in developing and elaborating a theory of *karma*, although it should also be emphasized that this has always been in the context of dialogue with other schools and sects. The Jain literature is surveyed in Glasenapp (1942), Tatia (1951), Jaini (1980), and Kalghati (1987). The distinctive Jain position on *karma* diverges from Vedism and from later Hinduism in rejecting both the *shraddha* ritual and the idea of merit transfer. Buddhism too rejected the former, but developed and elaborated the latter.

5. This is known as *samadhi maran* or *sallekhana* (among the Digambars). It is not a distant ideal but is occasionally carried out by both renouncers and devout members of the laity. *Samadhi maran* involves not just extreme abstinence, fasting to death, but a deliberate re-enactment, by means of the body, of the principle of renunciation represented by the Jina.

6. Digambars and Shvetambars are socially as well as religiously separate. They maintain their own temples and other institutions and rarely, if ever, visit those of the other group (except in the case of temples claimed by both groups, which is usually a matter of tension and conflict). Members of the two groups

hardly ever intermarry. The Digambar/Shvetambar divide is undoubtedly greater than the caste divisions which exist within either tradition.

7. Some of these differences are reflected in the temple idols. Digambar idols are naked while those of the Shvetambars have a small loin–cloth. Whereas Shvetambar idols stare blankly forwards through glassy eyes, on most Digambar statues the eyes are merely inscribed. They are downcast, suggesting inner contemplation, and this is seen by Jains as a diagnostic mark, differentiating them from statues of the Shvetambars. In both cases their eyes do not focus on the things of this world. There are many small differences between the statues of the two traditions and these become matters of concern when both groups claim ownership of a particular temple. A full discussion of all these tiny bodily signs is beyond the scope of this book, but the eyes have a special significance which is discussed below.

8. *Dada* means 'paternal grandfather' and thus more generally 'patriarch'; a *guru* is a spiritual preceptor; and *dev* (like *devta*) is a word used for powerful, miracle-working gods and deities. The temple and the *guru–dev* shrine are enclosed by a pleasant walled garden. There is also a preaching hall, used for religious sermons; a large covered courtyard used for the feasts which mark religious occasions and for wedding receptions; offices; houses for temple servants; and an *upashraya*, a suite of rooms where groups of renouncers live when they pass through.

9. *Yakshas* appear also in the mythology and iconography of Hindus and Buddhists. They are prominent in sculpture of the earliest Buddhist and Jain *stupa*s (commemorative funeral mounds) and are mentioned in the canonical texts of both traditions. There is evidence that in the medieval period worship of these godlings assumed as great a prominence as that of the Jinas themselves (J. P. Sharma 1989). Often thought of as animal and tree spirits, they are bad as well as good. Only a few are propitiated in Jain temples, and only a mere handful are popular today. But see below, Ch. 7.

10. As Obeyesekere (1984: 513–15) points out, just as a Buddhist and Jain deity, such as Pattini, could be taken over by Hindus, the Jains also absorbed cults such as that of Padmavati, which the Jains worship as *yakshi* of the Jina Parshvanath, from folk religion. Thus, 'there is nothing unusual, given the transformations of these religions, in both Buddhism and Jainism worshipping a common set of deities on a popular, subdoctrinal level'. In both cases many of these deities were borrowed from Hinduism. The religious practice of Jains is broader than the traditions of 'Jainism', and includes worship of powerful gods, exorcism of spirits, and a variety of tantric and magical practices. Although Jain canonical scripture does not give direct authority for many of these observances, they do in passing refer to many magical and miraculous events as well as to the gods and spirits responsible for them. However, many Jains consider a whole range of these practices to be non-religious. Gombrich and Obeyesekere (1988) give a vivid account of the comparable relation between 'Buddhism proper' and various folk-

religious elements in contemporary Sri Lanka. However, it should be noted that Jains, perhaps more than Buddhists, make a sustained attempt to see everything they do in life in a 'religious' (*dharmik*), that is, a specifically 'Jain', light.

11. Our respondents gave two explanations of this. One was that foul breath might offend and pollute the idol. The other was that the celebrant might inadvertently breathe in, and thus harm, insects while doing the *puja*.

12. *Pujari*s are often Brahmins, but are sometimes drawn from lower castes such as Malis (gardeners), though never from the lowest, 'untouchable', castes. One of their most important functions is to take away and consume, or dispose of, the rice, fruits, sweets, nuts, coins, and flowers left as offerings to the Jinas by worshippers.

13. Thus the elaborate *panc-kalyanak* ritual which is used, among other things, in the consecration of a Jina idol, is also called a *puja*, as are separate rites within it. All of these are elaborations on the basic *puja*, performed daily in the temple. The *diksha* initiation, on the other hand, is not in itself a *puja*, (though *puja*s may be performed to accompany it). It is a *samskar*, a life-cycle ritual. Strictly speaking, the *panc-kalyanak puja* consists of worship of the five *samskar*s of the Jina, while the *diksha* which actually effects an alteration of the status of the initiate, from lay person to renouncer, is itself a *samskar*. The term *upacar* (or *upachara*), which is commonly used for single offerings in Hindu *puja*, is not generally used by the Jains in Jaipur.

14. For instance, they cradle a mirror in their arms so that it reflects the statue (the baby) though the story mentions only a mirror being 'displayed'.

15. We discuss the role of printed *puja*-manuals and hymns in Ch. 8. The complete text of the *mantra* mentioned is as follows,

namo arihantanam	I bow before the Tirthankars (*arihant*s)
namo siddhanam	I bow before the perfected and liberated souls (*siddha*s)
namo ayariyanam	I bow before the leaders of the ascetic order (*acarya*s)
namo uvajjhayanam	I bow before ascetic religious teachers (*upadhyay*s)
namo loe savva-sahunam	I bow before all the renouncers (*sadhu*s) in the world.
eso panca namokkaro	This fivefold salutation,
savva-pavappanasano	Which destroys all sin,
mamgalanam ca savvesim	Is pre-eminent as the most auspicious
padhamam havai mangalam	of all auspicious things.

16. Some people use a string of rosary beads to count their recitations.

17. If the worshipper has come to the temple only to experience *darshan*, auspicious vision of the Tirthankar, then the *vandan* is usually performed at the beginning rather than the end of their time there.

18. The place in the home where drinking water is kept, the *parinda*, is pure and sacred. The family goddess (*kul devi*) or the ancestors (*pitra-ji*) are worshipped here. We should add that many Jain families, though not some of the more self-consciously religious, perform occasional *puja*s for Shital Mata, the smallpox goddess, or for the Hindu goddess Durga. These again are simple ceremonies. Geometric diagrams are drawn with red turmeric paste on the wall by the *parinda*, a stick of incense is lit and a lamp, some money, and some sweets are offered.

19. It should be said, however, that we saw many people using marigolds, which do not have much scent.

20. *Kusum* means 'soft' and is a Sanskritic word for flowers. The term *anjali* implies a specific hand gesture. The hands are placed next to each other, palms up, and squeezed together so as to form a steep-sided cup, with the fingers, pointing away from one, forming a sharp, spout-like point. The offering, held in the cup thus formed, is held up at eye level.

21. Offering flowers in *puja* is forbidden altogether by Digambar Jains, because picking them involves *himsa* and they may contain insects which would also be harmed.

22. On the rule-bound nature and automatic efficacy of Vedic sacrifice, see also Lévi (1966), Renou (1953), Biardeau and Malamoud (1976), Staal (1979, 1986), Herrenschmidt (1982), Das (1983), and Hevesterman (1985).

23. We use the term 'protestant' here following the example of Gombrich and Obeyesekere in their excellent book *Buddhism Transformed* (1988). There are many features which reformed Jainism has in common with reformed Buddhism, notably the influence of lay preachers and the playing-down of both temple ritual and the role of ordained ascetics. See Gombrich and Obeyesekere (1988: 4–11, 215–24).

24. This version of the well-known Ambika story was told by an elderly woman in Jaipur, just after she had performed *puja* in the Dadabari temple. A more elaborate and 'correct' version can be found in Granoff (1990: 183–5).

25. The earliest *shravakacar* text, the Digambar Samanthabhadra's *Ratna-karanda-shravakacara* dates from the 5th c.; the earliest devoted to the *puja* is Haribhadra Yakini-putra's *Puja-vidhana-pancasaka*, which has been dated at around AD 750 (Williams 1963).

26. Jaini (1979: 191–2) mentions that the earliest known Jain inscription, commissioned by the Orissan king Kharavela around 150 BC and therefore well before the redaction of the canon, tells how the king went to war to regain a famous statue of Anantanath, the fourteenth Jina, which had been carried off 250 years earlier by agents of the Nanda dynasty. Even if this does not quite show, as Jaini suggests, that a cult of image-worship existed among Jains even in Mahavir's time, it does suggest an early attempt to provide an authoritative pedigree for the *puja* in Jainism. The canon itself describes Mahavir as staying in *caitya*s, centres of *yaksha* worship.

27. *Samayik* (ritualized meditation), as it is practised by Jains today can take place separately from the *puja*, but all practitioners, including non-idolatrous Jains, begin it with the worship (*vandan*) of the twenty-four Jinas.

28. Herrenschmidt (1982: 28–9) sees the Judaic covenant, while requiring a sacrificial act, as essentially different from the effective sacrifice (of burnt and 'peaceful' offering, which expiates sin). The covenant is a symbolic sacrifice, a purely formal act marking a sworn word or commitment, while the expiatory sacrifice acts of itself, provided that it be correctly performed and adapted to its end.

29. Jaini (1979: 161) notes how the *namaskar-mantra* is used to initiate children into the *darshan-pratima* (the path of insight), and that prior to this initiation children in Jain households are referred to as nominal (*nama*) Jains. These remarks presumably refer to southern Digambar Jains, of whom the author himself is one. They do not apply to Shvetambars in Jaipur.

30. One of the more popular forms is to utter *asiausa namah*. 'A-si-a-u-sa' is formed from the first syllables of each of *arihant, siddha, acarya, upadhyaya* and *sadhu*. On the reduction of the *mantra* to *om*, see Williams (1963: 186) and for a more full discussion, see Ghoshal (1917: 112). Staal (1986: 57–9) describes the reduction of text to formulas, through formal operations such as these, in Vedic texts.

31. Everyone we spoke to was clear that this is the rule. But in answer to our queries about why this should be so, most people said they didn't know. One person said, 'This is what Indra (the king of the *devta*s) used when he did *puja*', others simply that 'Well-water is more pure than tap-water.'

32. Thus, for example, a movement is recorded in the 12th c., the Agamikas, who claimed that to be faithful to the ancient scriptures one should omit mention of traditional deities (*shruta-devta*s), such as the powerful protector goddesses, from Jain religious ritual (Schubring 1962: 67; Caillat 1978: 149; Cort 1987: 237).

33. The Terapanth was formed around the charismatic renouncer Bhikhshu, who broke from his Sthanakvasi teacher in Rajasthan in the 18th c.

34. The book is now available in a fine edition, translated, with an introduction and explanatory notes by the historian Mukund Lath.

35. Excerpts from Meghavijaya's *Yuktiprabodha* are published in translation as an appendix to Lath's edition of Banarsi's autobiography. The work is a diatribe against the Adhyatma movement.

36. Banarsi calls these rituals *vyarahar* – conventional (Lath 1981: 217).

37. This is a word for male renouncers in Jainism. It will be remembered that renouncers of the Digambar tradition go completely naked once they have reached the highest spiritual level.

38. Luther, for example, wrote, 'Now when God sends forth his holy Gospel, He deals with us in a twofold manner, the first outwardly, then inwardly. Outwardly He deals with us through the oral word of the Gospel and through material signs, that is, baptism and the sacrament of the altar. Inwardly He

deals with us through the Holy Spirit, faith, and other gifts. But whatever their measure or order the outward factors should and must precede. The inward experience follows and is effected by the outward. God has determined to give the inward to no-one except through the outward' (quoted in Eire 1986: 72).

39. *Prabhavana* means 'influence', the idea here being that seeing the generosity of Jains in giving out these sweets, others will be influenced to think well of the religion.

3

What Kind of Theory Do We Need?

RITUAL has been seen by anthropologists and others in broadly two ways: as a distinct category of events; and as an ever-present aspect of all actions. In this chapter we explain why we think both these approaches are mistaken. In both cases, moreover, the assumption has been that ritual is intrinsically a form of communication, and we further argue that ritual can be characterized without reference to communication. On these general conceptions, as if on two shifting underlays of fertile mud, a luxuriant jungle of theories about ritual has grown up. Though we may seem a bit like crocodiles snapping in the undergrowth, what we actually want to do is to cut through to find some firmer ground, without becoming entangled in the densely entwined branches of the theories, and without even attempting to clear the whole terrain. This involves charting a way to a new *kind* of theory of ritual. We shall explain how we think the category 'ritual' can be specified: not as a kind of event or as an aspect of all action, but as a quality which action can come to have—a special way in which acts may be performed. From this perspective theoretical attention focuses on ritualization, the process by which normal, everyday action is endowed with this quality and becomes ritual.

For anthropologists, and increasingly in recent years for historians, classicists, psychologists, and sociologists, ritual has occupied a prominent place in cultural studies. It would be easy to cite works of real brilliance, where description and exegesis of particular rituals aid the interpretation of a revolution, a political system, a type of agricultural production, or a system of gender relations. Nevertheless, we shall argue in this chapter that the theoretical discourse on which these studies routinely rely is in need of fairly fundamental reorientation, and we shall begin to explain our own ideas about the direction this reorientation should take. Much is known, from anthropological and other studies, about various kinds of ritual and the roles they can play in social and political processes, but the question of what ritual itself is—what is distinctive about ritual action—has hardly ever been posed in a helpful way. Until it is, the deep and alluring question of how and why ritual has the prominence it does in human affairs, a prominence which so-called 'secularization' has done nothing significant to diminish, will remain as it is at present, almost entirely opaque.

Our first task is therefore largely negative. Anthropology is littered with theories of ritual: a welter of labyrinthine arguments and complex, multi-clause definitions. We shall argue that most of them are trying to explain the wrong thing; but we shall not attempt a comprehensive critical review of these theories, which would anyway take a whole book, and still less shall we be detailing the many valuable insights which the literature undoubtedly does contain. Inevitably, then, our discussion will seem slighting and unjust to those who owe a particular debt to, or have a deep affection for one or other of the theorists we mention. Along the way we shall mention some works on ritual which we very much admire, a perhaps idiosyncratic genealogy which has helped us to reach our own ideas. Some of these authors will be mentioned only in passing and we shall refer to their ideas rather unsystematically in the service of our own argument. We can only hope that the argument will, in the end, justify the discourtesies we commit along the way.[1] The question we need to answer is what, on the most general level, will a theory of ritual have to look like? What kind of theory should it be?

Let us begin with the idea that ritual is a special kind of happening which requires a special interpretation or explanation. It has proved impossible to find criteria for this which yield a category of any analytical usefulness.[2] The starting point for most attempts to define a class of ritual events has been the perception that there are certain incontrovertible cases; events which when we look at them we are sure are rituals. If we can identify what makes them so, we can seek out these criteria in other events and institutions, and thus identify all the members of the class. One of the best-known definitions of ritual in anthropology is that given by Victor Turner in *The Forest of Symbols*. He defines ritual as 'formal behaviour for occasions not given over to technological routine, having reference to beliefs in mystical beings or powers. The symbol is the smallest unit of ritual' (1967: 19).[3] But other anthropologists, not to speak of industrial sociologists, ethologists, and psychiatrists, noting that events which are not religious can also be ritual, have looked for a definition which would include 'secular ritual'. While it is true that one could simply drop the phrase, 'having reference to mystical beings or powers', leaving the idea of formal behaviour in a non-technological realm, this results in a class of actions which is so compendious and varied that it is virtually useless. Jack Goody, in a playful critique of the way the term 'ritual' is used in the social sciences, cites the work of the industrial sociologist Bocock on ritualism in modern England:

If we include in our definition of ritual 'handshaking, teeth cleaning, taking medicines, car riding, eating, entertaining guests, drinking tea or coffee, beer, sherry, whisky, etc., taking a dog for a walk, watching television, going to the cinema, listening to records, visiting relatives, routines at work, singing at work, children's street games, hunting and so on,' then one can, as the author (Bocock, 1974: 15) rightly perceives 'go on adding activities *ad infinitum.* (1977: 27)

Goody concludes that a category defined in this way is without analytical value. In a similar vein, John Skorupski asks, 'What use does a term have which brings together a man shaking hands, a man praying to his god, a man refusing to walk under a ladder, a man clapping at the end of a concert, a man placing medicine on his crops?' As there is almost nothing which such a category would reliably exclude, we can only agree that the answer is, 'None at all' (Skorupski 1976: 171).

   If one returns in despair to the concept of ritual as 'having reference to mystical beings or powers', several problems still remain.[4] Whose idea of what counts as 'mystical' is to apply here? As Goody notes, to rely on 'our' ideas is to accept a simplistically dichotomous view of the world. The 'religious–secular' distinction is,

based on a we/they distinction, which operates in a temporal context (traditional/ modern), or in a geographical frame (we the people/they the savages), or by reference to a particular set of assumptions, for example, world religions (like Christianity) as against other local beliefs (like magic and witchcraft), until we reach the ultimate dichotomy on which so much thinking in this field is based: we = science/logic, they = irrationality (or non-rationality). (1977: 25)

Of course it may be the case that the particular culture under discussion itself makes a religious–secular distinction as applied to actions, but this is not always so; and even if such a distinction is made it may well not coincide with the observer's idea of 'having reference to mystical beings'. Since this idea turns on the question of what is and is not determined empirically, it is always possible for the intuitions of actor and observer to differ.[5] For example, the following action, which has gained a certain currency in the literature, is assumed by both Martin Hollis and Quentin Skinner to be a ritual: 'Certain Yoruba tribesmen carry about with them boxes covered with cowrie shells, which they treat with special regard. . . . The tribesmen believe that the boxes are their heads or souls and that what they are doing in treating the boxes in a reverent way is protecting their souls against witchcraft' (Skinner 1988: 85. See also Hollis 1968:

231). This 'example' of ritual action has appeared in debates (about rationality, social meaning, and so on) which are not our concern here, but it is striking that both these writers assume the action to be ritual mainly because they think there is something obviously unreasonable or odd about what the tribesmen are doing, and the sweeping language used ('the tribesmen believe that the boxes are their heads or souls') reveals a disregard for the fine grain of what in truth Yoruba people think they are doing. No useful analytical distinction or category of 'ritual' can rest on subjective judgements about reasonableness, whether ours or the Yorubas'. If 'ritual' is defined in this way it turns out, like 'taboo', 'totemism', and 'magic', not to be a useful analytical term at all; and the double abstraction whereby the anthropologist's idea of 'mystical' is added to the varieties of native metaphysics makes for a particularly unhelpful kind of nominalism. But although in each case a whole liter-ature exists dissolving such categories (Steiner on taboo, Lévi-Strauss on totemism, Skorupski on magic, Goody on ritual) they go on recurring *faute de mieux*.

Moore and Myerhoff attempt to define secular ritual. They observe that it is possible to see social behaviours as forming a continuum, with the extreme of prescribed formality at one end and the most open, optative, spontaneous behaviour at the other (1977: 22). But the problem here, if one tries to define 'a ritual' (a complex of actions) is that almost any complex social occasion involves acts at several locations on this con-tinuum, in various permutations and combinations. Which of such actions constitute rituals, and which merely have formal or ritualized elements? Moore and Myerhoff decide that locating the point where a given cere-mony lies on such a continuum 'does not have any heuristic importance'. However, they do think that it is of interest to consider the meaning of formal elements wherever they do occur. Here they cite with approval Rappaport's linking of sanctity with ritual—'Sanctity is the quality of unquestionable truthfulness imputed by the faithful to unverifiable propositions' (1975: 69)—and argue that leaving aside the question of belief, formality itself often conveys an element of presented certainty.

It is our conviction that one level of meaning of many formal actions is to present or refer to the culturally postulated and the socially unquestionable. It is an attempt to reify the man-made (see Berger and Luckmann 1966). That which is postulated and unquestionable may but need not be religious. It may but need not have to do with mystical forces and the spirit world. Unquestionability may instead be vested in a system of authority or a political ideology or other matters. If ritual is considered a set of formal acts which deal with or refer to postulated matters about society or ideology (or matters those mounting the ritual *want* to be unquestioned) then the notion of a secular ritual is not a contradiction in terms. (1977: 22)

In Rappaport's neo-Durkheimian view there are functions which only ritual can perform. Ritual is '*the* basic social act', because only in ritual are fundamental social conventions not only represented but also 'consummated'. By this he means that they are accepted by the participants, even if, as individuals, they do not actually practise them (1979: 197). We have much admiration for the many insights in Rappaport's paper. However, we have to reject his idea that ritual is essentially a kind of communication. Unfortunately, this assumption pervades his whole theory that the defining characteristic of ritual lies in the combination of formality and sanctity. We entirely agree with Rapaport as to the regulated (formal) nature of ritual action and the primal commitment which this imposes on participants. But does this imply sanctity? The question connects, of course, with the issues raised in the previous chapter about the nature of social convention and the religious evaluation and legitimacy of ritual itself.[6]

Rappaport insists that ritual is different from play. Ritual is in earnest. This is because authoritative social messages are transmitted by it.

Messages, although transmitted by the participants, are not encoded by them. They are found by participants already encoded in the liturgy. Since these messages are more or less invariant obviously they cannot in themselves reflect the transmitter's contemporary state. For instance, the order of the Roman mass does not, in itself, express anything about the current states of those performing it. In recognition of the regularity, propriety, and apparent durability and immutability of these messages I shall refer to them as 'canonical'. . . .

Since to perform a liturgical order, which is by definition a relatively *invariant* sequence of acts and utterances *encoded by someone other* than the performer himself, is to *conform* to it, authority or directive is *intrinsic* to liturgical order. (1979: 179, 192)

What are these messages? Is it not rather that to conform to liturgical order is to perform only the necessary acts, to leave a vacant space for new interpretations, and not necessarily so very pious ones either? The material we presented in the previous chapter illustrates Goody's general point, that while formalized acts may stay the same over a historical period, there is abundant ethnographic evidence that what they are said by the actors to refer to none the less changes. The same liturgical act changes meaning over time, or between communities at the same time: 'Any society, no matter how simple, experiences the continuous creation of meaning . . . a particular event, a new song, a topical phrase, will have its effect upon the network of meaning and thus change the system in one direction or another' (1977: 30).[7]

A defence of Rappaport's and of Moore and Myerhoff's position might reply that the momentous 'postulated matters about society or ideology' dealt with by ritual are nevertheless unquestioned at any given time. Yet a moment's thought will show that this is not the case. As Goody observes, while the exact recollection, formalization, and repetition of ritual may lead to social solidarity, it might also lead to loss of meaning. He cites the example of the election of the Master of a Cambridge college, a process which is perhaps not best known for being consensual:

The election in the chapel involved a declaration before God of one's belief that X was the right man. Nowadays the verbal vote seems an infringement of personal liberties (enshrined in the voting reforms of the 19th century). Yet ceremony preserves the emptied if not empty form, now shorn of meaning because that is how things are done. The formal repetitive character of 'ritual' leads to continuity, yes, but the pejorative implications of formal, ritual, convention, etiquette, are in fact embedded in their very substance, instrinsic to their nature. (1977: 31)

Not only can momentous acceptances of social values (a vow or oath, a religious conversion, a decision to become an American, even a marriage) take place in non-ritualized circumstances, it is also not the case that 'ritual' invariably involves unquestionable or sacrosanct theories of the world. To quote Goody once again,

It is misleading to assert that 'rituals' provide a key to deep values more than any other type of human behaviour. Indeed, I would be tempted to argue that they provide less of a clue, for the reasons I have stated, their formality, the element of culture lag, the component of public demonstration, their role as masks of the 'true' self . . . However this may be in non-literate societies . . . it is perhaps not only in 'secular' societies that rituals may be formal and repetitive, representative of the old rather than the new, occasions where action is automatic rather than thought out, hence probably less central to human life than the affliction or crises that have provided the occasion. (1977: 32)

What Goody's refreshing polemic side-steps here is the fundamental importance of ritualization as a way in which humans conduct affairs (even if certain cultures regard ritual with disdain, or a range of other attitudes). Rappaport rightly insists on this point, when he describes the social commitment implied by ritual action. 'The performance of ritual establishes the existence of conventions and accepts them simultaneously and inextricably' (1979: 194). What we are concerned to challenge here is the idea that accepting such conventions implies acceptance of any particular beliefs, ideas, or values. Ritual is not invariably evaluated in any particular way, either as necessarily efficacious, as always dubiously over-formal, or as imparting great social or spiritual truths. This is true even if people must commit themselves to the very formality of ritual in order to take part in it, and this is why we shall look, for an understanding of the distinctiveness of ritual, to the quality of ritualized action itself rather than to the beliefs, attitudes, or purposes which those who perform rituals might or might not have.

Let us now return more specifically to the idea that there is a class of events which we can call 'rituals'. Rodney Needham's brilliant essay, 'Remarks on Wittgenstein and Ritual', contains the following cheerless sentence:

What we isolate as 'ritual' in one or another form or context, is not more than the expression in social action of symbolic features which are by no means peculiar to it—whatever it may be. (1985: 156)

Needham has recourse to an idea used extensively elsewhere in his work, when he suggests that ritual is an example of a polythetic concept, which 'variously combines certain characteristic features, and the task of the comparativist is to identify these features and to register the patterns into which they combine' (1985: 156). This is certainly a possible solution, and Needham has shown it to be useful elsewhere. But in the case of ritual the 'characteristic features' can either be said to be few in number, in which case, whatever their combinations, they scarcely account for the heterogeneity of the phenomena; or they are can be said to be many, and we are more or less back where we started.

So the attempt to identify criteria by which a class of rituals may be isolated is, we think, fundamentally misguided. It will not help us to understand what 'ritual' means. This is because, even if we restrict ourselves to consideration of the easy or unambiguous cases, sequences of action which are ritualized do not have anything *else* in common, any more than do objects which are red. As events or institutions, they belong to different areas of life, and they fit in very disparate ways into the economic, social, political, cultural, and religious lives of the societies in which they are performed. One need only look at the range of interests anthropologists quite legitimately have in writing about particular rituals to see that these events and institutions are interesting for many more reasons than the fact that they are rituals. When anthropologists develop theories to meet these particular but disparate other interests, it is little wonder that their theories so seldom have anything to say about what it is that *makes* these events ritual. These authors are typically interested in the rituals they study because they are interested in politics, kinship, gender, class, cosmology, and so on; and this is a different thing from being interested in them *as* rituals (Much of what anthropologists do when they 'study ritual', is what chemists do when they 'study test tubes' or historians when they 'study documents'). Interest in the history, the social function, or the economic importance of rituals and in the religious symbolism, the cosmological ideas, or the ethical values which may be discerned by observing and by asking about them, are all important anthropological concerns and it is no part of our purpose here to disparage or discourage them (although what we say in this book will have implications for how they may be pursued), but we do insist that these various interests will not serve as a theory of ritual.

In our view 'ritual' is a quality which can in theory apply to any kind of action. Ritualization begins with a particular modification of the normal intentionality of human action. Action which has undergone this modification is ritual action. Action can be relaxed, ecstatic, communicative, or repetitive, quite independently of whether it is also ritual; just as an object can be red, and also spherical, wobbly, and expensive. Ritual action can also be religious, or not; performed by specialists, or not; performed regularly, or not; 'express the social order', or not. Just as different objects, though red, can be otherwise different, different actions, though they may all be ritual actions, need have nothing else in common. It is true that when a sequence of institutionalized action is ritualized this is usually one of the most interesting and significant things about it, and it is natural then to call it a rite, or, 'a ritual'. It will nevertheless always be a ritual 'something' and what this 'something' is can be very various indeed: thus there are life-cycle rituals, rituals of rebellion, imitative rites, rites of office, rites of commemoration, rites of purification, rites of affliction, worship, divination, sacrifice, namings, inaugurations, and so on. These 'rituals' are as various as the actions and operations of which they are ritualized versions.

But it may still be possible, without having to make any generalizations at all about the kinds of actions which tend to be ritualized, or the social implications of their being so, to say something both useful and general about the ritualization of action. We can know when an object is red, and know what it is for something to be red—in that sense we can 'understand redness'—without having to think we can have a theory of all the things which are red. Such a 'theory' could consist of nothing more than the observation that there is a wondrous range of very different objects which are red, and that they are put to an astonishingly wide range of uses. We have no reason to expect that because the term 'ritual' can with truth be applied to a sequence of action this will necessarily tell us anything else about its function, its history, or its sense. Things which are done in ritual (eating, washing, offering, and so on) and the things which are done by means of rituals (praising, changing status, greeting, and so forth) can be done in non-ritualized ways. What is the difference? Different kinds of events and actions can be ritualized, and we will be able to see the implications of this in each particular case only if we understand what is the difference between ritualized and unritualized action. What happens when you perform an act *as* a ritual? What is it about ritual acts that makes them ritual? The 'theory of ritual' which we shall present below will be an attempt to answer the question: of what does the ritualization of acts and processes consist?

Anthropologists have rarely approached ritual with this essentially phenomenological sort of question in mind, and have too often just assumed that social meaning can be 'read' in a direct and unproblematic way, from what people are observed to say and do during rituals. Exceptions to this rule include the works of Gilbert Lewis and S. J. Tambiah (see also two recent papers by Gerholm (1988) and Parkin (1992)). Another notable recent exception is Maurice Bloch (1986, 1989, 1992), whose works include specific consideration of the particular forms of action and expression used in ritual, and therefore some conjectures on *how* some of the particular effects so often and so easily attributed to rituals might actually come about.[8] But here as elsewhere some valuable observations on the character of ritual action are subordinate to, and pressed into the service of, generalizations about the function of *rituals*, as a category of events, and these generalizations are in turn an integral part of a theory of the symbolic content and the social function, and perhaps even the origin, of *religion*.[9]

Superficially, there might appear to be a similarity between our approach and the view we mentioned at the beginning of the chapter that ritual is an aspect of action, specifically, the communicative or expressive aspect. In this view, most prominently expressed by Edmund Leach, 'ritual' is a characteristic of all action, although its conspicuousness and its particular forms are variable.[10]

Almost every human action that takes place in culturally defined surroundings is divisible in this way; it has a technical aspect which does something and an aesthetic, communicative aspect which says something. In those types of behavior that are (typically) labelled ritual . . . the aesthetic, communicative aspect is particularly prominent. . . . But it is equally a matter of 'ritual' that whereas an Englishman would ordinarily eat with a knife and fork, a Chinese would use chopsticks . . . the term ritual is best used to denote this communicative aspect of behavior. (Leach 1968: 523–4)

On this view, ritual is not a special characteristic of some actions, as we shall be arguing, but a necessary characteristic of them all. For Leach then, ritual is like the propensity of physical objects to reflect light and so to have colour, rather than a particular colour which only some objects have. We shall argue in the next chapter that ritualization consists of a specific departure from how things are otherwise done: it is not an intrinsic feature of all action but a particular, occasional *modification* of an intrinsic feature of action, namely its intentionality, so Leach's formulation is clearly different from our own. It is also, as many have remarked, flagrantly counterintuitive. There are many everyday actions of which it seems quite contrived to suggest they have a ritual aspect. And it obscures the salient facts: that an ordinary meal can be turned into a ritual meal; that the participants, at any rate, think that something distinguishes the two events; and that the observable differences often include rules and practices—such as passing bottles always to the left—which are believed by everyone who participates to be arbitrary and quite without meaning. If every action is a ritual action and if the facts which make them so are an infinity of different 'messages', then has anything really been explained? We note, however, that Leach's characteristically bold and splendidly incautious formulation does have the virtue that it shows the logical consequences of equating ritual with communication.

The idea that ritual is essentially communicative and expressive is almost a social compact in anthropology, common as it is to the classic writings of Maurice Bloch, Mary Douglas, James Fernandez, Clifford Geertz, Max Gluckman, Edmund Leach, A. R. Radcliffe-Brown, Sherry Ortner, Roy Rappaport, S. J. Tambiah, and Victor Turner.[11] How anthropologists get themselves on this wrong track is obvious. Rituals are good things to do fieldwork on. Lots of people gather together; they do things which, when the anthropologist asks about them, involve informants going into details about all sorts of interesting things: cosmology, religious ideas, the social status of all the participants, and so on, and so forth. It almost seems that these events are arranged so that the anthropologist can learn from them. It is a short but utterly fallacious step to suppose that the purpose of the ritual is to communicate or express these ideas to the people, who already know them (and from whom, rather than from the ritual itself, the anthropologist in practice learns them). Even when a ritual can validly be cited as *evidence* that people hold this or that belief, it does not follow that the purpose of performing the ritual is to *communicate* the belief.[12] But anthropologists have been tempted to assert of ritual that it 'communicates' the theories or observations about the society in question which the anthropologists themselves want to communicate to their readership.[13] As Gilbert Lewis remarks, this attempt to interpret the ritual as functioning to communicate what the anthropologist has learned or surmised, 'can lead to a contrived intellectualisation of ritual in which the conviction that it is to be understood by means of a linguistic model distorts evaluation, and provokes such ingenuity in detection that the actors are told what they mean when they do not know it' (Lewis 1980: 117).[14]

Obviously, some actions which are ritualized are linguistic actions, saying prayers or singing hymns, for example. Clearly it would be absurd, however formalized these may be in some circumstances, to say that they are not examples of communication. A classic instance where an analysis in terms of communication is revealing is Tambiah's paper on the magical power of words, which works so well just because he focuses on the words. But the communication here is not intrinsic to the *ritual* character of these acts. It belongs rather to the as it were 'pre-existing' linguistic act which has been ritualized.

Woven into ritual sequences are numerous non-linguistic acts (waving a lamp, circumambulating a statue, and so on) which have no linguistic or quasi-linguistic meaning. It is obvious that all these acts, both those which use language and those which do not, in so far as they are ritualized, come to have new properties.[15] Understanding ritual involves identifying what these properties are, and as far as we can see they have nothing to do with communication. This is to recognize that ritualization is a quality of action, and not a special set of ideas. Ritualized action may include linguistic acts, such as saying a prayer or chanting a *mantra*, but we see no reason to accord primacy to the propositional ideas expressed in these, especially since ritualization very often obscures such ideas (the prayer may be in Latin, the *mantra* formalistically reduced to a single sound), rather than to attend to the evident fact of their being acts (of praying, of chanting, and so on). In a perspicacious passage Staal describes the affects of the ritualization of language in the case of Vedic literature.

Entire passages that originally were pregnant with meaning are reduced to long 'o's. This is precisely what distinguishes *mantras* from the original verse: to be made into a *mantra*, and thus fit for ritual consumption, a verse has to be subject to *formal* transformations, operations that apply to form and not to meaning . . . Ritual traditions have obvious social significance in that they identify groups and distinguish them from one another. They give people, in that hackneyed contemporary phrase, 'a sense of identity'. That identity, however, is often due to distinctions that rest upon meaningless phonetic variations. Thus the Jaiminiya and Kauthuma-Ranayaniya schools differ from each other by such characteristics as vowel length, or because the former uses 'a' when the latter uses 'o'. Up to the present time, the Vedic schools themselves are distinguished from each other by such variations of sound that can more easily be explained in grammatical than in religious terms. (Staal 1986: 57–9)

On initiating and ending the *puja* (and sometimes also stages within the *puja*) some worshippers make short declarations and salutations (such as '*nissahi*' and '*avassahi*') and we mentioned some other examples of preparatory and boundary-marking acts in Chapter 2: bathing, changing clothes, taking off shoes, touching the threshold, and just stepping into or out of a reserved physical space. One of the more sophisticated formulations of the idea that ritual is essentially a form of communication relies on the idea of a 'metacommunicative' message, carried by the boundary-marking actions which are so often found at the beginning and end of rituals. Gregory Bateson (1972), for example, suggested that they 'frame' episodes of action with a message—'all this is ritual'—and so effect an alteration of ordinary action, creating the phenomenon they contain. If this were true, boundary markers and the message they transmit would be an explanation of ritual itself.[16] However, we maintain that while these boundary devices do mark and announce a sequence of action as ritualized, they do not account for the ritualization of the action. There are two points to note.

First, many of the boundary-marking acts used by Jains are also employed outside the context of the *puja*. Jains, like all their Hindu neighbours, take off their shoes whenever they enter a house, change their clothes before attending many social events, and bathe to begin the day. That the use of reserved spaces marks out and bounds particular processes and events is similarly obvious.[17] Thus these acts are signals which do have agreed, conventional meanings[18] (in this they are unlike the ritualized acts which are within the 'boundary' and which may not be signifiers at all), but there is nothing essentially 'ritual' about the meaning of these acts. Second, there is nothing essentially boundary-marking (or indeed signifying) about them either. They can all be performed in order to achieve their own non-representational purposes in contexts where they have no such marking function. One can take off one's shoes to be more comfortable, or one can bathe to get clean. While it is true that, in context,

such acts point up the change between ritualized and normal action, it is
equally true that they can be recognized as marking this change only
because there is a change to mark.

Thus these boundary-marking acts have a propositional meaning which
they can convey in a number of contexts, including that of the *puja* ritual,
but the meaning they carry is a very general one. They announce that
what is to follow (or what has just happened) is different from unmarked
action, but they do not indicate in what way it is different. They say that
it is to be thought of as a unit, and taken as a whole, but they do not say
of what that whole consists. In the case of the *puja*, they do not indicate
that what is to follow will be 'ritual', as opposed to other activities for
which the same boundary signs are used, and thus it is clear that they
cannot be seen as constituting ritualization. Nor are they necessary for
ritualization to occur. Lesser sequences of ritualized action need have no
boundary markers at all. Consider saying grace or elaborate ceremonial
greetings: it is the way these acts are performed, the fact that they are
ritualized, that tells us that they are not just conversation.

Having said all this, we would be the last to deny that certain ritualized
enactments can *involve* communication, as many initiation rites, for instance, patently do. Perhaps we should discuss an example here in order
to come to a better understanding of what is involved. The example we
have in mind is the dance of the *devadasis* (female temple dancers) which
is still performed in a few Hindu temples in India. The dance is highly
stylized: the dancers learn a large number of gestures, eye positions, rigid
facial expressions, and percussive foot movements which, as Marglin
(1990: 220) points out, radically distance the dancer from her own subjective states of mind. In this way we can say the dance is ritualized. Combinations and sequences of gestures are known as *bhav*. Marglin states that the
word is used technically to refer to the total postural and gestural *gestalt*
which accompanies a particular emotional-cum-mental state, such as
anger, valour, and erotic love.[19]

Now the dances have as their aim to arouse in the audience an erotic
sensation which is transformed by the ritual to a spiritual-cosmic plane,
such that the spectators can participate in the 'divine play' of the gods. In
Marglin's analysis, the sensation is communicated to the spectators by the
fact that the *bhav* gestures are 'refinements' of everyday natural physical-
emotional-cognitive experiences.[20] However, we need to consider carefully the difference between two dances she describes. The evening dance,
which is still currently performed, is an interpretative accompaniment of
a sung poetic story and it is mimed, rather than fully danced. The midday

dance, now discontinued, was accompanied only by drumming, and was performed in a 'nonsemantic manner' (Marglin 1990: 221).

Although it is perhaps presumptuous to question an analysis of a ritual we have not seen, our interpretation would be slightly but crucially different from Marglin's. She uses Tambiah's (1985 [1981]) performative approach to ritual and assumes that indexical values are inferred by the spectators. We would argue that there is nothing in Marglin's ethnography to contradict our view that the *ritualization* of the dance does *not* contribute to communication. For the *bhav* states themselves to communicate they would have to be signs, that is, conventions so widespread and well understood that they can be 'read' by the spectators and this surely is a separate social process, not intrinsic to the states themselves. Formalization does not necessarily contribute to understanding. Apparently, these conventions were understood until the 1960s, but it is possible that one reason why the midday dance was discontinued is that they ceased to be so. Only the evening dance, where communication is much aided by explanatory songs, is now performed. We conclude that highly ritualized performance can certainly communicate to audiences, but that if the term 'communication' is understood to imply the transmission of ideas, as opposed say to the mental-emotional states conveyed by music and gesture, it requires special conditions, unconnected with ritualization, in order to do so. These conditions might include widespread understanding of a conventional sign-system, or association with a simultaneous performance in language.[21]

In the above example the identity of those who are to send and receive the message is clear, so describing the situation as involving communication makes some sense. Many rituals are not performances in this sense, and it is often not at all clear who is supposed to be communicating with whom (for more discussion see Lewis 1980). Rappaport (1979) has argued that the idea of ritual as communication may be salvaged by saying that what frequently happens is that people are communicating with themselves.[22] A lay Jain businessman reverently places a fruit in front of a statue and thinks, 'I accept that my body is separate from my soul, just as the skin of this fruit is separate from the kernel.' While noting again that such attribution of meaning to an act does not always happen, so that it is a poor candidate for a characteristic of all ritual, we can still ask, is this Jain *communicating* this idea to himself? Surely we must allow some constraints on what is to count as communication. We cannot admit that whenever people employ or act upon a belief, desire, or attitude, they are communicating that mental state to themselves or the notion of communication would lose all content. In this example, there is no gain in information and no transmission of knowledge. What is going on here is that the worshipper intends to *represent* an idea by means of a ritualized action, an action which could perfectly well represent other ideas.

John Searle demonstrates that it is possible to mean without intending to communicate (1983: 165–6). In Searle's view it is representation, not communication, which is the core of meaning. He uses the example of raising an arm as a representation of the belief that the enemy is retreating (1983: 167–9). This act remains a representation of this belief, it means 'the enemy is retreating' and is, like the belief, true or false depending on whether the enemy is indeed retreating, even if it is not communicated to anyone else. One can intend to mean something, which is to represent an idea, without intending to communicate, which is to produce beliefs in an audience. As we have seen, the Jain *puja* is a particularly good ethnographic demonstration of this possibility: celebrants certainly should give meanings to their ritualized actions (though a lazy or absent-minded person might not), but if they do, there is certainly no intention to communicate such meaning to anyone else.

A religious attitude might nevertheless suggest that people in rituals are communicating with God. This is an important idea in Christian theology, though it occurs hardly at all in Jain discussions because the Jinas, closest to divinity, no longer exist as such. The miraculous living teacher which the statue in a temple represents is dead. His liberated soul has gone to the topmost limit of the universe. It is not this pure soul which Jains worship in their temples, but the long-dead omniscient saviour. Nevertheless, it must be admitted that this does not stop many Jains from apparently talking to someone they believe no longer exists (see Gombrich 1971 for discussion of a similar situation in Buddhism). One man, for example, said that when he laid sweets before the statue he thought, 'O Bhagwan, I wish that like you I also shall have no hunger.' Here, while the worshipper is speaking *to* the Jina, there can be no intention to communicate. Nor does the analytical language of communication help us to understand what this man is doing in addressing his divinity thus. First of all, it does not add anything, or even make much sense, without the idea of reception as well as transmission, and here this is conspicuously absent. In addition, the vocabulary of transmitters and receivers, and the concern with the flow of information between individual *knowing* subjects, is quite wide of the mark. Even outside of ritual or religious contexts, we can speak to someone for reasons other than to communicate. As Charles Taylor illustrates, we can speak in order to place our thoughts before another, and so establish mutual space between us.

Let us say that you and I are strangers travelling together through some southern country. It is terribly hot, the atmosphere is stifling. I turn to you and say: 'Whew, it's hot'. This does not tell you anything you did not know. . . . What this expression has done is to create a rapport between us. . . . Previously I knew that you were hot, and you knew that I was hot, and I knew that you knew that, etc.: up to any level that you care to chase it. But now it is out there as a fact between *us* that it is stifling in here. (Taylor 1985: 259)

While the Jain man, in thinking as he did, was in a sense talking to the Jina, he was not, it seems to us, attempting to communicate with him. The thought he formulated was a response to the experience of a religious desire, and an attempt to create a space for religious experience. Such responses take many forms, not all of them necessarily in words, nor necessarily realized in a ritual context.

Of course, some ideas may be transmitted incidentally between participants during the course of a ritual. In the Church of England many people kneel when prayers are being said. But vicars have noticed that this is becoming less and less common. Kneeling may be given this or that meaning by the members of the congregation: it is reverential, it represents spiritual penitence, it is a kind of minor physical penance, it expresses subordination to God or acquiescence to the words of the prayer, and the reasons people have for doing it are probably related to whatever meaning they attribute. Such kneeling or not kneeling also indicates something about oneself to the other nearby members of the congregation, supposing they notice.[23] This could even be a reason for not kneeling, in which case we could certainly speak of communication, but surely no one sees *this* act of communication as expressing the meaning of the rite.

Most readers will probably think that the Jain *puja*, which can consist of an individual sitting in meditation, is pretty exceptional as rituals go and that the really interesting subject is those richly-laden, seemingly intrinsically symbolical rituals, such as Ndembu initiation, which have been so prominent in the anthropological literature. In response, we would first reiterate that for both words and actions occurring in rites it is not their being ritualized which makes them symbolic (and hence interesting to anthropologists primarily concerned with *what* they symbolize). Ritualization makes an action easier to use as a vehicle for the creative processes of symbolization (see Chapter 9), but these processes do not actually require ritualization: it is after all possible to make a symbolic gesture, for example wearing a black arm-band or giving a red rose, in a more or less unritualized context. What we are concerned with in this book is not whether an action is symbolic or not, but what difference it makes when actions are ritualized.[24]

From Durkheim's Australian 'totemic' rites, to Geertz's Balinese cockfights, and Turner's Ndembu initiations, the most influential anthropological studies of ritual have tended (accurately or not) to portray closed, local communities with a shared culture and symbolic code, and symbolic consensus has come to be seen as characteristic of ritual—even though some anthropologists have demonstrated that in particular cases symbolic consensus does not, in fact, obtain.[25] A recent paper by Tomas Gerholm (1988) suggests developing a perspective on ritual which could comprehend a range of more fragmented, divided, and historically self-conscious social situations, and takes as a paradigm a text by V. S. Naipaul—a description of his return to Trinidad to attend a 'Hindu' funeral rite for his sister. Naipaul describes the plurality of social experiences which the participants brought to the funeral rite; the fragmented and overlapping cultural and ethnic identities they drew upon; their more or less conscious desires to recover, reform, and reinvent 'their' traditions; and the way participants were united in performance although their notions of the meaning the rite might have were both incomplete and contradictory. Gerholm suggests, 'We should at least consider the possibility that what Naipaul describes is representative not only of Trinidad in the 1980's but also of other rituals in other places and at other times, even "traditional" places and "historical" times' (Gerholm 1988: 196). Gerholm proposes a 'post-modernist' perspective on ritual which would find, even in 'traditional' places, the kind of fragmentation of meaning which Naipaul highlights. We hope that our own discussion helps show why this should be so, and so develops what Gerholm calls for—'a useful antidote to the Ndembu paradigm'.

And it is also worth pointing out that anthropology has signally neglected the analysis of liturgical ritual in general, and in particular has neglected religious acts of worship, those plain and featureless rituals which offer few handles for virtuosity in symbolic interpretation and yet are so important to people's religious life. Here again the ritual is often assumed to have a profound meaning (sometimes conjectured to be too profound to be known), but on closer examination this kind of ritual turns out to lay bare an absence—perhaps a sacred absence—of semantic content of its own. An example is the Islamic ritual *salat*, worship by prostrations and recitations, which is required of all Muslims. Most anthropological studies of Islam tell one almost nothing of what goes on in a mosque, preferring to concentrate on the more dubiously 'Islamic' elements in the religious practice of Muslims. We have no quarrel with the wish to celebrate variety, which probably most often motivates this, but it does seem a pity that it distorts the anthropologist's picture of the range of ritualized acts there are. John Bowen, in a recent paper which does describe the forms which the *salat* takes, finds this rite recalcitrant to symbolic decoding.

The *salat* is not structured around an intrinsic propositional or semantic core. It cannot be 'decoded' semantically because it is not designed according to a single symbolic or iconic code. In particular times and places Muslims have construed the *salat* as conveying iconic or semantic meanings, but as part of particular spiritual, social and political discourses. The three Indonesian cases, and the brief perusal of examples elsewhere, suggest the wide variety of *salat* meanings. (1989: 615)

Our own view, which we shall develop further in subsequent chapters, is that the institutional imposition of meaning is a reaction religion can have to ritualization, not part of it. This chapter has been almost wholly negative. It is time now to begin to explain what we think ritualization is.

Notes

1. We shall give no consideration, for instance, to that substantial body of literature which, following the later writings of Victor Turner, subsumes the study of ritual into that of emotionally affecting performance. Not all rituals are theatrical in this way and not all 'theatrical' performances are profitably regarded as rituals. As studies of particular ritualized performances, these works can be subtle portraits of important institutions or wordy fantasies woven around the obvious, but in neither case do they contribute anything to the question of what distinguishes those more or less dramatic performances from others which are not ritualized, because the method consistently elides this distinction. The analogy of theatrical performance is so generously and prodigiously applied that Geertz (1983: 28) has aptly called it, 'a form for all seasons'. Much more useful, from our point of view, is Gilbert Lewis's (1980) careful exploration of the points of similarity and contrast between ritual and theatrical and musical performance. We shall ourselves several times draw comparisons between ritual and theatre, but this will be in the context of other comparisons, such as with acting under orders, and our purpose will be to point up the uniqueness of ritual, not to suggest that ritual is a genre of performance.

2. As a consequence, anthropologists have rarely felt constrained by their own definitions and characterizations of ritual, and have identified the 'rituals' they should study on intuitive grounds. Radcliffe-Brown proposed the use of the word 'ritual' as a qualifier for any actions, beliefs, values, sentiments, attitudes, and objects which other writers had identified as religion, magic, or ritual. Thus he wrote, 'Anything—a person, a material thing, a place, a word or name, an occasion or event, a day of the week or a period of the year—which is the object of a ritual avoidance or taboo can be said to have ritual value' (1952: 139). To talk of ritual attitudes and beliefs seems to us unnecessarily confusing. John Skorupski's suggestion seems pertinent. 'Ask', he writes, 'every time one feels inclined to talk of a "ritual" danger, a "ritual" precaution or a "ritual" prohibition, just what is added by the word—beyond a specious sense of understanding based on a confused idea that "ritual" dangers etc. are in some profound sense "Let's pretend" dangers' (Skorupski 1976: 171).

3. A year later Turner was defining ritual as, 'prescribed formal behaviour for occasions not given over to technological routine, having reference to beliefs in mystical (or non-empirical) beings or powers. But I shall also define a ritual or *a* kind of ritual as a corpus of beliefs or practices performed by a specific cult association' (1968: 15). Already we see atrophy and further confusion. Partly this is due to woolliness: 'mystical' does not cover all the cases, but Turner cannot bring himself to write 'imaginary', so confuses the issue by using another word which refers not to the existential status of the 'beings', but to *how they are known about*. So already a definition which began by specifying a kind of behaviour is opened out to include the status of knowledge about that behaviour (*whose* knowledge is left unstated); and by the next sentence we have ritual 'beliefs'.

4. Authors such as Robin Horton (1964, 1967), whom Tambiah rightly describes as Neo-Tylorian, stress this. An example of this approach is that of Lawson and McCauley (see Lawson and McCauley 1990). They take 'religious ritual' as the subject of their book, defining religion as a shared system of belief involving commitment to the idea of superhuman agents. Lawson and McCauley make the positive advance of treating religious rituals as actions. However, they say that, 'As actions, their [religious rituals'] general structures are not at all extraordinary' (1990: 6). What makes religious ritual different from ordinary actions is the metaphysical beliefs in superhuman agents which have semantic implications that in turn have an import on ritual form. This formulation makes it difficult for Lawson and McCauley to deal with cases such as Buddhism, where belief in superhuman agents may be absent. About this, they blithely observe, 'Religions without commitments to culturally postulated superhuman agents are (at least) extremely unlikely to have rich, highly constrained ritual systems. In fact, they are unlikely to have much ritual at all' (1990: 7–8). The Jain *puja* is a demonstration of how wrong this statement is. Apart from this, we disagree substantially with Lawson and

McCauley on their idea that strategies mimicking linguistic models provide the best approach to understanding ritual. They describe three analogies between ritual and language: (1) ritual as performative action, (2) as communication of information, and (3) as a formal system patterned on syntactic analyses of linguistic structures, but suggest that syntactic and competence models provide the best analogy for the analysis of ritual sequences. Our reasons for rejecting such formalist approaches should be clear from our discussions of how ritualization dissolves sequences in Chapters 4 and 5. Nevertheless, although we cannot accept their view of the semantic properties of ritual, we sympathize with their innovative use of cognitive research.

5. Malinowski, of course, claimed that the Trobriand Islanders he knew distinguished magical techniques from others, and insisted that all primitive peoples did the same (1954: 17). On the other hand, it is well known that many African peoples, including the Azande (Evans-Pritchard 1937) and the LoDagaa (Goody 1961: 145), have a single concept which can be translated as 'medicine' but includes things which one might call magic and ritual. Keith Thomas (1972: 668) denies that magic was a distinct category in early-modern England. And even if we could be sure that the Trobrianders drew the line of demarcation in the same place as did Malinowski, we cannot be sure that they *meant* the same thing by their distinction. As Skorupski notes (1976: 158) we cannot even be clear about what *we* mean by the distinction.

6. Bell (1992: 88–93) rightly argues that the features often cited by anthropologists, such as formality, fixity, and repetition, are only common and not invariant or intrinsic characteristics of ritual, something Needham (1985) has also argued. Bell also rightly insists that there must be many culturally different ways of constituting an action as ritualized (Chs. 8, 9, and 10 present our own discussion of the different ways we found among the Jains). But her own suggested invariant characteristic of ritualization is that it, 'specifically establishes a privileged contrast, differentiating itself as more important and powerful', and this, as she herself notes, requires a cultural consensus about the evaluation of things such as formality and personal sincerity. We would argue that consensus of this kind is not common (certainly less common than ritual) and that, indeed, as we suggested in the previous chapter, ritual is frequently the focus of discord about just such evaluations. So even Bell's 'privileged differentiation' is not an invariant characteristic of ritualization.

7. For an illustration that this applies even to very small-scale 'societies', see Barth (1987).

8. We have in mind especially Bloch's paper 'Symbol, Song, Dance, and Features of Articulation', but also several of the other papers in *Ritual, History and Power*. Despite the excellence of much of Bloch's analysis of ritual, his argument takes an odd and, we think, mistaken turn in this paper, perhaps precisely because phenomenological analysis is not separated from questions of social function. Speech-making, chanting, and singing are described by Bloch as increasing 'formalization' of natural speech. This formalization is

seen as 'impoverishing' language. But of course these formalizations are not *just* limitations, for they introduce new elements, like metre, melody, and various devices of rhetoric, which are absent or weak in everyday speech. In any case, it is difficult to see how Bloch thinks that 'choice' is reduced by these elements. How one might quantify 'choice' is a bit obscure, but even if we admit the idea it seems equally plausible that as a range of available options is narrowed, the significance of choosing between them might be increased. Nevertheless, having argued that ritual impoverishes the communicative resources of language, Bloch ingeniously attempts to explain ritual as an especially powerful system of communication and thus returns to the anthropological consensus. He argues that the point of ritual is to endow propositions (which are, he implies, vague and usually false) with persuasive power. This contention depends on the idea that with ritualization the propositional force (the range of what can be said) decreases, and illocutionary force increases. Again, quantification is inappropriate and seems to rest on a misapplication of 'speech-act' vocabulary. Bloch construes illocutionary 'force' as roughly equivalent to 'power' but the nearest equivalent is in fact, as Skinner glosses it, 'point', or what the speaker intends to do in saying what he or she says (see the next chapter). The different 'points' of locutions with different illocutionary forces include 'apologizing', 'warning', 'stating', and so on. Thus it seems mistaken to us to speak of illocutionary force as 'increasing'.

9. The concept of 'rebounding violence', which Bloch develops in *Prey Into Hunter*, is presented as a widespread *symbolic* structure, which has its most potent expression in rituals, but can also be found in mythology, and in various political institutions and kinship practices.

10. Leach believed that any distinction between what is normally called ritual or magic and communicative behaviour in general is 'either illusory or trivial'; thus 'speech itself is a form of ritual; non-verbal ritual is simply a signal system of a different, less specialised kind' (Leach 1966). See also Beattie (1966, 1970) for a similar view.

11. A few brief quotations: according to Radcliffe-Brown, 'ritual acts differ from technical acts in having in all instances some expressive or symbolic element in them' (1952: 143); and the function of rites and ceremonies is 'to regulate, maintain and transmit from one generation to another sentiments on which the constitution of the society depends' (1952: 157). Mary Douglas, with characteristic directness, asserts, 'Ritual is pre-eminently a form of communication' (1973: 41), and that, 'Magical rules always have an expressive function' (1973: 59). Leach: 'We engage in rituals in order to transmit collective messages to ourselves' (1976: 45). For Geertz (1973: 448–9), rites such as the Balinese cockfight encode 'a story they tell themselves about themselves' so that it acts as 'a kind of sentimental education'. When Tambiah observes that the formalization of ritual, 'puts in jeopardy the usefulness of the intentionality theory of meaning for understanding ritual' (1985: 132), he touches on what we shall argue below is the distinctive character of ritual; but the hope

that a solution could be found in information theory seems to have diverted him from this insight. So he begins his 'working definition' with the statement: 'Ritual is a culturally constructed system of symbolic communication' (1985: 128).

12. When you blush, this is evidence that you are embarrassed, because blushing is a natural sign of embarrassment. It does not follow that you blush in order to communicate your embarrassment. The notion of communication is tied to that of non-natural meaning. Communicative behaviour is *directed* towards a potential recipient, who is *intended* to understand the act in question in a particular way.

13. For general discussions of the dangers of projecting the academic stance and interest on to one's 'object' of study, and thus imagining 'it' in the image of one's own inquiry, see Bourdieu (1990), Fabian (1983).

14. Perhaps if ritual is not essentially communication, it would be better to say that it is expressive, that rituals present us with symptoms rather than messages? (Lewis 1980). Anthropologists have certainly been able to recognize and infer beliefs, desires, and attitudes in ritual by extrapolating from what is done and going beyond what their informants tell them about it, and they have written perceptively about the cosmology or the social structure using rituals as 'texts' on which to give commentary and exegesis. But the category of actions which is thus 'expressive' of facts about culture and society is much wider than ritual action. As Skorupski notes, 'A policeman's everyday uniform is not a ritual garment; a notice bearing the words "Private–No Entry", or a parking badge with a pictorial design on it, are not ritual objects; an armband marking out an official at a public meeting is not a ritual decoration; and the statement "I am the assistant secretary" is not a ritual utterance—but all are non-natural expressions of a social order' (Skorupski 1976: 163). Thus, if the claim that ritual action is 'expressive' is taken as proposing a criterion by which the observer can pick out a class of events or social institutions which are rituals, it fails like all other such attempts.

15. Tambiah (1985) has persuasively argued that the felt power and efficacy of magical spells and other ritual formulas can be attributed to the formalization of language which is often found in ritual, and indeed that ritual language often uses tropes and devices which are familiar also in poetry. Thus (1985: 138, 154–6, 385), he argues against Bloch's (1989) equation of formality with loss of semantic content. But the very fact that to make his point Tambiah stresses similarities with non-ritual language illustrates that he is not pointing to anything which is unique or distinctive about communication in ritual.

16. Bateson's discussion (1972: 177–93) is principally about play, but couched in general terms which he claims apply to ritual. Observing animals at play (that is, engaging in interactive sequences in which the unit actions are similar to, but not the same as, those of combat), Bateson distinguishes three types of message: (1) automatic physiological signs of the animal's mood, (2) voluntary signals which simulate mood-signs, and which can be trusted, distrusted,

falsified, denied, corrected, and so forth; and (3) messages which enable the receiver to discriminate between mood-signs and those other signs which resemble them. These last he calls 'framing gestures' (1972: 189). This is analogous to what Bateson, following Korzybski, calls the 'map–territory relation': the fact that a message, of whatever kind, does not consist of those objects which it denotes ('the word "cat" cannot scratch us'). Rather, language bears to the objects which it denotes a relationship comparable to that which a map bears to a territory. Play, histrionic behaviour, deceit, and ritual are all, in Bateson's view, examples of primitive map–territory differentiation, and hence steps in the evolution of communication.

17. Clearly, boundaries and frames cannot be equated simply with actual sacred spaces, such as the temple precinct, since non-ritualized actions also go on there (e.g. the *pujari* grinds his sandalwood paste in the temple).

18. By making such a sign, the actor intends to represent this idea, and whether this is communicated to anyone else is a secondary matter. One would still take off one's shoes even if no one else were present in the temple, or in the house.

19. Analogy with the Jain use of this word would suggest that the gloss should be the other way around, that is, that *bhav* is the emotional-cum-mental state that accompanies a gesture.

20. Marglin's idea of 'refinement' appears to follow an indigenous model, whereby the *devadasi*'s training, social position, and immediate preparations before the dance 'refine' her into the mobile goddess; transforming her, but 'without discontinuity between nature and supernature'. Even if this analogy is made by her informants, it does not follow that communication works like this, by 'refining' the 'raw material of spontaneously occurring expressive gestures' (we argue in Ch. 10 that even expressive gestures are mediated by culture). Marglin is more to the point when she emphasizes the intentional aspect of communication, 'The dance is rooted in a conception of a self engaged in a communicative act with both emotional and cognitive content' (1990: 221).

21. That ritual is a very opaque medium and a poor means of communication is an obvious point, which any anthropologist who has tried to 'read' one must surely know.

22. Wittgenstein (1968), of course, has pointed out the idea of communicating with oneself does not solve any of the problems of language. A private language is an impossibility because language must be sustained as such in a community's use for it to be meaningful. It is not really possible to have a private rule. This is because you cannot give yourself a means for telling the difference between actually following a rule and just thinking that you are. See also Kripke (1982).

23. This is a type of communication which, following Peirce, both Rapapport (1979: 180–1) and Tambiah (1981) call 'indexical'.

24. Rappaport makes a similar point when he writes, 'It would be well to make clear that I am raising no objections whatsoever to symbolic analyses of rituals as a class or to functional and adaptive analyses of ritual as a class. Both may surely increase our knowledge of the world. I am only asserting that to view ritual as simply a way to fulfill certain functions that may well or better be fulfilled by other means, or as an alternative symbolic medium for expressing what may just as well—or perhaps better—be expressed in other ways is, obviously, to ignore that which is distinctive of ritual itself' (1979: 174).

25. See for instance Fernandez (1965) and Keesing (1982). Watson (1988) argues that an emphasis in Chinese funeral rituals has generally been on performance rather than belief, that people often have no idea of what 'meanings' there might be in the rituals they perform. The claim is routinely made too that 'orthopraxy' rather than 'orthodoxy' characterizes popular Hinduism and Buddhism, but misled, perhaps, by the anthropological orthodoxy that ritual is generally about meaning, Watson suggests that his data on Chinese funeral rites demonstrate that cultural standardization in China shows a *unique* genius.

4

The Ritual Commitment

IN this chapter we begin to answer the question, 'What is the difference between acting in a ritualized and in an unritualized way?'. In attempting to describe what is distinctive about ritual action, we start with the subtle and yet pivotal transformation which ritualization effects in the relation between intention and action. The present chapter focuses on the theoretical delineation of this shift and some of its implications. This involves us in contrasting ritual with other kinds of action, such as games. In Chapter 5, 'Getting It Right', we try to understand, using the example of the *puja*, the actor's idea that there are specific acts to perform and rules to be followed. The chapter shows ethnographically how ritualization, by presenting action to experience as already-constituted and hence apprehensible elements, allows a wide variety of actual conduct to be counted unambiguously as successful performance, and that this is independent of the attribution of particular propositional meanings to the acts. A study of ritualization as a mode of action is, as far as we know, relatively new in anthropology and, rather than pretending to completeness, we acknowledge that at this stage what we have to say must be programmatic. It is in this spirit that we hope readers will approach Chapter 6, which follows up what we take to be the theoretical import of the idea of the 'ritual commitment' as it affects the relation between action and cognition. Further implications of our theory unfold through the subsequent chapters, in particular those which concern the ritual actor in religious liturgical contexts.

There follows now a condensed summary, which will be unpacked and explained in this and later chapters, of what we take to be the distinctive character of ritual action. Action may be said to be ritualized when the actor has taken up what we shall call the 'ritual commitment', a particular stance with respect to his or her own action. This has, so far as we can see, four main aspects. These are logically interdependent, and are actually just different ways of 'getting at' the same transformation. None the less, for the purposes of exposition we shall deal with them in turn, using the words 'non-intentional', 'stipulated', 'elemental' or 'archetypal', and 'apprehensible'; these words being not definitions, nor in any sense technical terms, but *aides-memoires*. (1) Ritualized action is non-intentional, in the sense that while people performing ritual acts do have intentions (thus the actions are not unintentional), the *identity* of a ritualized act does not depend, as is the case with normal action, on the agent's intention in acting. (2) Ritualized action is stipulated, in the sense that the constitution of separate acts out of the continuous flow of a person's action is not accomplished, as is the case with normal action, by processes of intentional understanding, but rather by constitutive rules which establish an ontology of ritual acts.

However, ritualization, because it is a quality of action and therefore a subjective as well as an objective phenomenon, requires more than the co-occurrence of these two features. It requires further that the action in question be enacted with an intention that means it will be in the above sense non-intentional. This may seem paradoxical, but it is of the first importance. Acting ritually is not a mistake or a consequence of inattention. The person performing ritual 'aims' at the realization of a pre-existing ritual act. Celebrants' acts appear, even to themselves, as 'external', as not of their own making. (3) Such acts are perceived as discrete, named entities, with their own characters and histories, and it is for this reason that we call such acts elemental and archetypal. (4) Because ritualized acts are felt, by those who perform them, to be external, they are also 'apprehensible'. That is, they are always available for a further reassimilation to the actors' intentions, attitudes, and beliefs. This can be done in a number of ways, described in turn in Chapters 8, 9, and 10: by constituting one's own act as a particular kind of representation, by consciously intending to mean some proposition by the act, or by a spontaneous 'thoughtless' identification with the act itself as a physical activity.

We believe ritualization to be a qualitative departure from the normal intentional character of human action. It is a distinctive way of 'going on'. Ritualization is not the only such departure, and later we shall give a brief discussion of some others, such as theatrical performance and acting under orders, in order to distinguish them from the case we have here. The analysis we give of ritualization derives from our attempt to understand the particular case of the Jain *puja*, and although we make some comparisons in passing with other religious traditions, we accept that a more detailed consideration of a wider range of cases might suggest some changes in our formulation. The institutional, and in particular the religious responses to ritualization vary across different cultural contexts and this in turn affects the character of ritualized action. Nevertheless, as we said in Chapter 1, we think that there is a sense in which different cultures are responding to the same phenomenon, and it is this, in the first instance, that we hope to describe.

Our first claim, that ritualization transforms the relation between intention and the meaning of action, can be explained by discussing the ways in which action in general can be said to be meaningful. We show how one of the ways in which action is normally meaningful does not obtain in the case of ritual. In anthropology, and in the human sciences more generally, we all tend to speak rather loosely about the 'meaningfulness' of social action, and while for most purposes this is fine, if we are to be clear about the peculiarity of ritualized action we need to distinguish different meanings of 'meaning'. In particular we must be careful when using linguistic terms to talk about non-linguistic phenomena. Just how, and under what conditions, do actions have meaning? In which ways is ritualized action different?

Non-linguistic action is limited in the ways it can mean. The sense, reference, and syntax of words and sentences in an utterance give its 'lexical' meaning (alternatively called its 'propositional' or 'locutionary' meaning).[1] In general actions do not have a lexical meaning (the sort of meaning found for words in dictionaries), and action in general has hardly any of the properties of syntax. There is a limited class of actions, basically signals, which have been given a meaning: a straightforward equivalent in language. Examples include the signals by which aircraft are guided around the tarmac, the 'thumbs-down', or punching the air in triumph. This translation into language may be a lexical meaning, like the dictionary definition of a word, or a locutionary meaning, like that of a sentence. Like their linguistic equivalents, these meanings can be, so to speak, 'carried around' by the action, with modification, from context to context. Like words, signals thus standardly 'express' in publicly agreed, conventional ways. Most of our action, however, does not express meanings of this kind. Furthermore, although signals can be arranged one after another to give a sequence of information or a series of instructions or requests, those with lexical meaning cannot be combined by the more complicated and creative operations of linguistic syntax. For actions to be used, as language is, primarily to signify and to communicate, requires in addition very constraining conventions and specialized contexts (like the *devadasi* dances mentioned in the previous chapter). Thus 'systems' of signifying actions are, in comparison to natural language, exceedingly simple, rare, and specialized.

The range and sophistication of locutionary meaning which signals can have is thus very limited, and most actions are not in any case signals and can thus have no locutionary meaning at all. But can they have other kinds of 'meaning'? Max Weber, of course, asserted that we may speak of action as distinct from mere movement 'in so far as the acting individual attaches subjective meaning to his behavior' (Weber 1978: 4), and while neither this way of putting the point nor the methodological implications which Weber drew from it have met with universal agreement in the human sciences (but then, what has?), pretty well everyone has been content to admit that some kind of meaning is definitional of action. We hope that what we have just said is enough to establish that whatever it means to say that everday social action is 'meaningful', it is not that it has locutionary meaning as does language, or that it expresses propositions. Thus although, as we have already seen for the case of the Jain *puja*, ritualized acts are frequently given lexical and propositional meanings this cannot tell us whether, or in what ways, ritual action is intrinsically meaningful. To add to the points about signals which we have just made, we can recall that many ritual acts are given no propositional meanings at all. In addition, those which are, as we saw in the case of the flower *puja* whose meanings are listed in Chapter 2, are often given not one but a variety of such meanings. It cannot be the case that such meanings are provided by the acts themselves. Our main objective in the first half of this chapter is to establish that there is an important sense in which the action in general has meaning, but ritualized action does not. This kind of meaning, which provides the identity for acts, we shall refer to as 'intentional meaning'. To explain what we mean by intentional meaning, we shall first describe it for linguistic acts, before going on to discuss non-linguistic action.

In order correctly to understand a linguistic utterance we must always understand something more than locutionary meaning; we need also to grasp its 'illocutionary force', or as Quentin Skinner says, its 'point'. We need to understand the kind of utterance it is. This is because to use language in speaking, writing, or whatever, is always to perform some kind of action. A young man is ice-skating and a policeman says to him, 'The ice is thin over there.'[2] We can see at once that it is possible for the skater to understand the locutionary meaning of this sentence, and yet, if he does not also grasp the illocutionary force of the utterance, he may misunderstand what the policeman intends to communicate. To understand the policeman, the skater must grasp that what the policeman is doing, in saying what he says, is warning him. He must, as one might say, 'take' what the policeman says as a warning. It is in grasping the illocutionary force or point of the utterance that the skater understands its meaning as an action, and it is this 'meaning as an action' that we call its intentional meaning.

The meaning of the policeman's utterance, as an action, although conveyed by means of a specific proposition about the thickness of ice, is not the same thing as the locutionary meaning of that proposition, and it might have been conveyed by a number of utterances with different locutionary meanings. Thus if we had to paraphrase the intentional meaning of this action, already an artificial exercise precisely because this meaning is not linguistic,[3] we could say for example, 'I wouldn't go over there, it's dangerous,' or 'Be careful if you go over there,' or 'If you go over there, you're likely to fall through the ice.' The policeman might have issued his warning by crying out, and thus by an utterance which had no locutionary meaning at all. In that case, as with a cry of pain or of surprise, or saying 'oops!', it is possible to make an utterance which is a communicative act by saying something which is, in linguistic terms, meaningless.[4] Communication here is possible when the addressee recognizes the illocutionary act being performed, when he or she understands the 'point' of the action.[5]

We have talked so far, in a rather loose sort of way, both of 'action' and of 'acts'. However, the identification of separate actions, from within the continuous flow of our physical and interpersonal 'going on', is itself an element of the intentionality of action. Since it is the intentionality of action, we claim, which is modified under ritualization, we need now to be clearer about the relation between action and actions. How do people distinguish and identify the 'actions' that they and others perform in the continuous flow of activity? The answer to this, for normal action, is that we attribute intentions to the agent. Both in watching and understanding the action of others, and in reflexively monitoring and understanding what we ourselves do (a process which is a chronic and intrinsic part of acting itself), we identify 'chunks' of what is done as actions ('I had lunch,' 'He agreed with Peter,' 'She opened the door'), and we do so on different levels of inclusiveness ('He handed him the book,' or 'He lent him the book,' and 'Taking a drag on her cigarette, and balancing her coffee-cup on her lap, she lifted the receiver, waited for the dialling tone, and dialled Jane's number, listened . . .', or we might just say 'She rang Jane'). Thus the boundaries between acts are not 'given' in the physical form of what is done. To identify actions we must form an intentional understanding of them—we must grasp their 'point'. To do this—to distinguish, for example, between 'lending' and 'giving'—requires that we *see* both ourselves and others as intentional agents, for it is with reference to the beliefs, desires, and intentions which we attribute to other actors that we grasp the intentional meaning of their action, and so identify their acts, and it is with reference to our own reflexively understood intentions-in-acting that we create and understand the acts we ourselves perform. If we do not attribute intentionality in this way—if we do not see a person's conduct as the intentional doings of an agent but merely as physical movement— then we have no grounds for distinguishing actions: no more grounds than a person who hears speech in an unknown language has for distinguishing words. It is because our doings are *seen as* intentional, that we may speak of discrete 'actions' (Giddens 1976: ch. 2; 1979: ch. 2).

Let us take a non-linguistic example: a boy puts a newspaper on your doorstep. In doing this, he is not sending you a message, his action does not express a proposition, but it does have what we have called intentional meaning. When you grasp that what he is doing is 'delivering', and not 'losing', 'donating', or 'leaving by mistake', you understand the intentional meaning of his action. We have called this kind of meaning of action its 'intentional meaning' because in the normal course of things, as in the case of newspaper delivery, when we form an understanding of the meaning of an action, the fact which makes that understanding true or false is a fact about the 'intention' of the agent.

So to understand the behaviour of our fellows we need to grasp the intentional content of action, and to do this we have to rely on the implicit ascription to them of beliefs, desires, and prior intentions (or purposes). These prior intentions or motives must be clearly distinguished from 'intentional meaning'. An intention *to* do something is not the same as an intention *in* doing it. Intentional meaning is not what someone intended to do before doing it, but what they understood themselves to be doing as they did it, their reflexive understanding of their conduct which is constitutive of the action as action. Following Skinner (1988: 60), let us give an example of this distinction. Farmer Ivanov is sitting over his breakfast planning his day. He has the prior intention of fulfilling his production target by ploughing four hectares of land. On the other hand, as he presses on the handle of the plough and whips his unwilling horse, he is enacting his intention-in-action ('ploughing').

This understanding of one's own action is not a separate reflection or observation, but springs directly from the intentionality of all purposive human action, from our being the agent and not just the medium of our action. Think of three people each moving their right arm about in what looks like a similar fashion. We might be inclined at first to say they are all doing the same thing. However, precisely because we (correctly) see all three as intentional agents, if we are then told (by them, say) that one was waving to his friend, one attempting to relieve cramp, and the other just moving her arm around so she could be part of this thought-experiment, we will be forced to change our initial view, and recognize that they were performing different actions. This is why we say that the intentional meaning is *in* the action, it is the intentional content of what we do and is *constitutive* of the acts we may be said to perform. Maurice Merleau-Ponty also characterizes normal human action as intrinsically intentional and the acting body as incarnate intentionality. It is a characteristic of action that every movement is, indissolubly, movement and consciousness of movement.

When I motion my friend to come nearer, my intention is not a thought prepared within me, and I do not perceive the signal in my body. I beckon across the world, I beckon over there, where my friend is; the distance between us, his consent or refusal are immediately read in my gesture; there is not perception followed by a movement, for both form a system which varies as a whole. (Merleau-Ponty 1962: 110–11)

It is the intention which *makes* this action a beckoning. There are not two things, an action and an intention, to be understood. A person may intend to beckon, or may only mean to move his arm, which Merleau-Ponty describes as an 'abstract' action.[6] The absence of the intention of beckoning, in performing this physical movement, results in a qualitatively different act. It follows therefore that when we attempt to understand what another's action is, to succeed in this we must grasp his or her intention in acting. *It is one of our central claims in this book that when an action is ritualized, this is not the case.*

   Now let us explain just what we mean by this radical claim. Under ritualization the relation which normally exists between intention and act is transformed. We should make clear, however, that this transformation is itself the result of a deliberate act: the adoption of a ritual stance. It may seem to be a paradox, but it is a result of the actor having adopted this stance that ritual acts are non-intentional. Intentions no longer play the immediate role which they normally do in determining the identity of the acts performed. We can illustrate just what we mean here by contrasting ritualized action with the following observation, which Stuart Hampshire makes, about the intentionality of normal human action:

While we are fully conscious, and in possession of all our faculties, this steady buzz of intentional activity continues, and we are to this extent necessarily and at all times in a position to answer the question 'What are you doing here?' or 'What are you doing now?', even though we had not previously formulated what we were doing in words. More often than not we have not previously expressed to our-selves our intention, or formulated it in words. But it is the *possibility* of our declaring, or expressing, our intentions from moment to moment, and if the question is asked, which gives sense to the notion of intention itself. (Hampshire 1959: 97)

When performing ritualized action one can still answer these questions, and as with everyday intentional action there is on any given occasion a determinate answer to them. But the way to give this answer will be to say, for instance, 'I am performing water *puja*', whatever you happen to be thinking, because for one and the same ritual act, as we shall show in detail in the chapters below, the actor's intentions can be very various indeed.

The same is true of different celebrants performing the same act. Consider the following example. A Jain woman performing *puja* stands before a Jina idol and takes a small oil lamp in her right hand. She lifts it up and holds it out towards the statue. What are her intentions as she does this? Is she shedding light on the idol? Is she offering the lamp to the idol? Is she shedding the light on herself? Is she representing the 'light' of doctrine by the light of the lamp? Any of these might be the case. We have met people who say they think of this action in each of these ways. In addition, it is quite possible to perform the act correctly without having any such intention, and we have met others who say no more than that they are doing *puja* with a lamp. Yet in each case they would all agree that they are performing the same act. Unlike in the case of newspaper delivery or the arm-raising experiment, their various thoughts about what they are doing, their various intentions in acting this way, make no difference to the correct description of what they do, to the kind of action they may be said to have performed. They are all performing *dip puja* (lamp *puja*) and whatever this woman's intention in doing it happens to be, her lifting this lamp remains unambiguously and determinately a token of this and only this stipulated type.

This is, to repeat, quite unlike unritualized action, in which to identify someone's action one must have a correct understanding of their intention in acting. In everyday life, if you see two people doing the same thing, but with different intentions in acting (say, 'driving away in a car' and 'stealing a car'), you will count these as different actions. The crucial point is that if two people do *dip puja*, the action, because ritualized, must be this alone. Let us be quite clear: the woman has the intention to perform the ritual. She may well also have an intention of, say, 'worshipping God', or 'shedding light on myself', but it is not in virtue of her having this kind of intention in performing *dip puja* that she counts as having performed this act. Her intention in acting is no longer constitutive of her action, and is no longer the key to its identity. This is what we meant when we said at the beginning of this chapter that ritualized acts are non-intentional.

The point is that the woman performing *dip puja* is not in a better position to answer Stuart Hampshire's questions ('What are you doing here?' and 'What are you doing now?') of herself, than she is of other participants in the ritual. The answer is, whatever her intention, 'I am doing *dip puja*.' The way for a ritual practitioner to answer these questions will always be to pick from a stipulated list of the ritual acts which he or she has learned: *jal puja, candan puja, dip puja*, and so on. Similarly, she has no privilege over an observer with regard to the correct designation of her own acts.[7] The agent, like an observer, recognizes ritualized acts as tokens of their type through experience of the act as a 'thing', through the sensations and feelings to which the encounter with it gives rise. How can it be that agents performing ritualized acts find themselves thus observing their actions from outside?

It is a commonplace of academic comment about ritual that it is 'prescribed'. By this it is usually meant that some series of instructions exists about how to perform the ritual. It is true that there are usually such rules in ritual, but we do not think they are in any interesting sense distinctive of ritual. They also exist in non-ritual contexts such as the law, the army, schools, cooking, and games. There is another quite different sense in which ritual action is 'prescribed', and which, unlike the idea of compulsory instructions, is a significant part of what is distinctive about ritual action. The important sense in which ritual is 'prescribed', the second of our four aspects of the ritual commitment, is not that there are rules restricting what people do, but that what their action *can be* is 'prescribed'. The kinds of acts they can be counted as being are prescribed, we shall say, by *ontological* stipulation. The reason this is so important is not just that this stipulation happens, for as we shall discuss in the next chapter something similar happens in games, but that it provides the identity for ritual acts, which intention fails to do. The ritual practitioner finds his or her acts already separated out, constituted, and named, for they are stipulated in the rules for performing the ritual. Thus the ontology of ritualized action (the range of essential entities of which it is composed) is ready-made and precedes the conduct of those who come to perform the ritual.[8]

Ritual action is therefore institutionalized action and is carried out in various ways in different societies and cultures. However, we do not think that this is all there is to it. Let us compare ritual acts with promising or thanking. As Sperber and Wilson (1986: 245) have pointed out, promising and thanking can occur only in societies with the requisite institutions: a promise is a particular, culturally defined form of commitment. 'Many societies have other forms of commitment, more akin to swearing, for instance, and other forms of expressing gratitude, more akin to blessing, for instance. . . . We have no doubt that a cross-cultural study of such speech acts would confirm their cultural specificity and institutional nature' (1986: 264). Ritualized action is different from this. It is socially and culturally institutionalized, but unlike promising and thanking, this cannot be all there is to it, since, although theoretically conceivable, societies entirely without ritualization are not in fact to be found. On the other hand, ritualized action is not like other apparently universal acts such as saying, asking, and telling, because the latter do not depend on social institutions. In its cross-cutting of these categories ritualized action seems to be *sui generis* (we return to this crucial point in subsequent chapters).

To return to the argument about ontology: what does this imply in relation to the *puja*? The *puja*, as we have said, is constituted by a series of named elements: *jal puja, candan puja, pushpa puja*, and so on. Exactly how people comport themselves in the performance of these acts is, as we have said, variable. The extent of this variability is perhaps quite unusual in religious ritual and many well-documented rituals are certainly more closely and firmly prescribed than is the *puja*. But even in this case, everything that people do in the course of a performance counts as instances of just those acts and nothing else, and this only serves to illustrate all the more strikingly the effect of ritualization. All that the performer of *puja* does, once he or she has embarked on a ritualized sequence, is identified with reference to a stipulated ontology which specifies the constituent units of the whole: a finite series of discrete, named, ritual acts.

We began this chapter by asking, 'What is the difference between acting in a ritualized and in an unritualized way?'. We are now in a position to offer an initial definition. Action is ritualized if the acts of which it is composed are constituted not by the intentions which the actor has in performing them, but by prior stipulation. We thus have a class of acts in which the intentions which normally serve to identify acts, that is to say, intentions in action, are discounted. By 'ritual commitment' we do not mean that the actor holds any particular beliefs, such as that the ritual is sacred or really will cure an illness, only that he or she is now committed to a particular attitude or stance, and that this is different from stances taken towards everyday actions (to which the actor is also committed when enacting them). A set of constitutive rules is accepted as determining the kinds of acts which he or she will perform. In adopting the ritual stance one accepts, that is, that in a very important sense, one will not be the author of one's acts.

There are cases in which something like this happens in language. Gareth Evans (1977: 200–1) pointed to the gap which can arise between what a speaker means to say by a certain utterance and what he in fact says when he utters it. Let us consider again our policeman. In addition to warning the skater, which was something he did intentionally, he has also, as it happens, informed him about the thickness of the ice. The skater now knows something he did not know before. The policeman will have informed him, but not in virtue of his intention, which was not to give this information, but to warn. Therefore conveying information about ice was not an action of his, just something that happened. So language displays a characteristic which is like that we are pointing to in ritual. If we use language, our words can have a meaning which is to some degree independent of our intention in using them—they can, so to speak, escape our intentions—so we can find we have performed a particular kind of linguistic act, but not intentionally.

Just how far does this similarity go? It seems to us there is a difference between these two cases which is of absolutely decisive importance. In all the linguistic examples we have seen, the gap between what the speaker means to say and what he or she does in fact say is the result of a mistake. Even if such gaps turn out to be humorous or are subsequently discovered to be otherwise delightful, they are none the less accidental.[9] In speaking you must accept, in one sense, that the words you utter will mean in a way that may escape your own intention, but it remains the case that you have a meaning in mind which you wish your words to reflect. It is with reference to this meaning that you choose the words you do. What you aim at, in using language, is that your words will indeed match your intended meaning. Gaps may open up, but the way we respond to them makes clear that this is not what we use language for. If I make a mistake, if I say 'uninterested' when I meant 'disinterested', I can with perfect cogency correct myself, saying 'that is not what I meant'. In ritual, on the other hand, you do not choose your acts in order to enact your intention, so that so long as you follow the rules, there is never any call to correct what you have done because it was not what you meant. Furthermore, in ritual it is not an accident or a mistake when the meaning of a ritual act diverges from the intention of the agent. It is the point of it that it should. When acting ritually, it is because your act is other than an ordinary intentional act that you perform it.

So the idea that in ritual you are not the author of your acts is inadequate. While it is true in the sense that your acts are not intentional, they do not just happen to you either. There are two elements to this. The first point is the obvious one that it is you as yourself who actually performs these acts. This is in fact of great importance and we shall return to it later. The other point is that it is also you, in intending to perform your act as a ritual, who constitutes your action as ritualized and thus *make it the case* that you are no longer, for a while, author of your acts. You set at one remove, or defer, rather than give up, what one might call the 'intentional sovereignty' of the agent. For both these reasons, the fact that ritual acts deflect intentionality does not make them non-actions such as absent-mindedly scratching your chin, or unintentional actions like clumsily knocking something over.[10] In ritual you both are and are not the author of your acts.

Let us expand briefly on this last point. A tourist wanders into a Jain temple. It is late in the morning and people have already been performing *puja*. The tourist sees a Jina idol, adorned with a silver crown, speckled with dots of sandalwood paste, and decked in fresh flowers. However, he notices that these flowers are not symmetrically arranged, so he takes a flower from a tray nearby and places it on the idol's left shoulder to balance one which is already on its right. To an observer he appears to have performed *pushpa puja*, but he has not. Why not? The obvious answer might seem to be that he did not have that particular intention. But let us think again about the lady who was performing lamp *puja*. She counts as having performed that act, even if she did not, as she lifted the lamp, have that intention. She might not know that '*dip puja*' is what it is called, she might mistakenly think of it as part of the same act as incense *puja*, she might perform it with some different, perhaps more elaborate intention, such as 'getting rid of my sins'. The overarching 'intention' she does have, and which distinguishes her from the tourist, is the ritual commitment. Her particular intentions no longer fix the act she is performing, as do the tourist's, and this is because she has already made an 'intentional' decision which makes this so. We are not trying to say that she need have some quixotically unrelated intention, only that she might have. It is this gap—a potential freedom from the everyday and inexorable suffusion of action with personal intentions—that provides a space which may suggest a reason why people perform ritual.

So the identity of ritual acts is not established by intentions, even though the action is performed intentionally. Our anthropological readers may feel that this is a niggling point, but we hope that as the book proceeds they will see that it has radical implications for the way we can write about ritual. For philosophers, 'Action' and 'Intention' stalk a well-trodden terrain, and here we have the rather more modest hope that we have pointed to a genuinely new case. Searle (1983: 101–2), for example, points to the fact that the same event can be both an intentional and an unintentional act. Oedipus married Jocasta intentionally, but when he did so, and by doing so, he married his mother. This, argues Searle, was Oedipus's action, but it was an unintentional action.[11] But his case, like every single one we have found in the philosophical literature, turns on mischance or a side effect. Ritual, whatever else it is, is not a mistake.

Nor is the point we are making restricted to religious ritual, in which the intentions are 'other-worldly' or perhaps inexpressible in an ordinary way. It is just as true of non-religious ritualization. If it is intended to name a ship, who could predict from everyday conventions that breaking a bottle over her bows would be the ritualized way to do it? Nor does the accomplishment of naming depend on any thoughts about ships and bottles which any of the participants might have. Nothing we might learn about the thoughts of the dignitary who broke the bottle will alter the fact that 'naming the ship' is what he or she *did*.[12]

Ritualization depends on a change of commitment. Laying fruit on a table, washing an object, giving something a name, and holding up a lamp, can all be done in non-ritual ways. These are all things which people do in the everyday world, and the source of their transformation is the actor's adoption of the ritual stance. What happens is that objects and acts within the ritual arena undergo a mental reclassification. Thus the observer in a Jain temple knows, if he or she sees a banana lying on the floor in front of an idol, that it is not just a banana: it is not just for eating nor was it left there by accident. Now the observer might make some interpretations about the purpose of this fruit, seeing it there, but as Gilbert Lewis (1986) has pointed out, seeing is not necessarily a good guide. We cannot share Frazer's confidence that he could detect the thought processes of magicians from an observer's report of the magical act itself. Talking to the actor does not necessarily help: quite often he or she will say simply that this is the way things are done and may have no beliefs or theories about why. But this very perception of the ritualized act as having its own facticity and independent existence, the 'elemental' or 'archetypal' quality which is our third characteristic of ritual action, seems to demand some kind of response. The conclusion seems inescapable that it is this which accounts for much of the felt 'power' of ritual, the sense that in doing it one is doing more than one seems. The actor feels there to be some reason for the act, that the ritual has its own point, or, to speak metaphorically, that the act has its own ritual 'intention'. The fact remains, however, that it is impossible to infer what that intention might be, if only because acts do not have intentions.[13] We shall see below that ritualized actions can be and are given meanings and intentions. Because ritualized acts present themselves as it were 'objectively' to experience, they may be felt to have their own character, to be there for some purpose, to 'be meaningful'. The actor might apprehend such 'objects' in a number of ways. To express this idea, the fourth dimension of the ritual commitment, we shall say that ritualized acts are 'apprehensible', waiting to be apprehended and, possibly, given meaning.

We now make some brief points, to be developed in later chapters, about the nature of these apprehensible acts.

One effect of the stipulative rules of ritualization is to divide up action into elements which can thereby appear 'distorted' or 'displaced' (a fact which aroused the interest of Freud, and to which we shall return below). Frits Staal illustrates this feature of ritualization when he shows that Vedic *mantra*s (spoken or sung religious formulas) are not just verses from the Vedic texts, but are bits and pieces from the Vedas, used ritually.

This ritual use of *mantra*s is very different from something else that is apparently similar, i.e. the ordinary use of a natural language such as Sanskrit or English. . . . Even if *mantras* derive from straightforward and intelligible sentences, their ritual uses are often unintelligible and 'crooked' (*vakra*). A verse is taken, but before it is half over, the reciter inserts a long 'o' and breathes; he then continues, but does not stop at the end of the line, linking it instead with the following and inserting other vowels and nazalisations. In addition, he recites the first and last verse of each sequence three times. . . . Such structural transformations result in expressions that have nothing to do with linguistic communication or the expression of thought. They are ritual. (Staal 1984)

Staal says that the ritual function of these *mantra*s does not lie in their language or even their metrical structure, but in their sounds, with their themes and variations, repetitions, inversions, and so on, all of these transformations being executed in accordance with fixed rules. His interpretation is that this essential musicality shows *mantra*s to be a form of ritual expression which preceded language. We do not need to agree with this last point to see that the structural facts he points to can only occur in acts and linguistic expressions which are already (1) removed from everyday intentionality and (2) separated into discrete units.[14] We will show later that the Jain *puja* consists of just such sequences, repetitions, interpolations, and variations, and we follow Lévi-Strauss (1981: 673), among others, in suggesting that this process is a feature of ritualization in general. We should stress, however, that this segmented and formal organization does not imply that there are underlying *principles* of design, or, as in language, a syntax. Its being structured does not make it decodable.

We have said that the component acts of *puja* are named, and this certainly emphasizes the parcelling out of ritual into discrete acts. A good number of the acts in *puja* are named after the substances of which they are acts of offering: rice, flowers, fruits, and so on. These substances are often given names in *puja* which differ from the words by which they are known in normal life. But knowing such special or sophisticated names is in no degree necessary, as knowing *some* name is, to one's ability to perform the ritual. The requirement is to refer to the act, not to attribute anything to it. One need have no knowledge or information about the act except that it *is*. We discuss this matter in greater detail in the next two chapters. Here we wish to say only that becoming conscious of ritualized acts as bounded 'entities' seems to us to be an implication of the ritual stance. Such consciousness is necessary in order to be able to accomplish and complete a stipulated action, and this is the case even if the actor classifies an act incorrectly (by giving it the 'wrong' name, for example).

For the actor, the ritualized act is seen as ready for him or her to do. He or she 'enacts' it, that is, does not simply do something as in everyday life ('eat a meal', 'deliver a newspaper'), but as it were mimics an idea of what should be done. Now this 'mimicry' can take many forms; in other words, the relation between the act as actually performed and the stipulated act is variable. It depends in part on the culture, in particular the religious culture, and in part on individual abilities and proclivities. One has only to think of the possibilities of the copy, the parody, the translation, the indexical sign, the theatrical presentation, the token, the act of public witness, or the memorial, to see the possible variation. As we discuss further over the next two chapters, people learning ritual acts start by copying, reproducing acts taught to them, but later what they do could better be described as the 'making manifest' of what has already become an idea (a prototype), which allows a greater freedom.

Here we should distinguish, as Hampshire (1959: 274–96) advises, the standpoint of observation from the standpoint of the reflective subject.[15]

From an observer's point of view, looking at the ritual action of someone else, it is difficult to distinguish these modes: that an act is a token of the prescribed action is all that can be known for sure. For the agent, on the other hand, although the identity of the ritual act is, as we have pointed out, pre-set, and stipulated, the mode of achieving such an act in practice is for this very reason the object of reflection. It is this reflective activity, which the agent is conscious of being able to change at will, which constitutes the difference between the ritual act as copy, parody, or memorial. The possibility of reflection is not a monopoly of ritual action, of course, but we would argue that in everyday life, in the flurry of purposive activity, it is often in abeyance, whereas the ritual commitment, which requires that acts be seen as 'given', and which eliminates unreflective intention, may well provoke it. In everyday life, Hampshire argues (1982: 281–3), as soon as one turns away from knowledge of causal connection (i.e. the observer's standpoint) to give attention to one's own desires and beliefs, one becomes aware that they are open to criticism and revision, in other words, one becomes aware of decision and intention, of 'the initiative that comes from the possession of language and therefore of the power of reflection', as well as a sense of freedom. In ritual the transition effected by reflection is different: it is to become aware of the relation between one's own act and the stipulated archetype, that is, of oneself as enacting the given act and thereby giving meaning to it as a mode of action.[16] This is one feature of ritualization which can provide for an inner debate, or a feeling of freedom, in the very context of prescriptive rules. This sense of liberty derives from a very actual freedom, which is to make sense of one's own acts to oneself. It includes in fact the possibility of non-reflection, of not having any religious thoughts or beliefs at all, and this results in the ritual act as a mere copy. This is what seems to have caused most anxiety for religious leaders.[17] It is what the Jain renouncer, in the text we cited in Chapter 2, was criticizing, when he described the Vedic ritual as a 'false sacrifice', because he knew all too well that it need not be accompanied by renunciatory attitudes or the will to relinquish what one has.

No doubt our readers may be thinking by now: but this is intention, creeping in again by the back door. They would be right. People often intend to perform ritual acts in a certain way (as a memorial, as a token, etc.), and we have not tried to deny that intentions are present in ritual action at specific junctures. But we would also point out that the question we have been discussing, the modes of ritual enactment, is still the back door. The central point remains: the identity of the ritual act, whatever people's intentions, is provided by stipulation, a prescriptive ontology.

Ritualization effects a change in the relation between action and time. The cutting up of continuous action into discrete, named acts is the prerequisite for the organization of sequences and structures. There is a clear and unambiguous sense, unusual in other contexts, in which each ritual act can be *completed*. Such a completion, though it may be done in some relatively fluid rituals such as the *puja* by individuals in their own time, is not just a matter of arbitrary decision. Each one is a pledge of order, referring to other completed and yet-to-be-initiated acts. Since ritualization has the effect of turning action into mimesis it has no 'natural' (everyday in that culture) relation to time or number. It can be multiplied, reversed, hierarchized, or dragged out for days on end, because, as we discuss further in Chapter 6, nothing need follow from whether such operations are performed or not (it is not that ritual acts cannot have practical effects, but that whether they do or not is a matter of what is being done in a ritualized way). Because the identity of ritual acts depends on a priori prescription, and not on intentional understanding, the elements can be arranged in purely formal structures which have no relation to the intentions and purposes for which the ritual as a whole is undertaken. Thus the number of times an act is performed within ritual sequences becomes a matter of invented order, rather than practical purposes.[18]

Chris Fuller, the noted anthropologist of Hinduism, has mentioned to us a common kind of devotionalist story whereby a ritual act is performed not just non-intentionally, but actually unintentionally: a bird is said to fly round a temple, circling it, and thus worships the deity without realizing it. The existence of this kind of story points to the distinction between our ideas about the transformation involved in adopting the ritual commitment and how things seem having adopted it. The story reflects the attitude, discussed further in Chapter 5, which sees the ritual act as being like a natural kind or thing, such that you might stumble across it by accident. But of course the story is not true. The bird was not performing a ritual. It was flying around. But a person, believing that rituals are such that a bird (or a Tibetan wind-flag) could have performed one, will perform his or her action with this attitude, in that peculiar way we call ritual. Our theory is designed to describe the real change in perspective and attitude which might make things seem this way. So the story misdescribes the situation in that it presents ritual, which, it is true, is qualitatively different from other action, as if this difference resulted from the way things are in the world, rather than being a product of human conduct and invention. Ritual can create a world which seems to *be* the world, and this is true with other types of overarching commitment that construct their own parameters of space or time. As Glenn Gould (1984: 5) wrote about music, 'The problem begins when one forgets the artificiality of it all . . . when we start to be so impressed by the strategies of our systematized thought that we forget that it does relate to an obverse, that it is hewn from . . . the void of negation which surrounds it.'

We therefore conclude this chapter by returning briefly to consider some points which arise from Bateson's discussion (1972) of framing. In the previous chapter we rejected the theory that boundary-marking actions can in themselves constitute ritualization, but Bateson does make several interesting observations. He observes that, 'Human beings operate more easily in a universe in which some of their psychological characteristics are externalised' (1972: 187), and with this we can happily agree. We have said that the adoption of the ritual stance is crucial to ritualization, and that this involves a process of mental reclassification. Boundary-marking acts, we suggest, are an institutionalized externalization of the psychological processes involved in this. Thus while they are not constitutive of ritualization itself, they do mark off a particular sequence of ritualized action as 'a ritual', and are thus part of the social processes whereby these institutionalized events are produced and reproduced.

Bateson's argument was developed to explain how animals know that certain actions are 'play', rather than fighting in earnest, and he referred to ritual only in passing, as another instance of a similar kind. This reminds us that ritualization is not the only modification of the intentional aspect of action. However, there are features unique to ritual, deriving both from society and from the situation of the self. One could summarize the difference between ritual and play by noting that in the latter the rules can be changed by institutional fiat, and while a church hierarchy might do the same, it cannot *see itself* as doing just this, but always has to argue for changes on the grounds that they are a return to an original, 'true', or scriptural form, or acting on divine authority, or otherwise recreating 'ordained action'. This 'archetypal' aspect of ritualization will be discussed further in Chapter 5.

Other instances of action in which the intentional content is different from the everyday include acting in a theatrical play or under military orders. An important difference between ritualization and these other cases is that in theatre and acting under orders the author (or giver of orders) is known, or at least it is understood that the responsibility for what is to be enacted does not rest with the actor. We shall return later to the contrasts between ritual and these other forms of action. Here we wish only to emphasize again that in ritual, despite the fact that the acts themselves are non-intentional, it is as himself or herself, rather than as Ophelia or as Private 22913527, that the celebrant enacts them. The ritual actor is not just carrying out someone else's designation. In plays or the army there is no requirement for the actor to take up an attitude towards the action. The performer in a play may like her character or not, believe in the play or despise it, and the same is true of military orders, but such attitudes are out of court. The same is not true about ritualized acts. This has two aspects: the actor in ritual is bound by what we have called the 'ritual commitment', that is, to seeing the acts as ritual in the ways we have described; and the actor also engages in ritual activity on his or her own account. This latter point is not affected by the question of whether or not his or her 'own account' is also some social role. People certainly act as representatives of groups and categories both in and outside ritual; but it remains the case with ritual, as it does not for acting both in a play and under orders, that the actor is also the acknowledged and responsible *agent*. We have seen this in the case of the Jain *puja*, where people choose which acts to perform and what meanings to give them. In Christian services we can see this when people who are taking part decide, for example, whether or not to say the words of some prayer with which they disagree. Even in great communal rituals, when social pressures may be such that it is impossible not to enact every element, the understanding in ritual is that one takes part as oneself. Now the ritualization of some social events, such as initiation or curing, may have the effect of modifying this 'self' in various ways (one may become 'an initiate', among others), but it does not displace the self. In other words, to return to our statement earlier, the special fascination of our subject is that in ritual one both is, and is not, the author of one's acts.

To recapitulate: action which is not ritualized has intentional meaning (warning, delivering, murder), and this is understandable by means of the ascription of intentional states to its agent. Ritualized action is not identified in this way, because we cannot link what the actor does with what his or her intentions might be. Instead of being guided and struc-tured by the intentions of actors, ritualized action is constituted and structured by prescription, not just in the sense that people follow rules, but in the much deeper sense that a reclassification takes place so that only following the rules counts as action. Nevertheless it is the actor as a conscious and thinking self who engages in this enactment. We move on now to try to show how this view of ritualization, as a transformation in the intentionality of action, explains some of the most puzzling and apparently paradoxical things about rituals.

Notes

1. To make our point here we use the vocabulary which has been developed by a number of writers, following Wittgenstein and Austin, to describe the features of language whereby, in making an utterance, a speaker is always also doing something. This vocabulary, as 'the theory of speech-acts', is now quite familiar in the human sciences, and we shall not embark on a thorough exposition here. The standard sources are Austin (1975) and Searle (1969, 1979). Note, however, that we do not endorse the way some anthropologists have applied this vocabulary, so to speak, *en bloc*, to the analysis of ritual.

2. We have borrowed here an example used by both P. F. Strawson (1971) and Quentin Skinner. We have drawn extensively in these pages on the works of Skinner (1970, 1971, 1988) and also on those of Anscombe (1963), Grice (1971), Papineau (1978: ch. 4), Blackburn (1984), Taylor (1985), McCulloch (1989), and Moya (1990).

3. It is important in general to guard against assuming that intentional states are like sentences somehow existing in our heads. It is part of understanding the meaning of this act to grasp the range of other actual sounds which could have enacted the same illocutionary act. Thus although the meaning of the action is not itself linguistic, we can try to express it in language by means of a number of possible sentences, but we should not therefore assume that the intended meaning, what was meant, is itself a sentence.

4. Ziff (1967) discusses this point. Austin gives examples of non-linguistic illocutionary acts, 'We can for example warn or order or appoint or give or protest or apologize by non-verbal means and these are illocutionary acts' (1975: 119).

5. This is something quite immediate: when you observe another person's action you do not normally first apprehend it as simple physical movement and then construe this movement as being a certain sort of action. In the same way, you do not first hear speech as sound, and then construe it as meaningful words and sentences.

6. 'If I then execute "the same" movement, but without having any present or even imaginary partner in mind, and treat it as "a set of movements in themselves"; if, that is, I perform a "flexion" of the forearm in relation to the upper arm . . . my body, which a moment ago was the vehicle of movement, now becomes its end' (Merleau-Ponty 1962: 111).

7. The thoughts of the actor no longer offer an explanation of the action, nor do they tell us what to call it. There is no need to infer what those thoughts may be in order to give a full and accurate description of what is done, and we will not be persuaded, by further information about what he or she is thinking, to

reclassify the act. Thus, there are no problems in the identification of ritualized action which parallel those involved in distinguishing between, say, 'chopping firewood', 'destroying Smith's chair', and 'making a lot of noise with an axe'.

8. The point is true, in relation to the *puja*, even of acts which have been introduced into it in recent times. For example, the decorating of the idol with silver foil, or the putting on of scent (*itr*), are both acknowledged by Jains to be recent additions to the *puja*. But both were taken on, as ritual acts, from the already-established popular regional religious repertoire of Hinduism.

9. The case is quite different when an author intentionally writes something which is ambiguous or has a double meaning. In such cases both meanings are intended.

10. The difference between action and non-action is discussed in the next chapter. We should note that we do not think, as Tambiah (1985: 134) suggests, that one can 'postulate a continuum of behavior, with intentional behavior at one pole and conventional behavior at the other . . . [and] locate formalized ritual behavior nearer the latter pole'. Intentionality is not just 'left behind' in ritual, or agents would be turned into automatons and the oft-noted improvisations and theatrical expressiveness of ritual (not to speak of its emotional power) would be incomprehensible. We have argued instead that intentionality in ritual is subtly transformed.

11. Searle points out that Oedipus also did a lot of other things unintentionally. He 'moved a lot of molecules, caused some neurophysiological changes in his brain and altered his spacial relationship to the North Pole'. Clearly, none of these were actions of Oedipus, even unintentional ones. But Searle remarks that he is 'inclined to feel' that 'marrying his mother' was an action which Oedipus performed, albeit unintentionally (Searle 1983: 102). It should be added that Oedipus, when he discovered it was the case, was rather more sure than Searle that this was indeed an action of his. For ritual, however, the distinction is easy to draw, for the range of acts a person has performed in virtue, not of their intentions but of the facts of the case, are clearly and unambiguously stipulated.

12. There is a 'Davidsonian' objection to our argument, and that of Searle, that all actions are necessarily intentional, because an action is defined as caused by an intention. We think that the language of causality is inappropriate here, as is shown by the examples of 'deviant' or 'wayward' causal chains (Chisholm 1966, see also the discussion in Moya 1990: ch. 11). Taylor gives the following example, 'I desire very much to smash your Ming vase because it will pay you out for being so mean to me. This powerful destructive desire of mine makes me so nervous that my grip is loosened on the vase and it smashes on the floor' (1979: 84). From the point of view of the 'causal' theory, this looks like an intentional action because the intention caused the event. Taylor argues in favour of the intuitive judgement that it is unintentional, and comments, 'In the normal, non-deviant case, our action expresses our intention. This

relation is a primitive, because it involves inseparability of the two. Consequently, it is futile to try to give an account of what non-deviance amounts to
in terms of a type of causal relation between separably identifiable terms. This
might serve as a neurophysiologically reductive account of what underlies the
distinction: but if we want to talk about what the distinction is about in our
experience, what underlies the intuitive distinction between deviant and
non-deviant chains, this kind of independent-term-causal account just *must* be
barking up the wrong tree' (Taylor 1979: 87–8).

13. Religious authorities can prescribe socially what the point of the ritual *should*
be. In Ch. 6 we call this a 'social purpose', but it is not possible for there to be
such a thing as a social intention.

14. While we cannot agree with Staal's conclusion that ritual is always and simply,
'pure activity, without meaning or goal' (1979: 9), and while we have no
sympathy at all for his resort to evolutionary biology for speculations about
the origin of ritual, he does, in the course of his work on ritual (1979, 1984,
1986, 1989) make many original and cogent observations. In particular his
close questioning of just what anthropologists and others mean when they talk
of ritual as 'meaningful'—often, on examination, they turn out to be saying
that it is *important* to those who perform it—gave us courage to press on with
ideas which we suspected might be unpopular.

15. Hampshire is referring here to the distinction between two kinds of knowledge, that of objects existing independently of anyone's knowledge of them or
beliefs about them (the standpoint of observers), and that of objects which are
modified by the agent's own beliefs about them, such as the knowledge a
person has of his or her own present and future action. The subject can also,
in retrospect, take up the standpoint of an observer of his own intentional
states (1982: 274–5).

16. See Ch. 8 for further discussion of this point and the difference between this
and attributing propositional meanings to ritual acts.

17. Reflection, which is always a possibility brought about by the ritual stance,
sometimes surfaces as public debate. The most familiar example is the early
stages of the Christian Reformation. The most passionate disagreements were
not about the stipulated acts (what needed to be done for a series of acts to
count, say, as communion), which remained largely unchanged from pre-
Reformation times, but about how what worshippers did was to be thought
about. To paraphrase Cameron (1991: 157–8), for late medieval thinkers a
sacrament consisted of a 'matter', the material element or action, combined
with a 'form', the correct verbal blessing, which if added to the appropriate
'intention' on the part of the participants, conferred 'grace' on those participants. But for thinkers in the Reformation the medieval interpretation wrongly
derived grace from a work performed apart from faith. For Zwingli, the
sacraments were no more than 'two external signs' bequeathed by Christ to
humanity as a concession to our frailty. The early Bucer similarly denied that
the sacraments achieved anything of themselves to aid salvation; he saw them

as 'protestations' and as 'memorials' of God's blessing. For Calvin, on the other hand, the sacraments were a means of enlightenment, a channel for the work of the Holy Spirit.

18. It might look as if a rite such as circumcision, for obvious practical reasons, can only be performed once, and that this might constrain the inventive and repetitive effects of ritualization. But this is not so. Circumcision can be done in a non-ritual way (for example for medical reasons) but if a person circumcised for these reasons subsequently converts to Judaism, this first operation does not count. The rite must be performed, but it is significant that the merest token (the drawing of blood) is sufficient. The limitation on number, normally due to the nature of the act being ritualized, is overcome.

5

Getting It Right

In previous chapters we made some brief remarks on the nature of prescription in ritual. Now we shall enlarge on these remarks and try to give an account of the kind of rules which govern the *puja*. While it is one of the most obvious things about ritualized action that it is prescribed, it is not so obvious quite how this compulsoriness or rigidity should be characterized. In liturgical traditions where authoritative figures are visibly present issuing instructions and orchestrating action, the thought that ritual is prescribed can seem unproblematic. As will become clear, Jain ritual practice is notably unauthoritarian, and readers will rightly feel that in this sense the Jain *puja* is a 'special case'; but as we suggested in Chapter 1, we think it is 'special' in a way which is instructive about ritual in general. We shall try to show that where, as in the Jain case, this kind of overt regulating instruction is more or less absent, and certainly no more conspicuously present than in other, non-ritual areas of life, it is possible to see that action can be 'prescribed' in a different way, one which is in part constitutive of ritualization. Moreover, the fact that the individual morning *puja* is not also a theatrical performance, unlike so many of the rituals which anthropologists have taken to be paradigmatic, means that the question of what you need to do in order to create an affecting display can be separated from the question of what you need to do in order to get a ritual right.

Let us begin by considering the idea that rituals are governed by 'scripts'. A script is a stereotyped sequence of events which the actor knows and uses as a guide to understanding and performance, for example 'going to the theatre'. This is a useful idea (although the term is unfortunate and misleading, as the 'script' need not be written down). We shall argue that ritualized action may be scripted, and that it is scripted in the *puja*. But once again, it is not in virtue of its being scripted that it is ritual. The idea of a script, while it does helpfully characterize much ritual action, does not identify the peculiar prescription of ritual as such. Many unritualized sequences of action are scripted, and indeed the idea of the script was developed in attempts to give cognitive descriptions of routine, everyday events like a visit to a restaurant or a trip to the dentist (Schank and Abelson 1977, Quinn and Holland 1987). If ritual is more prescribed than ordinary life, it might be the case that the scripts governing ritual are peculiarly clearly defined or unusually detailed. But this does not seem to be the case.

In Chapter 2 we gave two diagrams showing the scripts associated with the morning *puja*—structures for which we found a remarkable degree of agreement in the Dadabari temple when people were explaining things to us. As we observed, this shared understanding of the components and the structure of the rite does not lead to identical performances. While celebrants appear to follow rules in their performance of *puja*, and while many people can state explicitly the rules they think should apply, what they actually do varies: between different sects, different temple communities, different individuals, and even the same individual on different occasions. It is rare to find performance of the complete sequence. Here are three people, picked more or less at random from notes we jotted down, making their way about the Dadabari temple:

1. *A middle-aged woman.* Enters, waves incense, bathes statues with water, puts flowers on central Jina statue, makes rice in swastika pattern with fruits, waves incense again, waves a lamp before idol, goes out.

2. *A young girl.* Enters, waves incense before three Jinas, places flowers, puts sandalwood on forehead of left Jina idol, puts more flowers, waves incense again, goes out.

3. *An elderly woman.* Enters, rings bell, waves incense, circumambulates three Jina idols, puts on mouth covering, brushes right Jina idol with peacock feather, bathes it, applies scent, applies silver leaf, dabs sandalwood paste to nine parts of body, waves incense again, waves lamp, makes rice pattern, places sweets, fruit, sits praying, goes out.

We saw the elderly woman (3), whose *puja* was more or less 'complete', enacting the following 'reduced' *puja* on another day:

3. *Elderly woman.* Enters, waves incense, waves lamp, takes holy water and touches to forehead, back of head, and throat, touches floor of main Jina shrine with tips of fingers, prays with hands in front of face and over her head, goes over to image of Gautam Swami (one of Mahavir's disciples) and bows deeply, goes out.

Thus the same individual, applying the same rules, from day to day performs a slightly different sequence of acts and counts him or herself to have done the same thing (*puja*). This elderly lady's adherence to her daily *puja* script is variable, and we shall argue in the next chapter that it is not necessary to have a worked-up or explicit script at all in order to perform the rite. It seems probable that many people do not in practice think of it as a determinate sequence. There is some evidence that some people do feel it should have a beginning (the washing of the statue) and an end (a period of prayer). It was mentioned to us that some women, if they came too late to the temple to perform the bathing rite, would secretly wash the big toe of the statue to make up (though others said this was 'childish'), and a very large number of people indeed said that daily *puja* should end with a period of meditation. But despite these preferences, no one thought that missing out these elements invalidated a *puja*.

This observable diversity is not at all unique in ritual, and Tambiah (1985: 125, 141), Boyer (1990), and Parkin (1992: 19), have all pointed out that the repetition of rituals is not the unproblematic matter which anthropologists have tended to assume. So in what sense can ritual be peculiarly prescribed? We need to identify the kind of prescription which is not violated by this everyday variability. The knowledge persons have of their own action is qualitatively different from their knowledge of external objects and events, and since we argue that the actor's own attitude, his or her commitment or 'stance', is part of what ritualization is, it seems valid to draw on our own experience of knowing the *puja*. Of course we approached it with different background assumptions and different interests from those of devout Jain worshippers, but it none the less seems to us that the best way to begin our discussion of the character of the rules governing *puja* is to describe how we learned to perform it.[1]

One of our lay respondents offered to take us step-by-step through the whole ritual, so we agreed to meet him, early in the morning, at the Dadabari. We received our first instructions from our 'tutor' the day before, for we had to agree to prepare ourselves correctly before we arrived. On entering a temple, whether to perform *puja* or just to pray and take *darshan* of the idols, one should be free of certain sorts of pollution. Menstruating women may not come to the temple; neither may anyone who has attended a funeral (within three days), or anyone whose close relative has died (within twelve days), or who comes from a household in which a child has been born (again within twelve days).[2] To perform *puja* one must touch the Jina idol, so additional regulations on purity apply.[3] Before coming to the temple the worshipper must bathe. Before bathing, the bowels must be emptied, and no food taken thereafter; so we had to agree, for example, not to take breakfast before coming to the temple. Our tutor cheerfully informed us that in any case all this is 'good for health'. Everyone must put on clean clothes, and most people keep a set of clothes especially for *puja*. Women wear sarees, as they do at other times, but they must change from the one in which they cook and perform other house-hold chores. Men should not wear trousers or other stitched Western garments, but instead a plain white cotton loin-cloth, and a similar shawl on their upper body (although the occasional stitched vest is visible in winter and some of the younger men, a little uncertain perhaps of their skill with a loin-cloth, wear stitched underwear).

We arrived at the temple, suitably prepared and equipped with our newly-acquired clothing. We were helped into our clothes, we tied handkerchiefs over our mouth and nose, our friend provided us with the offerings we needed, and our instruction began. We started with *anga puja*, anointing the limbs of the statue. For this we collected some sandal-wood paste in a little metal dish from the *pujari*, and some flowers which our friend had brought for us. By watching and copying how they were performed, we learned the correct way to perform each prescribed act, and we learned about the mistakes we should avoid. For *anga puja* one should use the third finger, called the *anamika* ('nameless') finger, of the right hand.

Take the paste like this. Hold your other fingers down with your thumb, or they'll get in the way. Put the finger in the paste. . . . No, you should not plunge your finger in, you must not touch the paste with your fingernail. That is dirty. This side of the finger is connected with the mind. Oh yes, any scientist will tell you.[4] . . . Do it like this. Now you put the paste like this on nine parts of the *murti*. We begin with the right toe. . . . Good, that is *anga puja*.

The idol sits cross-legged in the lotus position so its left toe is on the right side of its body. When we moved on to the next idol one of us made the mistake of putting the paste first on the left toe. This did not cause any problems. We simply had to stop and do that particular act again. There was no requirement of fluency or facility. We stopped before each new stage while our friend checked that we were clear about what we had to do next. The fact that we were learning *puja* for the first time of course made the circumstances special. We could ask him questions and listen to his replies, while normally communication with others is avoided during *puja*. But even in this respect our experience is not atypical. If someone has a misfortune to avert, or some good fortune to celebrate, he or she may spend extra money on a slight elaboration of morning *puja*, and in such cases the patron has to be guided through the unfamiliar parts of the ritual by a *pujari* or a lay expert. Not infrequently, we would arrive at the Dadabari to find a husband and wife huddled in the *guru-dev* shrine, applying silver foil to the idol with the guidance and help of a *pujari*. Just as in our own learning of the *puja*, these patron–performers were guided through by others, and so long as the right thing was done in the end, their mistakes, delays, and breaks for consultation did not preclude correct enactment of the rite.

Similarly, whenever someone stages a public *puja*, a crowd gathers to sing devotional songs and chant prayers in the hall or courtyard in front of the shrine, but the *puja* itself is performed by the patron and members of his immediate family aided and instructed by *pujaris*, *yatis*, or lay religious experts. For these most prestigious, elaborate, and, it is believed, most efficacious forms of *puja*, most people never become proficient and their correct enactment always emerges out of a sea of delay, debate, and halting, faltering action. Most of the *puja* acts which are performed behind the scenes are exactly the same as those performed in more simple *puja*s, but there are always some unfamiliar elements, and the various acts of anointing, offering, and so on have to be co-ordinated with the prayers and sacred formulas. Those performing these *puja*s therefore spend a lot of their time just standing by the idol with a handkerchief tied over their mouth and nose, holding a jar of water, a lamp, a tray of offerings, or a garland of flowers, and waiting to be told when they should pour from it, wave it, present it, or drape it on the idol. Some of those who attend these *puja*s enjoy the singing very much and there is invariably a huddle of enthusiastic laymen who jostle for position with the paid musicians at the front and who loom as best they can over the microphones. They are always keen to prolong the singing, to repeat a verse, or to interject a popular devotional song. These rites are never rehearsed. They are regularly interrupted by debates about what is to happen next, who is to do what, and about the length of the singing; and they rarely finish until everyone has had their say (although occasionally the presence of a charismatic renouncer can quell this kind of discord[5]). In addition, these *puja*s are routinely interrupted by auctions at which the right to perform particular acts, usually *arti* (waving a fivefold lamp) and *mangal dip* (waving a single 'auspicious' camphor lamp), is sold to the highest bidder.

If renouncers are present at public *puja*s then although they can never perform any of the acts which involve touching the idol or making offerings, they are often asked to read the short Sanskrit prayers which punctuate the collective singing. At one public *puja* when no renouncers were present a young layman, well known for his religious learning, was reading these prayers. Then, half-way through, a small group of female ascetics came and sat down. When the next prayer came the young man proceeded with his recitation but was stopped in mid-flow as the opinion-forming members of the congregation decided that the ascetics should take over. The young man's weak protest, that it was better for the same person to perform all the prayers, was brushed aside, and a vague reference to 'the *shastras*' (religious treatises) disregarded. The ascetics, not especially keen to take on the work, were called upon to continue and one among their number began the disputed prayer again. No one thought there was any problem about stopping the recitation like this, or in delaying the continuation of the rite. The appropriate 'ruling' (Lewis 1980) having been made, the young man's recitation was simply counted invalid and replaced.

We noticed in our own case that our tutor simply disregarded any action (and a lot of inaction) on our part which did not count as the realization of a constituent *puja* act. If we did something which was specifically disallowed, he drew this to our attention and showed us again how to get it right, but no remedial action was required. This is why, even in elaborate *puja*s where a lot of time, money, and reputation may be invested, no one ever bothers to rehearse the rite. Our faltering and our mistakes had no effect on what was to come next. It was simply the case that when we had done the right thing we could move on to the next part. In a sense then, only when we got it right were we judged as having *done* anything. It was not of course that incorrect action became invisible, or our friend would not have been able to correct and instruct us, but it did not count as *ritual* action. So long as we correctly went through each named sequence any erroneous or extraneous action just didn't count. This gives a clue to the kind of rules at work. The crucial level at which ritual action is prescribed, the level at which it is prescribed in a specifically ritual way, is the level of the ritual *act*. While people can perform the same act in different ways, their doing so nevertheless counts as instances of the same act, and their performance therefore counts as correct.

The rules which are responsible for this effect are different from the boundary-marking rules which specify purity (bodily states, changes of clothing, removal of shoes, and so forth). The ideas about purity and pollution to which these latter rules apply, and the techniques they prescribe for how to prevent pollution, also apply in everyday life. They are quite stringent in *puja*, but conservative people apply the same or very similar restrictions on entry to the kitchen at home. Whether these ideas and practices may be called 'religious' or not, and most Jains would deny it, they are certainly not specific to ritual. In the context of *puja*, as in other contexts, if you break these rules you have committed a sin (either by showing disrespect or by causing harm). We would say, therefore, that these are regulative rules.

Here we employ a distinction, drawn from Searle (1969: 33–42), between regulative rules, which seek to constrain action in an already existing context, and constitutive rules, which create a context and hence a field of action.[6] An example of regulative rules is the Highway Code and the laws governing driving, which regulate what people do when driving cars. If you break these rules you have committed an offence, but even if you were to repudiate and pay no attention to the rules you would still be 'driving', and 'driving' would still be a possible form of activity if these rules did not exist. There is a kind of rule which is quite different. The basic rules of chess, for instance, do not regulate an already existing activity, for 'chess' exists only in so far as people accept these rules and act accordingly. These rules are therefore constitutive. Similarly, when we were told, 'This is *anga puja*, you take sandalwood paste on your finger like this, and do this with it,' what we were learning were constitutive rules. When we learned about which was the central idol in the temple and about how to perform the basic acts of *puja* we were learning essentially the same kind of thing as is contained in the rules of a game. Thus a rule book for tennis begins, 'There is a court of the following dimensions . . .' and continues, 'To serve, a player should . . .'. Even if you make a mistake, fail in your attempt, and thus act in a way not sanctioned by the rules, you are still playing the game, because you accept the authority and the relevance of these constitutive rules. You accept that if your foot is over the line when you serve it will be discounted.

To revert to the vocabulary we used in the previous chapter: the constitutive rules of the game establish an ontology of acts, they specify what kind of acts your physical movement *can be*. So it is in ritual. Constitutive rules create a form of activity, by defining the actions of which it is composed. We pointed out that ritualized action is composed of discrete acts which are disconnected from agents' intentions and we said that this feature of ritualization depends on stipulation. It is this stipulation, as distinct from mere regulation, which is constitutive of ritual. Only ritual acts (like valid moves in chess) count as having happened, so the celebrant proceeds from act to act, completing each in turn and then moving on to the next. This is unaffected by delays, false moves, extraneous happenings, or mishaps. Thus it is that *puja*s can be interrupted for a debate or an auction, delayed while performers are shown what to do, stopped and started after a mistake has been noticed or decided upon. Thus it is also that elements within the *puja* can be drawn out, hurried, or repeated, without altering the series of ritual acts which has occurred; without, it seems, these various intrusions or changes affecting what has happened. Just as one must accept a *commitment* to the constitutive rules of a game before one is playing the game at all, so performing ritual action involves a commitment to the prescribed acts. This commitment, that what one's action is to count as is a series of specified ritualized acts, is what we have called the ritual stance and is a matter, as we said in the last chapter, of how action is seen.[7] But as the fact that the rules are constitutive makes clear, this change in how the actor sees his or her own action guides what he or she does and is thus directly constitutive of a distinctive quality of action.

That the ritual stance is constitutive in the way we are suggesting can perhaps be illustrated by cases in which a celebrant does not actually, physically, do a *puja* act, but nevertheless counts as having performed it. There are two sorts of case of this. The first is where a person comes to the temple without making the prescribed preparation (bathing, changing clothes, and so on) and so cannot touch the idol. He or she cannot then perform *puja*. But we have seen people stand before an idol and make as if to lay a flower, or drop some rice grains, or toss some sandalwood powder. While this is clearly derivative of the physical act, and while those we spoke to justified their practice in ways that showed they thought of it as second best ('I didn't have time to do the full *puja* today'), it nevertheless counts for them as a valid *puja* act. The other, more highly regarded case, is where someone sets out only to perform *bhav puja*, by which some people mean sitting before the idol and performing *puja* as a meditational exercise. This is the normal practice of the renouncers, many of whom said that they do a series of acts like the physical actions performed by laypeople, but that they do only the *bhav* of them.[8]

In most games there are both constitutive and regulative rules, and the same is the case with *puja*. Unlike in a game however, there is no clear distinction in practice between these two kinds of rules; no clear difference, for example, between a written rule book and an unwritten etiquette. In general, we can note that constitutive rules are in practice taught ostensively ('This is flower *puja*') and the learner attempts to copy what is done. Constitutive rules can be explained in a roundabout way in language, but this is not the best way to learn them, and in practice it is not how they are taught. Regulative rules are usually more linguistically explicit, although for the learner they are mostly elicited by infringing them ('Do not put your fingernail in the paste, that is dirty'). While the constitutive rules are apparently arbitrary, reasons can be given for regulative rules, because they rely on bodies of convention and understanding which apply also outside *puja*. Thus many people told us that the flowers used in *puja* should not have been plucked, as this is a form of injury (*himsa*). Instead, fallen flowers should be used. While this rule is well known, few people follow it. Fallen flowers are not so pretty, their smell is faint, and they tend to fall apart when you handle them, so although they may be aware that there is some sin (*pap*) involved, most people use plucked flowers in their *puja*. We can see that this rule is regulative because breaking it does not destroy or disqualify the *puja*s they perform. It is secondary to the constitutive rule of what counts as a *pushpa puja*. If you think you can do your *puja* how you like, if you repudiate the commitment to realize and re-enact the act you have been shown, then you do not commit an offence against the *puja*, as you do if you use plucked flowers, you simply are no longer doing it.

The rule about using fallen flowers regulates action in *puja* by the application of Jain ethical concerns about injury to other creatures. There is a further class of regulative rules, called '*ashatana*', which proscribe other offences against the *puja*. An *ashatana* is a form of disrespect and the concept overlaps with the rules about purity we listed above. It is an *ashatana* not to wear a covering over one's mouth and nose (not everyone is too strict about the nose) when approaching an idol, lest one's stale breath or drops of saliva reach the idol. The point here is that these rules do not only apply in the *puja* or in other ritual contexts. Indeed, we were first introduced to the concept of *ashatana* when someone corrected us for leaving our bags on the floor along with our shoes when we entered a room. The bags contained our notebooks, and we had unwittingly treated these and so their contents (our notes about the Jain religion) with disrespect. The rules about *ashatana* are therefore regulative rules and they apply, although not with the same rigour, in all contexts. If you commit an *ashatana* during *puja* you have still performed *puja*, unlike the case when you disregard constitutive rules. You should correct the *ashatana* by performing a penance, but no remedial action is called for by mistakes in conforming to the constitutive rules.

Lists of *ashatana*s appear in the medieval *shravakacar*s. These are compendious catalogues, ranging from spitting, yawning, laughing, and vomiting, to tethering horses, forgetting to leave various objects outside the temple, and meeting old men to discuss marriage arrangements. The medieval texts give lists of eighty-four *ashatana*s (Williams 1963: 225–9; Cort 1989: 392). The number eighty-four is quite nominal; a general term for 'lots and lots' also used for the number of *gacch*s (religious orders) which are supposed to exist. There are several curious features of these *ashatana* lists, one being that some of the prohibited actions do perforce take place (yawning and stretching the limbs, for example) and others are, and were at the time, common practices (waving fly-whisks and saying *mantra*s). And it seems probable that even in the medieval period some of the actions prohibited by the *ashatana*s (like tethering horses) were very unlikely to happen in the temple during *puja*. Perhaps we could interpret this characteristic of the lists, together with the nominal number eight-four, as emphasizing the idea that there *are* rules, rather than in any serious or pressing sense themselves *being* rules. The rules can be about the most improbable things, but what you are supposed to understand is that the *puja* is a rule-bound universe.

In contrast with this, we found that what people actually learn is not rules (propositions of a general kind in language) but named actions they should copy. Where the names are words for the substances used, the words are distinct from their everyday equivalents. Rice, normally called *caval*, is renamed *akshat*, a Sanskrit word meaning 'indestructible'. For the water, flowers, lamp, and sweets the Hindi words of daily usage (*pani, phul, bati, mithai*[9]) give way to Sanskrit equivalents (*jal, pushpa, dipak, naivedya*[10]). In none of these cases, however, are the everyday words completely effaced. Children and less well-educated adults continue to use ordinary words. A woman doing the flower *puja* might call the act either the 'dignified' *pushpa puja* or ordinary *phul puja*.[11] Learning names for different acts of offering which distinguish them clearly from each other, and learning names for objects which dissociate them from their normal, non-ritual uses and contexts, conduce towards the adoption of the ritual commitment. The use of Sanskrit names is a mark of modest sophistication, of some limited specialized knowledge about the *puja*, but it is not necessary. What is necessary, we suggest, is the use of *some name* which stands for the concept of the act.

In games too the stream of action is segmented and labelled. But is it possible to play without knowing any such names? We suggest that taking part successfully depends on knowledge of the segments of action and the giving of some label to them at the level (or levels) at which they are stipulated. For example, in tennis a player needs to know that there are points and games and sets, and to have some way of identifying them shared with the opponent. The inclusivity of the action comprising a segment and labelled in this way is defined by the level at which constitutive rules operate. In tennis one needs to know that there are 'strokes', but performing a stroke can be done in many ways and it is quite possible, we can say from personal experience, to play tennis while being unsure about classifications within the category of a stroke (volleys, lobs, approach shots, cross-court backhands, and so forth). This is possible because the constitutive rules in tennis occur at the level of the stroke and above. Performers with some expertise know such technical names in tennis and we can see this as equivalent to the use of Sanskrit terms for acts in the *puja*. Thus we can say for ritual that although the naming of acts, at the level at which they are now perceived as objectively discrete, is an essential aspect of ritualization, renaming as such (for example in Sanskrit) is not.

It might be objected to the above argument that rituals such as the *puja* are not analogous to games, in that in their case there is no requirement to interact and communicate with an opponent. Might not ritual enactment be more like music, in which it is possible to learn a piece 'by ear' and play it without consciously understanding that it is made up of semiquavers, bars, a change into B flat minor, etc.? Ritual performance is like music in that it has its own time, created by the sequences and patterns of re-arranged and repeated elements, which is separated from that of ordinary life. Music is restricted to a single, on-flowing, and integral medium, that of sound, and can therefore exert a 'tremendous leverage on Time'.[12] It creates a time medium into which 'ordinary' time does not intrude (even if the listener is aware of the half an hour or so it takes to perform a symphony, for example). Ritual time has this quality too, but unlike music, it is based on the duration of physical acts which might in principle take place in everyday life (bowing, anointing, circumambulating). As we discuss further in the next chapter, ritualized acts are *ordinary* acts transformed by a different standpoint, the ritual stance. As we have just said, while 'rituals' are going on some actions are left out from the transformation effected by the ritual stance, such as walking between ritual sites, taking sandalwood paste from the *pujari*, or tying on a mouth-covering, and others, the *ashatanas*, are named and expressly forbidden. The acts which are ritualized must be distinguished from this background. We would therefore argue that the ritual transformation is not only intentional, as we have said, but that it also requires consciousness of each act that is transformed. Naming the acts is one aspect of this.

It is important for anthropologists to be aware of the level at which this is done. If we look, for example, at 'rituals of rebellion' like the popular Indian festival of Holi, it is clear that an infinite number of impudent and exuberant acts count as 'playing Holi'.

Rich, high-caste farmers find their shins beaten by the labourers' wives; respectable Brahman elders are chased by untouchable latrine-sweepers; a notoriously mean moneylender hears his death announced in parodic song by an ascetic; the anthropologist who asks too many questions is 'made to dance in the streets, fluting like Lord Krishna, with a garland of old shoes around his neck'. (Fuller 1992: 131, citing Marriott 1968)

As anthropologists have pointed out, these acts oppose the social norms and facts of everyday social organization, but their content is nowhere stipulated and obviously is a matter of considerable spur-of-the moment inventiveness. This does not make Holi any the less ritualized; it is just that the level of stipulation is not with these actions but 'higher'. During the day of Holi there is a prescribed time-period for all this saturnalian and humiliating activity, and as Fuller points out, 'Later in the day, the antics should always stop, so that order is restored and more conventional celebrations—such as worship of domestic deities and a collective meal— can take their place' (1992: 131). It is at this level, the blocks of kinds of activity (abuse, worship, communality), that prescription occurs in this case.

From talking to young Jains it became apparent that they learn to do the *puja* in much the same way as we had. They come to the temple with an older female member of the family and are shown, copy, and remember each constituent act. In time they build a comprehensive repertoire of acts, and can perform a full *puja*. We talked to one 9-year-old boy, for instance, who had been coming with his mother since the age of 6, and now comes occasionally to do *puja* on his own. He performs three of the eight *puja*s, having learnt these isolated and easily remembered reverential acts together with their names: '*kesar*'—dabbing with sandalwood paste,[13] '*mithai*'—placing small candy balls (*makana*s), and '*caval*'—placing rice on the table before the idol.[14] After he has done these, he sits in the temple for a few minutes and reads to himself from a book of devotional songs (*bhajan*s). Now, he told us, in addition to just placing a small pile of rice, he forms some rice into a crescent shape, which he calls *candrama*, but he has not yet learnt to form the rest of the rice pattern. With the paste, he usually dabs just the feet of God (Bhagwan), but occasionally, he said, he puts it on other parts of the body too. (In fact, he would have been unable to reach the other prescribed parts of most of the idols, but was reluctant to admit this). He knew no 'meanings' for any of these acts. He said he had come to do *puja* today because he had an exam to take at school that morning.

We noted above that even adults sometimes have to learn new segments of *puja*s, and that they are often instructed by the *pujari*. This is another element in the disjunction of action from either coherent total scripts (models) or religious meanings. Neither of the two *pujaris* at the Dadabari were Jains (they were both Brahmins) and they had been working there for one and three years respectively. They neither knew nor were interested in Jain religious ideas. They did not see it as part of their job to correct what 'they' (the Jains) did in the temple, only to help people with the more technically difficult actions, such as putting on silver leaf, and to tidy up and clear away. When describing the *puja* sequence to us they described what people did, not what they 'ought to do', and therefore missed out one or two elements which well-read lay Jains would regularly include. The meaning of the *puja*, on the other hand, is mostly taught to people by renouncers, who themselves do not practise it in its material form (they only do *bhav puja*). With the decline of the *yatis*, who are more equivalent to European priests, there is therefore no equivalent among the Jains for Christian confirmation classes, which teach actions, sequences, and meanings as a coherent whole. We have no wish to deny that the sense of an underlying structure which is arrived at by religious Jains—especially the transition from *dravya* (action with material objects) to *bhav* (meditation, devotion)—is highly important. For many people it comes to constitute the essential religious experience of *puja*. But it seems clear at the same time that this sense of structure is something which takes time to acquire and that for some people it appears to be absent.

Somewhat to our surprise, when we finished our halting and rather stumbling performance, we were congratulated that we had performed the *puja*. What we had done was not just a practice or a first attempt, but was actually an *instance* of *puja*. The fact that we had got things wrong, had not really known what we were doing, had had to be shown through the sequence, had stopped in the course of things to discuss what we were doing, and had missed out the beginning and meditation segments altogether, none of these invalidated our performance because amidst all this, we had got it right. What we had done counted as an instance of the ritual not because it was judged to have the appropriate intentional meaning: nothing in our fumbled doing-as-we-were-told would have justified the attribution of intentions which gave meaning to our conduct. We had done the prescribed ritual acts, so what we had done was *puja*.

Most anthropologists who have written about ritual have assumed that it is at the level of prescribed *sequences* that the prescriptiveness of ritual is to be found, but while the intuition that ritual is essentially prescribed seems justified, it does not seem to be the case that the sequences of actions in ritual are replicated more exactly than those in many unritualized contexts. This is because it is not at this level that ritualization, and so ritual prescription, applies. We have suggested instead that the ritualization of action is achieved by stipulation of ritual *units* (in the case of *puja* these are acts). This explains how it is possible to have 'snippets' of ritual embedded quite informally in everyday life (the grace before a meal, formal greetings, and so on). It also accounts for the fact that the young boy's enactment of three simplified segments, well under half of what we had been told the *puja* consists of, was also a *puja*.

This fact also explains why it is possible to repeat, change the order, or come back to a favourite section of the *puja*. The following example is utterly typical.

A middle-aged woman. Enters temple, takes incense holder and goes to main shrine and offers incense to all three Jinas, left to right; then to two of Mahavir's disciples; then to picture of pilgrimage site on left wall; passes Ganesh-like *yaksha*, but waves incense before the powerful god, Ghantarkaran; goes across the back of the temple and does the same before the Jina Shitalnath, then Nakoda *bhairu*; then Padmavati (a protector deity, *shasan-devi*).

Then takes sandalwood-paste and does *anga puja* for the Jina in the left-hand shrine (the others already have crowds around them).

Takes up incense again and goes to main Jina shrine. Puts down incense-holder and washes the left Jina in the central shrine with water. Dries the statue.

Recommences *anga puja* for the three Jinas by the left wall, and then goes straight over to Nakoda *bhairu* whom she anoints with paste on head and limbs.

Takes a lamp and wanders round the temple waving it at most images.

Takes a tray with rice and puts a small heap of this on the offering table before main Jinas (no swastika, fruit, or nuts); goes to Nakoda *bhairu* and leaves some grains on the floor, together with a few coins. Prays.

Prays at length before picture of burnt money. Goes out.

Some readers will certainly react: but this Jain *puja* is utterly atypical of ritual in general, where sequence is a crucial element of the structure. This has been argued by Chris Fuller for the Hindu *puja*, which is ethnographically one of the closest rituals to what we have been describing (1992: 57–82). In the Hindu *puja* the image is treated like the visit of an honoured guest. It is invoked, then bathed, dressed, adorned, offered food, honoured, and finally given a respectful leave-taking. Fuller draws from a body of theoretically authoritative Sanskrit texts a 'paradigmatic textual model' for the *puja*. There are sixteen acts, each of which is called an *upacar*, which should be performed in order. Now let us look at what actually happens. Even in the Minakshi temple in Madurai which, as

Fuller says, dwarfs most Hindu temples in size and resources, this model is not much followed. Fuller (1992: 67) writes that in the Minakshi temple numbers 1–5 and 14–16 are omitted, to leave only the central phase, numbers 6–13. Normally, in fact, only four rituals are conducted (bathing, decoration, food offering, and waving lamps) and these are considered to constitute a complete *puja*. The Hindu *puja*, then, can be compressed and stretched in just the same way as a Jain *puja*: as in the Jain case, acts of offering or bathing or anointing can be repeated over and over again.

Now even these drastic distortions of sequence are not quite the same as a reversal of order, such as we often observed in the Jain *puja*. In the Hindu *puja* one can bathe the idol umpteen times, but it would be just as unthinkable to reverse the order of bathing and dressing as it would in ordinary life. But it would be a mistake to underestimate just how far ritual practice can be from the discursive models which purport to describe it (see further discussion in Chapter 8). Fuller adds,

Moreover, although the 'full' worship in the Minakshi temple comprises only four rituals, which leaves out at least eight of the sixteen textual *upacar*s, it is common practice merely to offer food and wave the lamps. . . . Frequently, in the Minakshi temple and elsewhere, *puja* is further reduced to no more than the showing of a one-flame camphor lamp with a plantain on the side as food offering. . . . In the final analysis, the camphor flame, as the culmination of worship, stands synecdochically for the entire ritual. (1992: 68)

Thus sequence is often entirely obliterated, replaced by the simultaneous showing of food and lamp, or by the lamp alone. The thing to note is that seemingly inevitable sequences in ritual, such as the fact that bathing should always precede dressing, derive from two factors, both of which are extraneous to ritualization itself.

One of these, which is relevant to the comparative freedom of the Jain as opposed to the Hindu *puja*, has to do with the extent to which the rites are orchestrated (or not) by a priest or other religious authority (see also Chapter 7). The other point is that what makes for a complete sequence of ritualized action (a complete *puja*, a complete initiation, a complete 'ritual of rebellion') depends on the nature of the event which has been ritualized. Rites of passage have three stages (separation, a liminal period, and reaggregation) not because they are *rites* of passage, but because they are rites of *passage*. A ritual coronation or naming, divination or exorcism, commemoration or rebellion, must include elements which follow from the nature of the events ritualized. The Jain *panc-kalyanak* (celebration for the installation of a statue) is like this: it has a sequence because it is the commemoration of the five sacred events in the life of the Jina (conception, birth, renunciation, enlightenment, and release). On the other hand it does not follow even from a rite of passage that one could predict, given the purpose of a ritual, what its form will be.

This is because ritualization itself acts against, and tends to undermine, the orders of the everyday world. If there is a logic to a sequence of actions, then even missing out an element, let alone reversing some, will in normal circumstances be a breaking of the order. In such a case you would of course still have a list of actions, but the relations between the elements, which make the list an ordered *sequence*, would no longer obtain. If you were receiving and honouring a real guest you could not omit receiving them or bidding them farewell and still have honoured them. Similarly, you cannot omit bits of a symphony or a play, because each of the sections only makes sense or works if you have the other sections too (you can listen to just one movement of a symphony but you would not have 'listened to the symphony'). On the other hand, if a Hindu woman waves a camphor lamp and does nothing else, she would still have performed *puja*. Anthropology has tended to assume that there must be some structure or logic which provides rules about what you can omit in ritual, and how. Our point is that this structure, such as it is, inheres in the process or actions which had been ritualized. It is not a feature of ritual as such. Precisely because a sequence of actions has been ritualized, the ordering (the script) no longer plays the role or has the purchase that it would in everyday life. This is one feature which differentiates liturgy-centred ritual from performance-centred rituals, which we argue are weakly ritualized. Thus in the Hindu *puja* bathing must come before dressing (if either of them happen at all), because that's how things are with bathing and dressing. They come in that order in *puja* despite, not because they are in a ritual. So while it makes sense to say that the fact that bathing must come before dressing is necessary to the *puja*'s meaning, in so far as the meaning is that of 'receiving an honoured guest', it would be odd to say that it is constitutive of the *rite*, for what makes the rite different from receiving a real guest is just that adherence to this order is no longer necessary.

Rituals of worship are perhaps particularly arbitrary as regards sequence, since worship can be done in an infinity of ways. The Jain *puja* for example can be the classic eightfold worship, which comprises eight 'offerings': water, sandalwood, flowers, incense, light, rice, sweets, and fruit. This can also be extended by the addition of three or four extra items (a flag, a bell, water at the four corners of the shrine), or lengthened to various extents, such as to sixteen, forty-eight, or sixty-four items. Similarly, the pattern which is at the heart of the Anglican Office of worship can be seen as Psalms, Old Testament Reading, Canticle, New Testament Reading, Canticle; or it can be extended by the inclusion of music and other items—Introduction, Responses, Psalms, Old Testament Reading, Magnificat, New Testament Reading, Nunc Dimittis, Creed, Responses, Collects, Anthem, Prayers. All these variants can be construed as having 'the same structure', and might be given meanings in line with this, but because there is nothing to prevent the unlimited addition or repetition of elements it is difficult to escape the conclusion that the 'structure' is in fact a list. Like the Christian service, the eightfold worship of the Jains may come to have a feeling of inevitability for those who perform it daily, but this does not seem to be intrinsic to ritualization.

One man, who helps to officiate at collective *puja*s, described to us how he had learned it:

First from my family; it's a tradition (*parampara*) in my family; then from books, then from knowledgeable (*jankari*) renouncers. I learnt easily, sitting beside my family members 'Do that, do like this, do this, after that do this.' Ten days, five days, fifteen days it went on like that, and after that, on it goes (*vah calta hai*).

For him there was no question that his *puja* might not be correct. The sense of rightness was given by the continuity with what he had been taught. Because it was right before, it is right now if done in the same way. There can be variety and yet everyone feels they are performing the same archetypal act.

Thus, the scripts (or the 'discursive models') which people come to acquire are always programmatic and related to past exemplars rather than contemporary versions. When they depart from the temple after performing *puja* worshippers leave their offerings on the various tables and ledges in front of the idols, most on the large offering table in front of the central idol. Once or twice a friend of ours noticed 'a mistake' in one of these lay-outs and casually moved an offering to the 'correct' position. There was no idea that the departed worshipper had not performed *puja*, just a faintly embarrassed suggestion that some people are careless or ill-informed. We doubt he would even have bothered to do this if we had not been present. While each worshipper knows a set of rules, more or less elaborate, which he or she tries to follow, and most have an idea of a complete and comprehensive performance which, when they have time, they try to perform, they are remarkably relaxed about the fact that the precise sequences followed by their fellow temple-goers do not match their own. The attitude taken by most of our informants to other people's *puja*s was one of condescending or amused indulgence or generalized respect for those who are more learned or more devout. The 'mistake' in question was to have placed a piece of fruit on top of the swastika of rice grains. In *akshat puja* (rice *puja*) a pattern is laid out with rice grains: a swastika, above this three dots and above this a further dot, sitting in a crescent shape. Our friend insisted that *phal puja*, the placing of fruit, means 'I wish for the fruit of my *puja* to be release (*moksh*).' As the swastika, he said, represents the cycle of death and rebirth,[15] this was an inappropriate place to put the fruit, which, he said, should go on another pile of rice, the one in a crescent shape which itself represents release.

Most people in the Dadabari shared this view, and we have seen a number of recent pamphlets written by renouncers which recommend it, but it was not universal. We saw fruit left on the swastika several times, and there is evidence that the now dominant pattern is of relatively recent origin. The medieval *shravakacar*s, so far as we know, are silent on the matter, and when James Burgess saw Jains perform *puja* in Gujarat in the early 1880s, they regularly placed their offerings of fruit on the swastika and sweets on the crescent shape (1884: 191–6). Burgess quotes verses in Gujarati assigning appropriate meanings to these offerings, so the practice clearly had at least local religious sanction. Cort (1989: 376), citing three modern Gujarati pamphlets, reports that one prescribes the arrangement which Burgess saw, and two that which our friend in Jaipur was recommending.[16]

Even publicly agreed rules are not necessarily either clear or explicit. None the less, ritualization does require that people feel that somewhere there are rules telling you what to do and that the question of what is the correct thing to do can be settled by consulting them (however this might be done). It is this commitment to rules, rather than the production of a fixed series or sequence of actions, which is intrinsic to ritualization. 'Higher level' rules incorporating sequences are less definite than those which prescribe particular acts. This gives rise to the paradoxical character of the prescription of ritual. Ritual is prescribed action, you have to get it right, and yet sometimes it seems that so long as you try, so long as you accept the ritual commitment, it is almost impossible to get it wrong.[17] It is often the small things which are least problematic.

In the summer of 1986 Surendra, a retired gem trader and prominent member of the Dadabari community, performed a *puja* to replace the temple flag. James joined him on the temple roof, as did two female renouncers who were staying in the Dadabari at the time, a specialist Jain ritual adept, or *yati*, who lives in the walled city, and two of the Dadabari's regular *pujaris*. It was late morning in the middle of June: the sun was well up in an absolutely cloudless sky and a scalding hot dry wind was blowing in from the Rajasthan desert. Below in the temple, Surendra's sister was conducting a *panc-kalyanak puja* for one of the Jina idols there. There were two musicians; and a group of twenty or so neighbours, friends, and passers-by had gathered to join in the singing below. A large area in the roof of the temple is covered only with some iron bars, to let light into the chamber below, so the music could be heard faintly from the roof.

The *yati* was to instruct Surendra on how the *puja* should be performed, and was to be paid for this service. He had brought some notes to which he had frequent recourse, and had also brought some palm-leaf manuscripts. The renouncers, although they were barely audible in the wind as they stumbled through the unfamiliar words, read the Sanskrit prayers and formulae from this text.

The first stage was to be the sprinkling of water at a number of places around the roof, including the cardinal points, and after some discussion the location of these places was decided. While Surendra was sent off to do this, which as the action itself occurs in every-day *puja*s he could easily do without any further guidance, the *yati* drew geometric magical drawings (*yantra*s) on the flag with sandalwood paste. A mixture of grains was scattered after the water, and then the *pujari* tied a thread around the wrists of the two lay participants (the patron and the anthropologist) and placed the usual *tilak* mark, of sandalwood paste and rice grains, on their foreheads.

The *pujari*s had already removed the flagpole from its place and it was lying flat on the roof. At each stage the text was read out, looks exchanged, and guidance sought from the *yati*. He showed little confidence, peering quizzically at his notes and frequently changing his mind. Where the text supplied clues, the renouncers joined in and suggested what they thought it might imply, but mostly the *yati* demonstrated what should be done, and Surendra, sometimes helped by James, copied what he did and carried out similar operations around the temple roof or along the length of the flagpole. The flagpole was washed and anointed using water drawn from several different buckets, to which were added different perfumed powders, grains, leaves, and flowers. As at every *puja*, a coconut, with money tied onto it, was placed on an offering table near where the flag was to stand. All the usual elements of *puja* were used: a lamp, incense sticks, sweets, and fruits. These at least could be done with confidence and facility.

There were long delays while more water was brought from downstairs or while the next stage was determined, and much confusion, as instructions were re-issued and amended. It was getting hotter. Surendra filled many of the gaps with re-peated chanting of the *namaskar-mantra*. The ascetics read some final verses, and showed Surendra the prostrations which conventionally accompany these. The flag was fixed, and the *pujari*s began to hoist the pole back into place. Unfortunately, as they did so, the flag caught on some of the barbed-wire which covers the parapet around the roof, and tore. The *pujari*s looked contrite and apprehensive, but Surendra ignored the mishap and lustily joined the singing coming from below. The ascetics, now taking refuge at a distance in the single small area of shade, forbore to join him.

Surendra, the patron of the *puja*, decided that a photograph was called for, but the chains which hang from the top of the pole and are supposed to jangle beside the banner had become tangled, so before it could be taken he sent a reluctant *pujari* up the pole to free them and explained to James the importance of the ceremony, 'Every temple has a flag like this. If there is no flag, *puja* cannot be performed in the temple. Therefore this is a very important *puja*, costly too, and a very good thing to do.'

The flag would have to be replaced before long, but this *puja* to install it had been a success.

Occasionally, anthropologists have made positive use of some of the messiness of ritual performance (e.g. Geertz 1973: 142–69), but this has tended to be presented against the background assumption that normally rituals are miraculously perfect and effective performances so that messy ritual is presented as failed ritual, and as evidence of social erosion (for more discussion, see Bell 1992: 33–5). And generally, anthropologists have had great difficulty in treating rituals as anything more concrete than *types* of events, and have even persuaded many historians to do likewise (see Kelly and Kaplan 1990). Fredrik Barth, in an important recent book (1987), has taken the definite step forward of using the incremental changes which occur between performances of a ritual as a way of looking at the social organization of knowledge and practice in a particular cultural milieu. If you abandon the assumption of perfect order and perfect repetition, imperfection and variation become illuminating, rather than being noise that a well-honed interpretation dampens down and edits out.

Notes

1. The suggestion that we should learn to perform the *puja* came from our Jain respondents. While we got the impression that a few people were a little uneasy about non-Indians and non-Jains performing *puja* in the temple, most people were perfectly comfortable with the idea and if anything were amused and pleased by the spectacle. Moreover, it seemed to many people that properly to learn about *puja*, one had to learn to perform it, and that this must be the point of our asking all those questions about it.

2. In theory, no one who has taken food at a home in which a birth or death has recently occurred may perform *puja* for three days. This in general does not arise because such households will not normally offer food to visitors. Similarly, anyone who has recently infringed any of the multifarious dietary restrictions which lay Jains observe is considered polluted and should not

come to the temple until they have performed a ritualized confession (*pratikraman*) or undertaken a penance (*prayshcitt*). However, people choose for themselves the strictness of the dietary rules they observe, and penances, even when imposed by a renouncer, are usually fairly light: some prayers, a short period of meditation, or a fast.

3. In most Hindu traditions only consecrated priests may touch temple idols.

4. At this point he enlarged on the subject of the connections between different parts of the human organism, for example the toe and the stomach.

5. James witnessed a particularly memorable occasion of this kind, during a long eight-day festival in Jaipur in the early summer of 1986. A new idol was being installed and a vast crowd gathered from all over India. Each day there was a different long and elaborate *puja*, with worshippers squashed into every corner of a large hall. One day the electricity failed: the fans stopped and from most places in the hall it was difficult to hear the music or the prayers. It was very hot and a few people drifted away. Fewer and fewer joined in the singing, preferring to sit fanning themselves or chatting with their neighbours. Suddenly one female renouncer, well known for her vivid and fiery sermons, got to her feet and started berating the crowd for its inattentiveness—'Those who are not here to worship God', she said, 'should go home. You will get no fruit from sitting talking.' Order was restored, singing resumed, the renouncer sat down again, and the electricity promptly returned. Her popular standing was much improved.

6. The same distinction is used for slightly different purposes by Tambiah (1985: 135). We first saw that we needed this distinction as a result of conversations in Cambridge with Carlo Severi. This distinction has been used before in discussions of ritual, although usually for a purpose which is not our concern here, namely to argue that ritual is performatively efficacious in the context of questions and concerns about the rationality of religious and other beliefs. See Finnegan (1969), Tambiah (1981), Ahern (1982), and the critique of their arguments by Gardner (1983).

7. Searle (1969: 34) points out that the constitutive rules of a game include the rules which make clear 'the aim of the game', by which he means, for example, that in competitive games it is a matter of such a rule that each side is committed to trying to win. This aim is different from the purpose for which the game is played, which might be 'to win a championship', 'for fun', 'for money', 'to settle a bet', or whatever. We discuss the purposes of ritual in Ch. 8. Accepting what Searle here calls the aim of the game corresponds in the case of ritual to adopting the ritual stance.

8. We have mentioned above, in Ch. 2, the reasons why renouncers do not perform the 'material' parts of the *puja*.

9. In fact, the most common word now used for a lamp is taken straight from English: *laimp*.

10. Some people avoid the word '*naivedya*' and prefer to say '*mithai*' because they think of the former as having strong Hindu associations.

11. Alternative names for the sweets, and for the act of offering them, include *caru* and *navat*. Incense (*dhup*) and sandalwood (*candan*), which are rarely used outside some kind of ritual context, are called in *puja* too by these usual names. Fruit is referred to, both during *puja* and outside it, as *phal*. In addition, the words *dipak* and *dip* are not uncommon outside ritual contexts.
12. A phrase used by Stravinsky to describe Beethoven's music.
13. Sandalwood paste is called *candan*, after the wood itself. The paste also contains saffron (*kesar*). Saffron plays a greater part than does sandalwood in domestic ceremonies of a less distinctively Jain kind, and, as an especially valued food, would be familiar to a small boy. Saffron is also thought of as a 'hot', slightly stimulant substance, so despite its gorgeous smell and auspicious associations, some strict Jains are ambivalent about its use in Jain temples. One of the things that increased *religious* (as opposed to ritual) knowledge brings, is an awareness of issues such as this, and adoption of names which stress Jain themes and emphasize the discontinuity from more general Hindu practice.
14. A more knowledgeable person would call this *akshat*.
15. Of all the offerings and acts in the *puja* this had the most agreed meaning, and most people we met shared this man's view, but it was not universal. One respondent, an elderly lady who was quite sure of what she said, interpreted the four points of the swastika as *gyan, darshan, caritra*, and *arihant samsar*. These she translated as knowledge, philosophy, good character, and 'so I don't have to come into the world again'. In addition, by no means all people formed a swastika from their rice grains: some just left it in a pile, others formed three or four little swastikas together, others formed the more elaborate *nandyavarth*: a complicated hooked cross.
16. Cort himself, in search of a single 'meaning' for the *puja*, rejects the instruction given in the first pamphlet because it does not 'fit with' the meanings he gives for the offerings.
17. We said on p. 98 that there is never any call to correct what you have done in ritual on the grounds that it was not what you meant. This means that a certain kind of mistake does not happen. The 'mistakes' referred to in this chapter are of a different sort: they occur when one does not do what one thought the rule was, or when one learns one was mistaken about what the rule was, as distinct from not doing what one meant.

6

Apprehension and Cognition

WITH ritualization there is a new state of affairs which can be summed up by saying that actors both are and are not the authors of their acts. The relation between intention and action is transformed. This does not mean, as we have already remarked, that a person does not have thoughts and intentions when performing ritual. Such a person is not turned into an automaton or an unconscious subject of habit. Ritual acts are publicly stipulated cultural constructs, yet wide variations in how they are enacted and how they are thought about indicate that while they are in this sense not individual, they not completely shared either. In this chapter we compare the cognition of ritualized action with that of everyday action. We begin with a discussion of the physical nature of ritual action and its relation to language and narrative, then suggest the kinds of concepts people might hold of ritual acts, and finally explain why we have used the word archetype as an epithet for ritual action (it should be emphasized at the outset that we do not use this word in the Jungian sense).

Let us start with what Marcel Mauss called 'body techniques'. It is best to discuss these matters using an example, so we take up the flower *puja* again. As this occurs some way into a complete *puja*, the celebrant is already standing in a sacred space. Because she is to come close to the idol, she will be wearing a cloth mouth-covering. On a metal tray she has flowers, sandalwood paste, coins, and any other objects she is going to offer. She carries the tray in her left hand. With her right hand, in a gesture of wrist and fingers which it is very difficult for a European to imitate, she gently lays a flower-head on the idol or on a ledge in front of it. This prescribed act is not carried out irrespective of the external situation. So, for example, our celebrant may find that the statue has already been given flowers by other worshippers, and she must look for some cranny, perhaps the crook of an elbow, where there is space for her flower, where it will not fall off, and so forth. She has a certain amount of choice: it is not prescribed how many blooms should be placed, and a variety of kinds of flowers may be offered. The people we spoke to in the Dadabari temple said that the flowers should be whole and fresh, and have a sweet smell, so roses, jasmine, and frangipani blooms were preferred.

But we also saw marigolds, which have very little smell, being offered. The celebrant is not obliged to say any prayer when she makes this *puja*. If she likes, she might recite a verse she has learnt from her family or from a renouncer, or she might choose a verse from one of the booklets available at the temple. She is at liberty to think her own thoughts. Our task now is to explain what kind of act this is.

While action is perceived by an agent directly through his or her body, it nevertheless has an objective cultural dimension, and it is with this that we begin. Marcel Mauss long ago drew attention to what he called body techniques, 'the ways in which from society to society men know how to use their bodies' (1979: 97). Mauss observed that bodily movements, like walking, sitting, digging, and swimming, are specific to particular societies, and that even in one society they may change from generation to generation. Describing French swimming, he wrote,

The habit of swallowing water and spitting it out again has gone. In my day swimmers thought of themselves as a kind of steam-boat. It was stupid, but in fact I still do this: I cannot get rid of my technique. Here then we have a specific technique of the body, a gymnic art perfected in our own day . . .

But this specificity is characteristic of all techniques. An example: during the war I was able to make many observations, e.g. the techniques of digging. The English troops I was with did not know how to use French spades, which forced us to change 8,000 spades a division when we relieved a French division, and vice versa. This plainly shows that a manual knack can be learnt only slowly. Every technique properly so called has its own form. (1979: 99)

Mauss defines body techniques as actions which are 'effective' and 'traditional', which is to say that they are directed towards some goal and that they are learned, transmitted, and shared by all those in a particular social and cultural milieu. Thus, 'the constant adaptation to a physical, mechanical, or chemical aim (e.g. when we drink) is pursued in a series of assembled actions, and assembled for the individual not by himself alone but by all his education, by the whole society to which he belongs, in the place he occupies in it' (1979: 105). The ritualized acts of the *puja* consist of a substratum of just such body techniques, ways of sitting, walking, bowing, anointing, and so forth. The act of placing a flower could not be more simple, and yet it is done in a graceful Indian manner which is not the way a European would do it.

As far as we could tell, the physical actions in *puja* are not different from similar acts performed in other rituals and in everyday life. There are few actions in the *puja* which are not also done outside the temple.[1]

Perhaps anointing and waving lamps are the only ones which occur in this precise form only in ritual contexts.[2] Occasionally an action in the *puja* even seems to be 'modelled' on a secular activity, thus 'cradling' the mirror-image of the Jina is like the hugging and rocking of a baby. None of these body techniques, so far as we could tell, are restricted to Jains. They seem rather to be common to the broader regional and class groups of Indian society to which the Jains belong. Hindus and Buddhists all over the subcontinent also anoint statues with pastes made of various red and yellow substances. Although variation may be observed in the gestures employed, we suggest that these are not differences between religious groups, but rather differences between regions (between, say, north-west India and Sri Lanka) and between classes. All of this is to see the actions from outside, as objective 'social facts' in the Durkheimian tradition which Mauss helped to found. But people are also conscious of their actions.

While we argued in Chapter 4 that the intention with which a person performs a ritual act does not give their action identity or meaning, we tried to stress that such a person does, none the less, act intentionally. One of the ways he or she does this, which we have not yet mentioned, is the conscious 'direction' of the body. We find in Merleau-Ponty's *Phenomenology of Perception*, although the text is admittedly obscure, the most subtle account of this that we have come across. Merleau-Ponty, it may be remembered, described the difference between 'beckoning someone' and simply performing a flexion of the forearm without having any present or even imaginary partner in mind, an example of what he calls 'abstract movement'. We used this example in Chapter 4 to explain how the intentional quality in an action like beckoning is different in ritualized action. Here we wish to make a different point. Merleau-Ponty goes on to say that even abstract movement, action which is not relevant to any particular situation, involves consciousness.[3] 'To move one's body is to aim at things through it' (1962: 139). He argues that although people have concepts of space and time, it is not these 'worked-up' ideas which are at issue in bodily movement.

In so far as I have a body through which I act in the world, space and time are not, for me, a collection of adjacent points nor are they a limitless number of relations synthesized by my consciousness, and into which it draws my body. I am not in space and time, nor do I conceive space and time; I belong to them, my body combines with them and includes them. . . . My body has its world, or understands its world, without having to make use of my 'symbolic' or 'objectifying' function. (1962: 140–1)

This being in the world is prior and basic: 'Motility in its pure state, possesses the basic power of giving a meaning'. Merleau-Ponty argues that even if, subsequently, thoughts and perceptions of space and time are freed from this fundamental motility and spatial being, for us to be able to arrive at these developed conceptions of space it is first necessary that we should have been 'thrust into it by our body'.[4]

We suggest that this kind of basic, tied-to-movements 'directedness' persists in ritualized action, that is, it persists in the inseparable engagement of the individual with the very act he or she performs. This explains, for example, the irritated abruptness or careful gentleness with which someone may wash the idol, the large or small gestures with which they do lamp *puja*, or the fact that, if someone 'intends' to put sandalwood paste quickly on the forehead of the statue before rushing home to look after the children, they do in fact put the paste on this spot and do it quickly in their view.[5]

Merleau-Ponty makes clear, in his discussion of habit, that 'directed' motility need not imply consciousness of any very conceptual kind.[6] Just as the lady wearing a hat with a long feather 'knows' by habit how to keep a safe distance from things which might knock it off (1962: 143), so people enacting *puja*, at least by the time they are adults, have 'apprehended' with their bodies the acts they feel to be required. Imitation imperceptibly feeds an act into one's repertoire of activity so that it comes to seem that it had always been 'natural'. Thus adults 'know' without thinking about it how to take sandalwood paste without wetting the fingernail, and even if they do not know what to do next in a complex *puja*, they will probably feel they 'know' the stock of actions from which the ritual is built up. As Gilbert Ryle long ago pointed out (1949), in distinguishing 'knowing that' from 'knowing how', practical knowledge which people use in directing their action can be distinguished from knowledge they have about things in the world (which in this sense includes 'actions' as externally perceived objects of knowledge). Ritual acts are things of which people have both kinds of knowledge. The ritual commitment, a series of mental operations which can 'en-ritualize' any act, is thus a complex matter, because it is necessary to distinguish between the mental operations whereby people think about rituals (as constituted acts 'out there') and those by which their own actions are constituted as rituals. For example, someone might visit a temple and see *puja* going on and be able to give an account of it later; but this is different from taking part in the *puja*. The latter implies a commitment, which is, if you like, a kind of performative thinking (not a set of beliefs).

Our position thus differs somewhat from that of David Parkin in his interesting essay, 'Ritual as Spatial Direction and Bodily Division' (1992). Parkin observes that ritual, 'is an action that can only be understood as bodily movement towards or positioning with respect to other bodily movements and positions' (1992: 12). It is true that culturally established body techniques generally impose certain understandings: it would be difficult in Indian society to find someone worshipping a deity while turning her back to it, or making an offering by throwing a fruit at the statue. But Parkin's deduction from the fact of movement in time and space, that all rituals are in some way rites of passage and that participants necessarily 'make statements' through their movements, seems premature. We think that behind, as it were, the meaningful phasal sequences or gestural systems that can appear in ritual, there are simple acts to be done, with a cloud of diffused meanings before them as yet unrealized. Even directional acts in marked spaces do not necessarily make a vocabulary. Take a simple example from our own culture: the bishop ritually knocks at the cathedral door with his staff. Clearly he is going in. But why do we feel that there may be more to it than this, that maybe we should check with some knowledgeable person to find out what this rite is about? What after all is that staff with its strange shape? Is there a hint of aggressiveness in the way the bishop holds it? Why does he bang three times? We know that the bishop has actually been in and out of the cathedral before; in fact the ritualizing of entry subverts the simple movement of 'going in'.

To investigate the difference between acts and ritualized acts we need to step back from symbolism for a moment and discuss the relation between physical action and language. Cultural and cognitive anthropology has until recently more or less assumed that all conceptual thought is directly and necessarily dependent on language, both in the sense that linguistic categories provide the fundamental framework of thought (so that a study of a culture becomes an explication of a people's vocabulary) and in the sense that categories are represented in the mind in a 'language-like' form. Recent advances in cognitive psychology point in a different direction and prompt consideration of the variety of kinds of conceptual organization which we use to understand actions. We are indebted here to the collections and surveys by Johnson–Laird (1983), Quinn and Holland (1987), Neisser (1987), Lycan (1990), Stigler, Shweder, and Herdt (1990), Bloch (1991), and Boyer (1990, 1993), which outline and explore the significance of recent advances in cognitive psychology. A range of experimental evidence suggests that the knowledge we develop as we master practical tasks, and this includes the way children come to understand basic, everyday concepts, is not formulated in natural language (a child knows what a house is before knowing the word 'house'). Bloch stresses that the form this knowledge takes is not even like language, in that it does not have a sequential, logical form.

The knowledge which guides practice seems rather to take the form of loosely connected networks of meanings, or 'cognitive apparatuses', which are formed through the experience of, and through practice in, the external world, and which are dedicated to the particular tasks through which they are developed. As a result of repeated practice, the mind develops a dedicated apparatus to enable it to perform a familiar activity. Bloch describes how this process is reflected in the increased efficiency with which people perform such tasks.

When people are repeatedly asked to read a page of text upside down they gradually do this faster and faster, but the increase in speed is not continuous, nor does it go on for ever. At first there is a rapid increase in efficiency and this increase in efficiency continues for a while, then it begins to slow down, until eventually there is no further increase. (1991: 188)

Once formed, these networks enable us thereafter to perform these tasks with hitherto impossible facility and speed, but there is little or no improvment thereafter, indicating that the cognitive apparatus is now established. There is evidence that practical tasks can be transmitted in this way with little or no linguistic mediation (Lave 1990). This kind of process appears to happen in a wide variety of contexts where expertise in pattern recognition is a crucial cognitive task (Bechtel 1990), and these include such apparently intellectual processes as playing chess (Dreyfus and Dreyfus 1986). Bloch points out that under certain circumstances this non-linguistic knowledge can be rendered into language and thus take the form of explicit discourse; but in the process it changes its character. Reciprocally, in some circumstances the things we learn through language and the concepts we acquire in a linguistic form can be applied in developing practical mastery, but again this involves a definite transformation. Bloch remarks, 'If such transformations are commonplace, as I believe they are, we should then see culture as partly organised by connectionist networks and partly consisting of information organised by sentential logic, with a fluid transformative boundary between the two' (1991: 192).

Bloch argues that practical knowledge directing activity and discursive knowledge about it are fundamentally different in character, but that they are not independent. This is true both of a child's primary learning of concepts and of practical activity more generally. Bloch, characteristically, calls this interaction a 'dialectical' process. John Gatewood's paper on South Alaskan seine-net salmon fishing (1985) describes a process of just this kind, and we shall use his analysis, which gives a more substantive account of this interaction, to point to the differences between the cognition of ritualized and everyday intentional action. A ritual such as *puja* involves learned bodily tasks like those Gatewood describes, and the similarities between these two cases are also interesting.

Gatewood describes the cognitive organization of Alaskan purse seine fishing as divided first of all into tasks known by jargon names, such as 'making a set' or 'hauling gear'. After an initial period of confusion, the rookie (beginner) fisherman comes to think of a task such as 'making a set' as a linear order of jobs (what Gatewood calls a 'string of beads organization') and with practice he begins to understand each job as consisting of a distinct temporal segment which has its own character.

With experience, hauling gear, for example, becomes more than just a colorful addition to one's vocabulary and acquires all sorts of connotations. These connotations resonate through muscles that flex and contract in new ways. Thinking about hauling gear conjures moods of complex inner tensions. And these matters are distinct from simple linguistic mastery of the expression. When these kinds of feelings, these inner flowings, become patterned and regular through repeated activation, the seiner thinks of hauling gear in more than a linguistic framework. Now it is a temporal segment, an expression pregnant with meaning, a natural phase of seining. Its meaning is lodged in muscles as well as words. (1985: 208–9)

What is interesting about Gatewood's account is that he shows (1985: 209–10) for three different crew members that the linguistic expression 'making a set' does not denote a model, however malleable, which all seiners share. Rather, each seiner constructs his own version of the phases of a 'making a set', and each man does this on the basis of his own practical activity. Hence, each seiner builds up his own construction of 'making a set' out of the segments of activity he engages in. One man may divide 'making a set' into seven phases, another into only three, and each man's segmentation changes over time as he learns better how to do different parts of the whole procedure. A phase is always named, but this can be either by common seiners' jargon or by a fisherman's own phrase, which might be as vague as 'whole bunch of little things'. Such individualized segmentation occurs despite the fact that these men are working closely together, learning from observing one another, and all have a common goal. As Gatewood observes, his material seems to undermine two widely held views in anthropology: (1) that cognitive sharing is a prerequisite for successful social interaction and even more so for co-operative activities, and (2) that cognitive organization is simply internalized collective representations (1985: 210).

Collective representations of seining, on the other hand, are expressed in the narrative accounts which the fishermen use, when talking to one another, outsiders, and beginners, to represent seining discursively. These shared representations differ significantly from the personal representations which organize actions on the boat. But different fishermen's *narrative* accounts are substantially similar, even though the segmentations in terms of which they remember and understand their actions have neither the same elements, the same number of elements, nor coincident boundaries between elements. Gatewood concludes that the process of individual cognitive construction of segments of action involves an interaction between collective representations and one's own routine. Seiners' segmentations evolve as resolutions between two distinct modes of cognitive organization: (1) socially standardized but vague jargon terms for tasks, which are what seiners first encounter, and (2) the specifics of a given job routine, which vary from crew member to crew member and from year to year for the same person. But despite their vividness and subjective definiteness as chunks of action, the segments of which these representations are composed do not provide any sense of the process as a whole, nor do they ever become completely shared even between members of the same crew. The shared narrative 'story-like' accounts of fishing, on the other hand, can be learned and repeated by people— yarning in bars—who have never actually taken part in it (1985: 212–15).

What Gatewood describes is similar in important ways to what we observed and what we ourselves experienced as participants in the *puja*. The distinction he makes between narrative accounts and personal representations explains the fact that Jains could give us more or less common accounts of the structure of the *puja* as a whole (see the diagrams we gave in Chapter 2) which coincide in general with those described by Babb (1988) and Cort (1989) from Gujarat. Yet, as we observed, worshippers mostly do not follow these elaborate scripts or models in practice. Even when someone could give us a clear account of the *puja* structure, which was the case for around half of our respondents, the same person often did something observably quite different. Actual *puja* sequences were not defective forms of the narrated model, but more like a reshuffling of the pack of ritual acts. A celebrant would break off to repeat one segment ten times on different statues, or would miss out whole chunks, or would perform at the end some act which is 'meant to be' at the beginning, or vice versa. A complete sequential performance of the *puja* could of course occur, but in our experience this was quite rare and usually in a social or collective context, as when someone was demonstrating the *puja* or teaching it to someone else, or in collective *puja*s orchestrated by a specialist.

People do not start with models or scripts which they act out, but rather, through imitating acts which are previously named (but not necessarily well understood), they may gradually come to acquire more complex mental pictures of the act and its relations to other constituents of the whole. We do not claim that the practitioners simply observe ritual acts and accept them as being whatever they are told they are. Of course, people do have ideas of ritual acts, discuss them with one another, read books about them, and criticize and attempt to reform the practice of others. But the ability to do these things is based on having learned the sequential or nesting models contained in *discourse* about the ritual, and it is not necessary to have mastered such discourse, as we showed for the *puja* in the previous chapter, in order to be able to perform the rite. What comes first is a name attached to a jumble of actions. Particularly with lengthy, complex *puja*s, such as the *panc-kalyanak*, many non-specialist participants never get further than this. People can learn elaborate conceptual models of the *puja* without learning how to do it (by reading an article which describes them), but in practice most Jains learn these models, in so far as they do, only after they have learned to perform the rite. This is why we rejected the idea that discursive models of the *puja* are in any sense ontologically prior, that they underlie or explain what actually happens.

As Gatewood found with seine fishing, we became aware that ritual acts are seen as chunks ('First I do water *puja*, then sandalwood paste *puja*, then . . .'), and that such segments, as well as being foreclosed, are each felt to be different from each other and to have their own characteristic emotional tone. By 'foreclosed' we mean that the celebrant is aware of getting ready to enter such a segment and of emerging from it, and that these differ from the experience of 'being in', of doing, a segment. Gatewood writes,

The little tasks within a segment flow smoothly into one another and only rarely require conscious effort to remember what follows. By contrast, at the boundaries of segments, one typically has to think about where he is in the set and reorient psychologically to the upcoming, next segment. The little tasks within a segment are felt to be in some significant sense the same kind of work. (1985: 214)

The 'foreclosedness' which Gatewood points to is evident also in the *puja*. While people are in the midst of a segment such as flower *puja*, they are normally intently engaged, and when they have finished they look up, glance around, observe what other people are doing, and locate a free space in which to start the next act. It is at these interstitial points that they will cough, readjust their sarees round their heads, retie their mouth coverings, and so forth.

With ritualization indeed, this consciousness of the wholeness of a segment of activity is, we think, enhanced. As the *puja* shows, it is not simply the case in ritual that there are some acts which are ritualized and some which are not, but that those which are not (those which are excluded) must be definitely counteracted. This is different from everyday action. As we discussed in the previous chapter, many unritualized actions which take place in the temple, like putting money in collection boxes, combing one's hair to present a neat appearance, or tying on and taking off the mouth-covering are non-actions as far as the *puja* is concerned. In addition, there is the compendious category of unintentional faults (*ashatana*) such as yawning or stretching the limbs, which should not be allowed to occur and are punishable by minor penances. What this means is that ritualization does not simply ignore (as in everyday scripts) but also excludes, or represses, a great deal of what actually happens.[7] The stipulated acts are positively enhanced by being taught ostensively. They are learned in practice, and quite what comprises them is left conceptually unclear. A great deal of 'tacit knowledge' of what is happening is not accumulated and added to the picture of what is going on, but becomes psychologically irrelevant or suppressed. Thus, to go back to the flower *puja* example, carrying the tray, wearing a mouth-covering, not wearing shoes, and so forth, may be part of the flower *puja* schema when seen from outside, but to the celebrants they do not 'add up' to performing this ritual act in the way that digging, weeding, putting seeds in the ground, watering, and so on, contribute to gardening, or that pulling the breast line, helping Darrell, and hauling gear contribute to making a set.

One of the reasons we have chosen the seine fishing example is to emphasize that the distinctiveness of ritual action does not reside in its being in any sense 'impractical'. People achieve all kinds of very practical results by means of ritual, and no theory which presented it as intrinsically 'other worldly' could account for this. However, there are important differences between the cognitive organization of ritual acts and that of everyday activity. We can note, for example, that the mental segmentation of activity which Gatewood notes for fishing does occur in ritual, but it is not personal. As we pointed out earlier, the ontology of ritual action is socially stipulated. While, in learning the *puja*, you can see the stipulated acts as coming in sequences of different lengths or different kinds, and while you can 'reshuffle the pack' as we have described, you cannot break an act up or fuse it with another as you please. While it is possible to categorize the sequence of activities involved in fishing in various ways, it is not possible, say, for an individual to divide up bathing the statue into two halves and decide that only the first bit is *abhishek*, or to run bathing in with the offering of incense and call all this something else. Intervening in the interactive process described by Bloch, whereby discursively realized knowledge and the knowledge required to perform a task are mutually adjusted, is the fact that the basic repertoire of ritual acts is fixed. The celebrant accepts ritualized acts as already named and constituted.

When you learn to drive a car with manual transmission ('stick shift'), the account you are given in language starts with the general term 'changing gear'. This is broken down into two parts: 'moving the gear stick' and 'disengaging the clutch'. Initially, this second operation is quite difficult, and has to be explained as consisting of two separate things: pressing down the clutch pedal and at the same time releasing the accelerator just a little. In time these two things, with practice, are resolved into single action, which James's driving instructor, in his particular jargon, called 'a rocking motion'. Although this meant little at first, it was soon found helpful in co-ordinating the movement of the feet, and later came to be the name for what seemed like one action. We found the same to be true of the term '*candan puja*', which involves the actions of dipping the finger without wetting the finger-nail and putting a sufficiently large blob on the statue. The integration happens as the action enters the repertoire of what your body 'knows how' to do. With time, 'changing gear' becomes a single, integrated, and barely conscious action such that Caroline can no longer remember how she learned it. In ritual, this merging or differentiating of acts, as the focus of the actor's consciousness changes, is a psychological process but it does not affect the identity of acts, which are stipulated as wholes.

We have argued that this explains the 'filtering' effect, whereby all activity which does not contribute to the realization of a stipulated act is disregarded, and this in turn allows innovation and rearrangement on the level of action. But if a script or discursive model does not provide the initial framework for the understanding of ritual action, we still need to say quite what it is that is stipulated. People know a name for an act, they remember what they have been shown and can reproduce it. So what, apart from the name, do they remember? What does the name name? And how do people judge whether something they see counts as an instance of a particular ritual act? The answer we suggest, which will take up the middle third of this chapter, is that people learn a name for an action of which they have a simple mental representation or 'prototype', and that this prototype enables them to reproduce the act they have learned. This is true also for non-ritual acts. However, there is important difference in ritual action: the prototype does not, as is the case with everyday acts, enable people to confidently categorize observed actions by matching them against the range of prototypes they know.

We have more than once pointed out that ritual acts are named. As both Charles Taylor (1985: 187–8) and Sperber and Wilson (1986: 244) point out, actions in general are not always named, or indeed 'realized' linguistically at all. So what does the naming of ritualized acts imply? It is important not to assume that all words refer to the things they do in the same kind of way. This has been a familiar point in anthropology since Rodney Needham (1975) pointed out the relevance of Wittgenstein's celebrated discussion of family resemblance. Wittgenstein argued that there are no necessary features which all games have in common and in virtue of which a particular activity counts as a game. A family resemblance word such as 'game' can therefore be contrasted to analytical terms such as 'passport'. This word is fairly easy to define. It means, according to the *Shorter OED*, 'a document issued by competent authority, granting permission to the person specified in it to travel, and authenticating his or her right to protection'. The terms of this definition, if it is a good one, are necessary and sufficient conditions for inclusion in the class of passports. Philosophers used to take this kind of concept as paradigmatic, and anthropological analyses of cultural knowledge, such as the use of componential analysis, made parallel assumptions. But recent research suggests that the way we understand concepts rarely takes this form.

The work of Eleanor Rosch and others (see Rosch and Lloyd 1978) suggests that an important part is played in our understanding of everyday concepts by mental representations of typical instances, called prototypes, or schemata, and we suggest that the same is the case for ritual acts. The prototypical flower *puja* is represented as the simple action of placing a flower on a statue: this is the act which one is shown when learning the *puja*, and which one must be able to call to mind and reproduce subsequently. Similarly, we understand 'bachelor' with reference to a prototypical idea which is not the same as an analytic definition. So while it might be thought that we can simply define 'bachelor' as 'an unmarried man', we can see that while the Pope fulfils this definition, he is a long way from being a prototypical bachelor (see Quinn and Holland 1987: 23). There is no agreement in psychology about exactly what prototypes consist of, and some of the experimental evidence is conflicting, but the general idea, which at least in outline seems well established, is that they are 'representative samples' against which things in the world are matched. Instead of being composed of lists of necessary features, prototypes include 'default values', characteristics which we expect to be present unless there is evidence to the contrary. So we think of a dog as having four legs, fur, a tail, the ability to bark, and so on. A tailless or hairless dog can be recognized as a dog, although it would fail to be included in the category if what we did was to match it against a checklist of necessary conditions. Clearly, an idea of this kind would explain how we know how to use the word 'game'. The difference between prototypes and lists of necessary and sufficient conditions goes further than this, however, because the default values are not just listed, but arranged. Thus a table does more than just consist of legs and a top, the legs should actually support the top (Johnson-Laird 1983: 186). Similarly, 'Real objects, unlike the concepts studied in the psychological laboratory, have features that are correlated—feathers tend to be found on wings, scales on fins—and the pattern of correlations is reflected in the schema' (Johnson-Laird 1983: 190–1). As Johnson-Laird emphasizes, this means that our understanding of prototypical concepts involves us in making judgements, drawing on our experience of the way the world is (1983: 205–65).

This last point, however, does not apply to ritual acts, and here we begin to see how the cognition of these acts must differ from everyday examples like a 'dog', a 'bachelor', or a 'lie',[8] because complicated matters of context and everyday understanding, our knowledge of the way the world is, is actively suppressed. Ritual is a decontextualizing context.

Let us take an example which occurs in the *panc-kalyanak puja*. This elaborate rite, as we have mentioned before, commemorates the life of the Jina whose statue is being consecrated. Just before the celebration of the birth of the infant Jina, members of the congregation enact a scene in which, dressed as gods, they dig up some earth which they put in pots and 'sow' with seeds. According to Fischer and Jain (1977: 62) this represents 'fertility and all-round prosperity before the birth of a Jina'. However, it is not in its being ritualized that such an action is straightforwardly understandable—rather the reverse. If we see someone digging the earth in a garden, throwing away weeds and stones, putting on manure, watering the seeds, and so forth, we can understand what they are doing and would have no difficulty in identifying the script 'gardening'. On the other hand, we would definitely hesitate in attributing a symbolic or abstract meaning to the action, even one expressed in a sentence such as, 'This represents fertility and all-round prosperity.' It is different if the person, dressed in a tinsel crown, takes just a token spadeful from a marked off square of earth. Ritualization has stripped away most of the untidy activity of gardening, and this leaves a pared-down act, which is more suitable to carry a special meaning; but at the same time it has removed the clues to everyday understanding. Now we are not at all sure what is going on. Thus, although ritualized digging–sowing is not random as regards representing 'fertility' (it is a 'motivated sign' in Saussurean terms), it is not directly readable either. Nor would a postulated 'simplified world' of religious thought (a contradiction in terms in the case of the Jains) be a solution. In fact an observer knowing something about Jainism would still be very puzzled, since in real life Jains avoid actions like digging which destroy micro-organisms in the earth and they also tend to recoil in disgust from things teeming with life-matter such as live seeds. We would have to be *told*, as the Jain *pandit* told Fischer and Jain (1977: 17), that what is being represented is a religious idea, the miraculous increase in wealth and fertility on earth which accompanies the birth of a Jina.[9] And in lengthy or complicated pieces of ritualized action, despite massive and overt linguistic intervention, it is frequently the case that people are quite unable to connect what they see, or what they are told to do, in any intelligible way with the prototypes and schemata they have about the way the world is.

At a *panc-kalyanak* which Caroline attended the presiding *pandit* had a different idea about the episode of the seedlings from that reported by Fischer and Jain, and on this subject he gave a lengthy sermon. For him they represented religious rebirth: the growth of new souls in the devout Jains attending the rite. 'There are 50,000 people here,' he said, 'If just a few of them go away with new souls I shall be satisfied.' He preached vehemently against what he saw as his congregation's tendency to make literal intepretations of the rites: 'You say this is God's birthday. But the first rule of God is that he is never born. So how can he have a birthday?' He was making a distinction between physical birth, which is polluting, and the birth of new souls. 'A child is born,' he intoned, 'but God is never born.' People seemed mystified by this line of argument. In the somnolent heat of the huge marquee, the thousands of people present dozed or listened impassively. On the stage were similar pots to those 'planted' earlier in the morning, now with growing seedlings, and, following the sermon, people representing gods and goddesses took it in turns to read lines from slips of paper, 'Everywhere you look there is happiness and wealth,' 'When the god is born, what shall we do?', 'Rejoice! Rejoice!' (See Plate V.) One aged lady was silent when it came to her turn, perhaps she was too frightened or too old, or perhaps she could not read. After a pause an announcer declared through a megaphone, 'We are too happy to speak.' Another sermon followed. A few people in the congregation keeled over, frankly asleep. Then the king of the gods said, 'So many tens of thousands of people have come here to see the birth of the God,' and the queen followed with, 'No, they have come to see Ravindra Jain.'[10] This at least roused a smothered laugh, though the queen looked round, puzzled and abashed. No reference at all was made to the seedlings, which seemed to have a role like the accoutrements of royalty (crowns, fans, a throne) also present on the stage. The attribution of any meaning at all to this episode is, we feel sure, intermittent at best. Despite evident ritualization, it is only the apparent transparency of actions like planting seeds in pots, also done by Hindus in different ritual circumstances,[11] quite apart from the seemingly everyday character of the act, which could lead observers to think it must have meaning *in itself*. Our earlier arguments suggest that this is not just an ethnographic mistake but the wrong approach in principle to ritualized acts.

Thus while the action of digging some earth, or of planting seeds, is recognizable as a version of a similar act in the everyday world, such an act cannot be understood by drawing on the encyclopaedic knowledge, the schema, or the prototype we might have of the everyday action. The episode at which the seedlings are displayed has two parts, known as the *Indra Sabha* and the *Raja Sabha* (the assemblies of the gods and the kings) and both are part of the *garbha kalyanak* (the auspicious stage of conception of the Jina). Everyone is well aware of this from announcements and printed programmes. People accept that what they see going on at this point, whatever it is and however little sense it might make, just is the *garbha kalyanak*. According to the theory of prototypes you have a mental model of a prototypical dog, let us say, and you use the word 'dog' to refer to anything resembling your model. This has the advantage, as an account of everyday thinking, that it allows for marginal cases. 'A crucial datum corroborating the theory is that not all instances of a concept are deemed equally representative—a robin is a prototypical bird, whereas a chicken is not—and such judgments seem to depend on "distance" from the schema' (Johnson-Laird 1983: 191). A wide range of verb categories also

PL. IV. *Three Shvetambar nuns.* This photograph was taken in an *upashraya* at Palitana, Gujarat, in 1983. The nun in the foreground is demonstrating the use of a rosary. On her lap is the brush she uses for sweeping insects away before sitting down.

PL. V. *A layman and his wife as Mahavir's parents.* During the installation of a Jina idol in a *panc-kalyanak puja*, these people enact the parts of the Jina's parents. They are holding slips of paper from which they will read their lines.

show this 'graded structure' effect. In experiments, 'grasp' is consistently judged to be a better exemplar of 'hold' than is 'squeeze' or 'hug'; 'murder' is a better exemplar of 'kill' than is 'execute' or 'commit suicide' (Pulman 1983: 116, 132). But this, if it perhaps applies in many areas of everyday life, does not work for ritual acts. Although people must actually have a mental prototype of a ritual act like flower *puja*, which enables them to remember and reproduce the act, it does not follow that there are distant versions which are less representative as instances of the act. Not only the act of placing a flower on a statue is flower *puja*. Decorating a whole statue with a variety of different coloured blooms is flower *puja*. So is wandering round a temple, placing flowers here and there, or laying a single flower on a ledge, or dropping a huge bag of them from a helicopter on to the head of a giant monolithic statue.[12] It is still and no less a flower *puja* if you stand some distance from a statue and make the gesture of placing a flower, although you do not have one in your hand and you could not reach the statue if you did, or if you sit cross-legged on the floor of the temple and rehearse to yourself the meaning of the flower *puja*. They are all, by fiat, acts of flower *puja*. Thus, to return to the earlier example, there is no set of actions which *might* be *garbha kalyanak*, which you weigh up to see if they resemble your idea of *garbha kalyanak* or not. Nor does *garbha kalyanak* consist of a set of things such that some activity could come close to being it by having just some of these characteristics. One has to be told that some activity is *garbha kalyanak*, or to decide that this activity is it, and in performing an activity as *garbha kalyanak* these very actions do become it.

In some cases indeed the name may be *all* that is publicly agreed about a ritual and can provoke, rather than settle, doubt and dispute. Take blood sacrifice (*bali*), which although still widespread in Hinduism attracts much criticism and condemnation in India today, and is practised less than in the recent past (Fuller 1992: 83–105). In order both to conform to reformist pressure and so claim a high religious status, and yet at the same time to propitiate a deity who is believed to demand sacrifice, priests in Brahmanical temples carry out 'sacrifice' (*bali*) using vegetarian surrogates such as pumpkins or melons. But debate continues about whether these rites are 'really' *bali*, whether they are the same archetypal act, regardless of apparent surface differences, as the bloody slaughter of a buffalo. In the case of the Jains, whose deities are generally required to be as uncompromisingly vegetarian as they themselves are, even surrogate sacrifice is generally felt to be sacrifice, in that negative 'external' sense which Jainism has always rejected. One famous Jain epic poem is centrally concerned with the terrible consequences of a sacrifice of a chicken-shaped blob of dough (see Handiqui 1949).

So while ritual acts cannot be defined in terms of necessary and sufficient conditions, neither does the idea of a prototype quite capture all the characteristics of the cognition of ritual acts. Our use of the term 'archetypal' is intended to express a radical break from everyday action.[13] Ritualization creates a different form of knowledge: a different way of thinking about, and a different way of organizing acts. Thus, in the case of our ritualized planting of seeds, it can be seen that ritualized acts may be 'refined' in the sense that extraneous actions (watering, putting on manure) are cut away, but this is not to say that the ritualized act remains merely as a residue, which is the same as its everyday agricultural counterpart. The difference is that the ritualized act, which is socially prescribed and separately named, is already torn from instantaneous and purposeful everyday existence. It is archetypal in the following two senses. It is not the act which it mimics (no seeds actually grow, and the woman who 'cradles' during the *puja* does not hold a baby in her arms). Furthermore, the ritualized act is no longer just that action; it is now treated as a token of its stipulated type. As we have said, the stipulated act is something like an exemplar, and any enactment of it is an instance or example both of its previous appearances in the acting subject and of its performance by others. This is a result of the actor's progressively coming to have a mental picture of what the act is.

So we should treat with care Eichinger Ferro-Luzzi's idea (1981) that the problems in defining or categorizing ritual acts are solved by thinking of them, in the manner recommended by Needham (1972), as 'polythetic categories'. This idea designates overlapping assemblages of actions, none of which are universally present and none of which therefore defines the act. From an observer's point of view such an idea seems a correct designation, for example of 'the *puja*' as it is done by Jains, Hindus, and Buddhists in various ways all over the subcontinent. However, it does not work for the actors, who accept that certain key acts are prescribed for their own community, while being perfectly aware that other people do *puja* differently. People may or may not be able to give an account of the various components of *abhishek* and place them in a sequence. But woolliness on this point is not because the worshippers think, '*Abhishek* can be defined this way, and it can be defined that way'; rather, people will say that *abhishek* is certainly a specific thing, but that they have only imperfect knowledge of what it is.

We suggest that these contrasts between ritual and other practical activity can be explained by the idea that ritual acts are treated as elemental, that is, that each stipulated type of ritual act is thought of as if it were a separate 'thing' each with its own essential character. Our discussion of this point is necessarily provisional, and we want here only to point out that the ritual stance implies treating the acts as if this were the case (it implies no particular beliefs). We are aware that to take this idea further would require detailed psychological testing, preferably in a range of cultural and religious contexts, so our analysis here, which is largely conceptual, must therefore also be provisional. The best way to proceed for the present, we think, is to suggest that, as used by the actors, the names for ritual acts are in significant respects like the words we use for natural kinds.[14]

It has been argued (Kripke 1980; Putnam 1975, 1977, 1983; Schwartz 1977) that the terms we use to designate natural kinds work like proper names. It is important to distinguish the psychological and linguistic observations which are adduced in this literature from the metaphysical arguments which these observations have sometimes been used to advance. We shall argue only that ritual acts are treated in significant respects like natural kinds, not that they are really natural kinds, so none of the metaphysical issues (necessary truth and so on) arise. We do not need even to suppose that natural kinds really do exist, or really do have a common underlying structure. The point is just that they are treated differently from artefacts and other things of human invention. The difference may be explained as follows. Chairs, homes, and novels, let us say, are artefacts.[15] They all exist in the world, but they do not do so independently of social convention and human imagination. Their characteristics are the outcome of social negotiation and are open to change. Gold, lemons, and horses by contrast are, let us suppose, natural kinds. Their existence and their nature are natural facts. The idea we are interested in is that this distinction, whether or not it is metaphysically valid, is reflected both in linguistic usage and in the kind of prototype people have of these things. Scientists have theories about the molecular structure of gold, and the genetic properties of lemons and horses, and these 'underlying essences' are regarded as things which might eventually be discovered. Chairs, homes, and novels, by contrast, are things which people, collectively, invent. The idea is that use of these two kinds of term differs in a way which stems from a difference in the attitude which speakers take to the things the terms refer to. This is part of a more general point to the effect that the representations people have of things in the world are affected by the kind of things they are taken to be, so the relation between concepts and the things to which they refer works in various ways (Johnson–Laird 1983: 195).

Prototypes of artefacts and those of natural kinds consist of different elements and they play different roles in cognitive and linguistic practice (Keil 1987). Prototypes of artefacts depend on convention, intention, use, and function. A thing can diverge from the prototype of, say, a chair, in terms of observable features, yet still count as a chair. It does not have to have a flat seat and a more or less vertical back; it does not have to have four legs; it does not need to be made of any particular substances. It does have to be for sitting on, so that a Le Corbusier recliner and a tiny doll's chair are still chairs. The meaning of constructive or artefactual terms, their intensions (the sense of the words), are the prototypes we, in our language community, collectively sustain. Their extensions are whatever we agree with fellow speakers, broadly and at a given time, count as members of the class.

Prototypes of natural kinds (let us take the example, 'gold') do not refer to use or function (we would scarcely worry about 'fool's gold' if they did) but to more or less superficial observable features. They are designed to pick out a 'stuff' the true nature of which, although not securely known at least to most of us, is presumed to be an objective fact. This means that occasionally something may be revealed by a scientist to be a member of a natural kind which does not have the characteristics of the commonly held prototype. People's prototypes do not define what gold is; they are no more than the clues they have about what things might be made of gold.[16] Most people think of gold as being yellow, metallic, and shiny, but would acquiesce if told that something was 'white gold'. Thus in the case of natural kinds there is a 'social division of labour' about the features people have in their prototype, and experts look for other, harder to spot but none the less basically observable characteristics (like melting point or tarnishing). The intension of these terms is ultimately unknown—our scientists' theories are always corrigible—and their extension is whatever the experts say that they think, for the moment, ought to count. To count as what? Well, to count as being 'that stuff'.[17] What the use of these terms seeks to maintain is that people all refer to the same stuff as has been referred to before, using the same term. To be a competent user of the term 'gold' does not in fact require of people that they share the experts' or each other's theories about the stuff. Indeed, in using the term, they refer to just 'that stuff', whatever it is.

It may seem odd for us to suggest that ritual acts, which are after all things that are constructed by people, are nevertheless thought of in the same way that people conceive of natural kinds. This is a bold claim, but not any odder than the phenemenon of ritual itself. This transposition of a way of thinking about natural kinds on to a form of human action appears to endow these acts with a peculiar facticity, and it is this that we are pointing to in calling them elemental and archetypal. Let us be clear, we are not saying that ritual acts are natural kinds, but that people treat different instances of the same acts as objects sharing the same essence, and the result of this is that the acts may be given different meanings and purposes. In effect these different explanations are theories (like scientists' theories about molecular structure) about what that essence is.

To summarize our argument so far: natural-kind terms differ from artefactual terms in a way which does not rely on their actually having an underlying essence, but only in their being treated, cognitively and linguistically, as if they did. Let us repeat, our claim is not that ritual acts are, actually, distinct kinds of stuff like gold and salt, but that they are treated as if they were. Natural-kind terms are mentally represented by prototypes, and as we have said, people do seem to have ideas of proto-typical *puja* acts, but they do not use their prototypes to decide whether a certain act is or is not to count. Natural kind terms admit of a division of labour, a speaker can use the word 'elm' without knowing anything about how elms differ from other trees, and still successfully refer to just those trees. No one supposes that they can define 'elm' how they like, for they assume that there is a fact of the matter about what elms are. The idea that ritual acts are represented as natural kinds thus explains how a person can accept someone else's (ritual experts', parents', teachers') definitions or theories about the real or underlying 'essence' of his or her own acts (however, see Chapter 9). People can have terms to refer to, and proto-types to represent ritual acts, without knowing what they are. From the point of view of the ritual stance, the ritualized act has its own underlying and to some degree mysterious nature. It is what it is, irrespective of the actor's thoughts and intentions. This, we think, is what Lévi-Strauss had noticed when he remarked of magical and ritual actions that, 'From the point of view of the agent . . . [they] appear to him as additions to the objective order of the universe: they present the same necessity to those performing them as the sequence of natural causes, in which the agent believes himself simply to be inserting supplementary links through his rites' (1966: 220–1). That ritual acts should be thought about in a way which is parallel to thinking about natural kinds is thus directly implied by commitment to the ritual stance, by the way the actor in ritual sees his or her own action. As observers, however, we must add that it has these characteristics only because of the commitment with which it is enacted and which is constitutive of ritualization itself.

Our word 'commitment' does some of the same work as Rappaport's idea of 'acceptance' (1979: 194–5) and this has helped us in thinking about the question of why humans have ritual at all. Rappaport writes about 'acceptance of the liturgical order' that (1) it is not necessarily a grave matter (that is a question of whatever the liturgical order represents); (2) it does not imply any particular personal beliefs; (3) it is a public act, apparent to the performer and others; and (4) that acceptance is thus *the* fundamental social act, and it 'forms a basis for public orders which unknowable and volatile belief or conviction cannot'. Because acceptance of ritual order does not imply an inward state directly related to it, 'it is in some sense very profound, for it makes it possible for the performer to transcend his own doubt by accepting in defiance of it'. This makes deceit and insincerity also possible in ritual. But if ritual did not constitute itself this way there would be the certainty of disorder or non-order. Public order cannot rest on the constant acquiescence of individual belief. Thus Rappaport concludes that though the possibility of insincerity and deceit are the very acts that make social life possible, ritual renders them irrelevant.

In Chapter 4 we noted that ritual as a type of action has the particular characteristic of being both socially contingent and universal. The example we used to make this point is that ritual is socially and culturally institutionalized, like promising and thanking, but it must be more than this, because unlike them ritual is found in all societies. We can now go some way to saying what the 'more than this' consists in. It lies in the social (or perhaps we should write Social) act of commitment, which constitutes the acts to be performed as 'elemental' and 'archetypal', that is, understood as separated from one another and having some real essential nature in the same way that natural kinds are presumed to do.

We have refered to ritual acts as 'elemental', as being represented in the same way as a unique kind of stuff whose essential nature is unknown. However, it might be argued that however things are now, surely the form and occurrence were established at the beginning, at the inception of the rite, when people did know exactly what they were doing and why. Was there not an original moment when purposes, beliefs, and causes-in-the-world combined with intentions to establish the form of the rite?

We maintain that although such moments have of course occurred in history, what they established was a practice, not yet ritualized. For ritualization to set in there needs to be a distancing effect, whereby acts, materials, and even one's own body in ritual action become 'objects' and mentally reclassified, as we have said, differently from ordinary intentional action. How this happens—through pious repetition of the same acts, or governmental edict, or the common thinking only possible in very small groups, or the power of charismatic imagination—must vary in different social and historical circumstances.[18] Even with the best information, it is extremely difficult to specify for any given practice when this ritualization actually happens, and impossible for those like the Jain *puja* whose origin is unknown and probably piecemeal. Perhaps all we can say is that ritualization has occurred when it is possible to stand outside and comment on the practice, to regard it as an 'object', to give it one's own meaning or to change it (an 'object' is such when its presence entails a possible absence, that is, when its presence is no longer indissolubly tied to (is part of) the achievement of purposes).

This can be illustrated from what is probably the best-studied ritual of all, the Christian Eucharist. Even here the inception of the practice as a ritual activity is hidden in a thicket of different possibilities. Feeley-Harnik's study of early Christianity shows that right from the beginning there were several components in the practice of the commemorative meal which were chosen from a range of already ritualized practices.

When Christ enjoined his disciples, 'This do in remembrance of me', he was already drawing on a multifarious complex of meanings, centered on the Passover and on Judaic dietary laws and commensual practices; and in these respects he was not inventing an integral significance that would constitute the unique explanation of the subsequent enactment of the rite. (Feeley-Harnik 1981)[19]

How did this 'multifarious complex' become ritualized in a uniquely Christian way? As John Drury (1990) rightly observes, momentous events, the crucifixion of Jesus or the fall of Jerusalem, not only powerfully affect the existing symbolic structures by which the world is understood, but at the same time they must be made new sense of by means of these same existing structures in order to attain the 'significance' which persists in religion.[20] He asks, with reference to the origin of the Eucharist:

How can we locate the one point at which the event became significant? We may say that Jesus himself, by what he said and did at his Last Supper, stamped his death with significance. We may say that the coincidence of his death with the symbolic activities of Passover gave it such significance. A few bold spirits might even attribute that coincidence to Christian artifice . . . paying even more tribute to the vigour of early Christian imagination. We may say that the commemoration of that death in the symbolic Christian Supper which Paul found gave him his theology of the cross; or that Paul stamped that theology on the Supper (after all the Christian Supper in *The Didache* has a different and much less cross-centered theology).

The question asked here, about when 'the event' became significant, is not perhaps quite the same as asking when and how it became ritualized, but the series of possibilities is instructive none the less. In the years between Christ's death and the composition of the Gospels, the Lord's Supper was celebrated independently of the Temple and was, it seems, carried out in various quite informal ways in people's houses. The practice was not yet sacramental, though it was regulated by Jewish dietary laws. The purpose seems relatively straightforward: this was the occasion and means for the remembrance of Christ's living presence and of His death. We cannot know when the Lord's Supper started to become ritualized, but it was definitively so when, forty years later, Paul *chose* it to bear his own theology of sacrifice and his vision of Christianity as a universal religion. It makes no difference from our point of view whether, historically, Paul's decision was in fact the vital moment in constituting the Eucharist, or whether he found and stamped his authority on an already ritualized act.[21] We need only note that subsequent Christian ritual practice presumes that what Paul was doing was interpreting an already existing 'objective' ritual act. He was standing outside the rite and offering what he thought was the right theory of its 'underlying essence', not reflecting on an action of his own and telling people what he, as it happens, meant by it. What he did was to take up the commemorative purpose, combining it with the sacrificial Passover tradition celebrated in the Temple, and insisting on the inclusion of the Gentiles. He allegorized the bread in terms of moral qualities (as many of our Jain respondents did the objects used in *puja*).[22] So even if Paul's interpretation is not actually the baptism which many Christians would take it to be, and while it might be the case that no such single event could ever be identified, for the practice to be ritualized requires that the actors' attitude to it is that such a sacralizing event has happened.

The Last Supper itself cannot possibly be seen as a ritualized act,[23] but the subsequent commemoration of that supper did become so, and this can be said because it could now represent *various* and *symbolic* purposes and meanings. In the process of becoming the ritualized Eucharist, the practice of the Lord's Supper had to be codified or rigidified in a form which, precisely because that form became fixed irrespective of the purposes people had for performing it and of the meanings they attached to it, could admit, even at this early date, of the religious interpretation proposed by Paul as well as those other, different interpretations of other groups of Christians. Gerholm (1988: 195) has pointed to the fragmentation of meaning characteristic of ritual, to its 'hard surface' which allows, and indeed we would say provokes, a dispersal of experiences. We would agree with Parkin (1992: 18–19) who argues further that, 'for rituals in general, there must be contestation'.

While some of the participants in a ritual may well insist on the possibility of exact ritual replication, others are likely to see error and confusion in the conduct of a ritual. The standardizers and the disputants reproduce our own epistemological differences: between those seeking true representation in the correct reproduction of ritual and other events and those wrestling with the paradox of family resemblances between successive rituals.

'Protestantism' perhaps contains in itself the seed of this idea, since this cast of mind tends to constitute ritual as merely commemorative. Revisions always take the form of new theories about what the 'real' (original, ordained, authentic, divinely decreed, or 'reborn') nature of the act is. But despite this, for both Jains and Protestant Christians the unique first event, the death of Mahavir, the death of Christ, is utterly unlike any subsequent ritual commemoration or enactment. The line that is subsequently traced by the devout between the present enactment and the 'original' act should not blind us, as it does not blind these people, to the categorical change initiated by ritualization.

It is far more common for the real history of ritual acts to be ignored or systematically obliterated in order to give legitimacy to present practices, and sometimes new forms of ritual acts are presented as nothing other than the old.[24] Jains are unusual in acknowledging that they took on various parts of the *puja* from Hindu society, but the point is that they assimilated them as ready-formed acts, immemorial parts of Indian culture. There is another possibility: some religious traditions, such as certain branches within Judaism, acknowledge particular leaders as having ordained the rituals to be performed. Here, these leaders must be sanctified (in this case must be acknowledged as a messiah) and therefore their decisions about ritual stand for more than personal choice. Thus, in one way or another, ritualized acts stand beyond individual volition or invention. When new practices are established they must acquire this characteristic of distance or externality before we (or the practitioners) see them as ritual.

Let us consider now a less weighty example: a possible case of still incomplete ritualization. A trainee pilot in the RAF is taught, before entering the cockpit, to circumambulate his aircraft, and as he does so, to kick the tyres, wiggle a few of the catches (but not to touch some delicate pieces of machinery) and to look at some specific parts, like the rudder and the flaps. If he later moves to a civilian airline, he will still 'do the walk round' as it is called, of his jumbo jet, but will no longer be able to reach or see the things he is supposed to 'check'. His circumambulation will consist of little more than perhaps kicking the tyres and squinting far above him at the parts of the aircraft on the list he learned. It is probably now still possible to verify that the origin of this practice lies in a time when a pilot could check that his technicians and mechanics had done all they were supposed to. But the point at which this started to be ritualized, we suggest, is the moment when quite what the pilot touched and avoided touching, looked at and kicked, ceased to be a matter of his own technical competence or his confidence in the particular mechanics at work that day, and became instead, from his own point of view, a matter of stipulation. It is at this point too, when the acts to be performed were encountered 'ready made', that people would first have given the practice a 'symbolic' meaning, such as the ones which are popular today: that the pilot is taking over control of the aircraft and everything is now in his hands,[25] that it represents the idea of 'captaincy', that flight-crew are superior to technicians, or that nothing should happen on the aircraft that the pilot does not see or know about.

With these examples we try to convey the double character of the externality of ritual acts: they are thought of as both ontologically and historically prior to the actor's own performance of them. It is in this sense that we have used the word 'archetypal'. But we must repeat that we do not employ the term in its Jungian sense: we do not think our archetypes derive from particular collective experiences of humankind as a whole, nor, very emphatically, that they have universal symbolic meanings.

We have been emphasizing the externality, to individuals, of ritualized acts. The standard anthropological account of phenomena such as these, in the tradition derived from Durkheim and Mauss, is that they are objective sociocultural categories, parts of larger classifications, codes, or structures which function to maintain a particular cultural or social order. In such accounts the relation of these structures to the individual subject is of course notoriously obscure (a point to which we return in the next chapter). We have been proceeding here along a different path, attempting to outline the objective characteristics of ritual action as it is constituted by thinking subjects. Yet when Gatewood mentions the characteristic 'ethos' of practical actions, he points in effect to the limitations of a purely intellectualist analysis—and this is all the more evident when one is dealing with religious ritual. Charles Taylor rightly observes,

Human beings are self-representing animals. This means among other things that there is no adequate description of how it is with a human being in respect of his existence as a person which does not incorporate his self-understanding, that is, the descriptions which he or she is inclined to give of his emotions, aspirations, desire, aversions, admiration, etc. What we are at any moment is, one might say, partly constituted by our self-understanding. (1985: 189)

In other words, it is not sufficient to provide an explanation of how people understand action, we need also to think about what attitudes they have to it, and to themselves performing it. The following chapters of this book are in one way or another all attempts to understand ritualized action in this perspective. Up till now we have been discussing how people think about ritualized action, we now attempt to explain how they think about themselves performing it.

The fact that body movements are basically 'directed' in the way we described above, that they 'possess the basic power of giving a meaning' to use Merleau-Ponty's expression, does not mean that all actions are enveloped in a clear thought. Taylor (1985: 84) develops this idea more fully than Merleau-Ponty when he writes that action may be totally unreflecting; it may be something carried out almost without awareness. We may then become clearly aware of what we are doing, and formulate our ends. A degree of awareness is something we come to achieve. It is important for the argument of this book that the unreflectingness of everyday life, which may be a matter of deep-dyed habit, distraction, unfamiliarity, or perhaps even stupidity (all of which also occur in ritual), is qualitatively different from the absence of personal authoredness which confronts the actor when faced with a ritual act he or she should perform. When it is being done, an act like flower *puja* is 'comprehended' as the actor's own gesture of wrist and fingers directed towards relinquishing the flower on the statue, but *pushpa puja* as a concept may well be something of a blank,[26] and this is not because one is failing to concentrate or is the slave of habit but because the act in this stipulated form is not one's own. And yet it is 'I', as a self-reflecting being, who perform it. It is this which supplies a clue about the quality of the actor's relation with ritual acts. We describe ritual acts as 'apprehensible', to try to express the idea that they are, as it were, waiting for, and apt for, the achievement of self-interpretation.

This apprehension may be the starting point for more extended religious reflection. Although we leave a detailed discussion of this point until later, it is worth considering here what connection there may be between the ritual act as something physically enacted and as a socially prescribed archetype. The reader will notice that many of the meanings attributed to the flower *puja* have something to do with the physical nature of flowers and that they are always related to the self. For example,

A middle-aged man. 'The flower is soft. Like this our heart must be soft. By putting flowers we remove anger and put good morals in our heart.'

Or,

A young businessman: 'It is said that flowers have scent. We know many smells in this life. We put flowers so that we don't get distracted by beauty and pleasant scents. We give them to God instead.'

Although responses to our questions inevitably took the form of linguistic statements, it is possible, to judge from the frequency with which they referred to visual, olfactory, auditory, and taste sensations, that a central feature of attitudes to ritual acts is non-linguistic. This could be true even though people encounter ritual as named acts, since a name need not be seen as crystallizing a more complex conceptual schema but may function in a purely denotative way—the name denotes something which is observed and experienced. In this case the 'prior' encounter is with the phenomena, the physical acts and objects, denoted in this way, and what we know of how both children and adults learn the *puja*, as we described in the previous chapter, suggests that this is so for the Jains. Perhaps Wittgenstein (1979: 17) was on the right track after all when he wrote about the celebrated Beltane festival.

We feel like saying: it is too meaningless to have been invented in this form. Isn't it like this when I see a ruin and say: that must have been a house once, for nobody would have built up hewn and irregular stones into a heap constructed like this one. And if someone asked, how do you know that? I could only say: it is what my experience of people teaches me. And even where people really do build ruins, they give them the form of tumbledown houses.

Rodney Needham (1985: 175–6), we think, missed the point when he took Wittgenstein to task for assuming that the Beltane must once have had an intrinsic meaning which was the origin of the rite.[27] We agree with Needham that there is no reason to suppose the origin of a rite to be any clearer than present performances, but we think that Wittgenstein may have been getting at something else in this passage. Is he not, rather, saying that people feel rituals must be meaningful, and in the absence of any other clues they 'read back' from the muddling forms of what is actually done to some concept, to some whole idea? Some religions—and Jainism is an example—may encourage coherent formulation of religious ideas more than others.

What seems essential here is the feeling actors have when performing religious rituals that they are joining up with something outside themselves. This need not imply any particular concepts. Although Jains, being highly literate and interested in religious ideas, commonly do spontaneously come out with elaborate religious ideas (we observed this irrespective of our questioning), a more amorphous, feeling-based attitude is not foreign to them, 'Ritual . . . is the enjoyment of what is beyond us, until devotion becomes ecstasy and we feel that we are what we considered to exist outside us, that we are one with the goal, and that the ideal is realized within ourselves' (J. Jaini 1916: 74). It is with this idea, that the attitude to archetypal ritual acts need not (though it commonly does) imply the attribution of specific propositions or symbolic concepts, that we end this chapter. Ritual acts are apprehensible, but this does not mean that they are necessarily apprehended in a conceptual way. Several of our respondents said, for example, that the scent of flowers helps to concentrate the mind.

An elderly woman. 'We put flowers because of the smell. Flowers must smell or they are not allowed. If you have no flowers, then you can use cloves, as they have a flower shape and have a good smell. The smell helps to concentrate the mind; it fascinates and attracts people, so they will take pleasure in worshipping.'

Another woman said that she put scent on the idol so she should not get distracted, and many people observed how difficult it is to attain and maintain concentration during the *puja*. We cannot be sure what these people had in mind when they talked about 'concentration' (although some used the English word), but it seems evident that between the consciousness of performing a physical act and the realization of particular religious concepts there are intervening states of mind of various kinds.

Incomparably the most important of these, as virtually all our respondents made clear, is *bhav*, which means literally 'that which has come to be', but which our friends used in the sense of 'devotion' or 'religious sentiment'. *Bhav* is not already there; it has to be attained, or in the words of one of our friends, 'The aim of performing the *puja* is to make *bhav* rise in us.' We could perhaps say that *bhav* is in the enactment (the union of self and act). It seems to us, as we shall describe in detail in Chapter 9, that *bhav* precedes explicit concepts, and is the medium within which religious meanings come to be realized and attributed to ritual archetypes. But *bhav* is an emergent state of mind which can lead in another direction too, not towards explicit conceptual formulations, but to absorption in the physical act itself and trance-like altered states of consciousness. This we discuss in Chapter 10.

This chapter has attempted to outline the implications for a study of ritual acts of our conviction that humans are self-interpreting beings. People are inevitably conscious of themselves at some basic level as they engage in movements and actions, and in the case of ritual acts they further engage with the act as something in a sense outside themselves (as elemental or archetypal). The subsequent move to apprehend these archetypal acts takes place as people arrive at their senses of what the object (the act) is to them, a move which, as Wittgenstein so poetically expressed it, is analogous to seeing an irregular assemblage of stones and thinking there must have been a house once. The transition from implicit knowledge to clarified self-understandings takes place by means of mental states which are particular cultural idioms, such as the Jain notion of *bhav*. But before we discuss this and the issue of the status of the religious meanings people do attribute in understanding their acts, we need to say something about the reasons people have, and think that they legitimately may have, for performing ritualized acts.

Notes

1. Even the yogic postures which people adopt during *bhav puja* are also found in other contexts, such as at sermons or when meeting a renouncer, as well as when people practise yoga at home.

2. In *puja* sandalwood paste is applied with the third finger; the mark, which is made downwards, is different from the *tilak* mark which is made with vermilion paste when anointing the forehead of a returning family member who has been away for a long time. This mark is made upwards with the thumb. Both of these are slightly different as gestures from the mark which a woman makes on her own brow to indicate that she is married.

3. 'If we relate the act of pointing to consciousness, if once the stimulus can cease to be the cause of the reactions and become its intentional object, it becomes inconceivable that . . . the movement should be blind. For if "abstract" movements are possible, in which consciousness of the starting and finishing points

is present, we must at every moment of our lives know where our body is without having to look for it as we look for an object moved from place to place during our absence. Even "automatic" movements therefore must announce themselves to our consciousness, which means that there never occur, in our bodies, movements in themselves. . . . The distinction between abstract and concrete movement is therefore not to be confused with that between body and consciousness' (1962: 124–5).

4. It is this experience which provides us with the 'first model of those transpositions, equivalents and identifications which make space into an objective system' (Merleau-Ponty 1962: 142).

5. At the risk of being repetitious, we stress that this kind of bodily, maybe barely conscious, 'directedness' is different from the 'intentional meaning' whose modification we discussed in Ch. 5. If someone aims to hit a tennis ball into a square in the court, that aim 'directs' the movement of the arm, and this is similar to the aim of placing a flower on the statue's knee which also directs a wrist and hand movement, but this kind of low-level directedness is different from the *understanding* they would have of the kind of action it is (a volley or a service; a flower *puja*). Taylor's statement (1985: 196) that 'An act is essentially constituted by its purpose' is thus insufficiently precise to deal with the case of ritual (though it is true that he was addressing a different argument when he made this point). In the next chapter we distinguish prior intentions, purposes, and motives and we discuss the different ways in which they bear on ritual.

6. Merleau-Ponty (1962: 142) arrives at the conclusion that although habit involves a non-intellectual synthesis of component actions, it does not differ from the general power we exercise over our bodies. Habit only presents problems to philosophers who take the view that explicit thought is the cause of action.

7. We have already said that we do not think Bateson is right that the framing of actions constitutes a domain of 'ritual action', but it does look as if the presence of such ostentatiously precise regulative rules in a ritual like the *puja* has a framing effect, picking out some things as worthy of attention and actively excluding others. Bateson (1972: 187–8) makes the valuable point in this context that the processes of inclusion and exclusion which framing effects are not psychologically symmetrical, though logically they look as though they are. 'The frame around a picture, if we consider this frame as a message intended to order or organize the perception of the viewer, says, "Attend to what is within and do not attend to what is outside". Figure and ground, as those terms are used by gestalt psychologists, are not symmetrically related as are set and non-set of set theory. Perception of the ground must be positively inhibited and perception of the figure (in this case the picture) must be positively enhanced.'

8. Sweetser (1987) argues that the use of the English word 'lie' can only be explained as a prototype. She sketches out the elaborate 'folk theory' of

information and evidence against which our judgements about the applicability of this word are made.

9. For example, the last Jina, Mahavir, was named *Vardhaman* which means 'the increasing one', because while he was in his mother's womb worldly prosperity magically increased for his parents and indeed for their whole kingdom.

10. No one in the vicinity of the ethnographer had any idea as to who this was. Perhaps this slip of paper had been planted on the queen by a joker.

11. Ann Grodzins Gold reports that Hindus in Rajasthan also have complex *puja*s at which pots with seeds appear, to be followed by pots with growing seedlings in the next episode. They are given different meanings from the Jain case, since the context is the worship of a goddess, Path Mother, associated with the River Ganges and with death. The primary meaning assigned to the growing sprouts is that they symbolize the safe return of family members from the Ganges pilgrimage, though Gold also says that they are said to denote fertility (1988*a*: 198–200). Tapper (1987) reports that in the Telugu village whose rites he studied young rice plants are placed in pots and carried in procession at a goddess festival. Here too the meaning is hardly transparent. Although Tapper was told the purpose of the rite was to guarantee a good crop, the plants chosen were not ones bearing rice grains. Villagers explained to him that this was because plants without seeds stay green longer.

12. This version of flower *puja* was performed on the giant statue of Bahubali at Shravana Belgola (near Mysore), in 1975, to celebrate the 2,500th anniversary of the birth of Lord Mahavir.

13. Here we disagree with Marglin (1990), who argues that ritualization gives rise to acts which are 'refinements' of the body techniques of ordinary life. The implication of continuity with everyday life which the term 'refinement' conveys is, we think, misleading.

14. Pascal Boyer (1990) has argued that there is a significant structural similarity between cognitive assumptions governing natural-kind terms and the way people regard both the identities of certain ritual specialists and the kind of status acquired in *rites de passage*. Persons occupying positions defined by ritual contexts are represented, he argues, in the same way as living kinds. A detailed discussion of Boyer's admirable and complex argument would be out of place here, but we should say that while we were inspired by his work to look at the possible importance of natural-kind terms for an understanding of ritual, we have chosen to formulate the connection in a quite different way.

15. The words which we are contrasting here with names and natural-kind terms we call, following Putnam (1975), 'artefactual' terms. An essentially similar distinction is made by Schwartz (1977), who calls them 'nominal', and by Johnson-Laird (1983) who calls them 'constructive' terms.

16. Thus the identity of a natural kind is fixed. As Keil (1987: 187) remarks, 'if one takes a chair and carefully glues on leg extensions and saws off the back, most adults say that you have now turned it into a stool. By contrast, if one takes a racoon, dyes its fur appropriately, fluffs up its tail, sews a smelly sack

inside, and even trains it to secrete the contents when alarmed, most adults will say that you still have a racoon, albeit a strange one that looks and acts just like a skunk.'

17. Natural-kind terms have, as Putnam remarks, an unrecognized indexical component (1977: 131).

18. Jonathan Z. Smith (1982) discusses two contrasting possibilities. Both are models based on stories. In one, cited from Kafka, leopards break into the temple and drink the sacrificial chalices dry. This occurs repeatedly, again and again. Finally, it can be reckoned on beforehand and becomes part of the ceremony. In the other, cited from Plutarch, the priestess of Athene Polias, when asked for a drink by the mule drivers who had transported the sacred vessels, replied, 'No, for I fear it will get into the ritual.' However, we do not agree with his conclusion that ritual signification is above all a matter of placement, 'the ordinary . . . becomes significant, becomes sacred, simply by *being there*' (1982: 55).

19. Many Christians would no doubt dispute this point, claiming that the ritual of the sacraments constitutes a complete religious break with any previous ritual traditions. Nevertheless, the sustaining of a particular intepretation on this basis and its acceptance by a whole community depends on the existence of clerical institutional authority. Transmission by churches of certain interpretations through the centuries has not prevented the emergence and bifurcation of numerous claims to the truth, despite constant reference to the Bible itself. Participants in the Eucharist give multifarious and sometimes even conflicting interpretations of the ritual they perform. In our view, if a ritual action has, at a certain point in time, what seems like a unanimously accepted 'meaning' this is a consequence of the political economy of knowledge at that particular time and it is not an immutable fact about the action itself.

20. An analogous point is made by Obeyesekere (1981) in his discussion of subjective imagery and the invention of culture. He writes, 'Subjectification . . . is the process whereby cultural patterns and symbol systems are put back into the melting pot of consciousness and refashioned to create a culturally tolerated set of images that I designated subjective imagery. Subjective imagery is often protoculture, or culture in the making. While all forms of subjective imagery are innovative, not all of them end up as culture, for the latter depends on the acceptance of the subjective imagery by the group and its legitimation in terms of the larger culture. Subjective imagery, insofar as it is based on objective culture, has the potential for group acceptance, unlike fantasy or totally innovative acts, which have no prior cultural underpinnings' (1981: 169–70).

21. For example, new Jewish rituals at the Kabbalistic centre at Safed are associated with one Isaac Luria (1534–72). In this way a basically Sephardi liturgy came to be used even in Ashkenazi lands. It is significant that Luria was clearly not regarded as an ordinary man, because he was called the Holy Lion and the ritual he introduced was known as The Rite of the Lion (de Lange 1987: 42).

22. 'Christ our paschal lamb has been sacrificed. Let us, therefore, celebrate the festival, not with the old leaven, the leaven of malice and evil, but with the unleavened bread of sincerity and truth' (1 Cor. 5: 7, 8).

23. It occurred at the time of the Jewish Passover and this fact became part of the Eucharistic tradition. However, the Supper was not itself the Passover.

24. Brian Smith, discussing the relation between later Hindu ritual and the ancient Vedic sacrifice, notes, 'The Vedic sacrifice provides later Hinduism with a kind of standard of worth by which non-Vedic religious practices may be gauged. In the Mahabharata . . . the rewards of visiting various Hindu pilgrimage spots are couched in terms of the old sacrificial system. The mere appearance at one or another *tirtha* [sacred place] wins for the pilgrim "the fruit of the soma sacrifice" or "the fruit of the horse sacrifice" . . . In this way, the new and relatively simple religious practices of Hindu worship are said to resume in themselves the power of the most complex Vedic sacrifices. . . . The purpose of shrouding new Hindu practices in sacrificial clothing is not simply to prove the superiority of the new to the old, but first and foremost to present the new *as* the old. Sacrifice has functioned throughout Indian history as a marker for traditionalism and as a means for acceptable innovation' (1989: 215–16).

25. Actually, the pilot signs a document and at this point he legally takes over control of the aircraft, but this no more prevents 'the walking round' from coming to symbolize his assuming control than does the fact that marriage occurs legally with the signing of a register prevent the priest's words, 'I now pronounce you man and wife', from symbolizing that transition.

26. In other words, though understood in a referential way as a named action, it may have few attributes. See Donnellan (1977).

27. Tambiah, for example, seems to suggest this when he argues that rituals through time undergo 'meaning atrophy', which may however be reversed during movements of religious revivalism which serve to *reclarify* meaning (1981: 165). But Needham rightly rejects this thought. He criticizes the idea that the imagined house stands for the idea of the intrinsic significance which has been lost and argues that although the actors in a ritual may think this way, it is crucially misleading for the analyst to do so. The idea that ritual is analogous to a ruined house is just a presumption; it helps us to see why people do tend to assume that there must once have been an intact and identifiable meaning to a rite, and that what we now observe are 'ruins', relics, survivals, but still the question remains, why should a supposedly original form of a rite have had any more clear and instrinsic a meaning than does the present form? 'After all, if a rite can be performed today by participants who ascribe disparate and even conflicting meanings to it, or if it can be properly performed even while appearing to be meaningless, why should its perform-ance ever have been inspired by a clearer ascription of significance?' (1985: 175–6).

7

The Disconnection of Purpose and Form

ONE learns many ritual acts in *puja*, as physical movements, by being shown what to do and copying it. But unlike learning some other physical operations (those which require skill, like playing the piano, cooking, sewing, or driving a car) the notion of excellence or expertise cannot be applied unmodified to the performance of ritualized action; for ritualization itself tends to undermine the link between the purposes for which an action is performed and the form the action takes. In performing an act in ritualized form, *as* a ritual act, you perform it as you do, and not some other way, just because it is so prescribed, and not because it makes sense to you to do so, or because you have reasons for doing so. You have reasons only for 'enacting the ritual', and whatever those purposes may be, the way to 'get it right' as a physical act remains the same. Nevertheless, the relation between purposes and ritualized action is not altogether straightforward. This chapter discusses issues arising from the range of purposes people have in performing the *puja* and makes some comparisons with Christian ritual.

Now, there are a number of different categories which can be used to give an explanation of action (intention, purpose, motive, reason, and so on) and there is no firm consensus about how to distinguish between them.[1] We are indebted to the work of Quentin Skinner (1988) in clarifying the issues involved here, but we do not adopt his vocabulary, so we need to make clear how we will use these words. It is possible to distinguish, as discussed in Chapter 4, between the propositional (locutionary) meaning of a linguistic action and its intentional meaning. This is to distinguish, using the same example as before, between what the policeman said ('The ice is thin over there') and what he was doing in saying it (warning someone). Here, and in comparable non-verbal cases, we can speak of identifying the intention with which the action is performed. However, this intentional meaning is not the same as purpose. In the case of the policeman, his purpose may be supposed to be something like doing his duty or preventing an accident. Nor is it the same as his personal motive, which might be to get promotion.

Anthropology typically concerns itself with other categories, the supra-individual, cultural, and objective reasons why particular actions occur. One of these is the presence in society of legitimating values or ideas about the goals of actions, which we may call their 'social purposes': for example, 'Policemen are supposed to protect the public.' These may explain, at least to some extent, the policeman's individual purpose. Finally, there are the social-structural and coincidental circumstances of the situation: the role of the police in society, the fact that the policeman was on duty, and so forth. In this chapter we shall be concerned with individuals' motives and purposes and the socially held purposes which they may, to some degree, share.

All of the above categories apply to action in general, and we need to consider what is particular about ritualized action. We recognize of course, following Weber, that not all action is consciously directed at a goal, and this applies to ritualized as much as to any other kind of action. But with the Jains, and cultures like theirs oriented to individual respons-ibility and achievement, the presence of objectives, something to be striven for, is given strong social encouragement. So when, as here, pur-poses and objectives are part of the ethnographic reality, what difference does it make to the relation between such goal-related categories and action that the acts are ritualized?

We shall argue that individual worshippers' purposes in performing the *puja* cannot explain what is ritualized about either its occurrence or its form; and we shall suggest that the same is true of 'social purposes' (the legitimate goals of rituals as propounded by renouncers and teachers), although this question is more complicated. The two topics are related, since theories about the *puja* abound, both in the form of people's stated reasons for performing it and the theories about it which are put forward by religious authorities. Precisely because no theory, and certainly no particular theory, is in fact necessary for the performance of the ritual, those who perform it do so with a great variety of purposes, meanings, and interpretations in mind, and in some cases, of course, with none at all. For convenience of exposition, although it is perhaps rather an artificial division, we shall focus in this chapter on celebrants' motives and the available 'social purposes' for doing the *puja* at all, and in the following one on the relation between authoritative 'texts' and ritual action: a re-lation which provides the context in which meaning is given to elements within it.

It is evident that celebrants may have, concurrently, several motives and purposes for performing ritual, or they may have none at all (except to perform the rite itself). As we noted in Chapter 2, there have been through history completely different understandings about what the *puja* is for, and many of these are still current and to some extent inform individuals' purposes today. In religious communities it is common for a purpose to be publicly stated as part of the rite. The 'purpose' of fasting is itself ritualized by means of a formal statement of intent (*paccakkhan*). In both cases, the effect is to distinguish personal and actual purposes from those which have to be declared publicly. Despite this, the Jains we met in Jaipur not only gave a variety of reasons for performing *puja*, they each had purposes, on different occasions, of quite different orders. Some people only perform *puja* on special occasions, on auspicious days, or when they have a particular result they want to achieve (the rest of the time they might come to the temple only for *darshan*, to 'behold' the idols, to bow, and perhaps to mutter a short prayer to each one). Many of the regular celebrants of *puja*, most of the time, come to the temple not because they have any particular purpose in mind, but just because they do. It is a duty (*pharj*), part of the customary round of their everyday life (*nitya-karm*), and intrinsic to their sense of themselves as religious. These people gave us accounts of the effects they experienced: 'I get *shanti* (a feeling of peacefulness) for the day ahead'; 'I start the day with clean thoughts'; or they gave reasons for performing *puja*: 'It is for *punya* (merit)'; '*dharmik hai, zaruri hai* (It is religious, it is necessary)'; 'It is to know what our god is like'; 'It is to give honour to those we consider great.' But of course these statements express both more and less than their purposes and motives.

For the affluent, there is the option of sponsoring a collective *puja*, which involves paying for professional ritual officiants and musicians, and for large quantities of expensive offerings. Public *puja*s of this kind are sponsored by leading members of Jain communities both to celebrate calendrical religious festivals and to give thanks for fortunate events in their family. There are a number of different complex *puja*s which can be done in this way, and some are believed to have specific beneficial effects.[2] Patrons certainly choose which one to sponsor with this in mind, so they have reasons for performing *that* ritual. We might add that the sponsoring of a public *puja* brings considerable honour and renown, which is another motive for the wealthy. The same is not true of other people who attend. Their motives might include an expression of respect for the sponsor, or of solidarity with a local 'parish' community. They might wish to share in the greater merit of a grand and extravagent *puja*. They might have happened to be in the temple and felt moved to join in, or they might have thought it would be rude to leave, or they might have specific spiritual or worldly desires of their own, quite unconnected with the patron's, for which they want to offer a prayer during the *puja*. But as we have said, whatever the purpose an individual might have in mind on a particular occasion, for either an individual or a collective *puja*, the way to perform it correctly remains the same.

It is possible for worshippers to make choices with reference to the purposes they wish to achieve by ritual: this is particularly clear in Jain temples which always contain a large range of different types of deities. Like Buddhists, Jains differentiate between different kinds of purposes, some of which are considered to be religious while others are merely worldly, even though they are accomplished in a temple.[3] The Jains we met distinguished fairly rigorously between the idols of the Jinas on the one hand, and both more recent Jain saints and protector deities on the other. The Jinas do not intervene in worldly affairs, everyone was clear about this, and it would thus in theory be pointless as well as impious to pray or perform *puja* to their idols with the object of achieving a worldly end ('We can pray to them to give us only what they have attained'). In practice it seems that some Jains assign particular supernatural abilities to the different Jinas and pray to them for this-worldly help. We mentioned, in Chapter 2, how Banarsi addressed a Jina statue with a request for help in his failing business. But in our experience at the Dadabari Temple everyone rejected the idea that help of this kind might be forthcoming from the Jinas.[4] On the other hand, people do regularly perform *puja* to both the other categories of idols, Jain saints and powerful deities, with specific and quite worldly motives: for success in a merchant venture or in examinations, return of a lost or stolen object, recovery from an illness, or removal of a difficulty, and perhaps most commonly, success in arranging an auspicious marriage. But the point to note is that although performing *puja* to different idols is widely held to make possible different kinds of results, the way people actually perform their individual *puja*s integrates their attentions to *all* these different deities into a continuous series. The temple idols should be worshipped in descending order of religious status: the central Jina of the temple, other Jinas, disciples, other Jain saints, and finally powerful deities. Not everyone abides by this, and even among those who do, almost no one goes through the whole series of offerings in turn for the idols of each category. Most people interpret the rule to mean that one should perform each successive 'act' for the whole hierarchy in the right order. That is, they first bathe all the idols in turn, then use sandalwood paste to anoint all the idols in turn, and so on. Many people perform exactly the same acts in each case, right through the series of idols. They bow in the same manner, anoint in the same fashion, and pray in the same attitudes. Experientially then, the whole sequence of morning *puja* integrates rather than separates worship of these various classes of idol. Thus 'religious' and 'worldly' purposes, which are undoubtedly linked to worship of different classes of idol, are not tied to their own ritualized actions.

This cannot be seen as a recent debasement of religious principles. It is integral to the *puja* that it is a ritual act which can be performed to a variety of sacred objects with a variety of purposes. This can be seen from the fact that Jain texts note the enactment of *puja* for *yakshas*, the ambivalent nature deities, which have very little, if anything, which is specifically Jain about them. For example, the *Vivagasuya* says that,

One Gangadatta, who had no issue, visited the shrine of Umbaradatta *yaksha* outside the city of Patalikhanda, in the company of female friends of her class and worshipped the *yaksha*. She first bowed down to the image, then cleaned it with a brush of peacock feathers, bathed it with water, wiped it with a woollen cloth, dressed it with garments, adorned it with flowers, garlands, applied scents, scented powders, placed incense burners in front, and kneeling down, prayed for a child. She promised a sacrifice, a gift, and a special fund for the purposes of worship. (Cited in J. P. Sharma 1989: 55)

Sharma and also Shah (1953) note that this series of acts is the same as that for the Jina. But the meanings given to these actions in discussions about *puja* to Jinas would make no sense as applied to these deities.

Analogous disjunctions between act and purpose can be found even in Christian rituals of worship, despite the fact that much thought has gone towards tying them together by means of explicit statements of purpose. An example can be seen in a modern enactment which occurs in some Anglican churches at a certain stage in the Eucharist. One of the most sensitive issues of the Reformation was whether or not the act of remembering Jesus at the Lord's Supper involves offering the bread and wine to God. Many Reformation churches refused the idea of offering, with its implications of sacrifice, and consequently eliminated from their liturgy the 'presentation of the gifts'. The liturgical action which, at least in some churches, has taken the place of the 'presentation of the gifts' at this same moment in the rite is the collection (of money from the congregation). Commenting on the 'whimsicality' of this, Stevenson notes,

Sidespersons have for long regarded it as their privilege and ministry to handle the money, and there are occasions when, particularly in our great cathedrals, this part of the offertory is given such solemnity that the priest elevates the alms-dish in a way strongly reminiscent of the old elevation of bread and wine in the Mass. (1989: 64–5)

Perhaps this enactment is not merely whimsical: it indicates the re-emergence of a ritualized act, the procession of laypersons to the communion table bearing items they have provided. The manner of performance of this act, perhaps even the emotions with which it is done, may be common to the two traditions despite radical doctrinal difference in the propositional meaning given to the act.

To return to the *puja*, most people visiting the temple for worship would proceed from the main temple hall, through the garden outside, to a shrine for the four medieval saints, the *guru-dev*s.[5] The historical *guru-dev*s were founders of Khartar reformism. But how are they now worshipped? The idol in the Dadabari in Jaipur is of Jin Kushal Suri, the third *guru-dev*. He is a seated, clothed figure, holding a mouth covering (*muh-patti*) up towards his face in his right hand and a religious book (*sutra*) in his left. By the practice of *puja* his pure white marble body is covered with silver foil, encrusted with sandalwood paste, and decorated on every horizontal ledge with flowers and rice. Endowed with glittering mirror eyes and painted lips, the *guru-dev* sits in rigid brilliance (Plates I and II). With what sorts of purposes do people perform *puja* to him? One man said, 'We go to *guru-dev* for success, power, and attainment (*riddhi, siddhi, labdhi*).' Other people said they gave worship in order to attain, or in gratitude for having received, specific benefits: birth of a child, success in examinations, profit in a business deal. The *guru-dev*s themselves engaged in orthodox Jain ascetic practices directed towards attaining enlightenment, but the power they attained thereby has come to be seen in a magical light. They were particularly powerful, we were informed, on Mondays and full-moon days.[6] We were told one typical story. Far in the distant past there was a dispute between Hindus and Jains. A Brahmin put the body of a cow outside the gate of the Dadabari temple, preventing people from entering. When he was told about this, the *guru-dev*, by the power of his meditation, made the cow fly magically to come down to rest outside the doors of the Shiva temple. 'Serves them right!' was the Jain attitude to this.[7]

There is a way to think of the *guru-dev*s in a more orthodox religious sense. The *nav-anga-puja* (nine limbs *puja*) is performed to them in exactly the same way as it is to the Jinas, and people told us that each stage

PL. VI. *A standing Jina idol.* This statue has been anointed with sandalwood paste and decorated with flowers and silver paper.

PL. VII. *Idol of Manibhadra Vir.* This is a *yaksha*, a miracle-working deity. He too has been daubed with sandalwood paste, and decorated with flowers and silver foil. Photographs for Plates VI and VII were taken on the same day in the Tapa Gacch temple in Jaipur.

of anointing had the same meanings in either case. This is possible because the saints passed through similar stages of spiritual accomplishment to the Jinas (although they did not attain omniscience). The saints, some people said, in fact give peace to the soul, and the fulfilment of mundane desires is, as it were, an incidental benefit. It is the role of the saints to spread Jainism, and when one person has his or her desires fulfilled by a Jain saint, others will also have faith. This accommodation of dual purposes make the *guru-dev*s very popular. It was at their shrine that we saw the most fervent crowds of devotees, pressing forward to anoint the idol, and remaining to sing hymns and to dance.

But in the case of the protector deities and the fierce Rajasthani gods a *puja* is given directly and unequivocally in order to obtain some good: 'Ganesh-ji[8] is fulfilling our desires, giving prosperity to the people in domestic life. Nakoda-ji [a *bhairu*] gives magic power for the devotees, destroys the enemies using any means. But these things are the non-religious way.' There is no question of approaching these gods with the idea of transforming the self in a religious sense. Yet even here the distinction in ritual acts is minimal. The *anga puja* is not performed on nine parts of the body of these 'Hindu' deities, but single acts of dabbing sandalwood paste are done, usually on the forehead of the idol. The rice pattern of the swastika should not be formed for these gods either, although sometimes it is. Instead there is a different rice pattern, a trident, which is considered appropriate for the idols of fiercer deities.[9] But very commonly all the idols, from the Jinas, the emblems of peace and detachment, to the spooky formless *bhumiya*s who wreak vengeance on enemies, are given similar little piles of rice in no pattern at all. Thus we must conclude that the very same acts are performed in contexts which imply very different purposes, different background assumptions, and different attributed meanings.

The relation between an act and the successful achievement of its purpose is distinctive in ritualized action. In different ways this relation is both more and less constrained than in everyday life. It is not that ritualized actions are lacking in purposes, nor that no indigenous account can be given of how they achieve these ends, but the link becomes more or less *arbitrary* with respect to the conventions of the everyday world and to a lesser extent even to other ritualized acts. In ordinary, non-ritualized action this is true to a very much lesser extent. The policeman could have called, 'Hey!' instead of saying, 'The ice is thin over there,' but the range of actions he could perform to achieve his purpose successfully are quite narrowly limited by his having to get the other person actually to move away from the thin ice. It is very difficult to predict, on the other hand, knowing a person's reasons or purposes, what ritualized action he or she might perform. Nor is it possible to infer from the form of *puja* a person does what purpose he or she may have in mind. One reason for this is that nothing hangs on it (except of course for the worshipper). In the everyday world the policeman could not achieve his purpose if he did not in fact communicate a warning to the skater. But in individually oriented ritual such as the *puja* this is not the case; no one except the celebrant knows, or needs to know, when a purpose has been successfully achieved. In this respect, therefore, the performer of a ritualized act is freed from the necessity of conforming to the conventions and practical requirements of successful achievement of purposes.[10] On the other hand, he or she is constrained by the need to conform to the acts laid down for specific rituals.

Following the steps and obeying the rules of a ritual is crucially unlike using a list of instructions, like a recipe. The whole point of a recipe is that it is directed at a single goal and for this purpose one can learn to manipulate it. It is possible, indeed usual, to learn to improvise with a recipe, and this is easier the better one is at cooking. One learns to substitute one ingredient for another, to change some part of the recipe, to skip a stage, or to add an element of one's own, because one has learnt the kind of effects these changes will have, and it is to produce these desired effects that one diverges from the recipe. This is not possible in the kind of liturgical rituals we are discussing. The purposes of ritual-ized action inform no such regulatory feed-back on the way the action is performed. As Lévi-Strauss noted, 'The gestures are not being performed, or the objects manipulated, as in ordinary life, to obtain practical effects resulting from a series of operations, each following on from the preceding one through a causal link (1981: 671–2).'[11] This is what we meant when we said above that the relations between purposes and ritualized acts are arbitrary even in respect of other parts of the ritual sequence. It is true that celebrants of the *puja* do pick and choose which acts to perform, but it would be absurd to say that they do this in order to construct a more efficient *puja* for some given goal. Rather, they can select what to do on whim *because* their motives and purposes neither call for nor require particular acts. Thus ritualization, in two distinct ways, obscures the relation between action and the goals people might wish to achieve by it: first, the acts can be made symbolic, metaphorical, and so forth, because there is no need for them to conform to practical requirements; and second, ritualized acts need have no sequential rationality one in relation to another. They are, in respect of any particular purpose, apparently randomly repeated and inverted, lengthened or contracted, since there is no practical feedback from any of them.

There are two qualifications we should make to the above argument. One concerns speech-acts in ritual, such as prayers, invocations, and confessions. Here the purpose may be embedded in the content of what is said. The worshippers may also be enjoined in the liturgy to say what the act means. This can be seen as a reaction by the religious authorities to the very problem of disjunction which we have mentioned. Even so, it seems that explicit statements of purpose are not always a solution, as can be seen from the incessant changes in Western Christian liturgy. Not only do particular congregations and their priests have their own traditions and priorities, but it seems that even in one community spoken parts of a liturgy work best and are most stable when they too allow for numerous human and religious values. Stevenson observes,

Because of the inherently ambiguous character of good liturgical prayer, it has to bear repetition, it has to resound, it should not attempt to define, it needs to match many kinds of experience (or at least not confront them negatively). This means that there should be an element of the *paradoxical* about images in prayer, especially when used in relation to important theological areas, such as what the Eucharist is setting out to *do*. . . . Contrariwise, liturgies which are written with the express purpose of defining suffer from two deficiencies. They have evolved too rapidly, without real gestation. They narrow down meanings and contexts so that they lose their own freedom (different kinds of usage) and the freedom of the worshipper (different ways of relating to the language used). (1989: 8–10)

Stevenson suggests that liturgical languge is its own genre, which communicates by means of 'resonant paradox', and which is separate for example from doctrine used in non-ritual contexts. This implies that even when the language used in liturgy is not itself an archetypal ritual element such as praising or asking for forgiveness, but occurs as an adjunct, introduced to clarify the purpose of a rite for the congregation, it may in fact, particularly when resonant and successful, promote further ambiguity arising from the exigencies of its genre. In some cases, when such interpolations are repeated as parts of the ritual sequence, they themselves can become ritualized acts.

This is a complex subject on which it is difficult to generalize because of substantial cultural differences between religious traditions. The daily Jain *puja*, for example, makes no use of explanatory interpolations. However, we can see for almost all ritual activity the possibility of two contrary movements, the urge of religious specialists to sort out and clarify what is going on, as opposed to the tendency of ritualization itself to present acts as merely apprehensible and open to interpretation. In our view the use of clarificatory language is rarely completely 'successful' (in the specialists' terms). In the Jain case collective *puja*s make more use of language than the daily *puja*. Little verses may be sung for each act, but they are usually in Sanskrit which almost no one understands. Vernacular homilies are often added, but because they are given by low-status *pujari*s (temple servants) they have little authority (see also the next chapter), and certainly do not counteract or suppress the varied understandings which those present have developed in the course of their own regular devotions.

In Christian worship there have been far more serious and sustained attempts to prescribe meanings and purposes. A recent example is in the breaking of the bread offered in communion, called the fraction.[12] While this occurs during the words of institution in the Book of Common Prayer service ('who in the same night that he was betrayed, took bread, and when he had given thanks [the bread is broken at this point] brake it'), it occurs at a different point in the 1980 revision and is accompanied by these words of explanation from the priest, 'We break this bread to share in the body of Christ', and the people reply, 'Though we are many, we are one body, because we all share in the one bread.' Now it is true that the people's reply clarifies one aspect, the unity of sharing, but if we consider the previous sentence which gives a prescriptive meaning, 'We break this bread to share in the body of Christ', let alone the ritual acts themselves, of breaking and eating the bread, it is evident that essential mystery remains.

A second qualification to our argument above concerns sequences of acts, already referred to in Chapter 6. Undoubtedly most liturgical revisions in Christian services have involved the moving around of various elements in accordance with the purposes attributed to them. Looking historically at this, one is struck by the fact that the ritual acts, whether spoken or not, have lent themselves to a variety of positions, and this can only be because the acts themselves can be seen *ab initio* in so many ways. This is true not only of ordinary worshippers but also of religious leaders who thought deeply about liturgy. An example is the use of the Sanctus by Luther. In his first reform of the Mass, Formula Missae in 1523, Luther moved the Sanctus to a new position within the words of institution, but he later decided for his Deutsche Messe of 1526 to use it as an anthem sung as a conclusion. Spinks (1991: 150–1) comments that the reasons for this new position were twofold. The Sanctus came at the end of the institution during the elevation as a joyous response to the proclamation of the Gospel, as a thanksgiving. But secondly, Luther chose to use the version of the Sanctus from Isaiah 6, rather than the Heavenly Jerusalem of Revelation 4, and here he seems to have taken up the theme of Isaiah's sense of sin. The communion is seen as seal of the promise of forgiveness for sins, and after it the Christian is sent out as a servant of God. Thus the Sanctus was a fitting conclusion to the proclamation of the testament of forgiveness (the words of the institution). But, Spinks notes, 'It would be tempting for those who followed the Deutsche Messe to see any suitable hymn as an alternative to the sanctus at this point, and to omit the sanctus altogether' (1991: 151). He concludes that three possible treatments of the Sanctus are found in the *Kirchenordnungen* stemming from Luther: to retain the inherited medieval pattern intact, with the Sanctus before a reformed institution, as done in Brunswick 1528, Pomerania 1535, Osnabruck 1543, Buxtehude 1552, etc.; to follow the Formula Missae, which was done in various places in Germany and Sweden; and to follow the Deutsche Messe, using the Sanctus simply as a hymn either during the institution or after it. This brief summary of a complex history shows that while the positioning of an element of the liturgy may acquire a deep religious meaning from its juxtaposition with other elements in accordance with the aims of the church, the fact that this can be done is partly a consequence of the openness of the rite itself. Furthermore, the rite may be deliberately positioned, as in the Deutsche Messe, in such a way that it is open to two purposes or meanings.[13]

We should now address the question of the socially held purposes of rituals. Our idea of a 'social purpose' approximates to that of 'cultural models' as employed in Quinn and Holland (1987), but we wish to stress that these ideas are not indiscriminately 'present' in all members of the culture. Rather, they are upheld and propagated by people in certain socio-religious roles (renouncers, pandits, lay experts). Also, they differ from cultural models in general in that they are phrased as goals, aims, or purposes. It might well be argued that even if individuals' intentions and motives are divorced from the ritualized acts they perform, surely at some socio-cultural level these rituals are there for a reason and this is to be discovered by analysing the consensus of opinions and interpretations. The supposition of much anthropology is that an exercise of this kind will explain the form and the occurrence of ritualized action. To some extent this has to be true. For example, as we noted in Chapter 2, when reformist Jains of the Taranapanth undertook a radical rethinking of the *puja* and what was to be achieved by it, this had an immediate effect on the form of their ritual: for the focus of worship they substituted sacred books for the statue of the Jina.[14] But the relation between socially held purposes for rituals and the form and occurrence of ritualized acts is far from straightforward. We can only briefly discuss two of the issues here: one is whether or not there are self-evident purposes or functions for at least some rituals, and the second is the hold which 'social purposes' actually have over people.

From their perspective anthropologists may not be convinced that the potentiality for being put to different purposes is essential to ritual. Surely, they might argue, there are some ritual events, such as marriage, whose purpose, even if complex, is self-evident, or there are ritual events which are enveloped in total consensual common understanding. However, with regard to the question of the 'self-evident' social purposes of events such as marriage, their ritualization does nothing to make these purposes clearer, and in fact, if one looks at marriage ceremonies in detail, the ritualized acts often present puzzles to anthropologists. For example the Jains, not having a marriage ceremony of their own, use the Hindu one, and the crux of this is the circumambulation of a fire to the accompaniment of a Vedic chant. Jain interpretations of the sacredness of fire, those of Jinasena for example, of course have nothing to do with Vedism, but rather refer to its holiness in the context of the cremation of the divine body of the Jina, and hence are an obfuscation rather than an explanation of the marriage fire. Therefore we have to accept, as Jaini does, that the central element of the Jain marriage ritual has a social purpose which is nothing to do with marriage, but rather with 'providing a protective Hindu cloak, beneath which the beliefs and practices of Jainism could continue unabated' (Jaini 1979: 297–302). Thus even with marriage it is not that ritualized acts can be 'read off', knowing what marriage is supposed to achieve, it is rather that comprehensive knowledge of all sorts of other aspects of the society and culture must be employed before it is possible to understand them.

However, it might be suggested that this is just a problem for foreign anthropologists: the people themselves just 'know' what is going on. This is to address the second question asked above: are there not, somewhere, events which are ritualized and yet encompassed in total understanding and unanimity as to their purpose? It seems to us that this may sometimes happen, but nevertheless one cannot therefore conclude that this is a characteristic of any communal ritualized action. The closest our Jain congregation come is at evening *arti*, when people wave lamps before the god, and all of them, communally and with no other purpose, may work themselves into a trance-like state. At this moment they might have no other aim than performing the act and undergoing this mental and physical experience. They 'know' what is going on because there is at this point nothing to know apart from what they feel. But we cannot say that *arti* just has this single transparent purpose, since it is always also possible for worshippers to wish for some particular effect by means of it, such as making a promise to the god, or using the trance to call up a possessing spirit. At the other pole from self-generated organic unanimity would be common purpose imposed by fiat. Bad liturgical practice as it may be, as Stevenson maintains, there is no doubt it happens: the worshippers may simply be told, 'The purpose of this ritual is X.'

An alternative attempt to rescue consensus might suggest that people have a simple, but nevertheless basic shared understanding of a ritual to which they add their own elaborations. Our answer to this would be: Why should one assume that the shared meaning is basic? It might be just vague. There is no reason to suppose it is more precise than all the vaguely shared understandings which are necessary for all kinds of social processes, such as shopping, sunbathing on a beach, or passing each other on the pavement. The only reason we might be tempted to call these vague understandings of ritual 'basic' is that they seem to be about important things, like 'transubstantiation'.

We return now to the question raised in Chapter 6 about 'objective socio-cultural categories'. Anthropologists often identify 'symbolic structures' in ritual. Can we agree that social purposes can be given to rituals by such structures—either in the analysis of ideological domination through ritual, or in the cryptological analysis of symbolic correspondences? To take the first case, we would point out that there is a distinction between the discursive and rhetorical declarations imposed by authorities and the symbolic actions (such as penis bleeding in initiation) which appear in certain rituals as violent, repressive, or cruel. Such actions appear ideological and are often conflated by anthropologists with the overt statements of people in dominant social categories. However, their ontological status remains deeply unclear. And even where domination is not an issue, anthropologists engaged in symbolic analysis often singularly fail to provide realist information about what people actually say about such symbols, no doubt because the actors so frequently reply something along the lines, 'I know this means something, but I don't know what it is.' Anthropological interpretations have commonly covered up such unhelpful replies in order to produce a reading from their own deductions. The result of this is the kind of neo-Durkheimian analysis which in effect explains symbolic ritual action by a covert social functionalism (for example in the case of penis bleeding, the idea that men are ritually appropriating female reproductive power, and so strengthening male domination). One problem with this is that such anthropologically deduced purposes often end up by being so distant from the ethnography. A single notion, such as 'violence', used by Bloch (1992) to explain the 'radical transformations' which turn native into sacred vitality, can be exemplified both by real bloody killing and by a peaceful offering of rice. As Ohnuki-Tierney politely remarks, 'I do not know whether the rice offered during the imperial accession ritual . . . was seen to have been violently killed' (1992: 19). Of course we do not wish to deny the existence of cultural symbolism.

Indeed our theory suggests why it is particularly likely to accrete around ritualized acts and why religious authorities tend to intervene to prevent the dispersal of meanings. We also accept that it may be illuminating to describe ritual as having social functions. But we would claim that an across-the-board analysis, with no attention to the cognition of real participants, produces an occluded and ontologically unclear level of analysis. We prefer to remain with those 'social purposes' that are discursively expressed (by someone!).

We now return to the psychological question: what 'hold' do such religious purposes have over those who perform rituals? It is suggested here that this hold can be both greater and less than such purposes for everyday action. In our view, there is almost always a disjunction between the extent of the power religious purposes have in the worshippers' minds and the place those worshippers assign to rituals. This means that a unanimous dovetailing of purposes and ritual action is very unlikely to occur.

The Jains are a good example of this. On the one hand, people can be taken over by religious aims, which extend well beyond the performance of rituals and inform an encompassing attitude towards life in general. There is a sense in which people can 'know' and feel what religious activity is for, but at the same time they may not be able to relate this to the intricacies of any given rite. Devout Jains told us of the *same* great purposes when they explained why they did the *puja* as they did for their undertaking fasts, meditation, and confession. When talking of great religious aims many people described their goals as if they were floating over, enveloping, and directing all righteous action.

On the other hand, for other people ritual enactments were inconsequential, or even distracting in relation to their religious goals. Worshippers told us often that they had difficulty in concentrating on standardized purposes, even if they approved of the practice of idol-worship and found it helpful. Ritual in fact offers special opportunities for the mind to wander, precisely because the actions are simple, standardized, and habitual. Here again the distinction from everyday life is not perhaps one of principle but rests on the fact that what one's purpose is has very little effect on ritualized acts, whereas in daily life, even in routinized situations, people can improvise in order to avoid (or less frequently to bring about) dissociated mental activity. It seems that in everyday circumstances people often occupy themselves with trivial activities in order to avoid the inrush of thoughts (of things left undone or other longstanding preoccupations). Ritualized action usually provides no opportunities for such checks on reverie. Actually, our ethnography seems to show that very like the underlying nagging thoughts themselves, purposes realized through ritual cannot but be, to some extent, involuntary emanations from each person's state of self, as they are feeling or responding at a particular time. In other words, one is not entirely in control of one's purposes or motives, and except perhaps for the most mentally disciplined, there is a constant slippage back and forth between the religious goals people think they ought to have and their own wayward motives.

But if socially held goals are only temporarily grasped and held in the minds of laypeople, they are the domain, almost the 'property', of the renouncers who propagate them. Among renouncers we found a greater sureness and an ability to compose images for general edification, in effect a far greater identification with religious goals. Here is an authoritative voice talking about the *puja*, a voice which makes clear how this ritual is held to be efficacious independently of thoughts or purposes. The speaker is a young female renouncer:

The Jina's *puja* is only so as to become like him, and not for any other reason. Since we are all worldly beings, it is difficult for us to concentrate on the Jina and our minds wander. Now how does the *puja* help? If you have a new vessel and pour alcohol in it, it will stink. But if your pour in *panc amrit* (five auspicious nectars) it will smell delicious. *Puja* is like this—it *fills up* the human being. . . . Let me explain differently. If you buy a new vessel and put it away, if you don't clean it and look after it, then it will become tarnished yellow and black, even though the soul is there. This is very bad. But when Diwali comes, we clean the vessels.[15] So is *puja* like a Diwali for human life. To do *puja* is to cleanse the soul.

Here, rituals are seen as designed towards purposes (though it should be remembered that the renouncer does not perform *puja* herself), whereas for the layperson ritual acts are received as given, and purposes must be somehow fitted to them.

We have so far identified various levels, lay and expert, at which purposes and ritual actions relate in some way, and perhaps in order to tie these together it would be useful to end this chapter with discussion of one ritual act. We show here how purposes may be distinguished from symbolic meanings, and we consider the relation between the social purposes for rituals as standard performances and the recourse to ritual which individuals may have at a moment of extremity. Let us take the example of *abhishek*, the act of bathing the idol which begins the *puja*, as we observed it at the Dadabari temple in daily morning worship.[16] Please note that the Sanskrit term '*abhisheka*' is very difficult to define. It means essentially what is done in the ritual given this name (Eichinger Ferro-Luzzi 1981: 708). It can encompass what in many languages would be expressed by two terms, the bathing and the anointing of an idol, both of which are done in an enormous variety of ways in the many communities of the subcontinent.

After a preliminary burning of incense 'to cleanse the atmosphere' and a dusting of the idol 'to remove microscopic insects', the *abhishek* commences: first a pot of water is poured over the idol from above and wiped off with a special brush. Then a pot of milk is poured over, and some people will supplement this with a libation of ghee (clarified butter) or *panc amrit* (the five nectars[17]). This too is brushed off, and there is then a second pouring of water (Plate I). The idol should then be dried thoroughly, using three separate cloths. The water and milk flowing off the idol is collected and called *prakshal*. This is the prescribed ritual.[18]

An unprescribed but very common addition is the further use of *prakshal*: some people touch it to their foreheads or to their eyelids. It is said by many people to bring 'a feeling of peace (*shanti*)', and by others to afford 'protection'. Others take it home where it is applied in similar fashion to members of the family. The *prakshal* from certain *puja*s is said to cure even severe diseases. Taking away and using *prakshal* medicinally is thus enshrined in ritual practice and has its own clear social purpose. This is underwritten by an authoritative narrative concerning a leper cured by the *prakshal* brought by his devout wife.[19]

Raja Shripal somehow got associated with thieves, and he contracted leprosy from them. Wandering in this wretched state he reached a kingdom where there was a princess, Menasundari. Her father was angry with her for some reason and said he would marry her off badly, so he married her to Shripal. But Menasundari stayed with him. Then she met a guru and told him of her plight and asked him how she could get rid of her husband's illness. The guru gave her a *siddh cakra yantra* to do *puja* to, and told her that each six months she should fast for nine days. He told her all the rituals to do, and then she was to apply *prakshal* liquid to her husband's wounds. She did all this and her husband was cured. Ever since then people use *prakshal* as a medicine.

But even so the similarity between it and *prasad* (taking back as blessing food offerings made to deities) which is one of the key distinctions between Jains and Hindus, means that many Jains, especially among the religious leaders, are ambivalent about the practice. Among other purposes for *abhishek* mentioned to us were: to cleanse the soul; to give joy to God by bathing his idol in cooling and pleasurable substances; to adore

PL. VIII. *A collective* snatra puja *in the Dadabari temple.* A tiny Jina idol is seated on a stand representing Mount Meru, the centre of the universe. Men stand to the Jina's right, women to his left. On the tables in front of him can be seen water pots for *abhishek*, lamps, incense burners, a fly-whisk, and *puja* manuals. In the foreground, right, a young woman who is not participating in the *snatra puja* is forming her own arrangement with rice.

and honour the statue of the Jina; to purify the idol as a preparation for the emergence of religious sentiment; and to preserve the stone of the idol by giving it the smooth patina of greasy substances. Such 'social purposes' are not quite the same as meanings given to the rite. For example, when it is performed in the 'birth-*puja*', the *abhishek* is said by nuns to represent the washing clean of the Jina, the idol representing a baby which has to be cleansed of birth-pollution. Others see *abhishek* as a luxurious bath. In this, the five nectars are specified as the correct washing medium, because the ritual act our friends perform in the temple is a re-enactment of the bath given the baby on Mount Meru by deities, who would naturally use such a liquid (Plate VIII).

Now, as we have indicated, the actions people perform vary slightly: some people do not use milk, some put substances such as sandalwood powder or perfume in the water, some vary the water—milk—water order, and some, who arrive after the main *abhishek* has been performed, have to content themselves with bathing only the big toe of the idol. What we wish to reiterate here is that these acts do not change according to the purpose someone has in mind. Nor, of course, are the actions appropriate in an everyday sense for these purposes: to wash the idol one may nevertheless pour a greasy, sugary, perfumed mixture all over it, and in South India this on occasions has become a complete fruit-salad:

Baskets full of grated coconut kernel were emptied over the head of the image of Jina. Then again, slices of banana fruit, sugar, ghee, seeds of pomegranate and milk, were poured. (Srinivasan 1981: 49)[20]

The fact that different purposes, indeed whole different vocabularies, interpretations, and meanings, can attach to the same prescribed act, can cause considerable confusion. This senior nun, in conversation with James in 1987, clearly changes her mind in the course of speaking.

There are so many *yantra*s you can use in *puja* . . . you can drink the *prakshal* of the *yantra* (the water in which a sacred diagram has been bathed). But the *prakshal* of the Jina, this cannot be drunk, but the *prakshal* of *guru dev*, this can be drunk. We people [Jains] also don't use *tulsi* (sweet basil), as the Vaishnavas [Hindus] do in the water we use to bathe them. Actually, true Jains don't believe in any of these things. *Puja* is only for getting rid of our *karma*s. We don't believe in miracles (*camatkar*), only in *karma*.

Whether they share or not in the socially held purposes mentioned, people also have their own more worldly motives for performing the *abhishek*. Sheer competitiveness may push someone to participate in an auction for the right to take part, and there is certainly honour for the one who actually performs the rite.

One might have a perfectly clear purpose, like caring for a sick member of one's family, but how this might be pursued in ritual is not at all clear. A Digambar Jain worshipper at the Padampura Temple near Jaipur in 1982 gave Caroline this account of an *ad-hoc* recourse to *abhishek*:

They asked me, 'What is wrong with your wife?' And I had to tell them, a few days ago she delivered a child. In those fifteen impure days, something happened—she was caught with the defect of a spirit. I have taken her everywhere to find a cure, but nothing worked. When she came before God she [i.e. speaking the words of the spirit] suddenly shouted, 'Oh Baba, I won't leave this woman now unless you kill me, because I have got married to her. She was sitting at home in the room, with perfumes and all, and then I entered her and later married her.' It was terrible. So I made my wife sit before the Padampura Jina and I made her open her hairs [undo her plait]. We started doing *abhishek*, *puja*, *arti*, singing hymns, everything. Then we threw some *gandhadak* [scented water from *abhishek*] over her, and suddenly the spirit started excusing itself as though it was being prosecuted by the god. Soon it went away, and now my wife is well and does all her housework and cooking.

Among the many-layered desires of someone performing *abhishek* we have distinguished between socially held and individual aims, and it is likely, as Keesing (1987) proposes, that these may have different cognitive qualities.[21] Although we did not explore this question during fieldwork, thinking ourselves to be engaged on a rather different enterprise, the short account just cited does suggest that individual purposes, which are frequently thrown up by unique contingencies, may necessitate a synthesis of particularities rather than the application of prior schemas. The social purposes of ritual acts in regular liturgical contexts, on the other hand, are experienced as expositions of theological points, as general statements applicable in all circumstances (for an example, see the nun's statement above about what *puja* is for). But often people are not simply enacting a routine *puja*; they go to the temple for some unique reason, like the man whose wife was possessed by a sexually rapacious spirit.

In a devout community such as that of the Jains of Jaipur such haphazard events are incorporated into religious life, and are brought face to face with prescribed archetypal acts and the available 'meanings' to be attached to them. The case of the man whose wife was possessed is one for which the higher goals of Jainism have no practical answer. That situations of misfortune, strife, and illness are commonly enough brought to the *puja* can be seen from the whole popular development of the idea of *prakshal* and its curative effects, as well as the cults of non-Jain deities. But even this aspect of *prakshal* in its form as a socially held purpose for performing *abhishek*, does not explain the man's actual account. He did not describe what happened to himself and his wife as the application of a general rule, nor did he refer to the story of the leper Shripal. He describes himself rather as acting on hunch, and it is not clear if he made any conscious connection between the scents which attracted the evil spirit to his wife and the perfumed water, sanctified by *abhishek*, which drove it away. Nor do we know if the act of pouring holy *prakshal* water over his poor afflicted wife was seen by him as in any way analogous with its earlier pouring over the idol (probably most Jains would see such an analogy as deeply sacrilegious). But what he actually did has sufficient resonances. In other words, it is at least as likely that he imaginatively 'put together' the nexus of particular purpose and available acts he performed as that he 'deduced' what to do from generally held principles.

In this chapter we have tried to show how people's purposes in performing ritual acts, whether disciplined by religious goals or essentially untamed, are only partially aligned with the socially held aims which specialists attempt to tie down to particular rites. Purposes may have an effect on the available repertoire of ritual acts, such as when new rituals are invented, but they bear only a very attenuated relation, if they bear any at all, to expertise or to the way a rite is physically performed. However, though purposes do not account for *what* people do in rituals, it is nevertheless through performing these acts that purposes are achieved. People are therefore always likely, just because they do engage in self-interpretation, to attribute meaning to the rites they act out. We shall be discussing this compulsion to 'mean' in Chapter 9. But first we need to deal with the assumption which very many anthropologists would make, that there already is an underlying meaning to *puja* and that one does not have to go far to find it: it is there, expressed in all those sermons and commentaries, and the numerous manuals which lie in neat stacks in the temple.

Notes

1. Here, for the first time, we encounter the issue of the causal explanation of action. To grasp the intention in acting is to understand an action, and to discover or reveal that intention is to explain it, but the explanation here is not causal. An explanation is causal if one cites the motive which led an actor to form the intention with which he or she acted, or if one cites facts about the world, external to the actor.

2. For example, the performance of *vedniya-karma-puja*, on the twelfth day after the death of a member of one's family, is popularly believed to help secure for them a better rebirth. Although this practice is not at all discouraged by religious experts (who can be relied upon, if asked, to give a doctrinally acceptable 'social purpose' for it), they do firmly repudiate this popular motivation for performing it.

3. For discussion of this in the Buddhist case, see Gombrich and Obeyesekere (1988). Southwold (1983) also observes that Buddhists make this distinction, though he himself prefers to see the whole complex as 'religious'.

4. However, some people accepted the idea that the Jina's protector-deities (*shasan dev*s) help people 'on his behalf', and others allowed that though the Jina himself cannot intervene in human affairs some particular idols are magically powerful (Humphrey 1991). For excellent discussions of this issue see Babb (1988) and Cort (1989).

5. The identities of the four *guru-dev*s interpenetrate. Although there are specific stories attaching to each of them, they are always represented and worshipped together and addressed simply as *guru-dev*. Their statues are indistinguishable.

6. Some Hindu deities also enjoy enhanced powers, or are more inclined to use them, on specific days. Very close to the Dadabari is a celebrated Ganesh temple which attracts great crowds of devotees, including Jains, on Wednesdays. In the Jewellery Bazaar, the centre of the Jain district of the walled city, is a temple to Hanuman which is also particularly popular on Wednesdays.

7. The *guru-dev*s are not the only Jain saints to have undergone a transformation of the purposes for their worship. Gautam Swami, as helpmate and remover of obstacles, is worshipped along with Hanuman and Lakshmi, the goddess of wealth, at Diwali. At the same time, as Mahavir's closest disciple he was responsible for the establishment of the renouncer orders and in many ways is the archetypal Jain *sadhu* (Laidlaw, forthcoming). In this latter guise the notably worldly purposes of prayers to him offered by many worshippers are totally inappropriate, and there is no shortage of other Jains ready to point this out.

8. A deity also known by Jains as Shri Parshva Yaksha-ji Maharaj.

9. One informant told us that this represents strength. 'Bhairu' or 'Bhairav' is the name given to fierce manifestations of the great Hindu god Shiva, whose symbols include the trident spear. A number of the powerful gods worshipped by Jains are identified as Bhairu, although the connection between these gods and Lord Shiva is left unclear.

10. This is typically not the case in performance-centred rituals, and this fact supports the intuition that these events are less ritualized than liturgical rites. See Introduction.

11. To the extent that such goal-oriented diversions or inventions occur in performance-centred rituals, for example when a shaman improvises some act

which is designed to attract a spirit hitherto unknown to his audience in order to cure an illness, we would describe such situations as less ritualized (they violate the condition of there being only a limited set of 'acts' to perform, see Introduction).

12. We are endebted to Revd Stephen Cherry for this example, though we should add that the interpretation of it is ours and not his.

13. An analogous case in the daily worship of the Jains is the positioning of the incense and lamp *puja*s, which relate ambiguously to the categories of *anga puja* and *agra puja* (see Fig. 4).

14. For detailed analysis of changes in the form of a ritual deriving from radically different religious thinking about it, see the account given by Obeyesekere (1981: 169–75) and Gombrich and Obeyesekere (1988: 163–99) of the 'Buddhicization' of the hitherto Tamil Hindu fire-walking ritual at Kataragama in Sri Lanka. They make the important point that for the new ritual forms to become established it was necessary for the Buddhist religious leaders to posit the existence of a Buddhist book of rules (*katikavata*) which laid down the correct procedures. The book of rules was thought by many people actually to exist, but Obeyesekere discovered that it was accessible only by occult techniques (possession, trance, etc.). The point is made that ritual innovations must be legitimated by something other than the individual purposes and intentions of the innovators. In the case of the Jains, as we noted in Chapter 2, 'reforms' were also legitimated by reference to ancient texts.

15. Diwali, or Dipavali, is the Festival of Lights, a major festival celebrated by both Jains and Hindus. It marks the beginning of the Hindu calendar and many people clean out the whole house in the days leading up to it.

16. This is a simple form of the rite, which has elaborate variations in the communal *snatra puja* and the great public events of *panc-kalyanak*, the *anjan-shalaka* (a ritual for the 'enlivening' of the statue, turning it from mere stone to an idol worthy of worship), and the Digambar *mahamastakabhishek*, the consecratory bath given to the head of the statue of Gomateshvara at Shravana Belgola in Karnataka every twelve years.

17. This is offered comparatively rarely in individual *puja*, but is a requisite at the more festive *snatra puja*. Many of our informants were uncertain as to the components of *panc amrit*, perhaps because the mixture is made up for them by the *pujari*. One woman, for example, said that it is comprised of water, milk, sugar, curds, and a fifth element she could not remember. She did know, however, that it must not contain an element used by Hindus—honey—as this is procured by violent means: driving bees away from their homes. What is actually put in *panc amrit* seems to vary: sometimes jaggary (a crude, brown sugar made from palm sap) is used, sometimes molasses. Jains do not put *tulsi* (sweet basil) leaves in *amrit*, as Hindus often do. Cort (1989: 364) gives milk, curds, sugar, ghee, and flowers or sandalwood as the components used in Jain *panc amrit* in Gujarat. It is evident from Eichinger Ferro-Luzzi (1981) that

looking at India as a whole the composition is highly varied and that it often contains more than five elements.

18. Jains do not use the term *abhishek* for anointing the idol with sandalwood paste as seems to be the case in some Hindu rituals, nor for the application of dry sandalwood powder (*vasakshep-puja*) which is done during the *snatra* festivities. However, the latter action is clearly associated with *abhishek*, in that informants explained it as 'dry washing'.

19. Here, we give only a short version of the story, told to us spontaneously one day by a man who was talking about his *puja*. More complete versions of the story are rather long, with various sub-plots. For more discussion, see Laidlaw (forthcoming).

20. This is a description of the great *abhishek* at Shravana Belgola in 1780, but Eichinger Ferro–Luzzi makes clear that this use of fruit is common in South India to this day (1981: 720).

21. Discussing the relation between 'cultural models' and how people deal with the atypical and fortuitous, Keesing writes, 'But do we have, in addition to the models of culturally constructed common sense, deeper grammars to which we have recourse in the face of the atypical and complex? Do common-sense models, enabling us to deal with the world probabilistically on the basis of typical scenarios, 'canned' or formulaic routines, and ideal types, operate in conjunction with cognitive processes whereby we decompose situations into their deeper constituents and interpret them with an underlying grammar when we have to? Or, do we simply muddle through by extrapolation, approximation, and *ad hoc* invention?' (1987: 379).

8

Looking for Meanings

THE Jains of modern Jaipur are a highly literate community and behind them stand two and a half millennia of religious speculation. *Puja* has never been central to Jain doctrinal tradition and contemporary religious writing is devoted mostly to ethics and philosophy, but as we noted in Chapter 2, there is now also a substantial body of literature giving instruction on the subject of *puja*: treatises by learned ascetics, small manuals for the performance of the rite, prayer books, and hymnals. In addition there is a large, loose body of didactic narrative in which rituals such as *puja* often play a decisive part.[1] The great majority of these parables take their themes from a mythical vision of ancient India, ruled by kings, and peopled by princesses, paupers, religious Jain families (mostly stupendously wealthy merchants), bandits, Jain saints, and other figures from a stereotyped cast.

In addition to all this commentary from within Murti Pujak tradition, there are of course the writings of those who have opposed the *puja*: several quite separate schismatic Jain traditions whose sectarian identities and sense of religious mission have to a greater or lesser degree turned on opposition to rituals of idol worship. Finally, in this respect as in so many others, the place of the Jain community in particular sections and strata of the wider Indian society adds an enormous variety of literate comment on the *puja* and on ritual more generally, which informs Jain ideas about the ritual they perform.

We are concerned in this chapter with the relation between these widely available texts and ritual practice. Catherine Bell, in her interesting paper on Taoist liturgy (1988), notes the complexity of these relations,[2] and she points to two important processes: the textualization of ritual, whereby existing practices are selectively codified in writing, and the ritualization of texts, so that texts themselves become ritual objects and access to them becomes a ritualized act. With both these processes the text can no longer be seen simply as a reflection or expression of its historical context. 'By viewing the text as an entity that merely expresses a particular perspective on its time, we may miss how the text is *an actor* in those times' (1988: 368). Bell is discussing the codification by the fifth-century Taoist master,

Lu Hsiu-ching, of a body of scriptures, the Ling-pao. This mainly comprised the liturgy of life-renewal rites, themselves called Ling-pao. But intrinsic to this codification was a second process, which restricted access to these holy scriptures, and hence to their promises of immortality, within proper performance of the Ling-pao rituals under a liturgical master. If the first move, the textualization of rites, had the effect of defining orthodoxy while at the same time opening a regularized means of access to Taoist spirituality to anyone able to read, the second, the ritualization of texts, acted in an opposite way, to restrict participation to congregations subordinated to a Taoist master able to ensure the rites were correctly performed (1988: 391–2). Later in this chapter we shall discuss instances of the ritualization of text in Jain practice, but looking in the light of this brief discussion at the role of texts in Jain ritual practice generally, and at the daily morning *puja* in particular, we suggest that to a remarkable degree only the first of these processes, the textualization of ritual, is present. The result, paradoxically, is that specific liturgical texts are unnecessary for the correct performance of ritual.[3] No part of any ritual *requires* their presence, although they are helpful if one happens not to know or to have forgotten some passage. At the same time texts are superabundantly available, which acts perhaps to cancel out any claims for unique authority that might be made for any of them.

During our fieldwork we listened to extensive commentaries on *puja* from a variety of different people: ascetics, ritual specialists, and locally recognized savants as well as a large number of less well-informed 'lay' practitioners, and we consulted the pamphlets and manuals which are available in temples, and from which people draw some of their ideas about the ritual. It might be thought that an examination of these variously authoritative commentaries could reveal an essential or underlying meaning for the *puja*, and this is precisely what some of these texts and commentaries claim for themselves. We shall argue that this is not the case. We have already dismissed (in Chapter 2) the idea that the medieval guides for lay conduct (*shravakacar*) provide such a ready-made blueprint. Our account of ritualization suggests why actors should feel impelled to look for symbolic meanings, as one way of apprehending the ritual acts they perform. But it suggests too why symbolism, where it occurs in ritual, is highly unlikely to consist of the sort of all-explanatory hidden code which many anthropologists have seen it as their task to try to uncover. It is extremely unlikely to be much like a language. Actors' attribution of symbolic or propositional meanings to ritual acts—their attempt to imagine the building which the ruin once was—much more resembles Sperber's conception of symbolism as a cognitive mechanism involving creative improvisation, and the search for interpretations in a store of background and tacit knowledge (Sperber 1975, 1982, 1985). It seems, in line with this, that texts in general, including formal commentaries on rituals, provide the stock of images and ideas which people draw upon in order to attribute extremely various meanings to their ritual acts. Let us now discuss the texts which are closest to contemporary practice: manuals, liturgies, prayers, and hymns.

In any Jain temple there will be a number of *puja* manuals lying around, provided by the temple management, which the worshipper can consult. There are many versions of these booklets, some of which draw forms and tropes directly from Hindu devotional traditions, but the differences between them are not a subject of discussion, let alone controversy. They set out appropriate prayers and devotional songs which are intended for the most part for lengthy *puja*s for special occasions, and the majority by far of those performing daily morning *puja* do not consult them.[4] We were certainly taught some Hindi couplets and prayers for use in *puja*, which again show strong continuities with local Hindu practice, without reference to any manuals.[5] But some people do borrow excerpts from these manuals for their own individual *puja*s, mainly, we got the impression, to provide a general sense of order and correctness to their daily devotions. In addition, many (of the women especially) have little booklets of their own, often distributed by renouncers to their followers. These books contain pictures of the celebrated idols at Jain pilgrimage sites, both Jinas and protector deities, which are held to have special miraculous powers, together with short, simple prayers written by ascetics or learned laypeople, and mnemonic tables and grids. These diagrams, which are said to derive from abstruse tantric calculations, prescribe sequences in which the lines of prayers and *mantra*s should be recited (see Plates IX and X). Instead of reciting these texts in order, the worshipper, in a practice called *anapurvi*, follows the numbers in the boxes of each diagram from top left to bottom right (they might run, 1, 3, 4, 2, 5; 3, 1, 4, 2, 5; 1, 4, 3, 2, 5 . . .), reciting in different orders the lines from magical formulas as the numbers written in each box of the diagram instruct (the number 1 means you recite the first line, and so on). Different booklets give large numbers of such diagrams, often recommending them for worship of particular Jinas or deities, with each employing different patterned series, holding different elements constant and varying others. As in the Vedic case discussed by Staal, passages of meaningful text are submitted to the structuring and reshuffling effects of ritualization, and rendered meaningless. We noted in Chapter 2 that the only text in an ancient language which most people actually know and use is the *namaskar-mantra*, and that even this short prayer is often reduced in a formulaic manner.

When we learned the *puja*, we were taught a few short verses to recite, and these were treated and taught in exactly the same way as the other acts we had to learn: we merely had to remember them and recite them accurately.[6] It was not that there would be no merit in learning to understand them (those which were meaningful), but rather that to do so is quite separate from getting them right as ritual acts. One does not fail to perform them by having an incomplete or incorrect idea of what they mean. In many cases the prayers and *mantra*s are themselves in any case meaningless, or in languages which the worshipper does not understand. Many prayers are in Sanskrit or Prakrit, which are understood by very few lay Jains, and almost none of the people who performed *puja* daily could explain to us the meaning of what they were reciting.[7] Nor were they greatly troubled by this fact. Reciting a text is a distinct and valid ritual act independent of the apprehension of its meaning. Staal draws attention to similar treatment of texts in Vedic ritual, in which words are treated to purely formal arrangement and ordering (Staal 1986: 44–59), and if this does not mean, as Staal suggests, that utterances of language are turned into pure acts, devoid of semantic content, it does surely mean that the link between form and meaning is loosened to the point where the meaning attributed to the utterance is radically underdetermined in comparison with everyday language. These kinds of linguistic utterances in ritual, just like non-linguistic ritual acts, generally appear to *call* for interpretation, because no meaning, purpose, or intention can be either directly understood or uncontentiously inferred.

Now, some of these prayers are, and some are not, designated to accompany specific ritual acts in the *puja*. However, we found that because prayers are learnt separately from the actions, often as a whole group, these links frequently are not made immediately by people on a one-to-one basis. For example, people may learn a whole set of prayers which give meanings for the anointing of each of the limbs of the statue. But if we asked, 'What is the meaning of anointing the crown of the head?', the response, even if someone knew the prayers by heart, was often a puzzled pause. It was rather like asking whether N comes before L in the alphabet; the response was to run through the prayers in order, 'Crown of the head? Let me see . . . Toes . . . knees . . . arms . . . shoulders . . . ah, crown of the head, that means . . .'

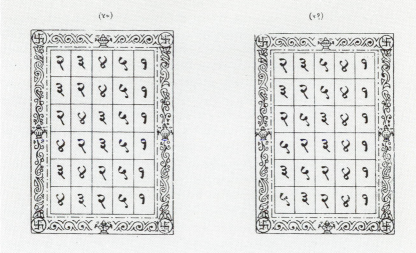

Pl. IX. *Pages from a* puja *manual.* The numbers on the page indicate the order in which lines from prayers and sacred formulas should be recited.

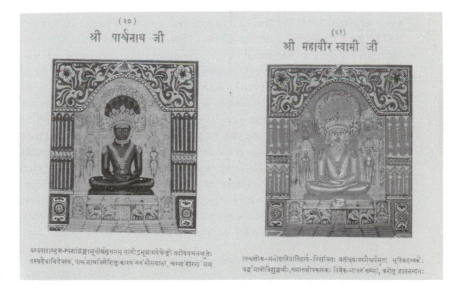

Pl. X. *Pages from the same* puja *manual.* Illustrations of the Jinas Parshvanath and Mahavir, with prayers in Sanskrit below.

There are also contemporary instructions or liturgies (*vidhi*) for the *puja* in Hindi and Gujarati, and probably in other modern languages. These are written mostly by renouncers. They consist of updatings of one or other variant of the medieval *shravakacar*s with the addition of prayers for each stage of the *puja*. However, we did not find that these books were in common circulation. Many people do not possess one, though they know of their existence, and in our experience worshippers very rarely, if ever, recite modern prayers for a whole *puja*, as they are instructed to in these texts. Any congregation, such as the worshippers at the Dadabari temple, has access to different variants. The prayer prescribed by one author for a given act might differ in import from that given by another. Because of this, and the restricted authority of these books, which are only considered as uniquely legitimate by the most devoted close followers of their various authors, we consider that it would be a mistake to salt these texts down, erasing or ignoring differences, and take the resulting synthesis to be the 'underlying meaning' of *puja*. This would be to assume that there really exists, in a quasi-metaphysical sense, a 'meaning' for the rite which the various authors are aiming at or approximating to. We prefer to recognize that in their various writings these authors are contributing to the creative processes of making, remaking, and disseminating *proposed* meanings, some of which are more successful that others and some of which lead, in turn, to changes in the way the rite is performed.

The *puja* manuals, which of all these texts are the most readily available, do not specify the ritual actions required, the 'archetypal actions', nor do they give comprehensive interpretations of these actions.[8] Ritual actions, as we have said, must be learned by practical demonstration. As the manuals are not descriptions of a liturgy, it is only by inference that people can use them to establish the correctness of a ritual action. This was true even of such an important point as the offerings to be made. Consider the role of written texts in the following account, abstracted from James's fieldnotes. The issue here is the presence or not of sweets and fruit at a specific *puja*. These two items are frequently said to represent the 'sweet things of life' which are given up, and the 'fruits' of renunciation. We give the account in detail, since it shows the complexity within which 'meanings' are (or are not) assigned.

Annual ceremony in which the small metal idol is taken in procession through the streets to a temple on the outskirts of the city. The next day, a *panc-kalyanak puja* is performed there.

(16/12) We all sit in a semicircle around the opening into the temple. The statue which was brought in procession, and is now inside the temple, has been covered with a white cloth.⁹ The *puja* is being performed by a *yati* and his assistants (*pujaris*). On the ground in front of the door to the temple hall, between the audience and the *puja* going on inside, are five small silver flags. Next to the idol is a metal tantric diagram (*yantra*), already anointed with sandalwood. One *pujari* is busy dabbing sandalwood paste on to a white cloth flag (which will later be hoist on the temple roof) . . . Each worshipper who arrives goes round all the permanent idols in the temple complex, making a short bow, before coming to join the *puja* . . . The congregation sings songs from a little book, copies of which are lying at the sides of the temple.

At the end of each of the five *puja*s a single Sanskrit verse (*shlok*) is recited by two female renouncers. Each time this is done one of the *pujari*s brings round a tray, containing the offerings which have been made in the foregoing *puja*, and each time he places this before one of the five silver flags. He then lays out these offerings in a pattern in front of the flag, before taking the tray inside again, ready for the offerings of the next *puja*.

The rice is laid out in the usual swastika pattern, the flag is then placed on the crescent of rice at the top. Fruit and sweets are not placed separately as they usually are in daily *puja*s. In the centre is a coconut, with a small piece of cloth, a leaf, and a coin tied on to it and with flowers on top. To its left is an orange, to its right a small pile of sweets.

Before the fourth *puja* (for enlightenment) is performed, the cloth flag, now prepared, is taken in procession around the temple by a small group of laywomen (from the family of the patron) dressed in especially grand orange and yellow saris . . .

(We break from the sequence of songs in the book twice: once to sing a popular Hindi devotional song which everyone seems to know by heart; and once to skip to the end of the book to sing a prayer called 'Sri Parshva Jin Stavan'.)

The fourth set of *puja* offerings appears. But there are no sweets this time, and no fruits other than the coconut. The rice is just placed in a pile, not arranged in the swastika pattern as on the previous trays . . . But at the fifth *puja* the full range of offerings with fruits and sweets appears again. At the same time a lay ritual specialist brings a separate large tray of offerings and places it on a table in front of the line of five *puja* trays. The man sitting next to me tells me this is wrong because he is sitting on the left as he does it . . . Next will be *arti* (waving a fivefold lamp before the idol), so suddenly a man has jumped to his feet and is yelling, taking bids from the congregation for the right to perform this . . .

(21/12) Met Ravinder (who had been present at the *panc-kalyanak puja*) in the morning. I asked him about it. He said, very grandly, that he could tell me all about this and indeed we talked for some time . . . I mentioned my puzzlement that at the fourth *puja*, the *keval-gyan puja* (for the enlightenment of the Jina) there had been no fruit or sweets. 'Oh yes', he said confidently, 'Only rice in *candrama* (the crescent-moon), because now none of these worldly things are wanted' (i.e. the Jina by this stage is now an enlightened soul, and desires only liberation from the world, to become a *siddha*, whose abode is represented by the crescent-moon). I mentioned that these things were present again at the fifth *puja* (the *moksh puja*, which is when the Jina actually becomes a *siddha*) and asked what this meant. He looked puzzled, and rummaged around among his books for one which would explain this. 'Yes, all eight items must be there,' he declared, equally confidently, 'This is *ashta-dravya* (eight-things) *puja*'. Why? Did this mean the fourth *puja* had been wrong? He didn't know, and his book did not explain, but he promised to ask the senior nun who was staying nearby.

Later, in the Dadabari, I found Ravinder going to meet Sajjan Sri ji (a very senior nun). 'Ah yes', he said, 'Come. We will ask your questions.' He was clearly excited by the prospect of the discussion. When I explained what I had seen to the nun she informed us straight away that this had been wrong, that all eight offerings should be present in each *puja*. When more books had been consulted, inconclusively, contributions were heard from other nuns, and this interpretation was agreed.

A number of points are worth noting. (1) If the experts running the *puja* were following a book (which, at least at the time, they were not), it was not the same as that from which the prayers were drawn, and which was provided for everyone to use. The prayer manuals provide no information on the correct ritual offerings. (2) There was no unanimity between the different books which were consulted by Ravinder and the nuns about the same ritual. (3) All these people, except the senior nun, were unaware of what was in their *puja* textbook until prompted to consult it. (4) Once consulted, the books are often inconclusive, giving only general instructions which might be executed in a number of ways. (5) Presented with a ritual act, our informant was able readily to produce a conventionally 'correct' meaning for what was later agreed to be an 'incorrect' action. (6) Finally, our friend was quite prepared to revise his proffered explanation of the reported act, with absolutely no embarrassment.

There is certainly a hierarchy of knowledge about the *puja*. The interpretations given by learned Jain ascetics, in person or in books, are regarded as authoritative. More authoritative still are the opinions of great teachers of the past, set out in their Sanskrit treatises. Still, it is not necessary to be acquainted with these views in order to perform *puja*. In any case, even more than the manuals in temples today, both the *shravakacar* texts and their updated *vidhi* variants disagree with each other, and offer a variety of conflicting instructions and interpretations. The largely oral tradition in the Jaipur Dadabari is much more agreed than are the texts to which the members of that same community could legitimately refer for authoritative guidance.

We found near unanimity, for example, on the general structure of the nesting hierarchy of acts in *puja* (the division into *anga-* and *agra puja*, their grouping to make up *dravya puja*, and their opposition, together, to *bhav puja*), whereas Williams outlines a plethora of confusing classifications in the *shravakacar* texts.[10] Perhaps it is for this reason that ordinary Jains, who perform *puja* every day, do not in our experience refer to the *shravakacar*s (another reason being the fact that so few read Sanskrit) and only rarely to modern Hindi textbooks derived from them. Both the rules people follow in the ritual, and the sources for their ideas about what they might mean, are drawn from practical instruction and a largely local didactic oral tradition, rather than the supposedly authoritative prescriptive texts. In brief, despite the existence of a sacred canon, a long history of debate on precisely these matters, and a corpus of liturgical writings, textually, the Jain *puja* is radically underprescribed. Ritual practice prescribes the ritual much more closely than does religious exegesis.

Fuller's description of Hindu ritual in the Minaksi temple in Madurai suggests that this relationship between texts and performance may be common to other traditions in South Asia. The priests of this temple are full-time ritual specialists in one of the most paradigmatic 'great-tradition' temples, and one might expect that the regular rites they perform might be quite closely guided by textual prescription, but as Fuller illustrates, this is not the case. His informants agreed that the *agama*s are the authoritative source on ritual performance. Yet Fuller writes, 'Probably the most important sociological and historical fact about the Agamic literature . . . is that it is nowadays largely unknown. . . . Neither the Agamas nor the ritual manuals actually contain the kind of explicit liturgical instruction that priests and others commonly suppose them to contain' (Fuller 1984: 136; 139–40). On the education of the priests who perform the rituals, he says, 'The pupils mainly learn by memorising exactly the passages recited to them by their teachers. It is considered vital that these passages' words, pronunciation and scansion are all memorized absolutely accurately, and this cannot be done by reading books' (Fuller 1984: 138). He also points out that there is a whole range of ritual rules, which all participants believe to be of the first importance and believe to be laid down in the *agama*s. For the most part they are not (Fuller 1984: 143).

Fuller recounts how he was criticized by a priest for taking notes of the latter's actions. The priest referred him instead to the rules in the *agama*s. He believed the correct instructions to be contained in the *agama*s, but he did not know what those instructions were. Against a background of recent criticism of priests by temple administrators, he was no longer confident that the instructions he had learnt from his *guru* and the prescriptions of the *agama*s were the same. We do not think, as David Gellner (1988) does, that this shows observation of ritual practice to be useful only as a check on the anthropologist's description of a 'cultural construct'— 'the model which guides actual practice'. It seems clear that far from being a guiding model, the *agama* literature is only theoretically authoritative and does not inform actual performance of the rite. If there is a 'cultural construct' for ritual actions, and we suggested in Chapter 6 that this should not always be assumed, it is not to be found in authoritative religious texts. The accepted idea that they are authoritative can well go along with almost universal ignorance about their content.[11]

There is thus an important distinction between ritual as practice and the set of organized metaphors, narratives, and argumentation which constitute religious commentary on particular rituals. A ritual does not necessarily or directly 'express' the meaning of the commentaries on it or codifications of it. This is especially clear in Jainism where the religious ideas expressed in commentary on ritual are unambiguously declared to have their proper place in non-ritual religious contexts. Whatever you can do in ritual, can be better done in another way—notably by leading a blameless life of detachment. Similarly, all the objects used in ritual, if they are given a commonly recognized religious meaning, can derive that meaning from sources (treatises, doctrinal speculation, or even mythological tales) which are not designed, principally or even at all, as ritual exegesis. Lévi-Strauss (1981: 668) protests against those who restrict the term 'mythology' to explicit mythological texts, and argues that the 'glosses or commentaries on ritual' are piecemeal 'implicit mythology', but anthropologists commonly link them with, or confuse them with, ritual proper. He writes that ritual 'consists of words uttered, gestures performed and objects manipulated, independently of any gloss or commentary that might be authorized or prompted by these three forms of activity, and which would belong not to ritual itself but to implicit mythology' (Lévi-Strauss 1981: 671).[12]

We said earlier that the sustaining of a particular interpretation and its acceptance by a whole community depends on the existence of clerical institutional authority. Where this is diffuse, as in Jain sects and schools, participants are free to give multifarious and sometimes even conflicting interpretations of the ritual they perform. We are not trying to say that these people are lacking in piety or respect for religious authorities—the reverse is true—but the institutional basis for consensus is lacking.

Another reason for the variety of interpretations is the embeddedness of Jain culture in that of the region and class to which they belong. Many notions to which people have recourse are not specifically Jain at all, a fact which is generally and readily acknowledged.

One prosperous, middle-aged lady, a member of one of the prominent gem-trading families in Jaipur, said,

I use peacock feathers to cleanse the idol. Why? The peacock is a pure bird. How do they reproduce? When there is water in his eyes, the female bird sucks the tears from his eyes, and that is how she gets pregnant.

He husband said that this was just silly stories. She retorted, 'But you use peacock feathers too.' She continued,

We use the peacock's tail feathers, not the feathers from his head—that is some other caste which does that. It will clean the smallest particles and insects away without harming them. You must brush very gently. But today I did not have time to do it gently. I bathe the idol with water straight from the tap, then with milk, which must not be boiled, and then with water again. Then we must dry the idol with three separate muslin cloths.[13] Sometimes people put saffron, micah, and sandalwood in the water, so there is a nice smell. Then I put scent, attar of roses, on the whole body of the Jina. This protects the marble of the statue. This is the influence of the Vaishnava Hinduism, earlier we Jains didn't do it. When Jains saw what the followers of Krishna did they thought their idols looked so beautiful and they should do it too. Jain teachers thought they would lose people if they did not agree. On special days I put on silver leaf, sometimes just on the forehead of the idol, sometimes on the whole body. This is something else we have taken from outside. It happened only about seventy years ago.

Most of the named acts of the Jain *puja* also seem to appear in the ritual sequences of other religious traditions. Some of them are common to the entire subcontinent, for example, *pranam* (performing obeisance to the god), *darshan* (experiencing 'sight' of the god), *abhishek* (anointing the idol or pouring a libation over it), *arti* (waving a lamp before it), *pushpa puja* (the offering of flowers) and *phal puja* (the offering of fruit). Perhaps the only act in the Jain *puja* which is unique to this religious tradition is the forming of the swastika, half-moon, and dot pattern in rice. On the other hand, the Hindu food-offering (*bhog*) and the consumption of the left-overs (*jutha*) of the god as a blessing (*prasad*) are foreign to Jainism, as, emphatically, is blood-sacrifice. As we noted in Chapter 6, this overlapping of ritual acts between different traditions allows them to be seen from an external observer's point of view as polythetic categories (Eichinger Ferro-Luzzi 1981), while within any given tradition they appear as prescribed acts. What we wish to point to here is that these ritual acts have all been given specifically Jain meanings, sometimes consciously contrasted with Hindu usage. They have appeared in Jainism as separate rites, elemental 'acts to be done', not as whole sequences, and they have been taken on at different times. For example, the use of scent and the application of silver foil appear to be recent additions to the Jain *puja* (and of course, not all traditions accept them). The question then arises as to how these detached elements, incorprated into Jain ritual sequences, are given meaning. Unfortunately we do not have the material to discuss this question historically, so we must be content with current practice. In the following discussion we shall be concerned first with the degree of spontaneity in assigning meanings and secondly with the range of individual meanings in relation to texts.

First, it is clear that particular objects used in the ritual do not have specific designated meanings *ab initio*. Let us take the prescribed act of placing fruit on the swastika of rice. A person will come to the temple bringing, say, a banana. Until it crosses the threshold this is simply fruit, and could be eaten. It will be recalled that at the top of the swastika, above the three dots, people form a crescent shape and a further dot within it, to indicate the curved domain at the edge of the universe and the liberated soul within it. Both the crescent and the dot are normally fashioned with rice grains, and fruit is placed on the dot to indicate that the liberation it represents is the 'fruit' which is desired. But we observed that in fact a banana can be used either as the crescent shape, the edge of the cosmos occupied by emancipated souls, or as 'spiritual fruit', depending on how the celebrant decides to place it. In other words, it has been made to represent, given meaning, but there is nothing about the act of 'placing a banana' *tout simple* to tell us which meaning the actor will give to it.

A more complex example is the *abhishek* (the ritual bath of the idol) which we use again because it will already be familiar to readers from the previous chapter. At the risk of being repetitious we cite again some of the meanings given there, but in this case using a tape-recording of a conversation among a group of people, since this illustrates something of the lively and yet essentially tolerant disagreements we found among Jain people. We suggest that a multiplicity of Jain texts and teachings provide a large, though not infinite, stock of possible meanings. These are chosen by people 'individually', but not, as it were, privately. In other words, the possibility of choice does not become transformed into subjectivity, as far as we could tell, because the meanings are selected from the assortment of publicly known alternatives. We talked to people both in public and alone on this topic, but even when away from the crowd and with people one or other of us knew well, we were not given meanings related idiosyncratically to the individual's life history.

We saw many people using a bunch of dried twigs to brush the statue. After it had been given a lustration of water, milk, and water again, it was then subjected to a vigorous scrubbing. It was then carefully dried, in all the crevices, using three cloths. A woman teacher said that she only used water, not milk. Rather carefully, and for the sake of our tape-recorder we felt, she said, 'Just as water is cold and takes away all the heat of the body when we bathe, so the water is supposed to take away the heat of anger and desire. When I wash the statue I think: water cleanses the body and in the same way I want the strength to cleanse my soul.' Milk and ghee are often used in bathing the statues. These greasy substances have a purpose, which most people would recognize: to give a patina to the stone of the idol and so to protect and preserve it. However, there is no acknowledged socially held propositional *meaning* for the act. People therefore cast around for things to say when asked about it. One person said that it is symbolic of the bathing, by the god Indra, of the baby Jina with *panc amrit* (five nectars), another that the milk is pure because it can counteract the poison of snake-bites. A third person referred to the story of Mula Jat, a farmer who discovered a Jain statue buried in his field. The statue could not be moved, but Mula Jat felt someone was saying to him, 'First give the statue a bath with milk,' and when this was done it was possible to move the statue and set it up for worship. A fierce old man said that the use of milk is altogether wrong, because 'germs will be there', and someone else muttered, 'Also it comes from the body, so how can it be pure?', but several other people said that it is used because it is pure, fresh, and straight from the cow. We provoked a brief debate about whether using milk was *himsa* (violence) because it deprived calves of their sustenance. Someone remarked that this would not be the case these days, because no one keeps cows in the cities anymore. All the milk goes to the milkman, so the sin, if there were any, would be his. This would not matter, because he would not be a Jain. The old man still looked disapproving.

The same man who spoke about the patina given by milk said that he also used curds and ghee to clean the idol and sandalwood oil to cool it. But he disapproved of people who brought attar of roses because, 'The rose has some warmness. That will spoil (the idol). It may crack. Even my warmness, as when I sit down and the place is warm, that will hurt God for up to one hour.' However, this same man brought rose flowers, plucked from his garden, to decorate his favourite statues.

It is true that one could extract characteristic themes from all this:

cleansing, cooling, and strengthening the idol, but these themes do not constitute a 'meaning' for the rite. First, it is clear that people have their own ways of enacting these ideas, if they hold them at all. They give their own meanings to customary actions. That is to say, the themes can be and are interpreted and applied in various, even contradictory ways. Secondly, the 'themes' are themselves mutually inconsistent. There is no 'grammar' or 'code'. The cleansing of the statue with 'auspicious' substances becomes problematic if people apply notions of non-violence to these substances, and the preoccupation with coolness and lack of passion are at odds with the whole idiom of *tapasya* (ascetic practice to 'burn off' *karma*, see Chapter 11). Finally, all this detailed and elaborate concern with the physical condition of the statue combines with assertions that the idol is merely stone, that it is the worshipper's *bhav* which is the important part of the *puja*.

We stated earlier that the meanings given to ritualized acts are not totally random. Most refer to some aspect of Jain doctrine, but people differ in what they see as the kernel of religion: some stress detachment, others peace, others even happiness (*sukh*). Frequently, especially in the collective *puja*s, meanings are drawn from 'cultural schemas', notably the story of the paradigmatic life of the Jinas. However, it should be realized that this is a vast corpus, comprising the lives (and previous lives) of the twenty-four Tirthankars, with all their happenings and trials, with a huge subcast of gods, demons, wives, kings, ministers, sages, animals, tempters, and disciples. There is no single theme, idiom, or symbolic code which is dominant in the *puja*, to which others are subordinated, and on to which they can be mapped. It is not even possible to sort out 'correct' or 'orthodox' meanings from others, because as we showed in Chapter 2, there are many orthodoxies. The same person could give several meanings for a single act, with no sense of contradiction between them.

In having a meaning for a ritual act, what people are doing is representing that idea to themselves. It is interesting that contemporary Jains maintain, as their primary 'world' of reference when elaborating parables about ethics and the self, the mythological kingdoms referred to above. Even contemporary religious tracts rely largely on stories about these never-never lands to make their points. This allows the making of religious judgements without constructing hypotheses about the real world round about, and leaves open to individual preference the question of interpretation of elements in the mythological picture as they affect practical ethics.

Thus the great and rich corpus of Indian culture provides a repertoire of propositions and discursive episodes to which people may refer. There are, however, certain limits to the range of appropriate meanings. An adequate treatment of this subject would fill another book, but we can briefly note some areas of regional culture which Jains avoid or incorporate only in a highly disguised or attenuated form: the sexual idioms and reproductive themes in much of Hinduism; the symbols of Hindu Shaivism, which emphasize destruction and creation (often in feminine forms); the whole idiom of animal sacrifice; and themes drawn from Muslim and 'tribal' cultures, both of which are valued negatively. Even predominantly Vaishnavite interpretations are skirted round. Thus, for example, the use of fresh milk in the *puja*, which goes against Jain principles of non-violence, and use of items which might contain life-forms, may well be covertly related to the Hindu reverence for the cow. But note that our respondents said only that milk is 'pure, fresh, and straight from the cow'. They did not go on to say that the cow is sacred, and in point of fact while Hindus in western India maintain cow-sanctuaries, Jains have established homes for animals in general (*pinjrapol*) and for birds and insects (Lodrick 1981). The Jain idea of the universal recycling of souls does not allow for the celebration of one species of animal over another.

Some segments of the *puja* are given tighter (more shared) interpretations than others, and this seems to be correlated with the more physically featureless actions, those which offer least purchase for individual imagination. Thus, while the flower offering is explained, as we have seen, in many different ways, the rice offering has a relatively coherent and agreed interpretation, perhaps because the Jains make a definite distinction between their view and that of the Hindus. Rice is regarded as itself a symbolic substance, irrespective of the pattern in which it is laid. In the ritual setting rice is usually called *akshat*, rather than *caval*, as it is in normal use. The grains should be unbroken, perfect, and uncooked, with the husk removed. The word *akshat* means 'perfect', 'unimpaired'. As in Hindu ritual contexts, it is often said to signify immortality. But unlike Hindu *akshat*, which is often coloured yellow, and where immortality is associated with auspiciousness, long life, and fertility, comments by Jain worshippers on the white rice they offer to the Jinas associate immortality with the end of reproduction and growth—the end, that is, of life.

1. *A young girl.* 'Just as this rice will not grow if planted in the ground, so we do not want to be reborn into the world.'

2. *A man.* 'When the husk is taken off rice, the *karma* attached to our hearts is removed.'

3. *A woman.* 'Rice cannot get rebirth. We want everlasting happiness, so we put it in front of God.'

4. *A nun.* 'Then there is *akshat puja*. Rice is clean because of its white colour. It should not be broken, that I would also be woundless. If people say harmful things to me, it causes a wound that might never be healed, but this does not belong to me. All is caused by *karma*. Rice is put so we should become unharmed, so all my wounds should be taken away.'

But despite this theme, which could perhaps be summarized as completeness surviving through the vicissitudes of *karma*, it cannot be concluded that the rice offering 'has this meaning'. Not only would this be to fudge the interesting differences in the interpretations given above, but we also found white rice liberally strewn at the shrines to all of the other deities in the temple, including even the 'non-Jain' fierce protectors of the locality. Here, since these deities have nothing to do with immortality, if rice is given any meaning at all it must be a different one.

Finally, we should address the case of collective *puja*s, at which people regularly pray and sing communally. The hymns and songs are tailored to the particular kind of *puja* that is taking place, recounting the deeds and praising the qualities of the *guru-dev*s or the Jina who is being worshipped, and expressing the hope that the *puja* will have its desired 'fruit'. The sequence of prayers and songs is taken from one of a number of books by ascetics which the temple has published or bought. Here, in many cases, printed texts propose a definite narrative or conceptual theme for the ritual: in the *panc-kalyanak puja*, such as is performed for the installation of a temple idol, there is the concept of the five auspicious moments, which summarize the story of a Jina's life; and in the *guru-dev puja*, which is staged quite often in Jaipur by wealthy families when they feel their prayers to the *guru-dev*s have borne fruit, a series of songs recounts the great deeds and miracles which are attributed to the *guru-dev* saints.

In these rituals there is then a coherent text which tells a well-known story, usually in language which people can understand, and, at least in any particular temple, the same text is generally used for each performance of the rite. But as we have seen, even if this vernacular text is read or sung in such a way that *its* meaning is plain and evident, this has little effect on the performance of other ritual acts, such as the ordering or the spacial arrangement of offerings. In a general sense, obviously, the content of the text is part of the meaning attributed to the events as a whole, but we should notice once again that this has nothing to do with the fact that the event is ritualized. A straight reading or singing of the text would much more clearly and unambiguously 'have' that meaning than such a reading does when it is enacted in a ritualized context.

And although these rituals are conducted or orchestrated, they are surprisingly undisciplined affairs. As at morning *puja*, people come and go as they please, there being no idea that one must stay for the whole sequence. The narrative contained in the text has only limited control over anything else that happens. Occasionally one or more of the gathering will get up and begin dancing, perhaps waving a *camar* before the idol. This prompts others to give small notes and coins as offerings to the idol. Both musicians and other self-appointed worshippers, who invariably have opinions about the correct way to proceed, play their part in controlling the *puja*. The space to the front of the congregation, before the idol and the microphones, is occupied (in addition to the paid musicians, who are usually not Jains) by the most enthusiastic male singers from among the temple community. From this little huddle a decision from time to time emerges to break off from the sequence prescribed in the book, at more or less any point in the 'story', for more popular devotional songs (*bhajan*s) in Hindi, usually to the tunes of the love songs in popular films. If these men feel moved by their *bhav* to do so, and if no pious or strict renouncer prevents it, they can extend an already long *puja* sequence for hours.

The songs and hymns do provide meanings which are collective and conventional, but they are not enforced in any way, and they do not govern the way the rite is performed. For instance, the *panc-kalyanak puja* celebrates the conception, birth, renunciation, omniscience, and final liberation of the Jina, but although the songs make reference to these events, the *puja* actions which are performed are generally the same as at any other *puja*. When a new idol is installed, certain 'dramatic' tableaux are staged, as we described in Chapter 6, but the more frequent *panc-kalyanak puja*s, performed annually to commemorate consecration and also at other times, dispense with these. On these occasions (such as the one discussed earlier in this chapter), each of the five stages is usually 'enacted' by the performance of exactly the same series of prescribed offerings and other acts.

And in the case of the *guru-dev puja*, as it is performed in Jaipur, the same text, which mixes up stories which each relate to a different saint, is performed in the same way, unamended, regardless of which of the four is the direct object of worship in the *puja* (either because he is thought to be responsible for the boon which is being celebrated, or because it is he who is represented in the idol). If the text is shortened, passages are cut because they have come to be associated, in an entirely formal way, with offerings. So if, for instance, no flag offering is being made, then the part of the narrative text which is printed under that heading, and would normally be sung in the period when the flag is being prepared, will be skipped, even though there is no semantic connection between them: they just happen to coincide in two parallel sequences. Here then, in a context where we do have what Bell calls the 'ritualization of text'—a text being incorporated as an intrinsic and prescribed part of a ritual—the effect is, as Staal describes for Vedic texts, that the text is subjected to purely formal treatment, which actually tends to undermine its conventional semantic content. So while the texts recited here plainly 'have meaning', and their place in ritual is partly responsible for the wide dissemination through Jain communities of the stories they contain, to say that the texts contain the 'meaning of the ritual', would actually be to pass over all the elements and features which those texts take on in a ritualized, as opposed to an everyday, context.

An officiant or an ascetic might also interrupt a collective *puja* with a disquisition of the purpose of the *puja*, an exegesis on the meaning of parts of it, or a reminder to the gathering that the important thing is that they should express their devotion to God. But this call that the *puja* should be done with devotion produces little more community of meaning than for the individual *puja*. Renouncers, if they are present, can be irritated by the 'filmy' hymns, and others may drift away from time to time to conduct private devotions in a quiet corner of the temple. Even in the centre of activity, as we have seen, by no means the same meaning is given by people to *puja* acts as they perform them. It is individual worshippers who *choose* to attend to these meanings and, if they wish, choose to make them their own. So how is this 'meaning to mean' carried out?

Notes

1. We cite some typical stories in Ch. 9, but to deal with this literature adequately is beyond the scope of this book. These works are published in all the major languages of India, including English. Often they consist of the discourses of renouncers. They explain how to be a good Jain in modern life, and are concerned with topics such as how not to be misled by external beauty, the need for tolerance and sincerity, avoidance of attachment and anger, respect for the renouncers, how to cope with sorrow, and the question 'Should happiness or goodness be one's goal in life?'

2. Especially so if one adds the texts produced by anthropologists and historians, 'recognition of a gap between their text and their rite, their rite and our text, or even their rite and our rite' (1988: 369). We do not address the matter of anthropological texts here, mainly because to date very few indeed have been written on the Jains and their effect is (and is likely to remain) negligible.

3. Texts are not ritualized in the sense Bell outlines, but religious books do have a ritual role outside the *puja* in signifying the corpus of Jain scripture. Thus renouncers and pandits give their sermons, their own inventions, seated behind a stand which an open book is placed, never looking at it, but as it were deriving inspiration from it. In the Taranapanth (see Ch. 2) this signifying role for marble representations of books is central, but the point here is not access to the texts as physical objects containing efficacious secrets, which is the case in the Taoist ritual, but to demonstrate that it is the religious ideas of the scripture rather than statues which should be worshipped.

4. A couple of examples of sung prayers: (1) 'Giver of religion, Maker of pilgrimages, Follower of complete wisdom, Most superior among men, Lion amongst men, Lotus among all people, Lord of the Universe, Giver of fearlessness, Giver of insight, Giver of shelter, Giver of Life.' (2) 'Giver of light to the whole world, creator of religion and pilgrimages, conqueror of desire and aversion, I shall pray to the twenty-four Tirthankars . . . [List of names of Jinas is recited] . . . I pray to these Tirthankars, who are free of sin, disease, and death, that they be happy with me. I pray to those who are supreme to grant me spiritual strength, and at some time to grant me the most coveted of gifts: to attain liberation. Cooler than the moon, brighter than the sun, calmer than the seas. I pray to the *siddhas* (liberated souls) to bestow on me perfection and liberation.'

5. For example:

> Do only what you want to do,
> If you like, only then give alms (*dan*),
> Worship the Jina only with devotion (*bhavana*),
> For *puja* will not bring you any fruits.

and:

> All these means of decoration,
> Such as things grown in the earth,
> Of what use are flowers
> When God is already sitting in a garden?

6. This differs from the process whereby religious texts are learned in non-ritual contexts. When religious students learn from their *guru*, a process called *svadhyaya*, they listen, memorize, understand, and ask questions about the meaning of the text, and then, the last stage of the learning process, teach it themselves.

7. Some of the most devout lay Jains memorize longish verses in Prakrit which are derived from the most ancient Jain canonical texts. They are the verses

which ascetics recite when they approach their superior to express reverence or to undertake confession. The manuals which ascetics write for *puja* often consist of arrangements and variations of these texts. Lay Jains often try to learn these verses to recite to ascetics, and many also recite them during *puja*. In this case many people have a general idea of what the verse says, without understanding the language or being able to translate it into the vernacular.

8. Even the *vidhi* instructions simply name acts to be carried out, rather than describing exactly how to do them.

9. This, it was said, is because the first stage of the *panc-kalyanak* is for the Jina still inside the mother's womb (*garbha-kalyanak*).

10. Williams provides Shvetambar lists of 8, 17, and 21 elements of *puja*; an unnumbered list given in the earliest text, the *Pancasaka*; a Digambar list of 11; and some other variants such as the 17 quoted by Yasovijaya. Cf. the various general structures for *puja*, and the various ways of conceiving its relation to the *caitya vandan*, outlined by Williams (1963: 216–18).

11. Elsewhere, Fuller describes priestly initiation ceremonies. He tries to construct an interpretation of the rites but is hampered by the fact that the priests who perform it 'have no grasp of the structure . . . and little cognizance of their intended purpose', Fuller (1985).

12. Feeley-Harnik mentions an example of this in modern Reform Judaism. The *haggadah*, the spoken commentary which accompanies the passover meal, was changed under the direction of Rabbi Herbert Bronstein. The Rabbi wanted the new commentary to have contemporary relevance, for he felt it had become 'dull and thin', and included in it passages from *The Diary of Anne Frank*. It is interesting that his justification for this explicitly distinguishes the *haggadah* from the essential rite: 'The Haggadah is like the libretto of an opera. The opera is the seder itself [the passover meal], and the head of the seder, like the producer of an opera, can alter the libretto.' Quoted in Feeley Harnik (1981: 62–3).

13. These cloths (called *anga luna*—limb cloth) should be specially washed and prepared for use in the temple.

9

Meaning to Mean It

MURTI PUJAK Jains insist that it is necessary that one means to mean. This idea was acknowledged by virtually all our informants at the Dadabari temple. At the same time however, there was no confidence that not having meant disqualifies the *puja* as a *puja*. It is no help to think of this as a 'contradiction' to be explained away as the result of a 'pure' intention-oriented Jainism having been corrupted by a ritual-oriented Hindu world. For it continues a debate about action and intention which has been conducted within Jainism and which has resurfaced right up to the present. In this chapter we shall attempt to show how alive these issues still are, how they compare with similar questioning during the Christian Reformation, and how their remaining unresolved gives rise to the extraordinary combination of behavioural discipline and imaginative freedom which characterizes Jain religious practice in general and the *puja* in particular.

'Meaning to mean' something by one's act is an act of intending. We have suggested, in previous chapters, that ritualized acts are 'non-intentional' in the sense that they are not directly constituted by the actors' intentions in acting. But as a possible reaction to the 'apprehensibility' of ritual acts, an intention, 'meaning to mean', may be superimposed. Perhaps all religious traditions exploit this possibility, to different extents and in different ways. In the Jain case, the worshipper's intention is not simply to hold in his or her mind some propositional religious statement which is applied to the ritual act, but actually to mean to mean it. This is the distinction pointed to by philosophers when they ask what is the difference between saying something and meaning it, and saying it without meaning it (Searle 1983: 169).[1] In ritual, it is impossible for an observer even to guess at whether or not this has happened in any particular case because, unlike in everyday life, the 'conditions of satisfaction' (usually, as we saw in earlier chapters, a change in the state of the self) are entirely subjective; no one except the actor knows if he or she feels that what is being thought is really meant in this sense. But for the actor the distinction is very important. In religion the human propensity for self-understanding does not necessarily take the form of achieving clear, discursive propositions. We noted at the end of Chapter 6 that there is a particular mental medium (*bhav*) by means of which Jains can apprehend ritual acts. *Bhav*, which is extremely difficult to define in English,[2] is undoubtedly as much an emotional as a cogitative state and is not ideational at all (it does not itself imply any particular ideas nor even the necessity of having 'ideas'). *Bhav*, as our Jain friends explained it to us, is something akin to devotion, the experience of deep sincerity, or knowing emotionally that one 'means it'.[3] We should add that notwithstanding the sense everyone has that they should 'mean to mean it', such an intentional component is not always present. As we go on to discuss in the next chapter, ritual acts are often performed without this intentional component and some acts in particular seem to lend themselves to quite another kind of non-intentional spontaneous experiencing. The intentional component which we have called 'meaning to mean' has to be superimposed on a ritual act.

We should clarify where 'meaning to mean' stands in relation to the mimetic re-enactment of ritual acts, which was alluded to in Chapter 4. One possible interpretation of the *puja* is that it is a memorial, but Murti Pujak Jains insist that this meaning must be meant. Similarly reformed Christianity also rejects the idea that there could be a fundamental meaning of a rite which is independent of whatever works within the human actor(s) performing it. Zwingli opposed the idea that the Eucharist is a sacrifice (of the body and blood of Christ), insisting rather that it is a memorial of Christ's once-and-for-all sacrifice (Stephens 1986: 219). For a ritual to be a memorial, those performing it must intend to re-create the primordial acts in this way. Yet the memorial is only one way of seeing the relation between one's own enactment and the original act. It can alternate with, coexist with, and be interpolated with, others. For example, some Jains talked to us of their desire, by their momentary re-creation of true spiritual attainments, to join themselves with God, which is not so much a memorial as a recognition of one's acts, and thus oneself, in another, sacred light. Yet other people spoke of their acts in *puja* as 'offerings', a common idiom which we have mentioned before and which will be discussed more fully in Chapter 11. It is not possible to discuss all of the modes of re-enactment which we encountered—that would belong to another book—but we should point out here that although these attitudes colour whole sequences of actions performed, they do not themselves constitute the propositional meanings given to individual acts which were discussed in the previous chapter, nor are they the same as the feeling of 'meaning it' which is the subject of this chapter. This can be seen from the fact that intentionally adopted modes of ritual re-enactment can include demonstration (for someone else) and ostentation (doing it for show).

'Meaning to mean' therefore is the culmination (in a religious sense) of a series of possible ways of responding to the apprehensibility of ritual acts. We have described these in various parts of this book and in order to be clear we now draw them together in a list:

1. simple copying the prescribed act, which can be done in an ignorant, habitual, or distracted way;
2. spontaneous mental and physical identification with the act resulting in an altered state of consciousness (see next chapter);
3. performing the ritual act in a particular mode of 'mimesis', for example as a symbolic sign, a token, a parody, a translation into one's own manner, a memorial, an offering;
4. giving a definite propositional meaning to the act, but without 'meaning it', for example as in accepting someone else's idea, or thinking of one's accustomed standard formula without experiencing its meaning;
5. meaning to mean, experiencing modes of enactment and propositional meanings as sincerely and emotionally felt (through *bhav*).

We have already discussed why people in general attribute meaning to ritual, responding to the 'apprehensible' character of ritualized acts. There are specific reasons why Jains in particular feel this is necessary, and the rest of this chapter is an attempt to understand how Jains come to the idea of *bhav* from within their religious philosophy. This derives from their interpretations of the doctrine of *karma*, of action and its consequences. Does *bhav* just happen to people, or can it be brought about intentionally?

The problem essentially turns on the question of whether one's action is seen as having an inevitable effect on the soul, irrespective of one's intentions, or whether it is necessary to intend that one's action be 'good' or 'bad', for it to be so. Jain canonical texts put both points of view and it is evident from our fieldwork in Jaipur that the issue has never been resolved. It is hardly a remarkable fact about Jainism, of course, that it has failed to 'resolve' the issues of free will and determinism: like all religions, Jainism has had to develop its own ways of living with both, and this is reflected in the Jains' way of thinking about the paradox of ritual in general. It would be a mistake to force ourselves, as some authors do, to characterize Jainism by a 'view' on this issue. It seems preferable to acknowledge that it is an enduring concern, a locus of debate and disagreement, and a problem, both interpretative and practical, which Jainism has bequeathed to its followers. Anthropologically speaking, this is to see that it is often as important to characterize a culture by what people worry about (and do not resolve) as by the categories, representations, or beliefs which they may share. It is also worth pointing out that many prevailing scholarly accounts, which represent Jainism as a simple, univocal, and determinist dogma, are very misleading.[4]

One side of Jain thought has always recognized, unlike the Buddhists, that whatever your good or bad intentions, any action, indeed life itself, will entrap you in sin. The *Sutrakritanga Sutra* ridicules Buddhists for maintaining an ethic exclusively concerned with intention.[5] 'If a savage puts a man on a spit and roasts him mistaking him for a fragment of the granary; or a baby, mistaking him for a gourd, he will not be guilty of murder according to our [i.e. Buddhist] views' (Jacobi 1895: 414–15). The same text is quite explicit that not only human beings, animals, and plants, but innumerable tiny forms of life in water, fire, air, and earth, being 'born in bodies, originating in bodies, grown in bodies, feeding on bodies, experience their *karma*, are actuated by it, have their form and duration of life determined by it' (Jacobi 1895: 388–98). Each soul is reborn in turn in innumerable different bodies, and carries with it the *karma* which has resulted from the actions of previous lives.

Beings . . . who were sentient in one existence will become senseless ones in another. Not getting rid of, nor shaking off, nor annihilating . . . their *karma*, the thoroughly wicked and ignorant wander from the body of a senseless being into that of sentient one, or from a sentient being into the body of a senseless one, or from a sentient being to that of another, or from a senseless being to that of another. The sentient beings and the senseless ones are both wrong in their conduct and commit sins through cruelty. (Jacobi 1895: 400)

Thus all forms of life, all *jivas*, whether conscious or not, commit sin (Jacobi 1895: 399). This seems unremittingly gloomy, and quite unequivocal as regards intention. However, although all action has effects, and every act binds the soul to *karma*, the precise effects of this depend also on the emotional condition of the soul. As the *Uttaradhyayana Sutra* puts it,

There is glue (as it were) in pleasure. . . . If you take two clods of clay, one wet, the other dry, and fling them against the wall, the wet one will stick to it. Thus foolish men, who love pleasures, will be fastened (to *karma*), but the passionless will not, even as the dry clod of clay (does not stick to the wall). (Jacobi 1895: 141)

The same text elsewhere asserts that it is first necessary to acquire spiritual qualities of mind which will cause subsequent thoughts and actions to be pure and virtuous (Jacobi 1895: 165–71). So Jain scripture contains both a vision of a determinist karmic universe and a contrasting idea of the transcendant qualities of the awakened soul. If even insentient beings commit sin, if action of all kinds produces *karma*, and if mere good intentions do not get one anywhere, how can a Jain escape from these natural, eternally self-reproducing bonds? How does a soul become awakened in this way, so that it can turn away from the karmic web in which it has been entangled since beginningless time?

Most Indian traditions have employed a theistic solution to this kind of problem: the intervention of divine agency turns human souls away from the path of ignorance and sin. But Jainism rejected this view in arguments which reveal much of the logical, egalitarian, and realist emphasis of the tradition.

For the non-Vedic *shramana* traditions of the Ganges Valley, however, the theory of divine intervention generated even more logical problems than it solved. The agent of grace, it was said, would have to be a special sort of being, unlike all other living beings in that it has been forever free of bondage. But how could an unbound being ever come into contact with the world of *samsara*—or influence it—since such actions are by definition limited to the embodied state? If it is admitted, moreover, that even a single being can exist outside the framework of *karmic* entrapment, that same possibility must be admitted for any number of other beings as well. Thus one would be driven into the theory that all souls are in reality unbound, and that we must understand bondage as illusory. But if this is so, if bondage is unreal, then why is there the experience of suffering? (Jaini 1979: 136)

Jainism thus rejected a theistic solution, and it also denied any fatalist notion of automatic salvation.

However, some Jain teachers do have recourse to a supernatural hope. The following passage comes from a sermon given by a Gujarati Jain renouncer, subsequently translated into English and printed as a book. The author explicitly refers to the inadequacy of human thought and speech to account for or convey the experience described.

The story of a very old woman of eighty years by age who was ordered by her mistress to go to the jungle to collect wood in the early hours of the morning is well known. One day, when she returned with the fuel, the mistress found it not enough and angrily snubbed the old woman, saying, 'Can't you see that these pieces of wood are not enough? I wonder if they could burn your dead body even in the cremation. Go back and fetch some more.'

The poor woman, tired, hungry and thirsty, was obliged to go back to the woods. She collected a big burden on her head and started back home. Meanwhile, one piece was isolated from the burden and fell to the ground. Just near that spot, the Divine Lord Mahavir was engaged in addressing the assembly of his devotees. The moment the old woman bent down to pick up the fallen wood, and balanced the tottering burden on her head with the other hand, the sweet nectarlike words of the Lord Mahavir flowed into her ears and that moment was the most blissful experience of her life. She was instantly free not only of the burden of the faggots on her head, but also of the heavier burden of *samsar* [the world of death and rebirth], which she had borne for eighty years. She was deeply immersed in meditation on the Lord's admonition. . . .

Where is the phrase or even a word to describe this sweetness? How can you imagine what is beyond the ken of imagination? Mind, with speech, returns baffled from this experience. The only way to describe it is to offer our quiet salutations to the Divine speech. Our humble silence alone can be our eloquence. (Chandrashekhar 1977: 255–6)

One can see that such a story is inspirational, in the sense that it provides hope for instant, ecstatic release that might come to us all, but Banarsi's autobiography shows how problematic it is to live by such a hope (see Chapter 2). A much more characteristic Jain answer to the determinism of *karma* focuses on and emphasizes the transformative, quasi-miraculous power of insight and understanding. The crucial experience is that of *samyak-darshan*, having the right view, by which the soul glimpses that its true nature is to work for its own salvation. 'Such an experience', writes Jaini, 'is compared to that of a blind man who is suddenly able to see; although the event is momentary, it involves nothing less than an undistorted view of reality' (1979: 142). One does not strive for this vision. It just happens.

There is an essential tension between the vision of spiritual bliss, like that of the old woman, as part of an entirely naturalistic (in Jain terms) cosmic order—a universe which includes the miraculous Jina—and the strictly speaking 'spiritual', almost perhaps 'mystical' importance of human intention. As Jaini writes, 'Consciousness attuned only to actions or the results of actions generates perpetual continuation of the *samsaric* cycle. Upon the attainment of *samyak-darshan*, the soul turns away from such concerns; it undergoes a deliberate and mindful reorientation of attention, coming to focus on nothing but its own nature' (1979: 149). Having achieved *samyak-darshan*, the soul is now free to work towards self-transformation. This is achieved through ascetic practice, but defined still as the work of consciousness, of those qualities of insight (*darshan*), knowledge (*gyan*), bliss (*sukh*), and energy (*virya*) which Jain doctrine holds to be innate to the soul. The human perfection achieved in this way is conceived as advance on the ladder of fourteen stages, or *gunasthana*, which, as we described in Chapter 2, so fascinated Banarsi. These stages consist of the attainment of mental states whereby it becomes possible to act intentionally against *karma*. This 'acting' often takes the form of ascetic discipline and practice, such as fasting and meditation—forms, that is, which can be seen in the characteristically Jain way both as action and as non-action. In either case, one 'acts' to overcome and remove *karma*, the consequences of previous actions, by the conscious ascetic withdrawal from action-in-the-world.

In practice, the progress towards non-action takes the form of re-nunciatory vows (intentional acts *par excellence*), each of which has subclauses explaining how they are to be understood and interpreted in daily life. The five great vows (*maha-vrat*s) are non-violence, not lying, not stealing, sexual restraint, and non-possession. The great vows are paralleled by less exacting equivalents (*anu-vrat*s) which are considered appropriate for especially religious laypeople. In both cases these vows are supplemented by a series of other vows (*guna-vrat*s) which aim to limit the area of a person's activities. Jaini notes (1979: 178) that teachers have likened a layman to a heated iron ball which 'burns' (injures) everything it touches, so it is important to restrict one's sphere of activities. The *guna-vrat*s include voluntary restrictions on travel, on numerous everyday activities,[6] and on minor sinful behaviour.[7]

During the history of Jainism different sects have stressed karmic determinism and transforming insight to different degrees, but the matter has never been settled. The essential point to note is that the main aim of Jain practice, in all schools and orders, is the removal of *karma* from the soul, and the extent to which this can be done depends on the (unknowable) spiritual state of the individual. Yet, arising from the same ideas about *karma* there are other attitudes to spirituality which reduce the role of intentional action. It seems to be possible to perform religiously good actions unintentionally, simply because of the kind of 'fortunate' person one is (the result of the influx of *karma* to one's soul during previous lifetimes as well as this), and chance contact with the divine, as the above story illustrates, can also bring about spiritual awakening. Some Jain teachers deny the value of both intention and action, leaving in their place only mystic contemplation of one's own soul. In other words, there is no separation of the two 'aspects' of Jain doctrine: they are combined in a *terra incognita* which people interpret in their own ways, to which they have their own solutions, and their own tone in which to voice them. Let us quote from a Jain middle-aged businessman talking to Caroline.

The eight kinds of *karma* make the soul (*atma*) heavy and mix up with its impurity. We are responsible for this, just the one man. No other person can give you happiness or trouble—it is only excuses if someone tells you so. If a rickshaw-wallah knocks you down, it is not his fault. It is your own fault: a bad thing was to come to you, from your own acts. . . . You can know if something good is coming to you, or bad. Your *atma* (soul) tells you. Every morning you ask yourself, talk to yourself, 'What have I done in the last twenty-four hours?' Hear the voice of *atma*. This gives us confidence. . . . You can go on doing good to others, but when do you do good to yourself? The main thing is to do good to yourself. Our eyes look outwards, but we forget ourselves. We clean the things which will perish, but what is it that survives in our next rebirth? It is our *atma*. We are misguided, though we have light within us. Lord Mahavir did not do good for others—he said, 'First let *me* be good, then I can do good for others.' This is the fundamental thing.

The Jains we met are more or less agreed that virtually all human beings cannot help but commit sins, whether they intend to or not. The whole intricate apparatus of Jain asceticism—ritualized vows, fasting, confession, and penance—presumes this. Yet all action, even actions of these kinds, are *karma*, and prevent the soul reaching enlightenment. This understanding of religious action emphasizes that the freeing of the soul from *karma* can only take place 'intentionally', on the basis of religious insight. The 'intention' which is conceived to play this role is a specifically religious intention which goes beyond the idea of merely purposive thought, to something akin to 'devotion'. This is the idea of *bhav* with which we began this chapter. It is as this category of *bhav* that the idea of 'enlightenment' enters ritual and, for most Jains, makes it a legitimate religious category of action.

The terms *dravya* (material) and *bhav* (quality) can be used in Jain thinking to designate abstract attributes of a thing, according to the point of view taken. The same terms are also used for substantive things like actions and states of mind. Thus they can be used, as was mentioned in Chapter 2, to denote stages in the performance of the *puja*. Still more germane is the fact that these terms are also used to describe the transformation which should take place in ritualized action itself, when *bhav*, which comes to be understood as a definite, self-perceptible, religious feeling, is generated by actions involving material things (*dravya*). Ritual acts must be deliberately saturated, so to speak, with *bhav*. Like vows, ritual acts in *puja* must be given meanings which define them as acts informed by religious insight, so that they too can become tiny steps on the road to enlightenment.

However, a quite different preoccupation with consciousness in the sense of intentional purpose is stressed by the mainly Digambar followers of Kanji Swami, who trace their spiritual descent back through the teaching of Pandit Todarmal and Banarsi (seventeenth century) to Kunda Kunda (second to third century). Although it does not have a very large following, this tradition is disproportionately influential in contemporary Jainism, largely because its vigorous proselytizing reaches all Jain communities and its combative style forces them to take notice. We give a brief account of what it has to say about intention and meaning.

There is an early Jain text, the *Tattvartha Sutra*, which is acknowledged by all Jains, Digambars, and Shvetambars. It compares the five great vows with ever-increasing 'breathing spaces' of non-action in the inflow of *karma*: a man carrying loads momentarily stops on his way by moving his burden from one shoulder to another, or he pauses to relieve himself, or to rest at a shrine, or to retire from active life for good. These images are open and can be interpreted in various ways.

Let us see how this is understood by the Kanji Swami tradition. A pandit from this group writes that ritual fasting alone is not a real penance: the avoidance of food should stand for the mental detachment from all passions and enjoyments. 'One with a right outlook is alone fit to practise penance' (Bharilla 1981*a*: 83). To this statement, Jains of all sects would assent, but in a Jesuitical argument characteristic of this group, the vows themselves are then rejected because even they may engender attachments (to the very doing of them) and are thus equivalent in a sense to not taking vows: 'The five non-vows (violence, etc.) give impious bondage while the five vows (like non-violence, etc.) give pious bondage. The exhaustion of both leads to *moksh*. So one covetous of *moksh* should not only give up non-vows but also vows' (Bharilla 1981*a*: 132). Thus this sect effectively undermines the whole apparatus of structured intentional austerity (including the orders of renouncers) by demanding that one should 'transcend' it.[8]

Again, religious teachers in all Jain traditions recognize the importance of acts of consciousness. Some contemporary teachers describe this spiritual activity as beginning with 'seeing' (*darshan*), which is superior to reasoning (Mahaprajna 1980: 3–11, 33).[9] Others, like Bharilla, the most prominent of the Kanji Swami movement's leaders in Rajasthan, emphasize 'knowing', where the object of knowledge is the Self, but the 'knowing' should be of a certain spiritual, non-intellectual kind which is illustrated by a story about a boy who lost his mother and was found by a policeman.

'What does your mother look like?' A boy who has lost his mother will readily say, 'My mother is like my mother.' 'What is her name?' 'Why, Mummy!' he will say at once. 'Is she white-skinned or dark-skinned, tall or short, fat or slim?' To these questions perhaps he can give no reply; for he has never seen or known his mother in these forms. He has known her only as his mother. . . . The policeman may say that the boy does not know his mother, what she looks like or what her name is. Then how do we search for her and find her? But is it necessary for the boy to know her name? Is it not enough that she is the 'Mummy' he has called her every day? Maybe he is unable to describe his mother in so many words, but then it is wrong, wholly wrong, to say that he does not recognise her. To know one is something different from to describe one. (Bharilla 1981*a*: 98)

And elsewhere he writes, 'The senses and the mind are not only useful in capturing, in grasping the supersensitive emotionless soul but are hindrances . . . because so long as the soul continues knowing and seeing through the media of the senses and the mind, till then the perception of the soul (self realization) will not be possible' (1981*b*: 178). The ideal here is to know the Self (*atma*, the immortal soul) in this way, which means to be lost in the Self, to acquire the 'feeling' of the Self, and to forget even the 'true gods, texts, and the guru'.[10]

Other Jain sects do not follow this line of reasoning. There certainly is a paradox in the Kanji Swami position since rejecting all forms of purposive action somehow leaves all the activity which does actually occur unattended to. The followers of this sect in fact perform rituals in abundance. These they continue willy-nilly, imitating what has gone on before, without a theory to explain these rituals and regardless of what the pandits say. Since rituals are ignored, the whole discourse of *bhav*, which attempts to deal with the emergent features of action, is also absent. But in the idol-worshipping sects, like the Khartar Gacch and the Tapa Gacch, ritual action is incorporated in religion, if not theoretically then at least by means of practical methods. Here, ascetic renouncers remain the paradigm of the religious teacher, and this is precisely because they do practise, rather than 'transcend', the ritualized forms of asceticism.

For our respondents, *bhav* refers to the mental state akin to 'devotion' in which the correct ideas can arise. It can thus also be seen as co-ordinate with the *gunasthana* stages: it enables the worshipper to proceed directly to experience of the divine by positing worshipful insight. This insight grows greater at each stage, it is true, but is still possible right at the beginning. Having the correct *bhav* is therefore the ordinary lay Jain's way of realizing the principle of religious 'non-action' which supersedes action. This can be done in a number of ways, and while some people describe *bhav puja* as a contentless meditation, or even an altered state of consciousness, for most ordinary Jains it consists precisely of 'meaning to mean' in ritual.

Perhaps we should quote some of our informants to show how they express these ideas. *Bhav* as a religious category is regarded as so sacred that the meaning it generates seems to be shared with the divine, even to derive from it. As used by the Jains we met, *bhav* has much in common with *bhakti* (devotional worship), which is a key idea in modern Hindu Vaishnavism. Occasionally our respondents used the word *bhakti* interchangeably with *bhav*, and undoubtedly many of them were influenced by the increasing popularity of devotionalism in northern India (see the next chapter).

1. *A middle-aged business man, Khartar Gacch.* '*Dravya* is when we put things out in *puja*, *bhav* is when we think about it with our heart. When we put water to clean the idol, we must think, "So my soul will be clean." The *dravya puja* is only for *bhav puja*.'

2. *A retired jeweller, Khartar Gacch.* 'Now we come to *agra puja*—I have told you all the meanings of this. But the important thing is, we have only to control this [points to his tongue], we have to control taste. [Laughs] Yesterday you said the food at the *ayambil* [ritual fast] was tasty—but it was not! We must not think it was delicious. My mouth is like a letter-box, food is like any parcel, letter, maybe a card—like this we should not taste it. This is action for the purification of the heart. If *bhav* is not there, we are thinking about other things, we are tasting, then *rag* [desire] and *dvesh* [aversion] will be there. That is useless.

3. *An elderly female ascetic, Khartar Gacch.* 'When we put sandalwood on the feet of the idol, we think, "This big toe of the god (Bhagwan) is so pure (*pavitra*), we do this *bhavana*,[11] that its *bhav* may come into me."'

How is *bhav puja* performed? The structure of ritualization, whereby distinct acts are separated out, appears to correspond with a deliberate stopping of the natural flow of thoughts, replacing them with concentration on a particular object. We have evidence of this from what was told us by a senior nun. She said she does *bhav puja* by placing an idol before her (she did not make clear whether she thought the idol need be physically present or not) and making it a symbol (*pratik*). She then chooses as her 'object' in turn each ritual act, which she does not perform (but which laypeople do perform), and 'having it in front of me as a model (*alamban*), I make contemplation of that'. She listed each of the acts of the entire *puja*, citing the meanings she gave them, some of which have been quoted elsewhere in this book. To give one last example, this is what she said about the final offering, the placing of fruit.

The eighth *puja* is fruit. Taking it as a symbol (*pratik*) we make contemplation on that, thinking, 'I offer fruit so that I should attain the fruit of liberation, *moksh*, the only fruit that I deserve'. And thinking, 'Oh, that I would not get attracted by these things.' We have been eating all these things, but it is not the soul (*jiv*) that eats them, only the body. As long as we are only this body we will be attracted to them. When we achieve *samyak darshan* then we are not attracted by tastes and eat only to sustain the body. The offering of this food is because I want to meditate and worship with the help of this body. And I am thinking, 'Oh, that I want the fruit of my actions.'

'Meaning to mean' (or *bhav*) is central for Jains not just because of the theological ideas we have been discussing but because Jains live in a world in which it is assumed that ritual has effects. The crucial issue is the legitimacy of these effects. With regard to ritual efficacy a similar tension exists within contemporary Jainism to that which dominated the Christian Reformation in the fifteenth and sixteenth centuries. Most Protestants in Europe and North America now find the idea of ritual efficacy independent of human subjectivity pretty well incomprehensible. But this was not so for Calvin or Zwingli, and modern Jains, as we have suggested, find the idea all too compelling. For Jains of a 'protestant' cast of mind in Jaipur today, the rejection and repudiation of intrinsic ritual efficacy is still as important and powerful a religious gesture as it was for Zwingli and Calvin. The gestures themselves, of course, are different. The Reformation was a reaction to an enormous growth in the cult of saints, images, relics, and use of indulgences in late-medieval Catholicism. Calvin, in his polemic against Catholic piety, developed a theory of reverential acts in which any act of worship is said to be objectively spiritual and to connect the human with God's sphere. This is the nature of any religious act, even one performed for a false deity. Since every act of worship is charged with this spiritual reality, which is related to God, it is wasted if it does not have the true God as its object. For Calvin, this transaction is as objective as the motion of one's hand. The subjective aspect of worship is the intention of the worshipper. But Calvin's conclusion is that the act of worship cannot be considered from this perspective. This is because the reality of God is the supreme reality. Every reverential act 'cannot but savour of something divine'.[12] Therefore, worship cannot but detract from God's honour if it is directed at the fictitious divinities dreamed up in man's subjectivity.

Jainism deals with this set of problems in a different way. The Jains have never been fierce about sacrilege, because they have always held that divinity is beyond offence. Wrong, careless, or ignorant actions can only harm one's own potential to become a 'god' (i.e. omniscient). The very habit of denunciation is foreign to our friends in the Khartar order. 'There is no difference between Issu [Jesus] and Mahavir,' said one old man, 'the end is the same, only the ways are different.' For Calvin the presence of a jealous God necessitates directing worship only to Him. But for Jains the requirement is different; it is to ride above merely worldly benefits of ritual. The Jain ideal is to take with one an all-encompassing religious mental attitude, thus superseding the world and *its* qualities. A prominent Khartar nun gave a sermon, at which James was present:

A boat will sink if it has holes in it. Likewise, if you lose concentration it is bad. If you are always thinking of your family your *puja* will fail. You will drown. Just as a lotus sits in the dirty water, but sits above it and doesn't sink into it, so we can live in the world. We may live in a family, but we can choose to be like a lotus.

> If I am in the world
> Then danger is far away.
> If the world is in me
> Then I'll surely sink.

This is like the difference between a boat in the water and water in the boat . . . living in the world we must do our own religious duty (*dharma*) but we must ignore the senses.

In practice, as the reader may already have noticed, the personal conviction that the ritual has been made meaningful, performed with *bhav*, is more important than specific assertions as to what the meaning might be. This accounts for the wide range of interpretations attached by Jains to any single ritual action, even where liturgically 'correct' meanings are available in allegedly authoritative literature. It is in these terms that we can understand both the equivocal 'emptiness' of the act itself and the boundless consequences of the mental attitude with which it is enacted.

What can we conclude about the 'meaning to mean' with which Jains feel they should approach their ritual acts? Religious authorities can provide their own interpretations, and these can be considered authoritative, but the religious requirement is not just that the ritual should be given meaning, it is that the worshipper should 'mean it', as he or she performs it. This protestant attitude has an important consequence. It implies that an account, like that given by Putnam, of a linguistic division of labour in the use of specialist terms, no longer applies: 'meaning to mean' strains to counteract it.

In such a division of labour I can rely on experts to guarantee that in speaking of an elm as different from a birch tree, my words have meaning, even if I have no notion of what the difference between the two kinds of tree might be. We explained in Chapter 6 how this does apply in the use of natural-kind terms, and hence, we suggested, in the initial apprehension of ritual acts. Ritual acts are referred to by the actors in terms analogous to natural-kind terms; that is, they are attached to classes of entity whose underlying nature is elucidated only by a theory, not in virtue of sets of necessary and sufficient conditions (Johnson–Laird 1983: 195). Putnam (1975) has pointed out the implication of this: such meanings 'just ain't in the head'. As Johnson–Laird put it,

Natural language would be a poor instrument for communication, or for externalizing thought, if it only contained terms specifying classes in virtue of sets of necessary and sufficient conditions. It is very useful to be able to point at some substance and say, 'Let's call that kind of stuff, whatever it is, *blodge* from now on.' However, the true intension of such a word—always supposing that it has one—is not very interesting; either it is in an expert's mind (though no one can know for sure that the right meaning is there), or it is in no one's mind and accordingly an idle wheel in the intellectual traffic of the world. (1983: 195).

If the terms for ritual acts are like this, our suggestion is that religious attitudes, especially protestant ones, may attempt to reappropriate meaning for the mind. The religious point is that you should take responsibility for your own meanings; you should learn what an elm (a *pushpa puja*, an *akshat puja*) is, rather than letting someone else know what it is for you. If you want to progress spiritually (or to 'talk with God'—one can imagine a number of different religious idioms here) you must attain a feeling both that you know what a term means and that *you* mean it. This does not actually alter the nature of the terms, whose objects remain ultimately and essentially unknowable, but it insists on the religious *feeling* of knowing by the self, which in the case of the Jains is accomplished by means of *bhav*. In this situation expert opinion, always voiced from somewhere outside the individual 'meaning-giving' subject, can no longer impose its meaning on the ritual. Indeed, in insisting that the meaning must be meant, that there must be personal and individual *bhav*, this route to consensus, through deference to authority, is effectively blocked.

In some religious traditions, the suspicion of ritual results in such insistent attempts to establish consensus about its meaning—attempts by religious authority to orchestrate the thoughts and intentions of practitioners—that the ritual itself is destroyed or ceases to be recognizably ritual. We have in mind here the extremes of 'lowness' in Christianity, or many events in Shvetambar Sthanakvasi religious life, in which worship resembles most a lecture or a class, and in which experience of the transcendent cedes its place entirely.

Notes

1. Searle writes, 'When I say something and mean it, my utterance has conditions of satisfaction in a way that it does not have any such conditions if I say it without meaning it. If I say "Es regnet" as a way of practicing German pronunciation, then the fact that the sun is shining when I utter this sentence is irrelevant. But if I say "Es regnet" and mean it, then the fact that the sun is shining is relevant, and it becomes relevant because saying something and meaning it is a matter of saying it with the conditions of satisfaction intentionally imposed on the utterance' (1983: 169).
2. '*Bhav*' is used in a wide variety of contexts, secular as well as religious. Its clutch of meanings include 'that which is manifest' or 'that which becomes', 'way', 'manner', 'meaning', 'emotion', and 'the inherent character of something'.
3. For a discussion of Indian merging of emotion and thought see Lynch (1990).
4. Paul Dundas (1985: 162) also makes this point and John Cort (1989: 18–41) gives an excellent discussion of the deficiencies of what he calls the 'standard portrait' of Jainism.
5. Authorities on modern Buddhism suggest that popular ethics in the Theravada tradition continues to be basically an ethic of intention. See especially Gombrich (1971).
6. Such as engaging in undesirable professions, eating many 'hot' foods, cooking after sunset, and drinking unfiltered water.
7. For example, brooding (contemplating harm to oneself or others), purposeless mischief, such as gambling, cutting trees, or digging in the ground for no reason, facilitation of destruction (by keeping or selling poisons, guns, etc.), giving harmful advice, helping hunters find animals, and 'purposeless listening' such as to lewd shows or music (Jaini 1979: 179–80).
8. Its teaching more or less bypasses the ascetic renouncers and the highly ritualized code of coduct which helps them to avoid, as much as is possible, the unavoidable sin to which all action in the world gives rise. Teaching in this sect is the preserve of lay pandits, who address (berate) their lay followers directly. Meanwhile, the few naked ascetics who occasionally wander into their religious functions are given relatively little attention. In this tradition

'conduct' (*caritra*) is redefined as a detached, passion-free state which is said to arise directly from having the right attitude (*samyak-darshan*). So the fact that the renouncers actually practise an extremely exacting code of conduct is downplayed in comparison with the lay teachers' emphasis on virtuous attitudes, such as forbearance, modesty, and straightforwardness.

9. Yuvacharya Mahaprajna is the heir apparent to the leadership of the Shvetambar Terapanth.

10. There is a tendency in Kanji Swami teaching to speak now and then of an encompassing mega-soul (*paramatma*) with which individual souls seek to merge, as in the Vedanta. But this is not clearly distinguished from the more orthodox Jain view that there are plural souls, each of which ultimately attains its own release.

11. *Bhavana*, which is derived from the same verb as is *bhav*, but which adds the feminine ending for abstract nouns -*na*, was also commonly used by our respondents. Its meanings include 'perception', 'consciousness', 'morale', a particular mood or emotion, and a (transient) mode of *bhav*.

12. Calvin: *Institutes* (1. 12. 3), quoted in Eire (1986: 213–14).

10

The Evocation of Mood

WE said earlier that people coming to the temple for *puja* encounter ritualized acts, as it were, ready for them to perform. These acts have no intrinsic meaning but they are 'apprehensible', waiting to be acted out in different modes and given symbolic meanings by the celebrants. This is an observation about the acts, not about the actor who performs them. But there are a few ritualized acts that are sometimes treated differently. Their apprehensibility rests not so much in their readiness for ideas to be attached to them as in the sensations and psychological states the acts themselves may induce, the very feelings aroused by enacting them. In a preliminary way we can describe this as becoming 'lost' in the act. Actually, this possibility is not much exploited in Jainism, but we devote a chapter to it because of its prominence in other more ecstatic traditions, and to show how the approach we are proposing applies in such cases. The initiation of these psychological states seems to be the result of an attitude or readiness in the actor, since not everyone takes up the apprehensibility of the acts in this way. We have called the episodes in which this occurs, 'emergent moods', a term which is meant to indicate not a particular type of act but an aspect of the ritual stance, that is, a special (emotional) way of constituting an act as ritualized.

The episodes of emergent moods can be seen as an alternative path by which the stipulated ritual acts are reappropriated by the self: instead of giving discursive meanings to the act, the celebrant here becomes absorbed in the act. Now it is true that one can become absorbed in any action, ritualized or not, indeed that some level of absorption (or paying attention) to what one is doing is the normal condition of intentional action. But ritualization seems to produce a different situation. We suggest that just as the meanings given to ritual acts are not everyday meanings, but symbolic and cultural meanings separated from the physical identity of the act, similarly the absorption of 'emergent mood' episodes is not at all a simple matter of paying attention to the point of what one is doing. The emotions aroused are in everyday terms inappropriate to the action, sometimes grossly so, such that an observer might well ask, how can such an act (which comes to appear trivial, as any non-purposeful action does) arouse such emotions? We shall venture the suggestion in our conclusion that this feature of ritualization, which is to provide a dynamic means for the emergence of disjunct meanings and emotions, is one reason why it exists at all.

The occasions for emergent moods are very various and we do not pretend that the examples we give below are all those which occur in Jain religious life. The more puritan of our informants disapproved of them, in much the same way, one imagines, that 'enthusiasm' was frostily dismissed in the eighteenth-century Church of England. Certainly, it is impossible not to see in much of what we describe below the influence of the devotional (*bhakti*) practices of certain branches of Hinduism, most particularly those currents of Vaishnavism that are popular among the merchant castes of western India. But despite the fact that 'Hindu influence' is frequently ascribed by certain learned Jains to 'the superstitions of the common people' we could find no evidence that emergent moods were the province only of certain social categories (such as gender, caste, or class). In the 1950s, G. M. Carstairs (1957) observed the repugnance of high-status Brahmins, Rajputs, and Jains in Rajasthan for *bhakti-marg* (Hindu devotional worship) and for the zealous singing of hymns (*bhajan*s). And Jains, as we note below, have negative attitudes towards the worldly emotions. However, the prevalence of what we have called 'emergent moods' shows that certain kinds of religious emotion are cultivated by some people, and it is the relation between this and ritualization that we seek to explain in this chapter.

An example of an 'emergent mood' can occur during the waving of a ceremonial fly-whisk (*camar*) before the idol, which is often done together with a celebratory dance for the god.[1] These dances surprised us at first; they were so different from the quiet, reflective *puja* we knew. A collection of people might be sitting praying, or singing hymns, when suddenly some matrons, a young girl, or a couple of dignified middle-aged men would get to their feet and sway into dance, twirling the *camar*s with both arms, and circling round. Dancing always consists of the same actions whatever the occasion, a swaying from foot to foot, waving the arms, and turning round on one spot. There are no formal dance steps as far as we could tell, and each person performs his or her dance alone, without reference to other people. Some people merely perform a few embarrassed circles. Others dance energetically, shooting their arms into the air. Their eyes would glaze over. Sometimes they would shout out, 'Victory to Lord Mahavir!' At the great public *puja*s, such as the *panc-kalyanak*, this dancing can be frenzied and wild. Men struggle and push one another to obtain the *camar*s, and having grabbed them, leap up and down to the insistently rhythmic music, whirling round and round. Men and women both dance, though usually in separate areas or at different times. Everyone else then sings or claps, a kind of joyful encouragement.

Let us describe a few more of these emergent moods. During the *snatra puja* for the birth of the Lord Jina we sometimes saw women sitting by themselves for long periods, absorbed in worlds of their own, crouched over, swaying rhythmically, hugging something to themselves. They were holding tiny mirrors, cradled in their arms. As with the other prescribed acts of the *puja*, this could have various meanings. When we later asked people about it they said that the mirrors showed the reflection of the idol. One woman said, 'We look at the reflection so that the baby God should be in our heart. The glass is pure (*shuddh*)—if we keep a glass at our heart we feel God is also in our heart.' Another said, 'God is spirit, so the mirror is a way to get the baby God into our lap—we want any way to hug the baby in our lap.'[2] During this episode of the *puja*, the *pujari* rings the temple bell which, 'is like the bell we ring for joy when a baby is born'. Anyone performing this act might give one of these explanations, but in the way that some people became immersed in what they were doing there seemed to be something else going on.

Another example of an 'emergent mood' happens at *darshan*, the auspicious 'sight' of the god. Shvetambar Murti Pujak Jains glue two (sometimes three) large eyes made of mirror-glass to the statues of the Jinas, the *guru-dev*s, and many of the protector deities. In a dimly lit temple this has the effect of making the eyes seem to glow, like animals' eyes at night. People told us that these mirror eyes are particularly important during *darshan*. As a ritual act *darshan* involves simply looking at the idol, and perhaps saying the *vandan* prayers, but since the term has many related meanings, including audience (with a king), insight, perception, and 'system of philosophy' we can infer that there is more to it than that.[3] One of our friends described his *darshan* of Mallinath, the seventeenth Jina, believed by Shvetambar Jains to have been a woman (Digambars deny this). As we were talking we were near the Mallinath statue, which is next to an absolutely identical statue of Shantinath, a male Jina.[4]

See the eyes! I feel those eyes are loving, yes, those eyes are loving me. So brilliant, everything is in those eyes. And when I look at her I see a woman. See the curve of her cheek, her neck is different from that of a man. You see it is completely different from this one [Shantinath].[5] My eyes meet her eyes and they shine into my soul. Her eyes draw me towards her. They draw me into her, and suddenly I experience bliss (*sukh*). I feel all these things, so many things, when I have *darshan* of this idol.

Darshan is not a passive 'seeing', but an act of positive visual and mental engagement with the god. When an image is installed in a Jain temple, one of the essential episodes of the *panc-kalyanak* consecration rites is the *anjan shalaka* (literally, 'the rod for applying kohl'), the enlivening of the image, and this takes place through fixing on the eyes. Without this ritual, people say, the statue is mere stone. We shall not go through the issues which this raises here (How can the deity be in the statue if he has left this world for *moksh*? What kind of power does the god in the statue have?) which are much the same in Buddhism and have been discussed by Gombrich (1966, 1971) and others.[6] But the fact is that the act of gazing at the reflecting eyes of the god seems often to engender a mental state which is more intense than that associated with, say, placing flowers or dabbing sandalwood paste upon it. We should emphasize that for many people *darshan* is a most perfunctory affair, the quickest and easiest way of putting in an appearance at the temple before rushing off to the day's work. For others it brings a sense of calm and peace to the beginning of the day. Only a few people described anything like the ecstatic experience noted above. But in all cases *darshan* was described as a feeling experienced rather than a proposition represented.

A fourth example occurs during *arti*, the 'offering' of lamps, which as we mentioned in Chapter 2 happens in the evening as a separate ritual, as well as punctuating the morning *puja*. For *arti*, five or seven small oil lamps are placed on a tray, together with some coins, and the worshipper stands in front of the idol holding the tray at shoulder height, making a circular movement in the air,[7] and chanting the *arti* prayer.[8] At this time, the *pujari* rings the bell, hard and insistently, with a deafening clanging (as anyone who has ever tried to work out what people are chanting during it will know). Like the cradling of the mirror, *arti* can be done in quite a perfunctory way, but very often it becomes much more than this: people bend and sway the whole top part of their bodies and seem to lose themselves in the act. It is quite tiring and difficult to keep one's balance while making such circular movements, particularly when the *arti* goes on for a long time.

Some Jains we knew went to other temples specially to perform evening *arti*. These are temples which have shrines for powerful deities of the land (*kshetrapal*) able to cure people of possession by evil spirits. Possessed people are explicitly forbidden to perform *puja*. They are thought no longer to be acting as themselves, but as dictated by the spirits which have taken up residence in their bodies.[9] However, we briefly describe the process of possession, as we observed it at the Jain temple at Padampura, outside Jaipur, because it illustrates how *arti* can be transformed as it is enacted, and because there is a complex area of psychology which it opens up. We should note that spirit possession occurs throughout South Asia, although the value which is placed on it in different religious contexts varies considerably. The contrast between the ecstatic scenes at Padampura and the usual round of quiet devotions could hardly be more marked. Many of our Hindu friends, and some Jains too, were as surprised as we were to discover such a flourishing possession cult in a Jain temple.

The temple is known as the court (*darbar*) of the god, that is Padmaprabhu Bhagwan, the sixth Jina, and his *kshetrapal*. Possessed people may spend months living in the temple precincts while spirits are gradually removed. Exorcisms take place in the evening, during *arti*, especially on full-moon nights. One afflicted Rajput said he had been staying there for three months and in that time 165 ghosts (*bhut*s) had been driven from him. The *kshetrapal* shrine is outside the temple, in a niche in the external wall near the door. But *arti* starts inside the temple, in front of the main Jina statue. Right at the front, before the Jina, are possessed women, now not standing but crouched on hands and knees on the floor, their hair untied, long and loose. Although the possessed women are not performing the *puja*, others in the temple are. These women are brought before the deity in the hope that *arti* will 'bring the spirit out', that is, will make it declare its desires so it can be satisfied and removed. To the rhythmic clapping of the congregation, including men and children, the possessed people bow their heads over until they nearly touch the ground and wave their heads in continuous rotating movements so that their hair flies in the air, round and round. They breathe convulsively and sometimes wail and moan, and a bell rings loudly, at walking pace, in time with the clapping. Some people in the crowd suddenly throw their arms in the air, crying, 'Victory to Lord Padmaprabhu', while others may drop to their knees and perform the same circular actions. We saw one small boy doggedly rotating his head, sagging and straightening himself weakly in the shadowy recesses of the temple. Meanwhile, sections of the crowd may rush to another Jina image, where frenzied clapping heralds another even more intense *arti*, but the possessed people stay where they are, seemingly incapable of stopping their obsessive movements. Suddenly, however, the Jina *arti* is over and everyone rushes outside to the shrine of the *kshetrapal*, the possessed people's family members helping them along as best they can. Here, the possessed resume the abandoned circular movements and their relatives, often aided by a *kshetrapal* medium, attempt by different means, sometimes violently, to make the spirits speak. They implore the deity to remove the spirits, vowing to offer *puja*s or donations in return. The most difficult part of the exorcism is getting the spirits to agree to relinquish their captive, and people told us that the 'court' punishes them if they are stubborn, and they often reply in kind. In effect this means 'punishing' the afflicted person. We saw husbands hitting their wives and sisters tearing one another's hair for this reason. The area in front of the *kshetrapal* shrine seethes with knots of shouting, screaming people, as families engage with the resentments and insults let out by the spirits. Sometimes the 'punishment' is self-inflicted. We were told of a Hindu temple near Jaipur where possessed women dig pits in the earth and put their heads in them, punishing the spirit by not eating and hardly breathing. This is known as 'hanging the spirit'. These 'punishments', observers say, do not hurt the possessed people, but it is difficult to believe this.

This description suggests that there are several different kinds of altered states of consciousness which form a continuum, initiated by *arti*. There is the exaltation of the rhythmic act, then the sudden inspiration which makes people oblivious to everything around them, then a kind of sympathetic 'possession' (seen by falling to the floor and making circular movements), which is not regarded as serious unless it is also manifest outside the temple and prevents normal functioning, and finally there is spirit possession, in which the subject's normal personality is replaced by some manifestation of the spirit or spirits. Jains seem to use the word *bhav*, or derivatives of it, for the states of mind short of actual possession. It is interesting that Gold (1988a: 95) notes that possessed women in her Rajasthani Hindu community were called simply *bhav*. We agree with Obeyesekere (1981: 169) that it is not really possible (at least at the present stage of research) to differentiate between the various psychological states involved and we take up his suggestion that they be called 'hypnomantic'.

At first we thought that these enactments had a different relation to intentionality from that which we have described for ritualized acts in general. Earlier we said that intention in ritualized action is disconnected from everyday intention, in that the identity of the act is unconnected to the intention of the actor. In the kind of emergent mood we are considering it seemed to us initially that this condition did not apply: the dance simply would not be performed if the celebrant did not feel like acting this way. Maybe in this case people were again simply authors of their own acts? Perhaps these emergent moods were purely intentional acts, bits of 'worldly emotion' which had seeped into the ritual? This might explain why they are disapproved of by the more ascetically minded Jains. From this point of view emergent moods seemed to be simply less ritualized, or non-ritualized, episodes inserted into the *puja*.

But we soon came to see that the 'emergent mood' episodes are as much ritualized acts as any other part of the *puja*. Indeed, we wonder if it may be largely through the presence of just such actions that performance-centred events in less liturgical religious traditions come to be, in so far as they are, ritualized. To begin with, they are not the everyday action of which they are a simulacrum: there is no baby, nothing has happened to occasion a dance for joy. Then, like other ritualized acts, all they have to be is something which 'counts as' the act. In all cases short of full possession, there are no consequences of their being done feebly as a token or passionately as the fervent act of a devotee. Furthermore, as in the rest of the *puja* these episodes are comprised of standardized acts. Gold observed possessed women at a Rajasthani Hindu festival of worship of the river Ganges (*Ganga puja*) where the actions are considerably more varied than those of Jain possessed people,[10] but even of this she comments that the seemingly erratic behaviour is in fact patterned and predictable (1988a: 96). Finally, these acts have their place in the sequence of the *puja* and they have the ritualized feature of being foreclosed (they can be completed on their own account without consequences for other ritual acts). In effect, they are divorced from 'intentional meaning', since as with other parts of the *puja*, emergent moods are culturally recognized psychological states cum physical actions which are available for people to switch into. They are widely believed—and we see no reason to doubt this—to have been part of Indian religious tradition for a very long time. Thus they are quite different in these ways from everyday acts which really do intrude on the *puja*, such as readjusting one's sari over one's head, or putting money in the collecting-boxes.

Still, the emergent moods episodes seemed different from the rest of the *puja*. Although symbolic propositional meanings were occasionally proffered for the prescribed acts, the focus of peoples' attention was not on these but on the psychological changes effected, through the actor's body, by the actions themselves. These changes occur spontaneously, and do not happen, unlike the attribution of propositional meanings, as the result of an act of intending. In our view, as with the elemental acts in the *puja* on which these moods may be superimposed, these emotional extensions have no intentional meaning. They are additional psychological reactions, which also have a ritualized 'archetypal' character, intervening in the enactment of the prescribed act.

Focus on physical acts is of course a recurring theme in Indian religions, from sophisticated yogic systems to trance behaviour (Kakar 1984). Jains do use yogic body positions (see the next chapter) but we are concerned here with something closer to the trance. The point that culturally patterned body movements can be used to produce specific psychological states is made in an interesting paper by Alfred Gell (1980). This describes among the Muria, a tribal people of Central India, the pursuit of a religiously valued state of vertigo by means of dance, swinging on a swing, certain postures of offering, and possession. The Muria achieve a state of 'deautomatized' or disembedded sensory-motor integration. Gell (1980: 223) notes the 'instrumental role of dance in Muria culture as a device for inducing non-normal psychological states in the performers, rather than as a means for communicating symbolic statements mimetically'. Gell describes the Muria as experiencing the presence of the god in communal dancing, not as an idea, but as a 'tangible physical quantity perceived somasthetically rather than intellectually constructed' (1980: 225), as a force acting directly on and through the body. The physical media used by Muria people to achieve the state of vertigo (communal dance, singing, oscillatory motions with a pole representing the god, ritual use of swings, the trembling of a possessed medium, and the circular movement by the priest when making offerings) are not the same as the Jain examples we are considering. But they have in common repetitive, circular, or oscillatory movements of the upper body. Such movements, if we accept the neurobiological evidence put forward by Gell, affect the normal functioning of the 'equilibrium sense' and the operation of the vestibular system. The vestibular system, to quote Gell (1980: 242), does not merely monitor equilibrium, 'it is closely keyed in with the control of the eye-muscles (ocularvestibular system) and also with the reflex control of the muscles of the head, neck and upper body, and the control of posture'. In our Jain cases, the bowed-over swaying movement of 'cradling', the sweeping arm movements of dance with whisks, the circular undulating rhythm of waving the lamp, even the crouched-over, to-and-fro movements of scrubbing the idol (often performed in an unbalanced posture since one has to climb on to ledges of the idol's pediment) all may conduce to weak forms of disturbance of the equilibrium sense, while the abandoned, lurching, swaying of the upper body, and circular tossing of the hair in possession must undoubtedly affect it strongly.

Except in spirit possession Jains do not enter full trance states during these ritual enactments, so they do just about have intelligible things to say about what goes on as they enter a hypnomantic state. Gell (1980: 224) notes that Muria people feel that the state attained, vertigo, is a 'surrender', and Jains use the same expression. Our friends rarely gave any explicit reason or discursive explanation of what they were doing. Even when asked, 'Why do you do this?', which for other *puja* acts normally gave rise to a flood of religious explanatory discourse, people in these cases would usually respond only by describing what they *did*. This response suggested to us that perhaps these emergent moods might have something in common with what Merleau-Ponty (1962: 103) calls 'abstract action', that is, 'movements not relevant to any particular situation' (See Chapters 4 and 6 where the idea of abstract action was introduced).

The idea of abstract action rests on how the body is seen. What is interesting for us is that Merleau-Ponty shows how the self is apprehended as both subject and object, as capable not only of 'seeing' and 'suffering' but also of abstracting its own action as an object, such as occurs with the parcelling of acts and the kind of displacement of intention we have mentioned for ritualization. The fact that the self is not only object but also subject, however, allows abstract action to create its own subjective 'projections'. In Chapter 6 we discussed Merleau-Ponty's description of the distinction between 'beckoning someone' and the abstract action of simply flexing of the forearm without having any present or even imaginary partner and we noted that even in the latter case, at some level of consciousness, a 'directedness' persists. The phenomenon of spirit-possession trance also demonstrates this: people coming out of these trances commonly say they do not know what they were doing and their family does not hold them responsible for their words and actions. Yet during the possession trance people act in specific, patterned ways (the circling of the head and shoulders) and not in the numberless other ways possible. This indicates that even ritualized possession is in some sense 'directed' and not totally formless, incoherent activity. But what is the nature of this 'directedness'?

If we return to the emergent moods which occur in the *puja*, when the subject is at some level aware of his or her actions, the following passage from Merleau-Ponty is relevant. He writes about abstract action as follows,

My body, which a moment ago was the vehicle of the movement, now becomes its end; its motor project is no longer directed at someone in the world, but towards my fore and upper arm, and my fingers; and it is directed towards them, furthermore, in so far as they are capable of breaking with their involvement in the given world and giving shape around me to an imaginary situation. . . . The abstract movement carves out within that plenum of the world in which concrete movement took place a zone of reflection and subjectivity: it superimposes upon physical space a potential or human space. Concrete movement is therefore centripetal whereas abstract movement is centrifugal. The former occurs in the realm of being or of the actual, the latter on the other hand in that of the possible or the non-existent; the first adheres to a given background, the second throws out its own background. (1962: 111)

Abstract action no longer involves intentional action towards things in the outside world, but Merleau-Ponty is suggesting that this is not merely negative but that it opens up a space, as it were, for its own projections. If we take up this insight, certain ritualized acts can be seen as 'apprehensible', not solely in the sense of their being apt for the attribution as yet unformulated, cultural, and symbolic meanings, but also (and alternatively) as potentially physically absorbing, an absorption which nevertheless may imply a subjective 'projection' or 'summoning'. Merleau-Ponty explains this as follows,

Abstract movement is endangered in so far as it presupposes awareness of an objective, is borne on by that awareness. . . . Indeed, it is not triggered off by any existing object, but is clearly centrifugal, outlining in space a gratuitous intention which has reference to one's own body, making an object of it [the abstract movement] instead of going through it to link up with things by means of it. It is then diffused with the power of objectification, a 'symbolical function', a 'representative function', a power of 'projection', which is, moreover, already at work in forming 'things'. (1962: 111–12, 121)

'Abstract action' is a category invented in order to explain features of action and consciousness. Nevertheless, the idea was a revelation for us in our attempt to explain the objective quality of ritualized acts, in particular when the ritual stance takes on the character of an emergent mood. Ritualized acts, if we see them for the moment as abstract action, require that the subject situates himself or herself differently from in everyday life: instead of intentions and external projects bringing a multitude of relevant facts to view in the world, actions-in-themselves give shape to a projected world and produce a phantasm around themselves. That is, to extrapolate from Merleau-Ponty's own account, in making a movement which has reference only to itself, it is necessary nevertheless for the subject to create the 'human' (i.e. not externally existing) space in which this act takes place. If we accept this idea, then 'apprehension' becomes not simply a matter of assigning meanings, as in other ritual acts, but alternatively, in the case of 'emergent moods', of allowing a particular kind of consciousness to arise through the act, a summoning of space, or rhythmicality, or time (the feeling, perhaps, that this is an 'immemorial act'). In the actions which are the basis for emergent moods there seems to be a characteristic projection outwards from the self: the circling of the arms in *arti*, the self-absorbed dance, the abandoned swaying of the head in possession, the rocking movement of the cradler, all of these, *as movements*, seem to operate centrifugally to create their own space, rather as Merleau-Ponty suggests.

Perhaps such ritualized acts come as near as anything in human conduct to Merleau-Ponty's 'abstract action'. However, it is impossible to describe emergent moods simply as abstract action, as 'not having relevance to any particular situation', because they are after all encountered by real people in the context of the ideas and practices of the Jain *puja*. The opening of the projected world which Merleau-Ponty describes for 'abstract action' is indiscriminate and undifferentiated—this has to be the case if 'abstract acts' are unrelated to particular situations. But in actual ritual situations we must first of all recognize that there are different named movements, and our ethnography would suggest that the emotions of emergent moods must also be very different from one another. The emotion engendered by seeing (*darshan*) for example, is unlikely to be the same as that achieved by cradling, and neither of these is similar to dancing. They may share the characteristic of minor rhythmic disturbance of the equilibrium sense, but we certainly do not wish, by calling these various actions 'emergent moods' and comparing them to 'abstract action', to force a nominal unity on what must be rather different phenomena.

Secondly, we must take into account that actual ritual action is carried out by individual people and by groups, not the unknown, abstract 'one' or 'I' of the theoretical category of 'abstract action'. Should we suppose that emergent moods are experienced variously by different individuals? Gell's analysis of Muria altered states of consciousness suggests that many ritual activities engender essentially common feelings and states of mind. Not only do different ritual activities, such as dancing and swinging, create the same psychological state, but individuals experience this in the same way. In the Muria case many rituals such as the communal dance seem to emphasize loss of individuality and the merging into a single, swaying body. Jain ritual action, on the other hand, generally avoids this depersonalization.[11] Nevertheless, we shall argue that in spite of the fact that this is ritual, any given act involving an emergent mood is probably experienced in something like the same way, so for example, the people 'cradling the baby Jina' are in all probability not only doing but feeling roughly the same thing.

There are peculiar difficulties, of course, in substantiating any such statement. Not only are other people's feelings ultimately unknowable, but in the case of Jains the whole area of emotion, as it relates to individuals, is suppressed. This is not the case in the surrounding Hindu world. There is abundant evidence from recent Indianist literature that the cultivation of specific emotions is part of culture, and that methods for perfecting them have been systematized and developed in a way that has not happened in Europe. A theory of the emotions, *rasa* (literally juice, flavour, essence) has been developed in the context of aesthetics and dramaturgy. It makes use of a categorization of primary and transitory emotions (*bhav*), such as love, humour, disgust, envy, and so on, which are enacted in such a way as to evoke an emotional response in the audience (Lynch 1990: 18).[12] It is interesting that these 'academies of emotion' chose the term *bhav* to develop a vocabulary and a culture of shared emotions. Jains, however, have on the whole been somewhat semi-detached from the whole Hindu culture of emotions, because for them worldly emotion is associated with 'attachment', and even worse with 'passions', which the religion is devoted to overcoming. But it is one of the paradoxes of religion that they do allow the cultivation of religious states of exaltation (which *we* can only see as emotional). The term *bhav* is sufficiently polysemous and vague to allow its use by Jains in several different contexts, in yogic techniques of meditation, in the predominantly intellectual-theological sense which we described in the previous chapter, or in an emotional sense. What we shall endeavour to show here is that the emotions involved in emergent moods are made quite specific, in that they are focused by the 'union' of the subject with the object of his or her devotion, that is, they take place in idol-worship. In other words, we suggest that religious culture intervenes to propose its own 'projections' to the self and this channels the emotions or imaginings flowing outwards from the self (to refer again to the analogy with Merleau-Ponty's idea of 'abstract action').

The whole tradition of teaching about the individual conscience, eliminating *karma* from one's own soul, and so forth, has accustomed most Jains to practise, if only intermittently, the lonely path of personal religion. The case of Banarsi, discussed in Chapter 2, shows how rocky this can be for the serious and devout. But contrary to modern Western presumptions, we have no evidence that the individualization of religious practice has led to the cultivation of private imagery or motifs. On the contrary, Jains seem to avoid exposure of, or engagement with, the sub-conscious in the Freudian sense, and sexuality, anger, and violence appear to be strongly repressed. Some support for this observation is found in Carstairs (1957: 318–24), who observes that, of the various Rajasthani communities to whom he gave word-association tests, the 'Banias' (*baniyas*), virtually all of whom were Jains, were made most anxious by sexual and violent themes. Our discussions with Jains, some of whom we knew well, suggest that what tends to happen is that they pass in silence over personal emotions while they welcome common religious symbols. The nun we quoted at the end of the previous chapter summed up this atttude when she lumped together all personal affections, ambitions, and fears as *samsar*, the ocean of suffering, over which the self should glide safely as in a boat.

It is significant that when unconscious desires and fears do nevertheless burst through, as in spirit possession, Jains do not incorporate this into normal ritual activity at their own temple. They travel to other places where no acquaintances but the immediate family are present. The Padampura temple outside Jaipur indeed seems to be a specialist temple for spirit possession. It is a huge temple out in the countryside, with only a few village houses nearby, nothing like enough to provide a regular congregation (and few of the inhabitants are in any case Jain). The worshippers at this temple virtually all come from elsewhere. Hindus, Jains, 'tribal' people, and even Muslims from cities all over Rajasthan come here to battle with their personal demons.

'Emergent moods' at the Dadabari temple, which are a regular part of worship for many people, cannot be seen, despite superficial similarities, as private obsessive rituals. We refer here to Freud's paper 'Obsessive Actions and Religious Practices' and anthropological work which employs some of Freud's insights (e.g. Obeyesekere 1981). Freud's idea in this paper is to make an explicit comparison between obsessive actions and religious practices: 'Obsessional neurosis presents a travesty, half comic and half tragic, of a private religion' (1985: 34). He writes that any action can become 'ceremonial' (and subsequently obsessive) if elaborated by small additions or given a rhythmic character by means of pauses and repetitions. These actions have to be carried out always in the same manner. They seem like mere formalities, and even the patient has no better explanation of them, and yet he is incapable of giving them up, 'for any deviation from the ceremonial is visited by intolerable anxiety, which obliges him at once to make his omission good' (1985: 32). For example, a woman who was living apart from her husband, over a period of time used to repeat an especially noticeable and senseless obsessive action.

She would run out of her room into another room in the middle of which there was a table. She would straighten the table-cloth on it in a particular manner and ring for the housemaid. The latter had to come up to the table, and the patient would then dismiss her on some indifferent errand. In the attempts to explain this compulsion, it occurred to her that at one place on the table-cloth there was a stain, and that she always arranged the cloth in such a way that the housemaid was bound to see the stain. The whole scene proved to be a reproduction of an experience in her married life which had later on given her thoughts a problem to solve. On her wedding night her husband had . . . found himself impotent . . . and said he would feel ashamed in front of the hotel housemaid who made the beds, and he took a bottle of red ink and poured its contents over the sheet. (1985: 35)

We are not competent to comment on Freud's idea that the ceremonial or obsessive act is a defensive measure, and we regard with great scepticism his theory that religion is a developed communal form of repressive and defence mechanisms, but on the other hand it does seem possible to accept the idea of private ritualization. Freud points to several similarities between obsessive action and ritual, notably the feeling of the actor that the act is prescribed and 'sacred', the mental isolation of such acts from other activities, and the conscientiousness with which they are carried out. But what is crucial, he writes, is that the point which seems at first to differentiate obsessive acts from religious ritual—that the former are foolish and senseless while the latter are full of significance and symbolic meaning—is a false distinction. The private ceremonial acts are revealed by psychoanalysis as neither foolish nor senseless but as the displaced expression of unconscious motives and desires. In the case of the woman who compulsively showed the stained cloth to her housemaid, although the act is in a sense unwilled by her and arbitrary (she could have adopted some other action), the whole subjective experience which is opened up by this act is indissoluably tied to her, her marriage, her husband, and her history.

Superficially there is perhaps something similar to this in emergent moods. These experiences are difficult to predict. They are repeated or rhythmic and sometimes seem, as they develop, to be compulsive or unwilled. But in every other way they are different. First of all the ritual actions which provoke them are regular and public. The emergent moods themselves are not pervaded, as far as we could tell, with a feeling of anxiety, but rather one of abandon, and most significantly, we failed to discover any personal symbolism associated with them. In this respect these emotional episodes contrast with the performance-centred events of the possession cult at Padampura, where the highly charged actions of all involved were part of a drama of caste and kinship relations, and with the case discussed by Obeyesekere (1981) in the context of Sri Lankan Buddhism, when subjective imagery deeply linked to personal experience is integrated at various levels with public symbolism and acted out in hypnomantic states of consciousness. We have no evidence that any of the possessed people at Padampura had successfully added to the public religious symbolism of Jainism in the area, although it is perfectly possible that such a thing might happen and Obeyesekere convincingly documents several cases. We are concerned here with regular ritual which nevertheless involves heightened emotionalism, and with the aspect of ritualization which can evoke an emotional response in the absence of dramatic and theatrical performance.

Of course we do not deny that private fantasy and reference to personal history are ever-present for all people, but the Jain religion, which encompasses temple ritual, urgently counteracts them. Perhaps we can say that Jainism, at least in present historical circumstances, more or less successfully remoulds or replaces them with its own imagery.[13] Many of the women who cradled the 'infant Jina', for example, were matrons with fine families of their own, but to us they never linked this ritual action to their own babies. Even childless women never said that 'cradling' the mirror-image reminded them of their longing for a child of their own, or of any particular moments or events in their own lives. The ritualized emergent mood seems to produce something different, to blot out the individual personality and replace idiosyncracies with a totalizing religious vision.

The writings of Jain teachers have given us some insight into this. The essential point is that the intellect is vulnerable and allows the infiltration into the self of suspect personal emotions. Muni Shri Chandrashekhar Vijay-ji compares the conscious self to a state with its own standing army.

All the inner guards should be posted only in those inward areas where there is the definite possibility of enemy attacks. And that inner vulnerable boundary is our 'Mind'. The check-posts must be erected in the mind, where the evil desires of sins are waiting in the bush with their strategy against us. If once these armies of sins go strong in the regions of mind and capture it, if they rush on into the area of our body, then there is sure defeat and ruin. (1977: 283–4)

Muni Shri Chandrashekhar Vijay-ji is a renouncer from the Shvetambar Murti Pujak tradition and his aim is to legitimate the worship of idols. Only the image of the deity, he writes, can remind worshippers of 'His' teachings. Other routes are distractions, to be blocked off. Using imagery which would not be out of place in a Vaishnava Hindu temple, this Jain renouncer describes how it is thus a religious duty to 'fill your mind' with the divine image and to avoid remembrance of anything else.

Only the image reflecting the form of the Lord can remind us of His glory. If there be any soul so unfortunate as not to be moved with the remembrance of God even by such a divine image, then in the whole world he cannot find even a single thing (except the image) capable of this bliss. The idol alone can remind us of the reality of God. . . . If the heart of a genuine *shravak* [layman] is filled with sincere gratitude in the form of constant remembrance of the merciful Lord who has bestowed his grace on us, then the devout soul . . . will be filled with the madness of worshipping the idol. He will always be engrossed in his contact through his holy idol. . . . In order to destroy evil attachments to the wordly things our hearts must be filled in every corner therein with the inward devotional feelings. In other words, the hearts which are occupied with images of woman, wealth, family, etc. must be refurnished with the holy images of the Lord. . . . And soon the upsurge of rolling waves of the spiritual joyous tides of the oceanic love in your heart will overwhelm those worldly unholy images and throw them out on the shores, never to return. (1977: 293–5)

Here the idea of intellectual meanings for ritual action is totally absent. Instead the layman is instructed to be wary of the 'mind' and its permeable borders which may allow the infiltrations of wordly desire. The devotee must 'submit' and 'surrender himself' (1977: 294), and the very 'refurnishing of the heart' with the image of the divine Jina will engender the joyous tides of religious love. Such writings are instructions to the laity, but they are also written from experience, and we suggest that it is this experience which is recreated in the episodes we have called 'emergent moods'.

This involvedness of the self is reflected in Jain writings. Muni Chandrashekhar-ji insists that worshippers should not buy the materials for *puja* from the temple but provide their own at their own cost, because it is not the god who has need of these things but man who needs to make some actual renunciation, however small, in order to experience non-attachment. Without this direct involvement worship is no longer genuine. For the same reason, the devotee should if possible make his own idol, of gold if he is rich, even of clay if he is poor, and this very having of an idol 'shaped after your own liking and wish will create in your mind a deep love' (1977: 295). The worshipper should become physically involved in the act: 'Mark the happy expression on the face of a devout soul who uses his own hands to rub the mixture of sandal and musk to prepare the anointment for the divine idol. Look at his divine happiness, his mystic concentration, during the ritual of worship, being performed by him' (1977: 299). It is therefore not a contradiction that the worshipper should see his or her own god in the image of the idol. This seems to be the experience of our Jain friends when the angular male figure is transformed into the curvaceous female Mallinath, when the shadowy statue is lit by the circling lamps of *arti*, and when the reflection in the 'cradled' mirror is seen not as the standard brass statue it is but as the beloved infant Jina. These, then, are perhaps analogous to the 'projections' and 'summonings' of which Merleau-Ponty writes, but in this case structured by learnt images. Jain statues are austere and uniform. The iconography of the Jina has not changed for millennia. Nevertheless, they do possess people's hearts. This is unlike the case in Sri Lankan religion, as described by Obeyesekere, who argues that hypnomantic fantasy is able to turn into public culture and this changes the iconography (1981: 177–9).

Reflecting on these moments of fervour in Jain practice, we asked ourselves whether emergent moods do not spread over into the *puja* as a whole. Perhaps the *puja*, for people inclined towards this devotionalism, should be seen as a succession of such experiences, or even as one single experience of adoration? However, we came to the conclusion that this is not the case. Jain puritanism, intellectualism, and the tendency to classify and categorize are too strong and pervasive. As we have noted earlier it is not that 'meaning to mean it' is devoid of emotion, rather that for the standard archetypal acts of *puja* there are constant injunctions to give them specific theological meanings and a consequent anxiety over meaninglessness. The inclination to surrender to the act seems to happen only when the prescribed acts require repetitive movements.

An implication of the above is that some kinds of physical movement may provide more fertile ground than others for emergent moods to occur. We are not sure why this is the case, but prescribed repetition of movements within a single 'elemental act' seems to be such a case, and this can be so even when there is an external object for the movement. An example occurs during the cleaning of the statue, which happens every morning. Again, like the dancing, this is an act which people vie to do. As we saw people at the Dadabari clambering over the statues, heartily scrubbing with bunches of grass, and purposefully threading their cloths repeatedly through the armpits, we couldn't help feeling that this was more than was needed simply to represent the idea of 'bathing'. There was a kind of concentrated exaltation about this cleaning. A woman said to us, 'It is for purity of the idol. Only when we have been doing this cleansing does the emotion (*bhavana*) rise in us.'

In this chapter we have tried to show that the Jain injunction to mean (and to 'mean to mean') in ritual action is interspersed with episodes when specific propositional 'meaning' is blotted out. At these moments, and perhaps for particular personalities only, the self is 'filled' with an emotionally experienced image created through particular, repeated, physical actions. We have argued that these episodes are nevertheless ritualized, and we can say this because in these instances emotional responses arise in stipulated action. They remain part of the *puja* sequence, standardized, repeatable, learnable, and 'elemental'. But within the framework of the elemental segment, a whole new set of psychological processes can take place, now involving channelled emotional projection and identification, rather than intellectual representation. Among these processes visual focusing and disturbance of the equilibrium sense seem to be particularly important. Our friends, like Muni Chandrashekhar-ji, talked about 'surrender' when referring to these experiences, but on the other hand of 'concentration' when talking about the *puja* generally. And even in these instances of surrender it is imperative that the self—the self weighed down by all the *karmas* produced by everyday life—must be present. A mere body is a non-self, for example when someone is possessed by evil spirits. People in a possessed state are forbidden from performing *puja*. This leads us to ask, how are we to understand the 'self' which undertakes worship? It is to this subject that we now turn.

Notes

1. A young girl said about this, 'We wave *camar*s for people in high posts. In history people waved *camar*s in honour of the Lord of Lords, so we wave it for the sake of honour.'

2. Men also perform this ritual act of 'cradling' the infant Jina, but we did not observe them becoming absorbed by the act in the same way as women.

3. *Darshan* in a Hindu context has been perceptively analysed by Eck (1981), Babb (1981), and Fuller (1992). Eck (1981) makes the point that Hindus speak of the god or idol 'giving' *darshan* and the devotee as 'taking' it. The same is true of the Jains. Bennett describes *darshan* in the Vaishnavite Pushti Marg as follows, 'Merely to observe the image does not amount to real *darshan*. Devotees stress that ideally the observer must feel that he or she is "in the deity's immediate presence" . . . This feeling was typically described as a sudden and

brief change of consciousness: at some stage of the *darshan* the devotee momentarily forgets mundane surroundings, the mind becoming completely engrossed in Krishna. *Darshan* as such is a subjective experience implying a heightened sense of awareness. For devotees blessed with the faculty of subtle sight the image is a sentient being, but for those with the limited faculty of gross sight it remains a lifeless statue' (1990: 192–3). The Jain case shares these characteristics, but is different from the Hindu version in several ways, notably that Hindu devotees observe a series of *darshan*s through the day as the priests occupy themselves behind the scenes with presenting a continuous drama (the waking, feeding, bathing, perfuming, dressing of the god; his taking cows to the pastures; his midday feast; his siesta; his evening refreshments; and so on). Jain idols do not go through this daily routine so the theatrical aspect of the Hindu mode of worship is absent.

4. For a discussion of the curious fact that Shvetambar statues of the female Jina Mallinath represent her as having a male body, see Laidlaw (forthcoming).

5. The informant added, 'And if you will go behind and look you will see that her statue has hairs down her back. There are no hairs on the male statue. This is my favourite *murti*; she is eight hundred years old, no, two thousand years old.' The statues were in a dark corner of the temple but try as we might we could see no difference between them.

6. Sometimes people would perform acts of the *puja*, especially dabbing with sandalwood paste, not on the idol itself but on a small pocket mirror. This was occasionally explained as a matter of convenience, 'I can see all the idols in the mirror, I can do *puja* for the whole temple.' But it was also said that 'The gaze of the *murti* is so powerful, even the mirror may crack.' This recalls the Buddhist case discussed by Gombrich (1966).

7. The movement may be vertical or horizontal, but is always circular in a clockwise direction.

8. As with the dancing, *arti* is done both for Jinas and for the *guru-dev*s, but the prayer is slightly different in the two cases. An *arti* prayer is written on the wall by each shrine.

9. In many of the cases we encountered these spirits are non-Jains. Indeed, they are spirits from the very cultures which Jains take some pains to exclude from their religious explanations (see Chapter 8). For example, one small boy was possessed by one Muslim and two Rajput spirits, another man by five Muslim spirits. However, there are also cases where people are possessed by close, deceased relatives.

10. 'The possessed woman holds her vessel of water tightly clasped over the lid, unlike the normal village woman's effortless style of balancing full open pots with hands free. Sometimes the possessed woman goes backwards, sometimes she leaves the road and strays into a field, sometimes she plants herself in one place with legs somewhat apart and sways from side to side, making small rhythmic breathing sounds. Her face is completely hidden by her wrap' Gold (1988*a*: 95).

11. The performance of *arti*, which is usually done in a group, and which can often lead to what seem to be communal states of exaltation, is a partial exception to this point.

12. Lynch comments, 'In this theory the major purpose of dance, drama, ritual and poetry is not mimetic, cathartic, or didactic; rather it is catalytic. Aesthetic forms ought to activate an emotion already present in participating members of the audience who must cultivate their own aesthetic sensibility' (1990: 17–18). He notes that the *rasa* theory, originally formulated between *circa* 200 BC and AD 200, was reinterpreted in the medieval devotional (*bhakti*) movements in which aesthetic experience became the mode of religious experience itself (1990: 18).

13. Jainism has not been the target for the kind of Christian missionary activity or the recipient of romanticized Orientalist enthusiasm which have between them provoked the crisis of confidence described by Gombrich and Obeyesekere for Sri Lankan Buddhism (1988). Nor is Jainism a national religion, and it has not had to bear a political load in India. To continue the contrast with Sri Lanka, where until very recently women have been unable to enter the Buddhist *sangha*, most Jain renouncers are women, who are actively encouraged to enter the order. Although we have adduced these factors to suggest why Jainism has not been altered by the incorporation of private imagery in recent years, we should add that it seems to have been remarkably conservative throughout its history.

11

Stances of the Self

IN ritual action, while people perform archetypal acts which are socially prescribed, they do not thereby leave aside the selves which are their everyday or 'real' selves. Indeed, ritual action seems to *require* some kind of awareness or situating of the self in relation to the act. This is true, at least in the Indian context, even of automatically efficacious ritual of the Vedic type.[1] Another way to put this would be to say that ritualized acts are there for the self-interpreting self, and not only some person-in-a-role, to enact. But what can be said about this self which engages in ritual acts?

We forbear even to attempt a general answer to this question for the whole range of human societies or for the range of institutions which have been called rituals. But we shall discuss how the issues lie for the major world religions and liturgical ritual, for which it is reasonable to assume the presence of a concept of the 'self' as conscious personal identity. This is not to assume any very substantive similarity between such concepts of the self, or that any of the others need necessarily be like the Western idea of the 'individual person' (an autonomous, legally and morally distinct personality). As Sanderson's perceptive paper (1985) on the Brahmins of Kashmir makes clear, even in that one society there are several theories of the referent of the 'I', none of which conform to the Maussian concept of the European category of the person, and all of which maintain a sophisticated sense of a conscious self.[2]

Let us describe how this works for the Jains. Readers may have noticed that we have been using the terms 'self' and 'soul' interchangeably. The reason for this is that the soul (*atma*), considered as an eternally existing conscious entity, is not divorced from the results of the actions of the self. On the contrary it is weighed down by the *karma*s which adhere to it and change its nature. Through this life, and the succession of previous and future lives, the soul is considered to be a highly complex entity structured by the *karma*s which obstruct and defile it and those which define it in a given birth. The latter essentially are those phenomena which define the self:

1. *nam karma* ('name', which means identity in a general sense and includes sex, size, shape, and the station in the world into which one is born: as a god, a hell-being, a plant or animal, or as a human being, rich or poor, Indian or foreign);
2. *gotra karma* (family or lineage);
3. *vedniya karma*, those *karma*s producing feelings of happiness and sadness; and
4. *ayu karma*, which determines the duration of one's existence in a given birth.

The soul is thus burdened, one might say, by being a self. This is very unlike the Western, essentially Christian, and positive concept of the 'person' as described by Mauss: the rational, indivisible, morally autonomous individual who is sovereign of his or her own consciousness and has the right to communicate directly with God (1985: 20–3).[3] A soul in Jain theology is valued in so far as it can lose or get rid of the self-defining *karma*s. This means, as Sanderson has noted of Indian religious doctrine in general, that theoretically speaking, individual conscious entities (souls) are not ultimately different from one another in more than a numerical sense (1985: 205).[4]

However, the theological or philosophical category of the self should be distinguished from concepts of the self which people hold, and which may or may not coincide with this category. Both of these are distinct from the sense of self, which we assume to be present for all human beings. All languages in all societies have had ways for a speaker to refer to himself or herself as an individual 'I' (Mauss 1985, Hollis 1985). Finally, the ongoing sense of the self which is present throughout a lifetime is distinct from the psychological awareness of the self at particular moments. All of these crudely delineated distinctions, perhaps especially the last, involve matters of extreme complexity: not only is it possible to lose awareness of the self, as seems to happen in possession trances for example, but it also is the case that one can perceive oneself 'as an observer' (to observe oneself) and alternatively be aware of oneself 'as an actor' (to be aware of one's agency).[5]

This book has suggested that ritual action brings all these distinctions into play. The present chapter focuses particularly on the relation between the individual sense of self and the categories of self presented in Jain (and more generally Indian) culture. The uniform essence of all souls is a theological abstraction: but it is the self-burdened soul of each individual which actually takes part in ritual. What we wish to point out here is that ritualized action, even such a relatively simple affair as the *puja*, presents an arena in which one individual may experience and 'work on' the self in a variety of ways, and we shall describe this below. Although Sanderson does not explicitly make this point, his discussion of the various modes by which Kashmiri Brahmins could conceive the 'I' refers constantly to ritual contexts (Mimamsaka ritual sacrifice, the Vaishnavite theistic middle ground, Tantric and cremation cults, and Vedantin renunciation) and it seems not implausible, in Sanderson's case too, that the ambiguous authorship of ritualized action provides a crucial terrain where these various senses of 'I' are made manifest. His paper investigates ideas of self by contrasting theories, adduced from texts, with 'principles implicit in social life which give soteriological sense to these idealizations' (1985: 193). We would add to these theoretical and discursive contexts that of the *practice* of ritual. Just as concepts of the self do not spring fully fledged from life or from sacred books, but must be learned, so also in ritual action it must be the case that agents' encounters with the acts which are ready to be performed can change how they think of themselves. In principle this is always possible, since ritual actors are conscious of themselves in relation to archetypal actions, but in religions like Jainism which exhort people to *measure* themselves against ideals it is all the more likely. As we described in the case of Banarsi (Ch. 2) enacting a ritual can lead to a sense of disillusionment with all ritual. But our concern here is with the people who do respond with an awareness of their own agency to stipulated, archetypal, and yet 'pointless' acts.

The most immediately striking feeling one has when entering a Jain temple, even an empty one, is that it is already peopled: there are the marble statues, standing and sitting, their eyes gleaming luminously from every side. The Jinas are at once predecessors, the representations of every quality the celebrant wishes to attain, and they are also preceptors, who taught the great truths of Jainism to an assembly of all creatures. This duality is created by two attitudes adopted towards the Jina statues by the worshippers, that is, they can situate themselves as 'attainers' or as 'listeners'.

Celebrants can see themselves as engaged in the sacred acts of attaining insight by means of symbolic mimesis of the path of enlightenment. This is particularly clear in the anointing of the limbs of the idol, one by one, bringing the worshipper to remembrance of the separate attainments of the Jina predecessor, with the devout wish that this be attained also by the self. In this attitude, the statue is a mirror of the self, or the self is a mirror of the statue. It is to allow this possibility that the body of the worshipper must be perfect and purified before the *puja*, and that the statue of the Jina should be perfect and unbroken. We can perhaps see in this attitude a quasi-Narcissistic engagement, the worship of the representation of what is ideally perfect in oneself. This aspect is heightened by the use of real pocket-mirrors in the ritual, which perforce must reflect the idol and oneself, by the building of some Jain temples in mirror-glass, and by the anointing of the self at a mirror at the beginning of the *puja*. Self-contemplation is valued by Jains as the re-enactment of the Jina's attainment: 'With supreme knowledge, with supreme intuition, with supreme conduct . . . the Venerable One meditated on himself for twelve years' (*Kalpa Sutra*, 120; see Jacobi 1884: 263). In this mirroring, just as the idol is not a portrait of the Jina but an assemblage of qualities, the self may be experienced as an aggregate rather than as a whole.[6] It is also the case, perhaps, that some people who experience the exultation of identity with the Jina may undergo a cosmic resituating of the self, a feeling of being at the very centre or the apex of the world, as the Jina is actually represented in the temple.

Perhaps it is not too far-fetched to draw an analogy between the despair of Narcissus and the disillusionment of Banarsi at the breaking of the charmed circle of mirror-like ritual.[7] Banarsi's realization that the desired spiritual transformation of ritual was not taking place, that he still desired to eat when he was engaged in a ritual fast, and that this was *his* desire, led him to analogous self-injury, and to impious mockery of the enactment of reflection itself. He and his friends pretended to be saints with profound mystical knowledge. Aping the naked Jina, he wrote, 'We would shut ourselves in a small room, shed our clothes and dance in the nude exclaiming that we had shed the world and had become *muni*s (renouncers). We would lustily rap each other with our shoes and loudly declare that here was a blow on the head of the man who dared blaspheme against us' (Lath 1981: 87).

However, it is not only by positing the self as the mirror of the divine that the *puja* engages with the self of the worshipper. The 'listener' to the doctrine relinquishes the dangerous equilibrium of mirror ritual. The self is placed away from the Jina, below him (represented in ritual by sitting opposite and below, or in paintings by following behind the Jina on the path upwards), and here the trailing web of *karma* attached to the self is fully acknowledged. The listener should respond by taking vows which will alter subsequent behaviour and block out inflowing *karma* or lessen that which is already there. The self appears now as 'someone bound by vows', that is as a dual unity, a Ulyssean self acting upon a self. The

PL. XI. *A* samavasarana-patta. This painting (from Rajasthan, dated AD 1800) shows the assembly which gathers to hear the Jina preach. In the inner ring are Jain monks and nuns, and pious laymen and laywomen.

vow-taking, striving listener also has a place in the great geographic shape of the cosmos, not on the rim like animals and the general traffic of the world, but somewhere in the front stalls, as it were, looking inwards to the centre, where the Jina sits (see Plate XI).[8]

But even vows, as we have seen in Chapter 9, can be understood as having the equivocal status of actions. Somehow the act should always be transfigured. We outline below the implications of this for the sense of self. The concern our informants expressed that *puja* should advance from *dravya* (external substance) to *bhav* (internal thought and feeling) has a long pedigree. The possibility appears early in Indian thought of transforming 'external' ritual action into an 'internal' generation of power in the self.

In the *Rig Veda* the ancient god of fire, Agni, who is also the sacrificial fire itself, consumes demonic energies by heat (*tapas*). In later literature the expulsion of the demons is directly correlated with purification, of both the sacrificial objects and the sacrifice itself. Reference to the god Agni becomes progressively more symbolic and figurative, and increasingly it is *tapas*, the creative/destructive power of heat, which itself comes to be seen as the power of purification. The *Brahmana* texts emphasize the need for the purification of the sacrificer himself. He is rendered 'fit for the sacrifice' through *diksha* (initiation) which is attained through *tapas*. *Tapas* is self-imposed suffering and pain which generates an inner heat. 'At *diksha*' writes Kaelber, 'The "human" condition, the sacrificer's impure condition, is overcome. More specifically and graphically, it is "consumed" or "burnt out" in the heat (*tapas*) of asceticism. . . . He is consumed and reborn through his own self-generated heat of asceticism' (Kaelber 1979: 202–3). In still later literature *tapas* is taken for granted as the primary means of ritual purification and therefore rapidly becomes the essential means by which to atone for specific transgressions. In particular fasting, sexual abstinence, and regulated breathing are means of generating 'heat' within the body. The fire imagery remains: Kaelber quotes the *Jaiminiya Upanishad-Brahmana* as saying that breath is man's essence or inner self, this inner self is *tapas*, and fire is the essence of *tapas* (1979: 212).

All this is taken deeply to heart in Jainism, which may indeed have provided the impulse for some of these ideas in Brahmanical thought. In Jain texts, the pure wandering monk (*shramana*) is frequently contrasted with brahminical sacrifiers. In a passage from the *Uttaradhyayana Sutra* which echoes another we discussed in Chapter 2, a Jain sage, emaciated by austerities, approaches a Brahman sacrifice but is turned away. When he then proves his magical powers, the Brahman priests ask him, 'Where is your fire, your fireplace, your sacrificial ladle? . . . What oblations can you offer to the fire?.' The monk replies as follows, 'Penance (*tapas*) is my fire; life my fireplace; right exertion my sacrificial ladle; the body the dried cowdung; *karma* is my fuel; self control, right exertion and tranquility are the oblations, praised by the sages, which I offer' (Jacobi 1895: 56). This vision of the self as the unique generator, by practices on one's own body, of a purifying transformation, is central to many Jains' attitude to *puja*. Many people told us that they wanted to 'burn away' their *karma*s. To the extent that individual morning *puja* is governed by this attitude, Jains will claim that it too is a form of yogic exercise and so is an austerity (*tapasya*). In the preparations and precautions which guarantee bodily purity and are required to perform the full *puja*, the intention to do this is, as it were, transferred to the body as well as retained in the mind. If one does not have the intention beforehand, and make these specific preparations, then one cannot perform *puja*, but only *darshan* (auspicious vision) of the idol.[9]

This is not the only kind of religious transformation of the self which Jains see as happening in ritual. One of our respondents, an exceedingly senior and respected nun, gave a different, cosmic and yogic, interpretation of the transformation effected in *puja*. She had just enumerated the significance of the nine parts of the body anointed in the *anga puja*. The last of these is the navel.

We worship the navel—it is considered the origin of creation. Brahma himself came from the navel. All parts of the body also originate from the navel, so that if it is pure, every cell of our being will be pure. As is the seed, so is the plant. So it is the point of origin which is responsible for evil as well as good. So unless this point is pure, and the *kundalini*[10] is pure, there is no point in *puja*.

She continued,

This is something from yoga. There are six *cakra*s in our being—the highest has one thousand petals, like a lotus, and is at the top of our heads.[11] The *kundalini* power is like a snake which lies coiled in the lowest region of our body. The *merudanda* (*axis mundi*) connects the lowest parts with the top of the head. Through yoga and meditation (*dhyan*) the *kundalini* will awaken, and we can make it rise, crossing *cakra* after *cakra*, and the ideal is for it to reach the highest one in our head, if our concentration is good enough. This leads to knowledge; the flowering of the lotus on the top of our head is *samyak-darshan* (true spiritual insight). When the *kundalini* rises there is a rain of *amrit* (blessed sweetness, nectar).

This nun was the only person to explain *puja* in a form drawing so elaborately on a yogic Tantric vocabulary which would be familiar too to her counterparts in many Hindu sects.

It was common, on the other hand, for people to interpret the *puja* in terms of the moral/spiritual renunciation—*tyag*. *Tyag* is a meaning given to an act of 'offering': it becomes 'giving up'. The importance of *tyag* for the Jain *puja* has been well stressed by Babb, 'The symbolism [of the *puja*] is reflexive, stressing one's own situation as represented or embodied by the physical materials employed in the rite. . . . The meaning of giving food, then, is ceasing to eat. The worshipper is therefore not "giving to" but symbolically modifying his or her condition by "giving up"' (Babb

1988: 75). But what, for some people and in some circumstances, are noble ideas, can seem less so in other contexts. The equivocal status of 'offering' things at *puja* is recognized by Jain scholars, one of whom said, 'A gift (*dan*) is for merit, but giving up (*tyag*) is for religion (*dharma*).' Other informants used *tyag* in two senses. It can mean the perfection possible in the human condition, the precious attainment of equanimity. The gods, because they live in bliss and satiation, are not capable of this. It can also mean a very practical kind of fast in everyday life, like giving up food for one day, giving up talking for five hours, or giving up salt in food for one day each week. That is, *tyag* can be given a *measurable* meaning in relation to the self, something which the 'offerings' in *puja*, seen symbolically, cannot.

The notion of relinquishment as applied to *puja* thus has a considerable range. But it is evident that there is not only one idiom which Jains can use. Or, to put this another way, the offering self can take different stances. The language of *tapasya* as fire, noted above, is at odds with the idea that the statue, which represents the qualities of the enlightened saviour to be emulated, should be cooled. In earlier chapters we have provided several examples of avoidance by some individuals of the use of 'hot' substances in the *puja* (glue, scent, and flowers are examples) and many people told us that the universally practised anointing with sandalwood paste cools the idol. In many cases, analogies were directly drawn with 'cooling' the passions in the self. In this idiom the statue is not simply a material object to be preserved physically by cooling substances but becomes an external model for operations on the self.

On the other hand, there is considerable evidence, both in the literature, and from our informants, that the bathing of the statue is often given the symbolic meaning of an enactment of the bathing of the infant Jina by the gods and goddesses (led by Indra/Shakra, king of the gods) which they performed on Mount Meru, with liquid from the milky ocean. These again are not interpretations just plucked out of the air, but the creation of a deliberate stance, recorded in one's own body. Jaini writes, 'While engaging in *abhishek* [bathing with holy liquid] the devotee visualises himself as Sakra [king of the gods] (a sandalwood paste mark on his forehead signifies this role) thus his action becomes . . . a re-enactment of the baby Jina's ritual bath atop Mount Meru' (1979: 200). The tinsel crowns which worshippers sometimes wear, most often in sponsored or collective *puja*s, is a material signal of this.

The self as a carefree god or goddess, satiated with happiness and wealth, is different from, and one has to say at odds with, a self visualized as a tense interaction of aspects of the soul caught in the causality of *karma*. This is perhaps less of a paradox than it seems. Many *pujas* are specifically designated as worship of one stage of the Tirthankar's holy life, for example *snatra puja* refers to his birth. The *panc-kalyanak puja*, which extends through several days, celebrates all five stages. At one level king and renouncer are successive stages. This fact to some extent can resolve the question of what has seemed to several observers the paradox- ical nature of the 'god' itself (Humphrey 1985). However, it is only to a limited extent that the worshipper follows these stages and represents them in his or her own body, by singing lullaby-like hymns at the birth stage. As we have already pointed out, the effect of ritualization is to reshuffle these carefully distinguished stages in time. For instance, the baby is always represented by an adult statue, and we observed crowns and ornaments even on the ascetic renouncer.

The religious problem of the self, the relation of the soul to the body, remains unsolved (as is its wont). This has been the subject of intense sectarian debates throughout the history of Jainism, especially between Shvetambars and Digambars, and we cannot enter into discussion of these here, except to point out that as a way of talking about religion in general and the *puja* in particular, our informants made liberal use of their own formulations of this problem. A nun said,

The soul (*atma*) has three forms; the outer (*bahya*), the inner (*antah*), and the supreme (*parama*). All the souls in the world are alike. The outer soul is that which does not know the other two, which does not know of its own independent existence, which only recognizes exterior joy (*sukh*), money, and so forth. The inner soul knows of its own independent existence, but it is in the body, and tied down by *karma*s. That which has come out of the body gradually, cleansing itself, just as a goldsmith puts metal in acid again and again until it comes out shining clean, that is the supreme soul, the *paramatma*. If we cleanse ourselves like this we become free of the body, and therefore *puja* is necessary.

For the Christian this would seem a very alien way of thinking about the soul (after all, a soul cannot really have much to do with money), but, as we have pointed out, for Jains the soul incorporates impurity or the bodily aspect of the self. We found that this nun's metaphor for the numbing extraction of the soul from the body is a very characteristic way of think- ing about the relationship among Jains. But we must point out that this attitude to the body, whereby it must be ignored, overcome, and burnt away, an attitude which is the basis of the ascetic way of life, is hardly congruent with the requirement of mirroring ritual that the body be pure and newly dressed in order to touch the idol at *puja*, the requirement that the body in some sense represent the perfected soul.[12]

In addition, there are attitudes whereby the *puja* can 'do you good', and of these we will note here only what one might call the medical variant. It may be recalled that the liquid which has been used to bathe the statue, called *prakshal*, can be collected, taken home, and used as a medicine. Women would set out in the morning with a special pot for this curative liquid. Men did this more rarely, but one assured us, in mythological vein,

Our ancestors' ways, those should be followed. If even a leper bathes with the *prakshal* of the *oli-ji puja* he will get rid of his illness. As it happened for Raja Shripal, and other lepers, so it would happen for us. So in our Jain theory the eight-offering *puja* has a medical value attached. Not only is your *karma* destroyed, but your illness is taken away. Jainism has a medicinal point of view, so if you do *ayambil* (a type of fast) it is the same as when a doctor tells you not to eat sugar or ghee—it is good for health.

At the house of a wealthy businessman we saw an elderly lady, looking pale and weak, sitting praying in a corner. 'She is fasting,' said her husband. 'For eight days she is taking only small amount of one kind of food. It is the change of weather. At this time the blood should be purified by a fast. That will be good for her.'

In this framework the *puja* is to be seen as a rite which brings a return, not the overt material return desired from the saints, nor even the lower-level religious return of merit (*punya*), but a return to the body itself. One should not understand this concern as irreligious, since, as we have seen, for the Jains body and soul are not easily divisible and the body can be seen as the instrument of religious progress. The bodily weakness brought about by fasting is itself a state of purity. It is worthy of honour, as can be seen by the fact that the women who have accomplished particularly gruelling fasts are taken in public processions through the town. Borne on a palanquin, unable probably to walk, they just allow themselves a smile of triumph amid the crowds, the dancers, and the blaring bands.

The range of stances taken by the self is not without limit. In the Jain case, for instance, one does not change gender when entering the ritual arena. If it is required to take a role men always take male ones and women females ones. Perhaps this requirement explains why neither of us have ever seen, nor heard of, enacted life-story *puja*s specifically dedicated to Mallinath, the one Jina supposed by Shvetambars to have been female. The cross-sex role enactment would be complex indeed, since Malli was first a man who achieved many prerequisites for Tirthankarhood, but because he cheated on the way, deviously accumulating more fasts than his fellow ascetics, was reborn as a woman. It was as a woman that he attained *keval-gyan*. This scenario would present difficulties of practical ritual enactment for the congregation, and it points to a central doctrinal difference—perhaps the central difference—between Shvetambars and Digambars: the question of whether clothes (and hence modesty) must be relinquished by the true ascetic, and thus whether women can, or cannot, proceed by this path. Among Shvetambars, since ascetics go clothed, women may be renouncers.

We further argue that role-playing in the *panc-kalyanak puja* does not dislodge the sense of self. It does not substitute a socially defined persona for the self of the agent (perhaps Plate VIII can illustrate this best, showing the row of sober, even grumpy-looking people in their roles of Indras, the kingly gods, who should be expressing joy at the birth of the Jina at this point). In this the *panc-kalyanak puja* performance is unlike ritual dramas, such as the Hindu *Ram-lila*. The boys who enact the parts of the main deities in the *lila* 'become' the gods: at a special preparatory *puja* two months before the performance they are initiated into the roles, their real names are forgotten for the time being, and they are expected to behave with the gravity suitable for their status. Strict rules regulate their behaviour. They are supposed to 'be' the gods whose parts they play, even when they are not on the stage. In the performance, their facial features are made unrecognizable by elaborate make-up; they are transformed into divine beings made evocative, fabulous, and strange (Kapur 1986: 60, 66).[13] Jains in their ceremony make no effort to become the gods, but remain themselves, only emblematically dressed up.

Both the *lila* and the *panc-kalyanak* can be contrasted with certain prominent approaches to acting in Western theatre, in which the actor 'identifies' in the Stanislavskian sense with the role. In this case the individual actor's own self informs his or her performance and permeates and transforms the role, so that the audience sees 'Olivier's Hamlet'. The boy playing Ram must not create a role in this way; rather he should represent the popular image and avoid any contribution of his own (Kapur 1986: 65). In the *panc-kalyanak* too the actors also must avoid making any singular contribution to the role, only in this case this is done by enacting it as a token. We have argued earlier that in ritualized action in general many modes of enactment are available to the celebrant, but perhaps it is this possibility in ritual, of a mere token being enough, which divides it from sacred drama. Otherwise, the two forms of enactment are very close.

We would suggest that a token is enough because the celebrant in ritual is addressing, not an audience primarily, but the self. For the self, a token may be just that, or it may be illuminated by religious thought and thereby become an act of penance, a memorial, or a renunciation. Thus, because the actor in ritual remains an agent, archetypal actions can serve to enhance the senses of self. Performing ritualized acts impels people to perceive themselves as doing something, and this opens the way for alternative interpretations of what the self can be.

Notes

1. Alexis Sanderson writes about Mimamsaka ritual, 'Securing the category of action from the language-dissolving void to which it was consigned by the Buddhist theory of impersonal flux, the Mimamsaka ritualist defined for the orthodox a self that was not only real but also absolutely self-determining. In harmony with his conviction that the Vedic rituals were mechanisms dependent for their results only on the exactitude of their performance, and that these results would accrue to him alone as their agent, he held that his present experience and all the perceptible aspects of his identity were the outcome of nothing but his own actions. . . . Thus in his self-representation, the most orthodox of Brahmans was the most individual of all individuals. . . . His "deity", his miraculous power of cosmic consistency, was nothing but the law of his own action. . . . Yet at the same time he exemplified all that was non-individual: he was the perfect man of the group. This contradicition, that of the "solipsistic conformist", was his self-representation as ritual agent' (1985:195–6).
2. Mauss (1985 (1938)) proposed a distinction between the sense of the self, which is always present, and the category of the person, which in Western society evolved via the notion of 'role' to the idea of the person as the possessor of rights in ancient Rome. The Western concept of the person was later underpinned by the Christian category (not simply the sense) of the self.
3. We are aware that there is much to criticize and qualify in this picture of the modern conception of the person or self (not to speak of Mauss's evolutionism), but we wish here simply to use this model as a contrast to Jain ideas. An adequate treament of this subject, which falls outside the scope of this book, would have to go far beyond our rough characterizations here.
4. For monistic doctrines like the Vedanta souls are not distinct even numerically.
5. O'Shaughnessy (1980: 15–38) claims that it is impossible to observe one's own actions (i.e. as actions involving a sense of agency). An idea of his argument can be gleaned from the following: 'It is not just that action and perception are antithetical . . . to disengage perception from its normal role of *handmaiden to action* and to involute it onto itself . . . would in general be to rob it of

its . . . very identity. Thus, looking at one's own actions must be a logically secondary activity that is parasitic upon the accomplice uses of
perception . . . (For the visual worlds of agent and observer, while sharing
much, are necessarily unlike; for the agent sees a dynamically organised world
and the observer does not). It follows that the attempt to situate one's actions
in a perceptual field that is being put to uses that actually *clash with* the
typifying basic uses is an attempt that must fail' (1980: 17). However, we feel
that the case of ritual action might be an awkward one for this line of thought.

6. 'It is the aggregate of qualities of the Perfect Man, of the Liberated Soul, that
is remembered, adored, and thereby developed in one's own self by the
worshipper by worshipping the idol of the Jina. The idol therefore serves
more the purpose of a symbol of aggregate of certain qualities than of a
portrait of a Tirthankara' (U. P. Shah 1975: 63).

7. When Narcissus realized that the beloved vision in the pool was his own
reflection, and knew that he still burned to embrace it, this awakening did not
resolve his agonizing predicament. He wept at his disenchantment, his tears
ruffled the surface of the water, and the image disappeared. In self-anger he
beat his breast, and the pool, resettling, mirrored his red blood, upon which
Narcissus wasted and died. He subsequently turned into a flower. As Stephen
Bann, in his illuminating book *The True Vine*, observes, the metamorphosis
into a flower is a radically different event from the play of resemblances in
mirroring. Such transformations do occur in rituals, but unlike mirroring,
they do not happen in all rituals. There are no such metamorphoses in the
Jain *puja*.

8. Parkin, in an illuminating paper, even makes spatiality and directionality
definitional of ritual (1992: 18).

9. The distinction between *darshan* and *bhav puja*, both of which are permitted
in an unprepared state, was elided by many of our informants. *Bhav puja*
for some seems simply to be more elaborate, to involve the mental saying
of prayers and contemplation of the qualities of the Jina. Others saw it as
requiring the adoption of specific body postures and performance of particular 'internal' recitations, like the *caitya-vandan*.

10. The source of spiritual energy in yoga.

11. *Cakra*s are 'circles' or 'centres' of cosmic significance. This whole account of
yogic power, the *kundalini* and so on, which is tantric in both vocabulary and
thought, is not without authority in Jain scriptural tradition.

12. Much more extended discussion of this will be found in Laidlaw
(forthcoming).

13. The *devadasi* dancers described by Marglin (1990), like the boys in the
Ram-lila, are trained so that all their expressions and gestures conform to a
stipulated repertoire.

12

Conclusion

THIS book has been an account of ritualization, and of the responses to it. The pivotal transformation which ritualization effects is to sever the link, which is present in everyday life, between the actors' intentions and the identity of the acts they perform. Commonly when this happens in everyday life, when you say something you do not intend to say, for example, it is a mistake. But ritual action is anything but a mistake: one of the definitive features of ritual is the *consistent* displacement of intentional meaning. So one of its enigmas, which we cannot claim to have solved comprehensively, is why people go on doing things in ritual ways when ritualization only serves to make them 'pointless'.

In reproducing ritual acts celebrants are no longer engaged in the constantly renewed compromise of everyday life whereby people endlessly adapt to new circumstances and attempt to turn them into familiar habits. Ritual acts are there to be performed, and in stepping into them, one stills an aspect of what Hampshire calls 'the steady buzz of intentional activity' (Hampshire 1959: 97). In ritual this disjunction between action and intentions occurs in a special way, different from other kinds of respite from everyday intentionality, like that found in acting in a play or under orders. A special characteristic of ritualized action is that the act to be performed is not just in store for us, it is also in store *in us*. It is still we, as ourselves, who enact it and are conscious of it. We have performed these acts before, they are part of our physical repertoires, and now they have come to be what we perform them as; they are not immutable objects but, to quote Beckett, are objects infected by our mobility.[1]

This intrinsic 'directedness' does not give ritual actions discursive meaning. It is a separate response which does this: the archetypal acts-to-be-performed are felt by those who perform them to be 'apprehensible', or recoverable. By 'meaning to mean' the ritual actor can reappropriate the ritual act and realign it with his or her intentions. In Chapter 8 we argued that scripture and the commentaries of religious authorities cannot alone account for this. Although they provide a pool of available material they cannot define how ritual actions are to be performed nor can they assign unique meanings to them. This work remains to be done by the actor. And the apprehension of ritual acts need not take the intellectual form of ascribing theological propositional meanings. As we showed in Chapter 10, there can be another, direct psychological response to the act, an identification with certain archetypal actions, in which repetitive motility generates culturally patterned emotions. The existence of this largely visual–emotional response demonstrates that discursive meanings do not 'underlie' ritual acts.

We claimed in Chapter 3 that the 'theory of ritualization' advanced in this book differs in kind from much of the writing about ritual in anthropology. What then does our theory imply for anthropological practice?

There have always been doubts, of course, about quite what anthropologists are doing in offering an analysis, an interpretation, or a 'reading' of a ritual. If this is what the ritual does, how does it do it? Who, if anyone, ever comes out with the supposed 'meaning'? If this is what the ritual says, who is it saying it to? Why keep repeating it? And why say it in this extraordinary way? Yet while some anthropologists have been troubled by these questions, and several have voiced at least some of them, for the most part we have all pressed on regardless. Ethnographers have displayed an almost puzzle–solving pleasure in 'decoding' rituals: the more bizarre and serpentine the better. Behind this lies the idea that rituals contain hidden messages about the societies in which they are performed. Our theory suggests that this is based on a mistake.

With Durkheim still lurking in the background as the most revered ancestor of the discipline, an anthropologist in the field looks around for 'social facts'. It is social facts, the theory says, which will elevate ethnography above the travelogue; and it is social facts which go beyond the account the people themselves could give of what they are doing and why. There are some very obvious reasons why rituals seem to fit this bill and there are others suggested by the account we have developed in this book. The ritual commitment itself is a social act. Obviously rituals are institutions, regularly or at any rate repeatedly performed. Ritual actors, we have said, are not directly authors of their acts, and their individual intentions do not define what it is that they do. Ritual is obviously social and cultural, not just the sum of the beliefs and desires of individuals and their consequent actions, as our discussion of the disconnection of ritual action from actors' purposes makes clear. Ritual is thus an escape for the ethnographer from the bewildering and dispiriting prospect of thinking about multifarious individuals, all with their own different reasons for conducting themselves in their own different ways. For those planning to 'commit a social science', the externality of ritual action is too good an opportunity to miss.

Rituals appear to have a unique charm in that not only are they social facts but also, unlike statistics about suicide, they are visible. Some rituals provide the attraction of being not only social facts which we can observe, but ones in which we can participate. The allure is certainly great: collective and often exuberant social action, mysterious, apparently inexplicable behaviour, an objective entity which people can endlessly discuss. Our own analysis in this book has also highlighted this last point, that ritual action appears to have an independent objective existence. Not only is this how the ritual practitioner sees his or her own action, but for similar reasons a ritual act appears to the outside observer, like a text, or a painting, or an artefact, to invite interpretation. And it is still more encouraging when the performers themselves can proffer interpretations of their own.

The standard practice has therefore been to collate the interpretations of different participants. Quite how this is best done depends first of all on the particular society in question. Sometimes most people have very little to say about the ritual, except to point to some locus of authoritative knowledge like a priesthood or a text (which may or may not exist, and may or may not in fact be helpful). In other cases, like that of the Jains, almost everyone has something to say, and constructing an interpretation involves distilling their accounts into a single model, a compromise between the authoritative and the widespread. From this model each individual could be said to diverge or deviate to a greater or lesser degree. Sometimes there are systematically varied interpretations which follow important social cleavages. In these cases a complete interpretation of the ritual must compare and contrast the accounts given by women and men, initiated and uninitiated, rich and poor, and so on. With this approach, the 'meaning' of the ritual resides in the systematic relation between these different models, and so in a greater and more complex model which lays bare the similarities and contrasts. Where changes in the interpretation of a ritual through time are included in the analysis, the result is a variant in this last method: the meaning of the ritual then becomes a model which displays the transformations between one model and the next; or it becomes a kernel of symbolic meaning which remains invariant from one period to the next. In all these cases the anthropologist can adduce additional facts about the society in which the rite is performed (mode of livelihood, class structure, gender relations, cosmology, other rituals and practices, and so on) which the participants themselves do not mention with respect to the ritual, but which the anthropologist judges to be relevant and illuminating; and then the anthropologist can add facts about neighbouring, similar, or very different societies which put the actors' interpretations of what they do in a complementary or a contrasting light.

All these modes of interpretation treat the ritual as an object or a social fact which is so because people in a given community are thought to have an underlying common idea of it, and common intentions and desires which it expresses. It is in this form, as conveying an underlying idea, that it is assumed to be interpretable. Anthropologists have thus behaved like theatre critics; but without paying attention to whether the conditions exist that would make 'criticism' a valid endeavour. But for a great many rituals, there is no performance intention of this kind. There is no individual intention to communicate on the part of the ritual actor, and no institutionalized arrangements to enact such an intention. Apart from the anthropologist, there is frequently no one who could plausibly be regarded as an audience, and certainly no one who is there as a critic. It would make absolutely no sense to 'criticize' a ritual.[2] And as we have said, as emphatically as we can, where given rituals do embody such communicative or performance intentions, these are not a function of the action's being ritualized.

One thing this interpretative approach suggests is that ritual is a mask for something else, that there is (somewhere else) a power structure, say, that ritual expresses or disguises. We think that where ritual is a field of power it is so in a direct way. If you bow during a state ritual you are by that very act constituting yourself as a subject, not just symbolizing a relation which 'really' exists elsewhere. However, this observation does not tell us anything general about ritualized action, since a bow is a bow in ritual or outside it. It would be ethnocentric to assume that bowing is necessarily 'a ritual' just because you yourself do it only in rituals. The ritualization of bowing is not what gives it its political efficacy. Our intention in this book is not to hinder or deflect attention from analyses of the ways in which ritual can be *directly* a negotiation of power (Atkinson 1989: 292; Bell 1992: 193–6), but to help in this endeavour by exploring the effects of ritualization itself.

Because anthropologists have thought of ritual as a class of events, they have picked out particular things called 'rituals', and then assumed that everything that happens in them is somehow 'ritual'. As a result, their 'theories of ritual' have had to account for all sorts of happenings and beliefs as integral to the theory, and this diverts their attention from ritualization itself. Say you have a 'ritual of rebellion'. You might want to develop an interpretation of the rebellion, and its historical, political, etc. importance; but it would be a mistake to assume that all of *that* added up to a theory of ritual. Conversely, you might be interested in a theory of ritual, in which case why burden yourself with all the historical, political, etc. phenomena, just because some of the things which are ritualized happen to be rebellions? Or, say you have a ritual, such as takes place in Mongolia, where a child's first fluffy, brownish hair is cut off to make way for adult hair. Hair and the cutting of it may have all sorts of symbolic associations, but the ritual itself will not tell you what these are, and nor will those associations be found only in ritual contexts. In fact the ritual takes place at some astrologically correct time, which may not coincide with when the first fluffy hair begins to grow thick and black, so that simply observing the ritual would not help you to find the symbolism. The Mongolians think that the strength, colour, and shininess of hair symbolizes human vitality, but they think this all the time, not just in the context of the hair-cutting ritual. On the other hand Mongols also cut their hair just to make it shorter. A theory of ritual does not have to account for all the facts about rebellions and all the facts about hair and hair-cutting; it has to explain what underlies these two differences: the difference between a ritualized and an unritualized rebellion, and the difference between a ritualized and unritualized act of haircutting.

Certain things follow from the view we have put forward. First, the varieties of explanation the actors themselves have of a ritual need no longer be suppressed or salted down. Where actors simply do not have an interpretation to offer, this need no longer been seen as an embarrassment. We can now see that variety, discordance, and even absence of interpretation are all integral to ritual. The whole distinction between 'knowledgeable' and 'unreliable' informants can be revealed for what it is: not a reflection of privileged access to 'really existing meaning', but a local construction put on a contest of intepretations. Why should anthropologists listen only to the winners of that contest? If there is no single underlying meaning to 'reveal' then the anthropologist's account does not have to be consistent: to represent only consistency when in fact there may be confusion and diversity has been a tempting short-cut to something which doesn't exist! In thinking of symbolism as a code, anthropologists miss the fact that in offering interpretations of a ritual their informants are actually being creative.

We began this book by noticing the fact that people have *attitudes* to ritual itself. The great wealth of varied interpretations just mentioned all derive from one kind of attitude, but as we have also pointed out, there can be others. We see the existence of consensus in the interpretation of ritual not as a given or essential fact about ritual, but as a socio-historical product which arises in the context of only certain kinds of attitude to ritual. And even attitudes are not enough. We have made the point that ritual itself tends towards a dispersal of meaning, and therefore one only gets consensus when social institutions that would produce consensus in any case are sufficiently powerful to counteract the effects of ritual. This can be done either by fiat from outside (Papal encyclicals) or by swamping the ritual with thought-reform (Jain Sthanakvasi preachings, school assembly, or a Nuremberg rally). But these social, institutional effects vary independently with attitudes to ritual itself. In the Jain case a devout desire that ritual should be meaningful has simply not been supported by the institutional conditions for consensus.

As we have tried to show in some detail for the *puja*, elaborate models, coherent meanings, and consistent interpretations of the rite are things which people *may come to have*, through, and as a reaction to, performing it. These models do not underlie it. We have argued that for the Jains, and for the other societies and religions we have touched upon in our discussion, it is better to see the discursive models and meanings of rituals as one of the possible responses to ritual, rather than as underlying its constitution. The Jain *puja* made us realize that reactions to, or the effect of 'being in' ritual need not consist of giving meaning but may appear in a number of ways. They can also take the form of an emotional/physical engagement with the acts (which may be more or less standardized), or of simple acceptance of the act as something to be done, or of the righteous rejection of ritual as such. Seeing things this way enables us to understand the varieties of meanings attaching to ritual, for it allows us (1) to distinguish the collective representations to which commentary and dispute about rituals can give rise, from the representations individuals may form of those ritual acts; (2) to distinguish these cognitive representations from the propositional meanings people may hang on their actions, and (3) to distinguish these from the practical know-how they must have in order to enact them; (4) to distinguish the above in turn from the purposes people have in performing ritual (whether socially sanctioned or not); and (5) to distinguish all of these from the reasons why ritual exists.

Let us end by speculating a little about this last subject, and here we refer not just to the immediate reasons for particular rituals but to the more general and unfathomable reasons for the continuation of ritual action. Why do people go on doing it when the first inkling that some action is ritualized is the realization of its arbitrariness? Why, for example, have a ritual in which the king begs the deities for rain which happens, not at times of drought, but regularly every year at the beginning of the rainy season? Wittgenstein's answer to this question was, 'Apart from any interpretation its queer pointlessness could make us uneasy' (1979: 18). He held that there is a psychological reaction to this pointlessness (a reaction which is not a hypothesis) which attributes 'depth' to rituals and gives them an ancestry. The depth lies solely in the idea of that ancestry, but this is not a matter of the real history or origin of the rite. 'No, this deep and sinister aspect is not obvious just from learning the history of the external action, but we impute it from an experience in ourselves' (1979: 16). Needham rightly points out that there are obscurities in this idea of 'depth'.

Evidently . . . the depth does not depend exclusively on a terrible character in what is commemorated. Suppose a symbolic action represents something sublime, such as the Ascension or the Enlightenment of the Buddha, then presumably this too will have 'depth'. So the particular evaluation placed on this prototypical event is not what confers depth. . . . It is a general finding in the study of symbolism, moreover, that anything can be made to stand for anything else; whatever it may be, a thing can bear practically any meaning in the eyes of those who use it for a given purpose. . . . On the one hand therefore, Wittgenstein has good reason to abjure an explanation by historical reconstruction; but on the other hand he has not supplied the grounds to accept that the character of a rite is to be elicited from our own experience. In particular, the character of 'depth' has not been shown to belong in a vocabulary for the comparative analysis of ritual. (1985: 168–70)

Needham's conclusion follows perhaps from his leaving aside, like most social anthropologists, the psychological aspect of response to ritual. But Wittgenstein had stressed that his point was psychological, and that 'depth' applies to the mystery of the act itself just as much as to the explanations of it, and it applies even if there is no explanation: 'the solution is not any more disquieting than the riddle' (1979: 18*e*). One expects him to say that the solution (the explanation) does not settle our unease, but what he actually says is that the riddle, the ritual act itself, is no less disquieting than the most mysterious or sinister event it may be thought to represent (for example, the sacrifice of a man). What Wittgenstein is getting at when he speaks of 'depth' may not be so different from our ideas of the archetypal quality of ritual acts. Perhaps some of the things we have tried to show in this book—that people may have a similar attitude to ritual acts as they have to natural kinds, thus endowing them with a strange facticity; that they learn how to perform ritual acts and have them inscribed in their bodies separately from the prototypical ideas they may come to have of them; and the fact that people can have such prototypes without knowing what the acts they represent 'really' are—perhaps all this is the beginning of a psychological explanation of Wittgenstein's 'an experience in ourselves'. But it still does not quite explain the riddle of the archetypal act itself.

We have suggested that ritual action is, in a sense, like an object. This is not because people have a common idea of it, but because they do not. (Thus in our view, it is not the existence of collective ideas about ritual action which constitutes it as a social fact, but common acceptance of rules about ritual action). Such an object-like quality is peculiarly difficult to perceive, even for objects which really are physical objects, because it is constantly on the point of being overwhelmed by the rushing in of personal and conventional symbolism. We can illustrate this point by quoting from D. H. Lawrence writing about Cézanne.

The actual fact is that in Cézanne modern French art made its first tiny step back to real substance, to objective substance, if we may call it so. Van Gogh's earth was still subjective earth, himself projected into the earth. But Cézanne's apples are a real attempt to let the apple exist in its own separate entity, without transfusing it with personal emotion. Cézanne's great effort was, as it were, to shove the apple away from him, and let it live of itself. It seems a small thing to do: yet it is the first real sign that man has made for several thousands of years that he is willing to admit that matter *actually* exists. Strange as it may seem, for thousands of years, in short ever since the mythological 'Fall', man has been preoccupied with the constant preoccupations of the denial of the existence of matter, and the proof that matter is only a form of spirit. And then, the moment is done, and we realize finally that matter is only a form of energy, whatever that may be, in the same instant matter rises up and hits us over the head and makes us realize that it exists absolutely, since it is compact energy itself.[3]

Clearly rituals are not really objects, but an object-like existence is given to them by the fact that they are ontologically constituted beyond individual intentions. Thus, metaphorically, they too can 'rise up and hit us over the head' with their presence, with their being there for us to enact in that particular form. The patterns rituals take, beyond our purposes, beliefs, or intentions, propose their own time, and to step into this, to enact it ourselves, is perhaps to defy our transience and death. And this is not just some trick, because we learn and remember ritual actions; we enact them as ourselves, and in that sense they are in us too.

Sorting all this out is dependent on the exercise of understanding the *ritual mode* of action. The idea that there is such a mode is perhaps the most controversial claim in this book. We do not think we need to be committed to the claim that the difference between ritualized and unritualized action is the same in all circumstances or in all societies, any more than one needs to think that 'play', 'humour', 'drama', 'love', 'war', or 'religion' are always and everywhere the same, in order to think that the difference between something which is play and something which is not is always one that it is well to understand. We therefore think that ritual is universally a possibility as a mode of action; but because the attitude you have to ritual is part of it, this will be culturally constituted in different ways, and therefore ritual is universal, but is not always the same. We shall be happy enough to be told that ritualization as a mode of action takes different forms, or mixes the characteristics we have pointed to in different ways, in other societies which others know better than we. We shall be content, because that, we think, rather than more observations about the functions and interpretations of ritualized institutions, will be a contribution towards an understanding of ritual.

Notes

1. This, and the idea that objects of desire (hope, fear, etc.) may be stored in us, comes from Samuel Beckett's essay on Proust: 'Exemption from intrinsic flux in a given object does not change the fact that it is the correlative of a subject that does not enjoy such immunity. The observer infects the observed with his own mobility' (Beckett 1965: 17).
2. Grimes (1990) suggests otherwise, and in so doing shows up, because he exceeds, the limitations of the equation between ritual and theatre. Because it is assumed that the purpose of ritual is to communicate to an audience, the academic observer, by analogy, takes on the role of adjudicating and evaluating how clearly and persuasively he or she has received a message.
3. Quoted in Stephen Bann's *The True Vine* (1989). We are much indebted to Bann's book for insights that have helped us think about representation.

GLOSSARY

abhishek: act of anointing: by daubing paste, sprinkling powder, or pouring liquid.

ācārya: spiritual teacher; senior male renouncer; leader of a renouncer lineage.

āgama: sacred or 'canonical' text; scriptural tradition.

agra pūjā: that part of *pūjā* which is performed in front of an idol.

ahiṃsā: 'non-harming'; an all-encompassing ethical principle in Jainism which enjoins avoidance of harm to all living beings.

akshat: 'indestructible'; a name for the whole white grains of rice used in *pūjā*.

anga pūjā: 'limb' *pūjā*; that part of *pūjā* which involves bathing and decorating the body of an idol.

ārtī: waving a (usually multiple) oil or camphor lamp in front of an idol in worship.

āshātanā: 'disrespect'; fault or mistake in performance of ritual; breaking a rule.

ashta prakāri pūjā: 'eightfold' *pūjā*.

baniyā: trader or merchant; member of a caste traditionally associated with trade or money-lending.

Bhagwān: 'God'; word most commonly used to address a Jina in prayer.

bhairu: a fierce male deity, widely believed to be a form of Shiva.

bhakti: devotion; fervent emotion of loving supplication and worship; tradition of religious practice which emphasizes such emotion, and of poetic writing which evokes and celebrates it.

bhāv: meaning, essence, sincerity, emotion, internal; logically opposed to *dravya* (q.v.).

bhāv pūjā: that part of *pūjā* which consists of adopting specified bodily postures, saying prayers, singing hymns, and silent devotion.

bhūmiya: 'lord of the soil'—male deity, usually guardian of a particular village, temple, or place.

boli: auction, usually for the right to perform honoured roles in ritual.

caitya: temple or sacred image.

caitya-vandan: rite for worshipping Jina (idol); a part of many Jain rituals, including *pūjā* and *pratikraman* (q.v.).

caitya-vāsi: 'temple-dweller'; allegedly 'lax' medieval Shvetāmbar Jain renouncers, opponents of the renouncers who founded the Khartar Gacch (q.v.), and forerunners of the *yatis* (q.v.).

cakra: wheel or circle; a term of tantric religious discourse referring to a point in the body which is a centre of spiritual 'energy'; also a term for certain (especially circular) magical diagrams, such as the *siddha-cakra* (q.v.).

camār: fly-whisk; traditional symbol of royalty in India; waved during *pūjā*.

candan: sandalwood and, in *pūjā*, yellow paste made from sandalwood.

caraṅ: a shrine in which a dead person is represented by a carving of footprints; used mostly by Jains for dead saints such as *gūrū-dev*s (q.v.) but also occasionally for Jinas.

Dādābārī: garden or complex housing a shrine to a *Dādā-gūrū-dev* (q.v.), usually built outside a town or village and often marking the place where he was cremated or has appeared miraculously after death.

Dādā-gūrū-dev (also *gūrū-dev*): patron saint of the Khartar Gacch.

dān: charity, alms-giving, religious or ritual gift.

darshan: 'beholding' an idol, a saint, or a renouncer; worship by seeing and being seen; also insight and system of philosophy.

devadāsī: professional female temple dancer.

devtā / devī: male/female deity.

dharma: '*Dharma* can be and has been translated in a thousand ways: "righteousness", "truth", the "Way", etc. It is best not translated at all' (Gombrich 1971: 60).

Digambar: 'sky-clad'; the branch of Jain tradition whose most advanced male renouncers go about naked.

dīkshā: the rites at which people are initiated into a renouncer lineage.

dīp pūjā: waving a lamp in front of the idol during *pūjā*.

dravya: substance, material, appearance, outer; opposed to *bhāv* (q.v.).

gacch: a renouncer lineage; the term is commonly used only of those Shvetāmbar traditions which build temples and worship idols.

garbha-kalyāṇak: the auspicious moment at which a future Jina enters his or her mother's womb; the rite at which this is re-enacted.

guṇasthāna: fourteen stages of spiritual purification.

gūrū-dev: see *Dādā-gūrū-dev*.

gūrū-vandan: ritualized obeisance to living renouncer or to the shrine of deceased saint.

gyān: knowledge.

himsā: violence; aggression; any infringment of the principle of *ahimsā* (q.v.).

jāp: repeated recitation of a prayer or *mantra* (q.v.); telling a rosary while reciting prayers.

jīva: soul; sentient being.

Jina: 'conqueror'; one who has overcome all spiritual obstacles, subdued all desires, and will attain the state of *moksh* (q.v.); a synonym of Tīrthaṅkar (q.v.).

karma: action; the particles of matter which adhere to the soul as a consequence of action; the moral 'trace' of action; the law which brings to one the just 'fruit' of one's former actions; hence, loosely, 'fate'.

keval-gyān: omniscience.

Khartar Gacch: a particular Shvetāmbar renouncer lineage and the lay followers thereof.

kshetrapāl: 'guardian of the place'; a kind of male protector deity whose idols are often found by the door of Jain temples.

Mahāvīr: 'Great Hero'; the twenty-fourth and last Jina of our era; an elder contemporary of the Buddha.

Mallinath: the nineteenth Jina, held by the Shvetāmbars to have been a woman.

maṇḍala: a magical diagram.

maṅgal dīp: waving an ('auspicious') lamp before an idol in worship, usually at the end of a *pūjā*.

mantra: sacred chant; formulaic contraction of a prayer; sacred syllable; magical spell.

moksh: liberation; salvation; permanent release from earthly life and suffering.

muni: a male renouncer.

mūrti: sacred statue or picture; idol.

naivedya: food (and in Jain contexts specifically sweets) offered during *pūjā*.

namaskār-mantra: nine-line prayer, the most sacred and most frequently used sacred formula in Jainism.

nissahi: a word spoken on entering temple to worship, to signal that one is leaving worldly cares behind.

pañc-kalyāṇak: the five 'auspicious moments' in the life of a Jina: conception, birth, renunciation, omniscience, and death and final release; the ritual re-enactment of these five events in *pūjā*.

Pārshvanāth: the twenty-third Jina of our era.

prabhāvana: 'influence'; any act which increases the fame and prestige of the Jain religion; a euphemism for *prasād* (q.v.).

Prakrit: a general term for a group of Middle Indo-Aryan vernacular languages, in which early Jain texts were composed.

prakshāl: liquid in which an idol or sacred image has been bathed.

prasād: 'grace'; sanctified offering (usually food) returned to worshippers or distributed to family and friends at the end of *pūjā*.

pratikramaṇ: ritualized confession.

pūjārī: ritual officiant; temple servant. A *pūjārī* in a Hindu temple would be a 'priest' but this is not a sacred office in Jainism.

pushpa-pūjā: placing a flower on or before an idol in worship.

sādhu/sādhvī: male/female renouncer of any Jain order, who has taken the five 'great vows': non-violence, truth, not taking anything which is not given, sexual restraint, and non-possession or non-attachment.

samavasaraṇa: assembly of gods, men, and animals to hear a Jina preach; model replica of this event; synonym of *samosaraṇ*.

sāmāyik: 'equanimity'; lay ritual of meditation and prayer.

samosaraṇ: synonym of *samavasaraṇa* (q.v.).

saṃsār: the world of death and rebirth; the ocean of suffering.

samyak darshan: perfect insight; correct view of reality; faith in Jain teaching.

sangh: religious community, that is, male and female renouncers together with their lay following.

shāsan-devtā/shāsan-devī: male/female guardian deities associated with the Jinas; often referred to as *yakshas/yakshīs* (q.v.).

shramana: 'striver'; term for variety of non-Vedic renouncer movements which include the Jains and Buddhists.

shrāvak/shrāvikā: 'listener'; man/woman who accepts Jain teaching; a lay Jain, especially a pious and devout lay Jain.

shrāvakācār: text prescribing righteous conduct for lay Jains; the whole body of such literature written in Sanskrit between the fifth and thirteenth centuries.

Shvetāmbar: 'white-clad'; the branch of the Jain tradition whose renouncers all wear white robes. This tradition includes the Khartar Gacch, the Tapa Gacch, the Sthanakvasis, and one of the groups called the Terapanth.

siddha: 'perfected', liberated soul; soul in the state of *moksh* (q.v.).

siddha cakra: magical diagram used in *pūjā* and as an amulet; represents the Jina, the *siddha* (q.v.), the levels of the monastic hierarchy among renouncers, together with the qualities of spiritual insight, knowledge, good conduct, and asceticism.

snātra pūjā: daily morning ritual which re-enacts the bathing of the infant Jina by deities.

Sthānakvāsi: 'hall-dweller'; a Shvetambar renouncer order which does not keep temples or practise *pūjā*.

syādvāda: the Jain doctrine sometimes referred to as 'relativism', or 'qualified assertion', according to which different aspects of the complex truth about an object or a question are grasped when it is considered from different points of view.

Tapā Gacch: a particular Shvetāmbar renouncer lineage and the lay followers thereof.

tapas/tapasya: 'heat'; austerity; ascetic practice.

Tarānapanth: a Digambar sect which does not keep idols of the Jinas, but performs *pūjā* instead to carved representations of sacred books.

Terāpanth (1): a Shvetāmbar sect, under the leadership of a single *ācārya* (q.v.) which does not keep temples or practise *pūjā*.

Terāpanth (2): a Digambar sect which does keep temples and practise *pūjā*, but with certain restrictions.

tilak: forehead mark; identifies members of particular Hindu sects; (when red) identifies women as married; (when formed of a paste used during worship) identifies those who have attended and taken part in a religious ritual that day.

Tīrthaṅkar: 'ford-builder'; one who founds or refounds the Jain tradition; a synonym for Jina (q.v.).

tyāg: renunciation; relinquishing or giving something up.

upāshraya: dwelling-hall for Jain renouncers; used also for renouncers' sermons and for the laity to undertake fasts and religious rituals.

vandan: obeisance; ritualized form of respectful salutation.

vidhi: ritual, and also law, method, and system; rules for performing a ritual correctly; manual containing instructions on ritual performance.

vrat: restraint; a vow to observe some set of religious prohibitions.

yaksha/yakshī: male/female spirit or demon, associated especially with tree-cult and found in the mythology of Jainism, Hinduism, and Buddhism; another name for *shāsan devtā*s/*shāsan devī*s (q.v.).

yantra: magical diagram.

yati: male Shvetambar cleric who differs from a Jain *sādhu* in having a permanent home, keeping personal property, and travelling in vehicles, and who tends to work as a ritual officiant and to practise esoteric and magical arts; present-day representative of *caitya-vāsi* (q.v.) tradition.

REFERENCES

AHERN, EMILY MARTIN (1982), 'Rules in Oracles and Games', *Man: The Journal of the Royal Anthropological Institute*, NS 17.

ALSDORF, LUDWIG (1973), 'Niksepa: A Jaina Contribution to Scholastic Methodology', *Journal of the Oriental Institute of Baroda*, 22.

AMES, MICHAEL M. (1966), 'Ritual Prestations and the Structure of the Sinhalese Pantheon', in Manning Nash (ed.), *Anthropological Studies in Theravada Buddhism* (Yale University Press, New Haven, Conn.).

ANSCOMBE, G. E. M. (1963 (1957)), *Intention* (Basil Blackwell, Oxford).

ATAL, YOGESH (1961), 'The Cult of Bheru in a Mewar Village and its Vicinage', in L. P. Vidyarthi (ed.), *Aspects of Religion in Indian Society* (Kedar Nath Ram Nath, Meerut).

ATKINSON, JANE MONNIG (1989), *The Art and Politics of Wana Shamanship* (University of California Press, Berkeley, Calif.).

AUSTIN, J. L. (1975 (1962)), *How to Do Things with Words*, ed. J. O. Urmson and Marina Sbisa (Oxford University Press, Oxford).

BABB, LAWRENCE A. (1975), *The Divine Hierarchy: Popular Hinduism in Central India* (Columbia University Press, New York).

—— (1981), 'Glancing: Visual Interaction in Hinduism', *Journal of Anthropological Research*, 37.

—— (1988), 'Giving and Giving Up: The Eightfold Worship among Svetambar Murtipujak Jains', *Journal of Anthropological Research*, 44.

BANKS, MARCUS (1992), *Organizing Jainism in India and England* (Clarendon Press, Oxford).

BANN, STEPHEN (1989), *The True Vine: On Visual Representation and Western Tradition* (Cambridge University Press, Cambridge).

BARTH, FREDRIK (1987), *Cosmologies in the Making: A Generative Approach to Cultural Variation in Inner New Guinea* (Cambridge University Press, Cambridge).

BASHAM, A. L. (1951), *History and Doctrines of the Ajivikas* (Luzac & Co. Ltd., London).

BATESON, GREGORY (1972), *Steps to an Ecology of Mind* (Ballantine Books, New York).

BEATTIE, J. H. (1966), 'Ritual and Social Change', *Man: The Journal of the Royal Anthropological Institute*, NS 1.

—— (1970), 'On Understanding Ritual', in Bryan R. Wilson (ed.), *Rationality* (Basil Blackwell, Oxford).

BECHERT, HEINZ (1983), 'A Remark on the Problem of the Date of Mahavira', *Indologica Taurinensia*, 11.

BECHTEL, WILLIAM (1990), 'Connectionism and the Philosophy of Mind: An

Overview', in William G. Lycan (ed.), *Mind and Cognition* (Basil Blackwell, Oxford).

BECKETT, SAMUEL (1965), *Proust: Three Dialogues* (London).

BELL, CATHERINE (1988), 'Ritualisation of Texts and Textualisation of Ritual in the Codification of Taoist Liturgy', *History of Religions*, 27.

—— (1992), *Ritual Theory, Ritual Practice* (Oxford University Press, New York).

BENNETT, PETER (1990), 'In Nanda Baba's House: The Devotional Experience in Pushti Marg Temples', in Owen M. Lynch (ed.), *Divine Passions: The Social Construction of Emotion in India* (University of California Press, Berkeley, Calif.).

BHARILLA, HUKAMCHAND (1981*a*), *Tirthankara Mahavira and his Sarvodaya Tirtha* (Shri Kundkund-Kahan Digambar Jain Tirtha Suraksha Trust, Bombay).

—— (1981*b*), *Dharma Ke Dashalakshana* (Shri Kundkund-Kahan Digambar Jain Tirtha Suraksha Trust, Bombay).

BHATT, BANSIDHAR (1978), *The Canonical Niksepa: Studies in Jaina Dialectics*, Indologia Berolinensis, v. (Brill, Leiden).

BHATTACHARYA, NARENDRA NATH (1976), *Jain Philosophy in Historical Outline* (Munshiram Manoharlal, Delhi).

BIARDEAU, MADELAINE, and MALAMOUD, CHARLES (1976), *Le Sacrifice dans l'Inde anciènne* (Presses Universitaires de France, Paris).

BLACKBURN, SIMON (1984), *Spreading the Word: Groundings in the Philosophy of Language* (Clarendon Press, Oxford).

BLOCH, MAURICE (1986), *From Blessing to Violence: History and Ideology in the Circumcision Ritual of the Merina of Madagascar* (Cambridge University Press, Cambridge).

—— (1989), *Ritual, History and Power: Selected Papers in Anthropology* (Athlone, London).

—— (1991), 'Language, Anthropology and Cognitive Science', *Man: The Journal of the Royal Anthropological Institute*, NS 26.

—— (1992), *Prey into Hunter: The Politics of Religious Experience* (Cambridge University Press, Cambridge).

BLOOMFIELD, MAURICE (1919), *The Life and Stories of the Jaina Savior Parcvanatha* (Johns Hopkins University Press, Baltimore).

BOCOCK, J. (1974), *Ritual in Industrial Society* (Chatto & Windus, London).

BOURDIEU, PIERRE (1990), *The Logic of Practice* (Polity Press, Oxford).

BOWEN, JOHN R. (1989), 'Salat in Indonesia: The Social Meanings of an Islamic Ritual', *Man: The Journal of the Royal Anthropological Institute*, NS 24.

BOYER, PASCAL (1990), *Tradition as Truth and Communication: A Cognitive Description of Traditional Discourse* (Cambridge University Press, Cambridge).

—— (ed.) (1993), *Cognitive Aspects of Religious Symbolism* (Cambridge University Press, Cambridge).

—— (forthcoming), *The Naturalness of Religious Ideas: A Cognitive Theory* (University of California Press, Berkeley, Calif.).

BUHLER, J. G. (1936), *Life of Hemacandracarya*, trans. M. Patel (Singhi Jaina

Jnanapitha, Shantiniketan).

BURGESS, JAMES (1873), 'Papers on Satrunjaya and the Jains', *Indian Antiquary*, 2.

—— (1884), 'Papers on Satrunjaya and the Jains: IV', *Indian Antiquary*, 13.

CAILLAT, COLETTE (1975), *Atonements in the Ancient Ritual of the Jaina Monks* (LD Institute of Indology, Ahmedabad).

—— (1978), 'Les Mouvements de reforme dans la communauté Indienne des Jaina', *Académie des Inscriptions et Belles Lettres, Comtes-rendus des séances de l'année*.

CAILLAT, COLETTE, and KUMAR, RAVI (1981), *The Jain Cosmology* (Harmony Books, New York).

CAMERON, EUAN (1991), *The European Reformation* (Clarendon Press, Oxford).

CARRITHERS, MICHAEL, and HUMPHREY, CAROLINE (eds.) (1991), *The Assembly of Listeners: Jains in Society* (Cambridge University Press, Cambridge).

CARSTAIRS, G. MORRIS (1957), *The Twice-Born: A Study of a Community of High-Caste Hindus* (Hogarth Press, London).

—— (1961), 'Patterns of Religious Observance in Three Villages of Rajasthan', in L. P. Vidyarthi (ed.), *Aspects of Religion in Indian Society* (Kedar Nath Ram Nath, Meerut).

CHANDRASHEKHAR VIJAY-JI, MUNI SHRI (1977), *Call for Vigilance*, trans. S. R. Falniker (Kamal Prakashan, Ahmedabad).

CHARPENTIER, JARL (1927), 'The Meaning and Etymology of Puja', *Indian Antiquary*, 56.

CHISHOLM, R. M. (1966), 'Freedom and Action', in K. Lehrer (ed.), *Freedom and Determinism* (Random House, New York).

CLOTHEY, FRED (1969), 'Skanda-Sasti: A Festival in Tamil India', *History of Religions*, 8.

CORT, JOHN EDWARD (1987), 'Medieval Jaina Goddess Traditions', *Numen*, 34.

—— (1989), 'Liberation and Wellbeing: A Study of the Svetambar Murtipujak Jains of North Gujarat', unpublished Doctoral Dissertation, Harvard University.

COURTRIGHT, PAUL B. (1984), 'On This Holy Day in My Humble Way: Aspects of Puja', in Joana P. Waghorne and Norman Cutler (eds.), *Gods of Flesh/Gods of Stone: The Embodiment of Divinity in India* (Anima, Chambersburg, Pa.).

—— (1985), *Ganesa: Lord of Obstacles, Lord of Beginnings* (Oxford University Press, New York).

DAS, VEENA (1983), 'Language of Sacrifice', *Man: The Journal of the Royal Anthropological Institute*, NS 18.

DENNETT, DANIEL C. (1990 (1981)), 'True Believers: The Intentional Strategy and Why it Works', in William G. Lycan (ed.), *Mind and Cognition* (Basil Blackwell, Oxford).

DIMOCK, EDWARD C. (1966), 'Doctrine and Practice Among the Vaisnavas of Bengal', in Milton Singer (ed.), *Krishna: Myths, Rites and Attitudes* (University of Chicago Press, Chicago).

DONNELLAN, KEITH S. (1977), 'Reference and Definite Descriptions', in Stephen

P. Schwartz (ed.), *Naming, Necessity and Natural Kinds* (Cornell University Press, Ithaca, NY).

Douglas, Mary (1973), *Natural Symbols: Explorations in Cosmology* (Barrie & Jenkins, London).

Dreyfus, H. L., and Dreyfus, Stuart E. (1986), *Mind over Machine: The Power of Human Intuition and Expertise in the Era of the Computer* (Free Press, New York).

Drury, John (1990), 'Christ our Passover', unpublished paper.

Dumont, Louis (1960), 'World Renunciation in Indian Religions', printed as Appendix B in *Homo Hierarchicus*, comp. rev. edn. (University of Chicago Press, Chicago). First published in *Contributions to Indian Sociology*, 4.

—— (1965), 'The Functional Equivalents of the Individual in Caste Society', *Contributions to Indian Sociology*, 8.

—— (1985), 'A Modified View of Our Origins: The Christian Beginnings of Modern Individualism', in Michael Carrithers, Steven Collins, and Steven Lukes (eds.), *The Category of the Person* (Cambridge University Press, Cambridge).

Dundas, Paul (1985), 'Food and Freedom: The Jaina Sectarian Debate on the Nature of the Kevalin', *Religion*, 15.

—— (1987), 'The Tenth Wonder: Domestication and Reform in Medieval Svetambara Jainism', *Indologica Taurinensia*, 14.

—— (1992), *The Jains* (Routledge, London).

Eck, Diana L. (1981), *Darsan: Seeing the Divine Image in India* (Anima Books, Chambersburg, Pa.).

Eichinger Ferro-Luzzi, Gabriella (1977), 'Ritual as Language: The Case of South Indian Food Offerings', *Current Anthropology*, 18.

—— (1981), 'Abhiseka, the Indian Rite that Defies Definition', *Anthropos*, 76.

Eire, Carlos M. N. (1986), *War Against the Idols: The Reformation of Worship from Erasmus to Calvin* (Cambridge University Press, Cambridge).

Evans, Gareth (1977), 'The Causal Theory of Names', in Stephen P. Schwartz (ed.), *Naming, Necessity and Natural Kinds* (Cornell University Press, Ithaca, NY).

—— (1982), *The Varieties of Reference*, ed. John McDowell (Clarendon Press, Oxford).

Evans-Pritchard, E. E. (1937), *Witchcraft, Oracles, and Magic among the Azande* (Clarendon Press, Oxford).

Fabian, Johannes (1983), *Time and the Other: How Anthropology Makes its Object* (Columbia University Press, New York).

Feeley-Harnik, Gillian (1981), *The Lord's Table: Eucharist and Passover in Early Christianity* (University of Pennsylvania Press, Philadelphia).

Fernandez, James W. (1965), 'Symbolic Consensus in a Fang Reformative Cult', *American Anthropologist*, 67.

—— (1986), *Persuasions and Performances: The Play of Tropes in Culture* (Indiana

University Press, Bloomington, Ind.).

FISCHER, EBERHARD, and JAIN, JYOTINDRA (1977), *Art and Rituals: 2500 Years of Jainism in India* (Sterling Publishers, New Delhi).

FRAZER, JAMES (1957), *The Golden Bough*, abridged edn (Macmillan, London).

FREUD, SIGMUND (1985 (1907)), 'Obsessive Actions and Religious Practices' repr. in *The Origins of Religion*, Pelican Freud Library, 13 (Penguin Books, Harmondsworth).

FULLER, C. J. (1979), 'Gods, Priests and Purity: On the Relation between Hinduism and the Caste System', *Man: The Journal of the Royal Anthropological Institute*, NS 14.

—— (1984), *Servants of the Goddess: The Priests of a South Indian Temple* (Cambridge University Press, Cambridge).

—— (1985), 'Initiation and Consecration: Priestly Rituals in a South Indian Temple', in Richard Burghart and Audrey Cantlie (eds.), *Indian Religion* (Curzon Press, London).

—— (1992), *The Camphor Flame: Popular Hinduism and Society in India* Princeton University Press, Princeton, NJ).

GARDNER, D. S. (1983), 'Performativity in Ritual: The Mianmin Case', *Man: The Journal of the Royal Anthropological Institute*, NS 18.

GATEWOOD, JOHN B. (1985), 'Actions Speak Louder than Words', in Janet W. D. Dougherty (ed.), *Directions in Cognitive Anthropology* (University of Illinois Press, Urbana, Ill.).

GEERTZ, CLIFFORD (1973), *The Interpretation of Cultures: Essays in Interpretive Anthropology* (Basic Books, New York).

—— (1983), *Local Knowledge: Further Essays in Interpretive Anthropology* (Basic Books, New York).

GELL, ALFRED (1980), 'The Gods at Play: Vertigo and Possession in Muria Religion', *Man: The Journal of the Royal Anthropological Institute*, NS 15.

GELLNER, DAVID N. (1988), 'Monastic Initiation in Newar Buddhism', in Richard F. Gombrich (ed.), *Indian Ritual and its Exegesis* (Oxford University Press, Delhi).

GERHOLM, TOMAS (1988), 'On Ritual: A Postmodernist View', *Ethnos*, 53.

GHOSHAL, SARAT CHANDA (trans. and ed.) (1917), *Davrya-Samgraha*, The Sacred Books of the Jainas, i (CJP House, Arrah).

GIDDENS, ANTHONY (1976), *New Rules of Sociological Method* (Hutchinson, London).

—— (1979), *Central Problems in Social Theory: Action, Structure, and Contradiction in Social Analysis* (Macmillan, London).

GLASENAPP, HELMUTH VON (1942), *The Doctrine of Karma in Jain Philosophy*, trans. G. Barry Gifford (Bai Vijibhai Jivanlal Pannalal Charity Fund, Bombay).

GOLD, ANN GRODZINS (1988*a*), *Fruitful Journeys: The Ways of Rajasthani Pilgrims* (University of California Press, Berkeley, Calif.).

—— (1988*b*), 'Spirit Possession Perceived and Performed in Rural Rajasthan',

Contributions to Indian Sociology, NS 22.

GOMBRICH, RICHARD F. (1966), 'The Consecration of a Buddhist Image', *Journal of Asian Studies*, 26.

—— (1971), *Precept and Practice: Traditional Buddhism in the Rural Highlands of Ceylon* (Clarendon Press, Oxford).

GOMBRICH, RICHARD, and OBEYESEKERE, GANANATH (1988), *Buddhism Transformed: Religious Change in Sri Lanka* (Princeton University Press, Princeton, NJ).

GOODY, JACK (1961), 'Religion and Ritual: The Definitional Problem', in *British Journal of Sociology*, 12.

—— (1977), 'Against "Ritual": Loosely Structured Thoughts on a Loosely Defined Topic', in Sally F. Moore and Barbara G. Myerhoff (eds.), *Secular Ritual* (Van Gorcum, Assen).

GOULD, GLENN (1984, repr. 1988), *The Glenn Gould Reader*, ed. Tim Page (Faber & Faber, London).

GRANOFF, PHYLLIS (ed.) (1990), *The Clever Adulteress: A Treasury of Jain Literature* (Mosaic Press, Oakville).

GRICE, H. P. (1957), 'Meaning', *Philosophical Review*, 66.

—— (1971), 'Utterer's Meaning, Sentence-Meaning, and Word-Meaning', in John R. Searle (ed.), *The Philosophy of Language* (Oxford University Press, Oxford).

GRIMES, RONALD L. (1990), *Ritual Criticism: Case Studies in its Practice, Essays on its Theory* (University of South Carolina Press, Columbia, SC).

HAMERTON-KELLY, ROBERT G. (ed.) (1987), *Violent Origins: Ritual Killing and Cultural Formation* (Stanford University Press, Stanford, Calif.).

HAMPSHIRE, STUART (1959), *Thought and Action* (Chatto & Windus, London).

HANCHETT, SUZANNE (1988), *Coloured Rice: Symbolic Structure in Hindu Family Festivals* (Hindustan Publishing Corporation, Delhi).

HANDIQUI, K. K. (1949), *Yasastilaka-campu and Indian Culture* (Jivaraj Jaina Granthamala, Sholapur).

HARLE, J. C. (1986), *The Art and Architecture of the Indian Subcontinent* (Penguin Books, Harmondsworth).

HEESTERMAN, J. C. (1985), *The Inner Conflict of Tradition: Essays in Indian Ritual, Kingship and Society* (University of Chicago Press, Chicago).

HERRENSCHMIDT, OLIVIER (1982), 'Sacrifice: Symbolic or Effective?', in Michel Izard and Pierre Smith (eds.), *Between Belief and Transgression: Structuralist Essays in Religion, History and Myth*, trans. John Leavitt (The University of Chicago Press, Chicago).

HILTEBEITEL, ALF (1988), 'South Indian Gardens of Adonis Revisited', in M. Biardeau and K. Schipper (eds.), *Essais sur le Rituel* (Peeters, Paris).

HOLLIS, MARTIN (1968), 'Reason and Ritual', *Philosophy*, 43.

—— (1985), 'Of Masks and Men', in Michael Carrithers, Steven Collins, and Steven Lukes (eds.), *The Category of the Person* (Cambridge University Press,

Cambridge).

HORTON, ROBIN (1964), 'Ritual Man in Africa', *Africa*, 34.

—— (1967), 'African Traditional Thought and Western Science', *Africa*, 37.

HOUSEMAN, MICHAEL (1993), 'The Interactive Basis of Ritual Effectiveness in a Male Initiation Rite', in Pascal Boyer (ed.), *Cognitive Aspects of Religious Symbolism* (Cambridge University Press, Cambridge).

HUMPHREY, CAROLINE (1985), 'Some Aspects of the Jain Puja: The Idea of "God" and the Symbolism of Offerings', *Cambridge Anthropology*, 9.

—— (1991), 'Fairs and Miracles: At the Boundaries of the Jain Community in Rajasthan', in Michael Carrithers and Caroline Humphrey (eds.), *The Assembly of Listeners: Jains in Society* (Cambridge University Press, Cambridge).

JACOBI, HERMANN (trans. and ed.) (1884), *Gaina Sutras: Part I, The Akaranga Sutra and the Kalpa Sutra*, Sacred Books of the East, 22 (Clarendon Press, Oxford).

—— (1895), *Gaina Sutras: Part II, The Uttaradhyayana Sutra and the Sutrakritanga Sutra.* Sacred Books of the East, 45 (Clarendon Press, Oxford).

JAIN, B. K. (1983), 'Ethics and Narrative Literature in the Daily Life of a Traditional Jain Family in Agra during the 1930s, a Study Based on my Personal Childhood Experiences', *Indologica Taurinensia*, 11.

JAIN, SHOBHITA (1971), 'A Social Anthropological Study of Jainism in North India', unpublished B. Litt. Dissertation, University of Oxford.

JAIN, (MUNI) UTTAM KAMAL (1975), *Jaina Sects and Schools* (Concept Publishing Co., Delhi).

JAINI, JAGMANDERLAL (1916), *Outlines of Jainism*, ed. F. W. Thomas (Cambridge University Press, Cambridge).

JAINI, PADMANABH S. (1974), 'On the Sarvajnatva (Omniscience) of Mahavira and the Buddha', in L. Cousins *et al.* (eds.), *Buddhist Studies in Honor of I. B. Horner* (Reidel, Dortrecht).

—— (1977), 'Bhavyatva and Abhavyatva: A Jaina Doctrine of "Predestination"', in A. N. Upadhye *et al.* (eds.), *Mahavira and his Teachings* (Bhagwan Mahavira 2500 Nirvana Mahotsava Samiti, Bombay).

—— (1979), *The Jaina Path of Purification* (University of California Press, Berkeley, Calif.).

—— (1980), 'Karma and the Problem of Rebirth in Jainism', in Wendy Doniger O'Flaherty (ed.), *Karma and Rebirth in Classical Indian Traditions* (University of California Press, Berkeley, Calif.).

—— (1985), 'The Pure and the Auspicious in the Jaina Tradition', in John B. Carman and Frederique Apffel Marglin (eds.), *Purity and Auspiciousness in Indian Society* (Brill, Leiden).

—— (1991), 'Is There a Popular Jainism?', in Michael Carrithers and Caroline Humphrey (eds.), *The Assembly of Listeners: Jains in Society* (Cambridge University Press, Cambridge).

JOHNSON-LAIRD, P. N. (1983), *Mental Models* (Cambridge University Press,

Cambridge).

KAELBER, WALTER O. (1979), 'Tapas and Purification in Early Hinduism', *Numen*, 26.

KAKAR, SUDHIR (1984), *Shamans, Mystics and Doctors: A Psychological Inquiry into India and its Healing Traditions* (Unwin, London).

KALGHATGI, T. G. (1987), 'Karma in Jaina Thought', in S. S. Rama Rao Pappu (ed.), *The Dimensions of Karma* (Chanakya, Delhi).

KAPFERER, BRUCE (1983), *A Celebration of Demons: Exorcism and the Aesthetics of Healing in Sri Lanka* (Indiana University Press, Bloomington, Ind.).

KAPUR, ANURADHA (1986), 'Acts, Pilgrims, Kings and Gods: The Ramlila at Ramnagar', in Veena Das (ed.), *The Word and the World* (Sage Publications, New Delhi).

KEESING, ROGER M. (1982), *Kwaio Religion: The Living and the Dead in a Solomon Island Community* (Columbia University Press, New York).

—— (1987) 'Models, "Folk" and "Cultural": Paradigms Regained?', in Dorothy Holland and Naomi Quinn (eds.), *Cultural Models in Language and Thought* (Cambridge University Press, Cambridge).

KEIL, FRANK C. (1987), 'Conceptual Development and Category Structure', in Ulric Neisser (ed.), *Concepts and Conceptual Development: Ecological and Intellectual Factors in Categorization* (Cambridge University Press, Cambridge).

KELLY, JOHN D., and MARTHA KAPLAN (1990), 'History, Structure, and Ritual', *Annual Review of Anthropology*, 19.

KLATT, JOHANNES (1882), 'Extracts from the Historical Records of the Jainas', *The Indian Antiquary*, 11.

KRIPKE, SAUL A. (1980 (1972)) *Naming and Necessity* (Basil Blackwell, Oxford).

—— (1982), *Wittgenstein on Rules and Private Language* (Basil Blackwell, Oxford).

LA FONTAINE, J. S. (1985), 'Person and Individual: Some Anthropological Reflections', in Michael Carrithers, Steven Collins, and Steven Lukes (eds.), *The Category of the Person* (Cambridge University Press, Cambridge).

LAIDLAW, JAMES (forthcoming), *Gentle Conquest: Religion and Economy among the Jains*.

DE LANGE, NICHOLAS (1987 (1986)), *Judaism* (Oxford University Press, Oxford).

LATH, MUKUND (trans. and ed.) (1981), *Ardhakathanaka: Half a Tale, a Study in the Interrelationship between Autobiography and History* (Rajasthan Prakrit Bharati Sansthan, Jaipur).

LAVE, JEAN (1990), 'The Culture of Acquisition and the Practice of Understanding', in James W. Stigler, Richard A. Shweder, and Hilbert Herdt (eds.), *Cultural Psychology: Essays in Comparative Human Development* (Cambridge University Press, Cambridge).

LAWSON, E. THOMAS (1993), 'Cognitive Categories, Cultural Forms and Ritual Structures', in Pascal Boyer (ed.), *Cognitive Aspects of Religious Symbolism* (Cambridge University Press, Cambridge).

LAWSON, E. THOMAS, and McCAULEY, ROBERT N. (1990), *Rethinking Religion: Connecting Cognition and Culture* (Cambridge University Press, Cambridge).

LEACH, E. R. (1954), *Political Systems of Highland Burma: A Study of Kachin Social Structure* (G. Bell, London).

—— (1966), 'Ritualisation in Man in Relation to Conceptual and Social Development', in J. Huxley (ed.), *Ritualisation of Behaviour in Man and Animals* (Philosophical Transactions of the Royal Society, London).

—— (1968), 'Ritual', in *International Encyclopedia of the Social Sciences* (Macmillan and Free Press, New York).

—— (1976), *Culture and Communication: The Logic by which Symbols are Connected* (Cambridge University Press, Cambridge).

LÉVI, S. (1966), *La Doctrine du sacrifice dans les Brahmanas*, 2nd edn. (Bibliothèque de l'École des Hautes Études, Paris).

LEVINSON, STEPHEN C. (1983), *Pragmatics* (Cambridge University Press, Cambridge).

LÉVI-STRAUSS, CLAUDE (1966), *The Savage Mind* (Weidenfeld & Nicolson, London).

—— (1968), 'The Sorcerer and His Magic', in *Structural Anthropology* (Penguin, Harmondsworth).

—— (1981), *The Naked Man: Introduction to a Science of Mythology*, iv. (Jonathan Cape, London).

LEWIS, GILBERT (1980), *Day of Shining Red: An Essay on Understanding Ritual* (Cambridge University Press, Cambridge).

—— (1986), 'The Look of Magic', *Man: The Journal of the Royal Anthropological Institute*, NS 21.

LODRICK, DERYCK O. (1981), *Sacred Cows, Sacred Places: The Origin and Survival of Animal Homes in India* (University of California Press, Berkeley, Calif.).

LUKES, STEVEN (1985), 'Conclusion', in Michael Carrithers, Steven Collins, and Steven Lukes (eds.), *The Category of the Person* (Cambridge University Press, Cambridge).

LYCAN, WILLIAM W. (ed.) (1990), *Mind and Cognition: A Reader* (Basil Blackwell, Oxford).

LYNCH, OWEN M. (1990), 'The Social Construction of Emotion in India', in Owen M. Lynch (ed.), *Divine Passions: The Social Construction of Emotion in India* (University of California Press, Berkeley, Calif.).

MCCULLOCH, GREGORY (1989), *The Game of the Name* (Clarendon Press, Oxford).

MAHAPRAJNA, YUVACHARYA (1980), *Mind: Beyond Mind*, trans. S. K. L. Goswami (Adarsh Sahitya Sangh Prakashan, Churu, Rajasthan).

MALINOWSKI, BRONISLOW (1954 (1927)) *Magic, Science and Religion* (Routledge & Kegan Paul, London).

MALVANIA, D. D. (1975), 'The Jaina Concept of the Deity', in U. P. Shah and M. A. Dhaky (eds.), *Aspects of Jaina Art and Architecture* (LD Institute of Indology, Ahmedabad).

MANIPRABHASHRI (SADHVI) (1988), *Pravacan Prabha: A Series of Discourses*, trans. Gyan Jain (Shri Vichakshan Prakashan, Indore).

MARGLIN, FREDERIQUE APFFEL (1990), 'Refining the Body: Transformative Emotion in Ritual Dance', in Owen M. Lynch (ed.), *Divine Passions: The social construction of emotion in India* (University of California Press, Berkeley, Calif.).

MARRIOTT, MCKIM (1968), 'The Feast of Love', in Milton Singer (ed.), *Krishna: Myths, Rites, and Attitudes* (Chicago University Press, Chicago).

MASSON-OURSEL, PIERRE (1948), *La Philosophie en Orient* (PUF, Paris).

MAUSS, MARCEL (1972 (1950)) *A General Theory of Magic*, trans. Robert Brain (Routledge & Kegan Paul, London).

—— (1979), *Sociology and Psychology*, trans. Ben Brewster (Routledge & Kegan Paul, London).

—— (1985 (1938)), 'A Category of the Human Mind: The Notion of Person; The Notion of Self', in Michael Carrithers, Steven Collins, and Steven Lukes (eds.), *The Category of the Person* (Cambridge University Press, Cambridge).

MERLEAU-PONTY, M. (1962), *Phenomenology of Perception*, trans. Colin Smith (Routledge & Kegan Paul, London).

MONIER-WILLIAMS, MONIER (1899), *A Sanskrit–English Dictionary*, 2nd edn. (Oxford University Press, Oxford).

MOORE, SALLY FALK, and MYERHOFF, BARBARA G. (1977), 'Introduction', in Sally F. Moore and Barbara G. Myerhoff (eds.), *Secular Ritual* (Van Gorcum, Assen).

MOYA, CARLOS J. (1990), *The Philosophy of Action* (Polity Press, Oxford).

NAIR, V. G. (n.d.) *Jainism and Terehpanthism* (Shri Adinath Jain Swetambar Temple, Chikpet-Bangalore).

NEEDHAM, RODNEY (1967), 'Percussion and Transition', *Man: The Journal of the Royal Anthropological Institute*, NS 2.

—— (1972), *Belief, Language and Experience* (Basil Blackwell, Oxford).

—— (1975), 'Polythetic Classification: Convergence and Consequences', *Man: The Journal of the Royal Anthropological Institute*, NS 10.

—— (1985), 'Remarks on Wittgenstein and Ritual', in *Exemplars* (University of California Press, Berkeley, Calif.).

NEISSER, ULRIC (ed.) (1987), *Concepts and Conceptual Development: Ecological and Intellectual Factors in Categorization* (Cambridge University Press, Cambridge).

OBEYESEKERE, GANANATH (1981), *Medusa's Hair: An Essay on Personal Symbols and Religious Experience* (University of Chicago Press, Chicago).

—— (1984), *The Cult of the Goddess Pattini* (University of Chicago Press, Chicago).

O'FLAHERTY, WENDY DONIGER (1980), 'Karma and Rebirth in the Vedas and Puranas', in Wendy Doniger O'Flaherty (ed.), *Karma and Rebirth in Classical Indian Traditions* (University of California Press, Berkeley, Calif.).

OHNUKI-TIERNEY, EMIKO (1992), 'Vitality on the Rebound: Ritual's Core?', *Anthropology Today*, 8/5.

ORTNER, SHERRY B. (1978), *Sherpas Through Their Rituals* (Cambridge University Press, Cambridge).

O'SHAUGHNESSY, BRIAN (1980), *The Will: A Dual Aspect Theory*, ii (Cambridge University Press, Cambridge).

PAPINEAU, DAVID (1978), *For Science in Social Science* (Macmillan, London).

PARKIN, DAVID (1992), 'Ritual as Spatial Direction and Bodily Division', in Daniel de Coppet (ed.), *Understanding Rituals* (Routledge, London).

PULMAN, S. G. (1983), *Word Meaning and Belief* (Croom Helm, London).

PUTNAM, HILARY (1975), 'The Meaning of "Meaning"', in K. Gunderson (ed.), *Language, Mind and Knowledge* (University of Minnesota Press, Minneapolis).

—— (1977), 'Meaning and Reference', in Stephen P. Schwartz (ed.), *Naming, Necessity and Natural Kinds* (Cornell University Press, Ithaca, NY).

—— (1983), 'Reference and Truth', in *Realism and Reason*, Philosophical Papers, 3 (Cambridge University Press, Cambridge).

QUINN, NAOMI, and HOLLAND, DOROTHY (1987), 'Culture and Cognition', in Dorothy Holland and Naomi Quinn (eds.), *Cultural Models in Language and Thought* (Cambridge University Press, Cambridge).

RADCLIFFE-BROWN, A. R. (1952), *Structure and Function in Primitive Society* (Routledge & Kegan Paul, London).

RAPPAPORT, ROY A. (1975), 'Obvious Aspects of Ritual', *Cambridge Anthropology*, 2.

—— (1979), *Ecology, Meaning, and Religion* (North Atlantic Books, Berkeley, Calif.).

RATNA PRABHA VIJAY, MUNI SHRI (1950), *Sramana Bhagawan Mahavira Series*, 5/1 (Sri Jaina Siddhanta Society, Ahmedabad).

RENOU, LOUIS (1953), *Religions of Ancient India* (London).

ROSCH, E., and LLOYD, B. (eds.) (1978), *Cognition and Categorisation* (Lawrence Erlbaum, Hillsdale, NJ).

RYLE, GILBERT (1949), *The Concept of Mind* (Hutchinson, London).

SANDERSON, ALEXIS (1985), 'Purity and Power among Brahmans of Kashmir', in Michael Carrithers, Steven Collins, and Steven Lukes (eds.), *The Category of the Person* (Cambridge University Press, Cambridge).

SANGAVE, VILAS ADINATH (1980), *Jaina Community: A Social Survey*, 2nd rev. edn. (Popular Prakashan, Bombay).

SCHANK, R., and ABELSON, R. (1977), *Scripts, Plans, Goals and Understanding: An Inquiry into Human Knowledge Structures* (Lawrence Erlbaum, Hillsdale, NJ).

SCHIPPER, KRISTOFER, and STAAL, FRITS (1986), 'Vedic and Taoist Ritual', in Michael Strickmann (ed.), *Classical Asian Rituals and the Theory of Ritual* (Berlin).

SCHUBRING, WALTHER (1962), *The Doctrine of the Jainas* (Motilal Banarsidass, Delhi).

SCHWARTZ, STEPHEN P. (ed.) (1977), *Naming, Necessity and Natural Kinds* (Cornell University Press, Ithaca, NY).

SEARLE, JOHN R. (1969), *Speech Acts* (Cambridge University Press, Cambridge).

—— (1979), *Expression and Meaning: Studies in the Theory of Speech Acts*

(Cambridge University Press, Cambridge).

SEARLE, JOHN R. (1983), *Intentionality: An Essay in the Philosophy of Mind* (Cambridge University Press, Cambridge).

SHAH, UMAKANT PREMANAND (1953), 'Yaksa Worship in Early Jain Literature', *Journal of the Oriental Institute of Baroda*, 3.

—— (1955), *Studies in Jaina Art* (Benares).

—— (1975), 'Evolution of Jaina Iconography and Symbolism', in U. P. Shah and M. A. Dhaky (eds.), *Aspects of Jaina Art and Architecture* (LD Institute of Indology, Ahmedabad).

SHARMA, J. P. (1975), 'Hemacandra: Life and Scholarship of a Jaina Monk', *Asian Profile*, 3.

—— (1989), *Jaina Yaksas* (Kusumanjali Prakashan, Meerut).

SINGER, JEROME L. (1985), 'The Conscious and Unconscious Stream of Thought', in D. Pines (ed.), *Emerging Syntheses in Science* (Santa Fe Institute, Santa Fe).

SKINNER, QUENTIN (1970), 'Conventions and the Understanding of Speech Acts', *Philosophical Quarterly*, 20.

—— (1971), 'On Performing and Explaining Linguistic Actions', *Philosophical Quarterly*, 21.

—— (1988), 'Meaning and Understanding in the History of Ideas'; 'Motives, Intentions and the Interpretation of Texts'; ' "Social Meaning" and the Explanation of Social Action'; and 'A Reply to my Critics', in James Tully (ed.), *Meaning and Context: Quentin Skinner and his Critics* (Polity Press, Oxford).

SKORUPSKI, JOHN (1976), *Symbol and Theory: A Philosophical Study of Theories of Religion in Social Anthropology* (Cambridge University Press, Cambridge).

SMITH, BRIAN K. (1989), *Reflections on Resemblance, Ritual and Religion* (Oxford University Press, New York).

SMITH, JONATHAN Z. (1982), *Imagining Religion: From Babylon to Jonestown* (University of Chicago Press, Chicago).

SMITH, PIERRE (1982), 'Aspects of the Organisation of Rites', in Michel Izard and Pierre Smith (eds.), *Between Belief and Transgression: Structuralist Essays in Religion, History and Myth*, trans. John Leavitt (University of Chicago Press, Chicago).

SMITH, VINCENT A. (1901), *The Jain Stupa and Other Antiquities of Mathura* (Archaeological Survey of India, Allahabad).

—— (1917), 'The Jain Teachers of Akbar', in *Commemorative Essays Presented to Sir Ramkrishna Gopal Bhandarkar* (Bhandarkar Oriental Research Institute, Poona).

SOUTHWOLD, MARTIN (1983), *Buddhism in Life: The Anthropological Study of Religion and the Sinhalese Practice of Buddhism* (Manchester University Press, Manchester).

SPERBER, DAN (1975), *Rethinking Symbolism* (Cambridge University Press, Cambridge).

—— (1982), 'Is Symbolic Thought Pre-rational?', in Michel Izard and Pierre Smith (eds.), *Between Belief and Transgression: Structuralist Essays in Religion,*

History and Myth, trans. John Leavitt (University of Chicago Press, Chicago).

—— (1985), 'Anthropology and Psychology: Towards an Epidemiology of Representations', *Man: The Journal of the Royal Anthropological Institute*, NS 20.

SPERBER, DAN, and WILSON, DEIRDRE (1986), *Relevance: Communication and Cognition* (Basil Blackwell, Oxford).

SPINKS, BRYAN D. (1991), *The Sanctus in the Eucharist Prayer* (Cambridge University Press, Cambridge).

SRINIVASAN, AMRIT (1981), 'Ascetic Passion: The Devadasi and her Dance in a Comparative Context', unpublished paper.

STAAL, FRITS (1979), 'The Meaninglessness of Ritual', *Numen*, 26.

—— (1986), 'The Sound of Religion', *Numen*, 33 (in two parts).

—— (1989), *Rules Without Meaning: Ritual, Mantras and the Human Sciences* (Mouton, Leiden).

STEPHENS, W. P. (1986), *The Theology of Huldrych Zwingli* (Clarendon Press, Oxford).

STEVENSON, KENNETH (1989), *Accept This Offering: The Eucharist as Sacrifice Today* (SPCK, London).

STIGLER, JAMES W., SHWEDER, RICHARD A., and HERDT, GILBERT (eds.) (1990), *Cultural Psychology: Essays in Comparative Human Developent* (Cambridge University Press, Cambridge).

STRAWSON, P. F. (1964), 'Intention and Convention in Speech Acts', *Philosophical Quarterly*, 73.

—— (1971), 'Meaning and Truth', in *Logico-Linguistic Papers* (Methuen, London).

SWEESTER, EVE E. (1987), 'The Definition of Lie: An Examination of the Folk Models Underlying a Semantic Prototype', in Dorothy Holland and Naomi Quinn (eds.), *Cultural Models in Language and Thought* (Cambridge University Press, Cambridge).

TAMBIAH, STANLEY JEYARAJA (1985), 'The Magical Power of Words' (1968), 'Form and Meaning of Magical Acts' (1973), and 'A Performative Approach to Ritual' (1981), all repr. in *Culture, Thought, and Social Action: An Anthropological Perspective* (Harvard University Press, Cambridge, Mass., and London).

—— (1990), *Magic, Science, Religion, and the Scope of Rationality* (Cambridge University Press, Cambridge).

TAPPER, BRUCE ELLIOT (1987), *Rivalry and Tribute: Society and Ritual in a Telugu Village in South India* (Hindustan Publishing Corporation, Delhi).

TATIA, NATHMAL (1951), *Studies in Jaina Philosophy* (Jain Cultural Research Society, Benares).

TAYLOR, CHARLES (1979), 'Action as Expression', in Cora Diamond and Jenny Teichman (eds.), *Intention and Intentionality* (Harvester, Brighton).

—— (1985), *Human Agency and Language*, Philosophical Papers, 1 (Cambridge University Press, Cambridge).

THAPAR, ROMILA (1987), *Cultural Transaction and Early India* (Oxford University Press, Delhi).

THOMAS, KEITH (1972), *Religion and the Decline of Magic* (Penguin Books, Harmondsworth).

THOMAS, NICHOLAS (1988), 'Marginal Powers: Shamanism and the Disintegration of Hierarchy', *Critique of Anthropology*, 8.

TURNER, VICTOR (1967), *The Forest of Symbols: Aspects of Ndembu Ritual* (Cornell University Press, Ithaca, NY).

—— (1968), *The Drums of Affliction* (Clarendon Press, Oxford).

MAHOPADHYAYA VINAYA SAGAR (ed.) (1977), *Kalpa Sutra* (Prakrit Bharati, Jaipur).

WATSON, JAMES L. (1988), 'The Structure of Chinese Funerary Rites: Elementary Forms, Ritual Sequence, and the Primacy of Performance', in James L. Watson and Evelyn S. Rawski (eds.), *Death Ritual in Late Imperial and Modern China* (University of California Press, Berkeley, Calif.).

WEBER, MAX (1978), *Economy and Society*. ed., in two vols., by Guenther Roth and Claus Wittich (University of California Press, Berkeley, Calif.).

WILLIAMS, R. (1963), *Jaina Yoga: A Survey of the Mediaeval Sravakacaras* (Oxford University Press, London).

—— (1966), 'Before Mahavira', *Journal of the Royal Asiatic Society of Great Britain and Ireland*.

WINTERNITZ, MAURICE (1983), *A History of Indian Literature*, ii. *Buddhist and Jaina Literature*, new edn., trans. V. Srinivasa Sarma (Motilal Banarsidass, Delhi).

WITTGENSTEIN, LUDWIG (1968 (1958)), *Philosophical Investigations* (Basil Blackwell, Oxford).

—— (1979), *Remarks on Frazer's Golden Bough*, trans. A C Miles, ed. Rush Rhees (Brynmill, Retford).

ZIFF, PAUL (1967), 'On H. P. Grice's Account of Meaning', *Analysis*, 28.

INDEX

abhishek 150, 182–7, 190, 201, 202–4
abstract action 94, 135, 162–3, 235–7
acting under orders 105–6, 260
action: and acts distinguished 92–3, 104;
   cognition of 133, 162; and *karma* 39;
   and non-action 99, 108, 142, 217, 219;
   qualitative view 4–5; segments
   'foreclosed' 141, 142; segments in *puja*
   120, 140; segments in seine fishing
   139–40; and thought 3–4, 14–15; *see
   also* abstract action; body techniques
agency 4–5, 10, 263
agent 5, 93–4, 99, 103, 106, 153, 258
agra puja 27, 32, 199
anga puja 26, 32, 114, 172–3, 199, 253
anthropological interpretations of ritual
   70–1, 73–4, 261–4
apprehensibility, *see* ritualized action:
   apprehensible
archetypes, *see* ritualized action, archetypal
arti 28–9, 179, 186, 197, 201, 230–2, 237,
   243, 245, 246
Atkinson, Jane Monnig 8, 10–11, 15
Austin, J. L. 107
authority in ritual 111, 125, 157, 165, 180,
   182, 198

Babb, Lawrence A. 6, 140, 188, 244, 253
Banarsidas 48, 51–5, 62, 170, 219, 239,
   249, 250
Banks, Marcus 58
Bann, Stephen 259, 268
Barth, Fredrik 83, 130
Bateson, Gregory 75, 85–6, 105, 163
Beattie, J. H. 84
Beckett, Samuel 268
Bell, Catherine 3–4, 83, 191–2, 208, 209,
   263
Bennett, Peter 244
bhakti 42, 48, 221, 228
Bharilla, Hukamchand 219–20
bhav 76, 86, 161–2, 204, 207, 212, 213,
   218, 220–3, 224, 225, 226, 232, 238,
   251
bhav puja 28, 33, 47, 118, 162, 199,
   221–2, 259
Bloch, Maurice 72, 73, 83–4, 85, 138–9,
   143, 180

Bocock, J. 66
body 94, 116, 234, 255–6; body
   techniques 133–5, 137
Bowen, John R. 81
Boyer, Pascal 8, 9–10, 113, 164
Buddhism 17–18, 46, 58, 59, 61, 78, 82,
   188, 189, 214, 225, 230, 241, 245, 246
Burgess, James 128

Calvin, John 110, 222, 223
Cameron, Euan 109
Carrithers, Michael 58
Carstairs, G. Morris 228, 239
Cézanne, Paul 267
Chandrashekhar Vijay-ji, Muni Shri
   241–2, 244
Cherry, Stephen 189
Christian Reformation 13, 52, 54, 56, 109,
   222
Christian ritual 7, 56, 79, 109, 127,
   155–7, 171–2, 175–7, 212, 222; *see also*
   sacrifice
circumcision 110
clothing 113–14
cognitive apparatuses 138
cognitive psychology 137; *see also*
   prototypes; scripts
communication: and action 90;
   distinguished from representation
   78, 86; ritual 64, 68, 73–4, 76–7,
   114, 263; with God 78; with oneself
   77
consciousness 136, 219, 232, 236
consensus in ritual 80, 83, 87, 115, 165,
   179–80, 200, 224–5, 264–5
constitutive rules 117–21, 131; *see also*
   ontological stipulation; ritualized action:
   stipulated
Cort, John Edward 6, 128, 131, 132, 140,
   188, 189, 225
cradling, as a ritual act 60, 135, 229, 237,
   241, 243
culture of emotions 238

Dadabari temple: description 21–4
dance 66–7, 76, 86, 228, 237
darshan 26, 60, 201, 219, 229–30, 237,
   244, 259

deities, local 23–4; *see also* Hinduism, deities shared with Jainism; *kshetrapal*; *yaksha*s
*devadasi*s 76, 259
Digambar Terapanth 55
Digambars 19–20, 47, 51, 53, 62, 186, 219, 229, 255
discursive models 31–4, 123, 127, 141, 143, 265
Diwali 182, 189
Donnellan, Keith S. 166
Douglas, Mary 73, 84
dravya 218, 251, *see also bhav*
dravya puja 32, 47, 199
Drury, John 155
Dundas, Paul 16, 48, 49–50, 58, 225
Durkheim, Émile 135, 158, 261

Eck, Diana L. 244
efficacy of ritual 1, 13, 37, 38–9, 40, 45, 85, 142, 222, 263
Eichinger Ferro-Luzzi, Gabriella 150, 189, 190
elemental acts, *see* ritualized action, elemental
emergent moods 227–44; ritualized 233
emotion 227–44, 261; theory of 238, 246
Evans, Gareth 98
Evans-Pritchard, E. E. 83

Feeley-Harnik, Gillian 155, 210
Fernandez, James, W. 73, 87
flower *puja* 118, 119, 142, 164, 201; example of body technique 133–5; meanings 34–5; meanings related to physicality and the self 160–1; prototype 144, 149
framing 163; not intrinsic to ritualization 75–6; part of ritualization 105
freedom of interpretation in ritual 99, 103, 202–8; *see also* meaning
Freud, Sigmund 101, 239–40
Fuller, C. J. 58, 104, 122, 124–6, 199, 210, 244

games: and ritual 105, 117–18, 120–1, 131
Gatewood, John B. 139–43
Gautam Swami 22, 112, 188
Geertz, Clifford 73, 81, 84, 130
Gell, Alfred 234–5, 237
Gellner, David N. 200
Gerholm, Tomas 72, 80, 157
Giddens, Anthony 93

Gold, Ann Grodzins 164, 232, 233, 245
Gombrich, Richard F. 59, 61, 78, 188, 189, 225, 230, 245, 246
Goody, Jack 65–9, 83
Gould Glenn 105
guru-dev puja 206–7, 208
*guru-dev*s 21, 50, 59, 172–3, 188

habit 136, 163
Hampshire, Stuart 94–5, 96, 102–3, 109
Hegel, Georg Wilhelm Friedrich 4
Herrenschmidt, Olivier 40, 62
Hinduism 53, 58, 61; as counterpoint for Jain identity 42, 55–5, 131–2, 172, 183, 185, 202, 205; deities shared with Jainism 22, 23–4, 55, 59, 174, 188, 206; Holi 121–2; *Ram-lila* ceremony 257; rituals with seedlings 164; sequence in Hindu *puja* 124–6; as source of Jain ritual acts 1, 29, 43, 108, 135, 157, 179, 183, 193, 201, 228; texts and ritual performance 199–200
Holi 121–2
Hollis, Martin 66
Horton, Robin 82
Humphrey, Caroline 6, 58, 188, 255
hypnomantic states 232

illocutionary force 84, 91
image-worship 48–9, 115, 249–50, 259; and 'idol-worship' 57–8
initiation ceremonies 8, 252
intention 88–110; and action in Jain religious discourse 211–18; and consciousness in different Jain traditions 219–21; fixes identity of everyday but not ritual acts 92–4, 108; and *karma* 39
intentional meaning 91; constitutive of action 93–4; displaced by ritualization 94–6; distinguished from directedness of action 163; distinguished from locutionary meaning 92; distinguished from prior intentions and motives 93; distinguished from purpose 167–8
intentionality: of action 107, 135–6; of emergent moods 232–3; in ritual 71; transformed but not absent in ritual 99, 100, 108

Jain marriage ceremony 179
Jain renouncers 17–18, 58; authoritative in interpreting *puja* 198; may not perform *dravya puja* 46–7; participants in *puja*

115–16, 128–30, 131; performing *bhav puja* 118, 123; propounding social purposes for ritual 182; writing instruction manuals for *puja* 196

Jain society, wealth of 20–1

Jaini, Padmanabh S. 16, 58, 61, 62, 179, 216, 217

Johnson-Laird, P. N. 145, 164, 224

Judaism 40, 44, 62, 110, 165, 210

Jung, Carl 133, 158

Kanji Swami tradition 219

Kapferer, Bruce 9

karma 18–19, 39, 45, 58, 213–15, 217, 218, 244, 247–8, 250

Keesing, Roger M. 87, 186, 190

Keil, Frank C. 164

Khartar Gacch 20, 21, 48–50, 220

kshetrapal 23, 230–2

Laidlaw, James 188, 190, 245, 259

de Lange, Nicholas 165

language, and intention 98; and physical action, 137–40, 194; and purposes for performing ritual 175–7; and ritual acts 2, 74, 101–2, 175–7; *see also* texts and ritual performance

Lath, Mukund 53, 54, 62; *see also* Banarsidas

Lawrence, D. H. 267, 268

Lawson, E. Thomas 82–3

Leach, E. R. 72–3, 84

learning *puja* 113–14, 120–3, 127, 167, 194

Lévi-Strauss, Claude 8, 9, 102, 153, 175, 200

Lewis, Gilbert 72, 74, 77, 81, 85, 100, 116

linguistic/cognitive division of labour 152, 153, 224

liturgy 12–13, 37, 42, 68, 175–8, 192, 196, 199

Lonka Gacch 50

Luther, Martin 54, 62–3

Lynch, William W. 225, 246

McCauley, Robert N. 82–3

Mahavir Swami 17, 22, 61, 112, 164, 188, 216, 223

Malinowski, Bronislaw 83

Mallinath 20, 229, 243, 245, 256–7

Marglin, Frederique Apffel 76, 86, 164, 259

Mauss, Marcel 11, 133–5, 247, 248, 258

meaning: of action in general 90;

dispersed in ritual 2, 41, 80, 156–7; intentional, *see* intentional meaning, 91; lexical/propositional/locutionary 90–2; in *puja* 1, 34, 36, 128, 196, 204, 244; of rice offering 205–6; in ritual 6, 137, 262; of signals 90

meditation 28, 144

Merleau-Ponty, Maurice 94, 107, 135–6, 159, 162, 163, 235–7, 243

mistakes in performing *puja* 114–15, 127–8

models in ritual 31–4, 178, 180; *see also* prototypes

modes of ritual enactment 102–3, 212–13, 257; *see also* ritualized action: apprehensible

Moore, Sally Falk 67–9

Moya, Carlos J. 14

Myerhoff, Barbara G. 67–9

myth 200, 204

Naipaul, V. S. 80

namaskar-mantra 26, 44–5, 60, 62, 129, 194

naming: of action in seine fishing 139; and natural kinds 151; part of ritualization, 120–1; of *puja* acts 120, 131, 132; of ritual acts 102, 144, 149

Narcissism 250, 259

natural kinds, ritual acts conceptualized as 104, 151–4, 267

Needham, Rodney 70, 83, 144, 150, 160, 166, 266

Obeyesekere, Gananath 59, 61, 165, 188, 189, 232, 239, 241, 243, 246

object-like quality of ritual acts 96, 100–1, 156, 267

Ohnuki-Tierney, Emiko 180

ontological stipulation 96, 97, 103, 117

oral tradition 198

orthopraxy 87

O'Shaughnessy, Brian 258

panc-kalyanak puja 17, 60, 125–6, 129, 196, 206, 207, 228, 230, 255, 257; meanings attributed 145–9

Parkin, David 72, 113, 137, 157, 259

Parshvanath 21, 59

phenomenology 72, 83, 135

play 105

pollution 113, 116

prakshal 32, 183, 185, 186–7, 256

prasad 14, 56–7, 183

pratikraman 39, 41–2, 53
prayer 26, 206, 209
prescription in ritual, *see* ritualized action, stipulated
private ritual 239–40
prototypes 102, 144, 145, 147–50, 152, 153; different for natural kinds and artefacts 152
puja: ceremonial performances 29–31, 115, 145, 169, 206–7; discursive models 32–3; general description of daily rite 24–9; Jain interpretations of 42–6, 191–210; 249–55; of temple flag 128–30; theoretical importance of 41–2
pujaris 24–5, 60, 123, 129, 197
purity: requirement for performing *puja* 113–14; rules 116
purposes: individual 186–7; linked to different deities 170–1, 173–4; and motives distinguished 167–8; more or less religiously valid 170; for performing *puja* 169–70; in ritual distinguished from those in everyday life 167, 174; ritual distinguished from other rule-bound activities 175; 'self-evident' 178–9; *see also* social purposes
Putnam, Hilary 164, 165, 224

Radcliffe-Brown, A. R. 73, 82, 84
Ram-lila 257, 259
Rappaport, Roy A. 67–9, 73, 77, 87, 154
regulative rules 116–20
religious reaction to ritual 1, 8, 11, 12–13, 36–42, 46–57, 191
religious–secular distinction 66
renouncers, *see* Jain renouncers
rites of passage 125, 137
reverie 181–2, 241
ritual: and context, 145; defined as a category of event 65–7, 70; defined as a characteristic of all action 72–3; defined as expressive action 85; defined as framed action 75–6; defined as genre of theatrical performance 81; defined as polythetic concept 70, 150, 201; defined by reasonableness/rationality 66–7; defined with reference to communication 64, 67, 68, 73–9, 83–4, 85; defined with reference to sanctity 67–9; efficacy 1, 13, 37, 38–9, 40, 45, 85, 142, 222, 263; expertise not applicable 167; haphazard events and 186–7, 190; liturgy-centred 8, 80–1;

and music 101, 121; performance-centred 8, 11, 188; and power 6–7, 84, 111; as power 10–11, 263; as a quality of action 2–3, 5, 71–2; reasons for existence of 99, 265–8; reforms of 12, 46–57
ritual commitment 97, 99–100, 128, 136, 154; compared to commitment in games 118; initial characterization 88–90
ritual of rebellion 121–2, 263–4
ritualization: distinguished from mistakes 98–100; excludes background activity 142, 145–6; focus of theoretical attention 3, 64, 263–4; as historical process 56, 155–8; implies social committment 69, 97, 154; private 239–40; and time 104, 155, 166 and universal process 13, 97, 154
ritualization of text 45, 74–5, 83–4, 101, 191–2, 208
ritualized action: apprehensible 89, 101, 160–2, 211, 213, 227, 236, 260; archetypal 89, 100, 135, 149, 150, 153, 154, 158, 196, 234, 266; elemental 89, 100, 151, 153, 154, 202, 267; non-intentional 89, 94, 96, 99, 100, 108; stipulated 12, 89, 96, 117, 121–2, 143
Rosch, E. 144
Ryle, Gilbert 136

sacred drama 257
sacrifice 40–1, 62, 166, 252; controversy about what counts 149; Eucharist as, 171, 212; *puja* as 43, 252; as renunciation 38; Vedic 8, 13, 17, 36–8, 42, 61, 166, 251
salat 81
samayik 39, 42, 44, 53, 62
Sanderson, Alexis 247–8, 249, 258
Schwartz, Stephen P. 164
scripts 111–13, 122, 127, 140–1
Searle, John R. 78, 100, 107, 108, 117, 131, 211, 225
sectarian divisions in Jainism 19, 20, 50–1, 191, 219, 255, 257
secular ritual 65, 67
seine fishing 139–40
self, in ritual 5, 103, 106, 159–60, 211–12, 219–20, 238, 242, 247–9, 267
sequences of ritual acts 32, 101–2, 104, 113, 117, 123–7, 140, 175, 177, 193, 255
shamanism 8, 10, 11
*shravakacar*s 42, 61, 119, 192, 196, 198–9

Shvetambar Terapanth 20, 51, 62, 226
signals 90
Skinner, Quentin 66, 84, 91, 93, 107, 167
Skorupski, John 11, 66, 82, 83, 85
Smith, Brian 166
Smith, Jonathan Z. 165
Smith, Pierre 8, 9
snatra puja 25–6, 189, 255
social facts 261–2, 263
social purposes 168, 177–87; hold over
    celebrants' minds 181; prescribed in
    ritual 176–7, 179
soul 247–8, 255; Jain conception of
    18–19
Southwold, Martin 188
Sperber, Dan 97, 144, 193
spirit possession 186, 230–2, 233, 235,
    237, 239, 244, 245
Staal, Frits 62, 74–5, 101, 109, 193–4,
    208
Stevenson, Kenneth 179
Sthanakvasis 20, 51, 56
stipulation, *see* ritualized action, stipulated
Sweester, Eve E. 163
symbolism 172, 192–3, 204, 233, 254,
    264, 267; functionalist analysis of
    180–1; ideological, 180; not definitional
    of ritual 79–80; not private in *puja*
    202–3

Tambiah, Stanley Jeyaraja 13, 72, 73, 74,
    77, 82, 83, 84, 85, 108, 113, 131, 166
Tantrism 253
Tapa Gacch 20, 220

Tapper, Bruce Elliot 164
Taranapanth 51, 56, 209
Taylor, Charles 4–5, 78–9, 108–9, 144,
    159
texts and ritual performance 26, 28,
    49–50, 57, 191–208
theatre 81, 105–6, 111, 257, 260, 263
time, Jain concept of 16–17
theism 215
Thomas, Keith 83
Thomas, Nicholas 15
trance 179; *see also* emergent moods; spirit
    possession
Turner, Victor 65, 73, 81, 82
tyag 253–4

violence 180

Watson, James, L. 87
Weber, Max 11, 91, 168
Williams, R. 43, 44, 62, 210
Wilson, Deirdre 97, 144
Wittgenstein, Ludwig 86, 107, 144
    266–7; on the Beltane festival 160–1,
    162
worship 80–1

*yaksha*s 22, 59, 171
*yati*s 48, 50, 51, 123, 129, 197
yoga 253, 259

Ziff Paul 107
Zwingli, Huldrych 52, 54, 109, 212, 222